LIGHTS ON

LIGHTS ON

Norwegian Contemporary Art

SKIRA

Cover
Jan Christensen
LIGHTS ON – norsk samtidskunst
2008

Design
Marcello Francone

Editorial Coordination
Eva Vanzella

Editing
Emanuela di Lallo

Layout
Sabina Brucoli

First published in Italy in 2008 by
Skira Editore S.p.A.
Palazzo Casati Stampa
via Torino 61
20123 Milano
Italy
www.skira.net

Printed and bound in Italy.
First edition

ISBN: 978-82-91-43054-6
(Astrup Fearnley Museum of Modern
Art, Catalogue no. 61);
978-88-6130-792-6 (Skira)

Distributed in North America
by Rizzoli International Publications,
Inc., 300 Park Avenue South,
New York, NY 10010, USA.
Distributed elsewhere in the world
by Thames and Hudson Ltd., 181A
High Holborn, London WC1V 7QX,
United Kingdom.

LIGHTS ON
Norwegian Contemporary Art

Astrup Fearnley Museum of Modern Art, Oslo
12 January – 23 March 2008

ASTRUP FEARNLEY MUSEUM OF MODERN ART

Dronningens gate 4,
PB 1158 Sentrum,
N-0107 Oslo
Ph. (+47) 22 93 60 60
Fax (+47) 22 93 60 65
info@fearnleys.no
www.afmuseet.no

*The Museum is generously supported by
the Thomas Fearnley, Heddy and Nils Astrup Foundation,
and Astrup Fearnley AS*

Exhibition Curators
Gunnar B. Kvaran
Hanne Beate Ueland
Grete Årbu

Crew
Audun Erikstad
Roger Høyer
Ulf Holbrook
Øivind Haaland
Cai Jerner
Kai Mikalsen
Berit Wilhelmsen

Catalogue Editors
Gunnar B. Kvaran
Hanne Beate Ueland
Grete Årbu

Text editor
Marit Woltmann

Photographs
The artists
Tom Henning Bratlie
Niklas Lello
Hans Petter Smeby
Anders Valde

Translations
Arlyne Moi
Nina Schjønsby

Editing
Melissa Larner

*Education / mobile telephone
information*
Hanne Beate Ueland

Reception – bookshop
Ann-Christine Oveland

Thank you to
Akira Ikeda Gallery, Berlin
Anders Smebye
Anne-Karin Furunes
Bergen Kunsthall:
Solveig Øvstebø
Bergen Kunstmuseum:
Eli Okkenhaug,
Bodø Kunstforening:
Irena Jovic
Bomuldsfabriken Kunsthall,
Arendal: Harald Solberg
Børre Sæthre
Fotogalleriet, Oslo:
Ida Kierulf
Galerie c/o Atle Gerhardsen,
Berlin
Galerie Eva Hober, Paris
Galerie Katharina Bittel,
Hamburg
Galleri By The Way, Bergen:
Annette Kierulf
Galleri Erik Steen, Oslo
Galleri Fimbul, Oslo:
Ole Robert Fimbul-Kiserud
Galleri GAD, Oslo
Galleri Gann, Sandnes: Sveinung
Nygaard
Galleri LNM, Oslo:
Gørild R. Skavhaug
Galleri MGM, Oslo
Galleri Opdahl, Stavanger:
Monica Berntsen
Galleri Riis, Oslo Espen
Ryvarden, Ulrikke T. Berg,
Kristin Elisabeth Bråten,
Eva Refsahl
Galleri STANDARD (OSLO):
Eivind Furnesvik
Hordaland Kunstsenter, Bergen:
Mari Aarre

Inger Lena Gåsemyr
Jan Christensen
Kjetil Skøien
Kunstverket, Oslo:
Mette Cecilie Monsen
Laura Bartlett Gallery, London
Lautom Contemporary, Oslo:
Randi Thommessen
Luxe Gallery, New York
Nils Stærk Contemporary,
Copenhagen
Per Gunnar Tverbakk
Porsgrunn Kunstforening:
Andreas Rishovd
PSM, Berlin
Rogaland Kunstmuseum,
Stavanger: Jan Windsholt
Transit Art Space, Stavanger:
Einar Børresen
Knut Åsdam

Contents

9   Lights On – Norwegian Contemporary Art
Gunnar B. Kvaran
Hanne Beate Ueland
Grete Årbu

Art Works

14   Jesper Alvær & Isabela Grosseová
18   Tobias Arnell & Jørgen Craig Lello
22   Thora Dolven Balke
24   Siri Berqvam
26   Kyrre Bjørkås & Rune Andreassen
28   Ole Martin Lund Bø
30   Bjørn Båsen
32   Jan Christensen
36   Gardar Eide Einarsson
40   Ida Ekblad
44   Jan Hakon Erichsen
46   Matias Faldbakken
50   Jan Freuchen
54   Ivan Galuzin
58   Anna Sigmond Gudmundsdottir
62   Ane Mette Hol
66   Håvard Homstvedt
68   Lars Kjemphol & Espen Henningsen
72   Maren Juell Kristensen
74   Hjørdis Kurås
76   Ingvild Langgård
78   Trine Lise Nedreaas
80   Martin Skauen
82   Eirin Støen
84   Stian Ådlandsvik
86   Øystein Aasan

Articles

91 Pissing on the Nordic Miracle
Power Ekroth

97 New Ways to Work Together
Pragmatism, Quality and
Relational Aesthetics
Erlend Hammer

103 Institutional Critique's
Knowledge and Interest
Trude Schjelderup Iversen

109 Art Criticism: A Picture
Kjetil Røed

115 Untitled (Rendering Things
from Memory due to a Lack
of Facts and Other Sources)
Leif Magne Tangen

123 The Spirit that Returns
Line Ulekleiv

Bookshop

130 One for the Books

Artist Spaces

136 Bastard
142 Blunk
148 Rakett
154 Rekord

163 Gallery Overview
Ida Sannes Hansen

169 Alternative Art Spaces
Ida Sannes Hansen

177 Mo Money Mo Problems
Subsidy Schemes for Young
Norwegian Artists
Ingrid Pettersen

184 Short Biographies
189 List of Works

Lights On – Norwegian Contemporary Art

Gunnar B. Kvaran, Hanne Beate Ueland, Grete Årbu
The Curators

Astrup Fearnley Museum of Modern Art first directed its attention to up-and-coming American artists in 2005, through the exhibition *Uncertain States of America*, and then in the autumn of 2007 devoted an exhibition to the youngest generation of Chinese contemporary artists. The time has now come to look at things closer to home and to follow up with a presentation of Norwegian contemporary art.

Each and every generation of artists has its own approach to the concept of art, but their art also reflects the era in which they live. Sometimes this is deliberately thought through and staged, yet the contemporary era – with its complicated intellectual, spiritual, populist and material production – also influences artists without them being consciously aware of it.

Through the last decade we have witnessed a steadily increasing globalization of contemporary art. Throughout the world artists focus on research problems with similar contents, forms and artistic idioms, even if not exactly the same. Norwegian artists have been acknowledged as being part of a larger artistic milieu – a milieu in which they, with increasing enthusiasm, have become visible and active participants.

During this period the situation and conditions for Norwegian contemporary art have undergone great changes – not only in relation to the artwork as a creative production, but also in relation to 'the Norwegian artworld'. New commercial and non-commercial galleries have appeared on the art scene, a new generation of young and capable curators and critics have distinguished themselves, and the Museum of Contemporary Art – for a time the main arena for Norwegian contemporary art – has now become part of the National Museum of Art, Architecture and Design. And it doesn't stop there. Norwegian artists not only share ideas and concepts with their international colleagues, but also spaces, discourses and markets. While it has become completely natural for young Norwegian artists to observe what is happening internationally, it is also normal for them to participate in and influence the international art scene. Astrup Fearnley Museum of Modern Art found the time ripe to look more closely at the emerging generation of artists in Norway. We have therefore once again included a group exhibition in our 2008 programme, this time for Norwegian contemporary art. We attempt to present the emerging generation and its artistic research problems, along with the dynamism, enthusiasm and complexity found in the Norwegian art milieu, a milieu that 'lives and breathes' as never before.

As with art in general, contemporary art concerns originality and qualities in relation to the artist's intentions: concept, visualization, concretization and contents. We have sought to find young Norwegian contemporary artists who represent our era, a continuity or a breach with history: artists who have found, or are in the process of finding, a new approach to the concept of art.

This required research. We, the exhibition curators, made use of many channels for finding information about the Norwegian contemporary art scene. The response was surprisingly good and several hundred portfolios on Norwegian contemporary art have been compiled.

After a thorough evaluation, and of course long discussions, we came up with the following constellation of artists who could be said to represent a new era in Norwegian contemporary art: Jesper Alvær & Isabela Grosseová, Jørgen Craig Lello & Tobias Arnell, Thora Dolven Balke, Siri Berqvam, Kyrre Bjørkås & Rune Andreassen, Ole Martin Lund Bø, Bjørn Båsen, Jan Christensen, Gardar Eide Einarsson, Ida Ekblad, Jan Hakon Erichsen, Matias Faldbakken, Jan Freuchen, Ivan Galuzin, Anna Sigmond Gudmundsdottir, Ane Mette Hol, Håvard Homstvedt, Lars Kjemphol & Espen Henningsen, Maren Juell Kristensen, Hjørdis Kurås, Ingvild Langgård, Trine Lise Nedreaas, Martin Skauen, Eirin Støen, Stian Ådlandsvik and Øystein Aasan.

At the start of a 'decade yet to be named', we believe it is possible to present a creative, intelligent and rich manifold of contemporary art, created by ambitious artists who are self-confident and cognizant of their contribution to, and participation in, the international contemporary art scene.

Young Norwegian contemporary artists – many with impressive academic education – seem to be more concerned with object-based art more than process-oriented art. Most work from post-conceptual premises and realize their artistic ideas through sculpture, architecture/installation, video, sound, photography and painting. The artists in this exhibition largely work with a narrative pictorial language, often including text references and pictograms firmly rooted in everyday memories and popular culture. Some of the artists reflect over the appropriation of pictures, objects and art-historical references; others focus on perception and the physicality of objects. Another tendency is to explore metaphysical and mystical conditions. Yet, in spite of the copious variety and forms of expression, in almost all of the artists one finds a critical closeness to society and a will to create meaningful, socially relevant art.

Where is the Norwegianness in Norwegian contemporary art? Clearly, Norwegian art in general is a part of Western art and cultural history (at times it has been a very important part). Throughout history Norwegian artists have participated, with greater or lesser distance, in the development of international art. It is therefore not easy, especially in today's globalized art world, to point to specific elements which would lead to a Norwegian identity. This difficulty particularly arises on account of the close connection with Anglo-American art and culture, and the English language's internationally dominant position (the latter can also to some extent bring about a transference of reality and identity).

One can of course speculate and point to the use of materials and basic techniques. Many artists use wood rather than man-made or synthetic materials in their sculptures and pictures, and they also employ modern technology. Does this involve a form of identity inviting reflection over the artist's sensibility and his or her rootedness in a milieu, or is it more a question of accessible resources? Or could Norwegianness lie more explicitly in the artist's relation to themes and contents? In contrast to their international colleagues, Norwegian artists are often profiled as having a stronger critical engagement, social involvement and consciousness. This could be due to the robust democratic tradition we have in Norway.

An exhibition is always based on the curators' knowledge, experience, intuition and taste. Our selection of artists presenting a theme such as 'Norwegian contemporary art' is of course a selection we as curators stand for, but it is far from being the only possible way of presenting this theme. Norwegian contemporary art is luckily more complicated than this. We have therefore sought to expand and create a dynamic exhibition concept by inviting young curators to make 'exhibitions within the exhibition'. We have reserved a primary exhibition space in the museum and called it 'The Guest Room': this has been devoted to temporary exhibitions under the aegis of artist-driven, non-commercial galleries. Throughout the exhibition period we have presented shows by *Bastard*, with curator Anders Smebye (12–27 January), based in Oslo; *Blunk* with curators Lina Berglund, Kristoffer Henriksson, Freia Uta Beer and Aylin Soyer Tangen (31 January – 10 February), based in Trondheim; *Rakett* with curators Åse Løvgren and Karolin Tampere (14 February – 2 March), based in Bergen; and *Rekord*, with Thora Dolven Balke, Ingvild Langgård and Eirin Støen (6–23 March), based in Oslo. These galleries have received a carte blanche to present what they see as the most interesting and significant contemporary Norwegian art. In this way the exhibition has extended beyond our initial intentions and has, for short periods, added surprising glimpses into aspects of Norwegian contemporary art which were not initially planned as part of the exhibition.

LIGHTS ON – norsk samtidskunst is not merely focused on artists and artworks. It also aims to present 'the Norwegian art world' in greater breadth. A 'book project' is therefore also included in the exhibition. The bookshop 'One for the Books', curated by artist Marte Johnslien, presents and sells 'artist books' and other Norwegian and international books by and about Norwegian contemporary artists.

Throughout the exhibition period various lectures and panel discussions have been organized to illuminate aspects of Norwegian contemporary art. These were held in our new conference room, 'the Corner Room' (the space formerly occupied by *Mother and Child Divided*). Themes include the relation between the young generation of Norwegian contemporary art and 'the global art world', 'the new critics', 'private collectors' and 'the alternative art space'.

In this comprehensive catalogue, we present the exhibition *LIGHTS ON – norsk samtidskunst* through texts and pictures, artists' statements and articles by young Norwegian artists, curators and critics: Power Ekroth writes about Norwegian contemporary art in relation to the international contemporary art scene and Erlend Hammer discusses galleries, collaborations and relational aesthetics. Trude Iversen's essay focuses on the third generation of institutional critique while Kjetil Røed's deals more generally with contemporary art criticism. The essay by Leif Magne Tangen addresses critical moments in Norwegian contemporary art in recent years, whereas Line Ulekleiv's text sheds light on Norwegian mysticism in contemporary art. Along with these contributions, we have tried to elucidate 'how young Norwegian artists survive': Ingrid Pettersen explains the myriad of support schemes for young Norwegian contemporary artists and Ida Sannes Hansen provides an overview of Norwegian contemporary art spaces and commercial galleries mediating contemporary art.

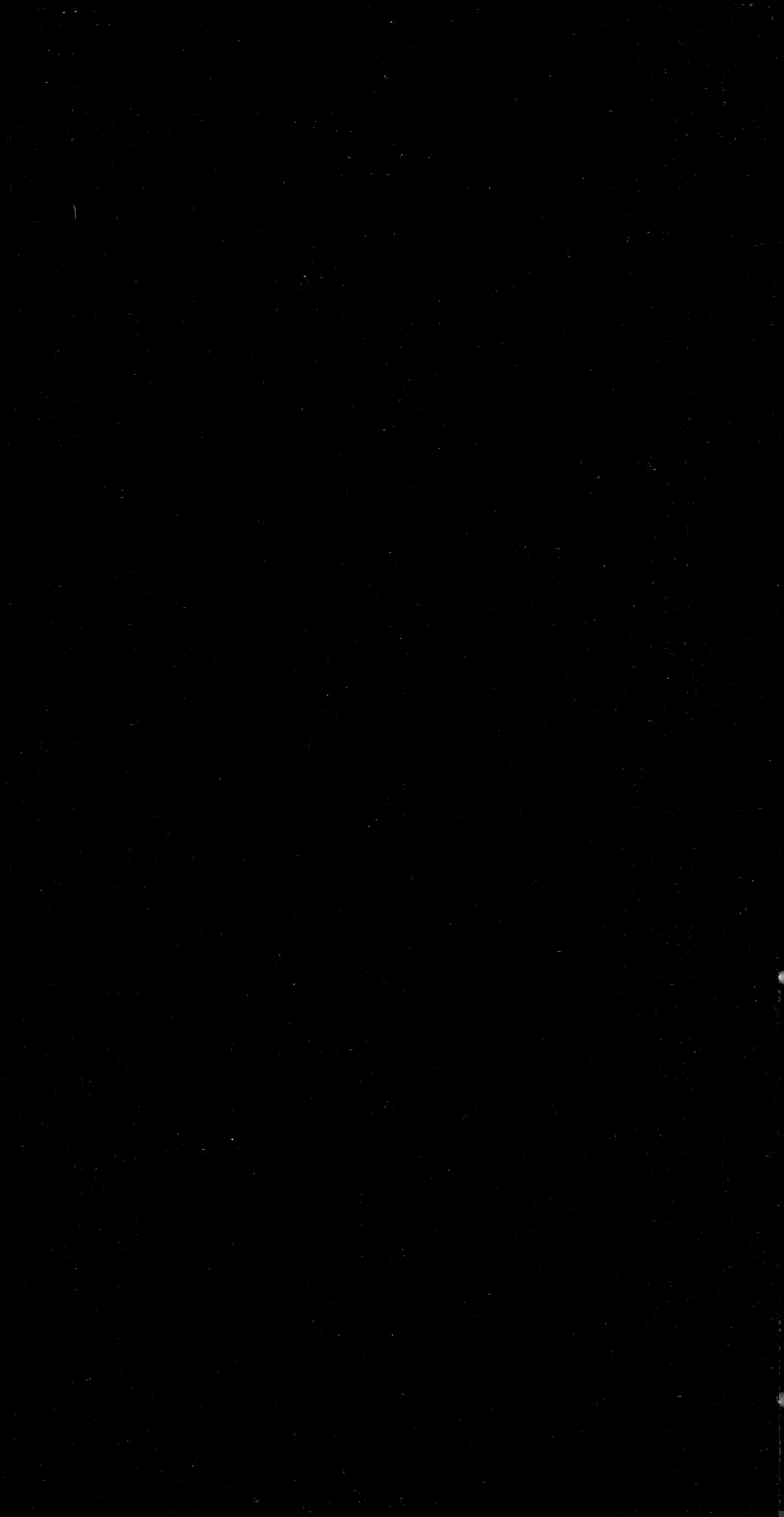

Art Works

Jesper Alvær
Isabela Grosseová

Born 1973 Copenhagen
Born 1976 Prague
Live and work in Prague

Trademarks can be understood in the context of a certain kind of inherent creativity used for various ends, all in relation to the situation at hand. Decorating for Easter, refurbishing a room or puttering about in the workshop – this sort of multi-dimensional activity can be found throughout the world in manifold variations. *Trademarks* concretely refers to different constructive occupations reflecting a flexible modernity with regional adaptations. The work can also lead one to think of medieval guild emblems and seals with symbolic pictures of professional occupations. Examples are the shoemaker's double eagles, the baker's crown and pretzel and the carpenter's compass and set-square. The advent of strong European nations with jurisdiction to regulate patents and copyrights caused the guilds to loose some of their power. After the French Revolution they disbanded. Norwegian artisans often continued to use *laug* (guilds) to describe

their professional organizations, e.g. labour unions or bodies of accreditation. In the pictures, one can see each individual trademark in its original mode of display. All the various elements in *Trademarks* are from Egyptians working in Bengjazi, Libya. In recent years we, as a collaborative artist practice, have mostly worked in Central Europe, and have been influenced by an art scene addressing several fundamental social, political and economic themes. Typical examples of these are the great collective experiences such as European Union membership, the fall of Communism, revolutions and the phenomena of countries approaching a more Western style of Europeanism. These themes are combined with new historical constructions and national retrospective views, and are often addressed from a single subject's perspective. Sporadic experiences of art institutions in Norway, Japan, France, China and the USA have also influenced our work.

Jesper Alvær & Isabela Grosseová
Trademarks, 2006
Appropriated objects, video stills
Dimensions vary
Courtesy of the artists

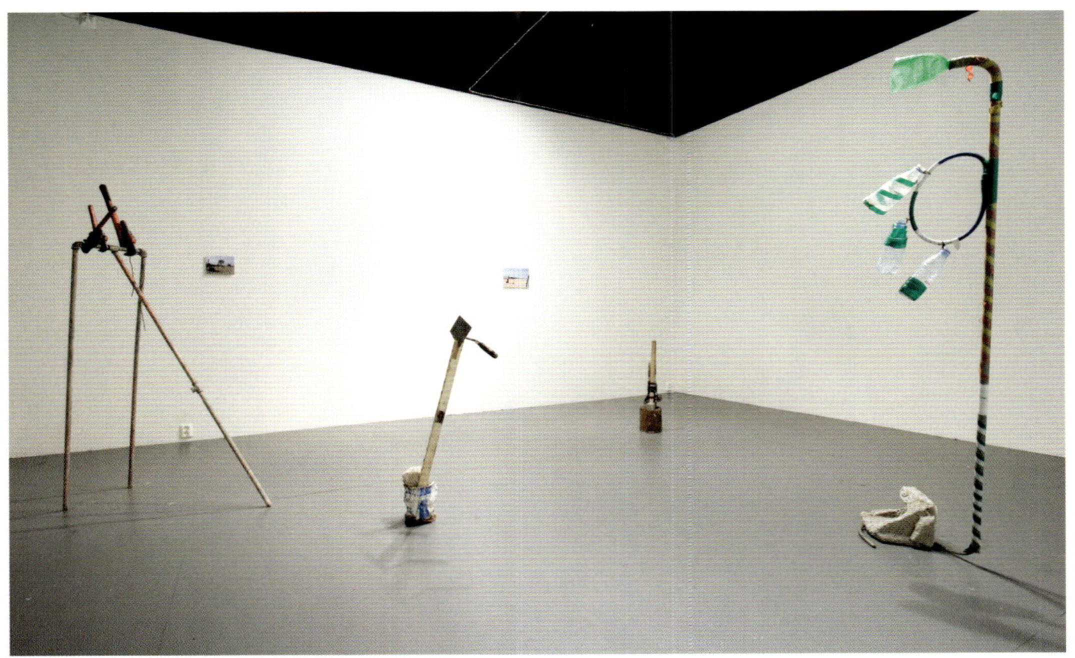

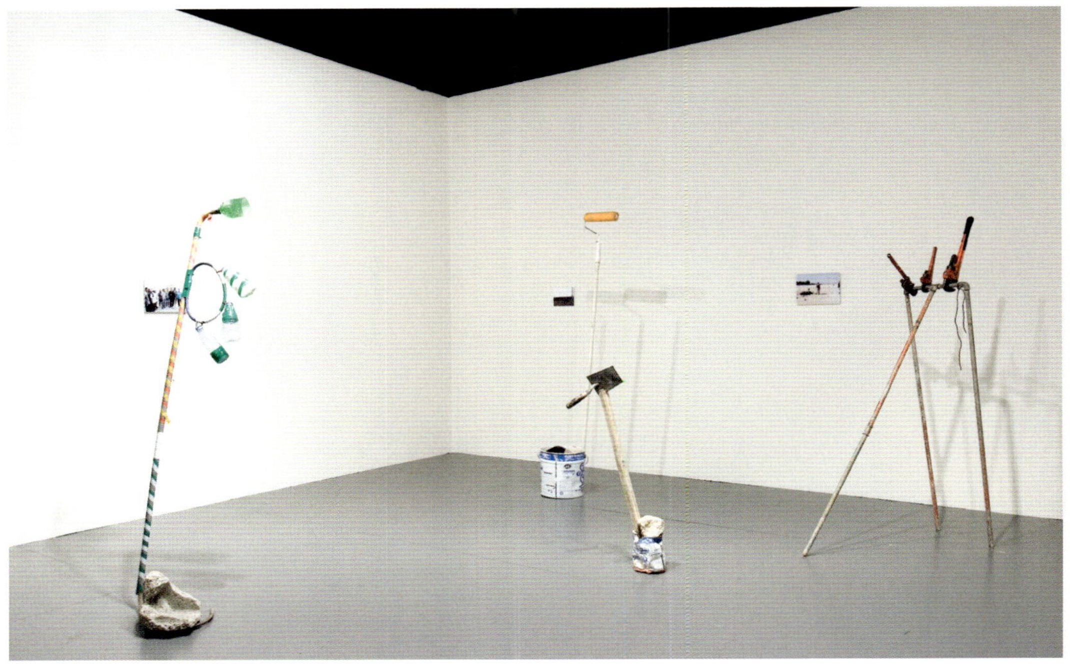

Jesper Alvær & Isabela Grosseová

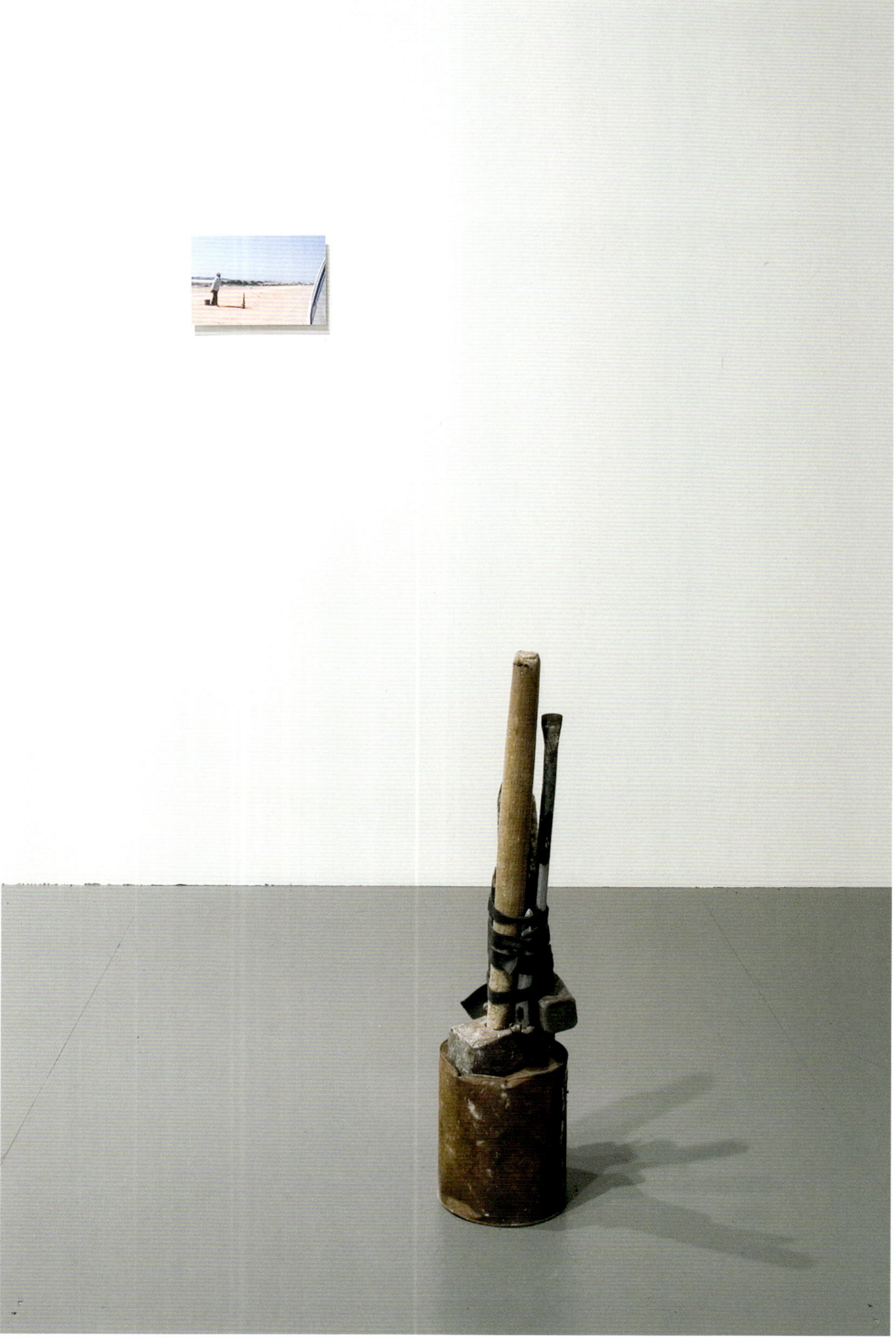

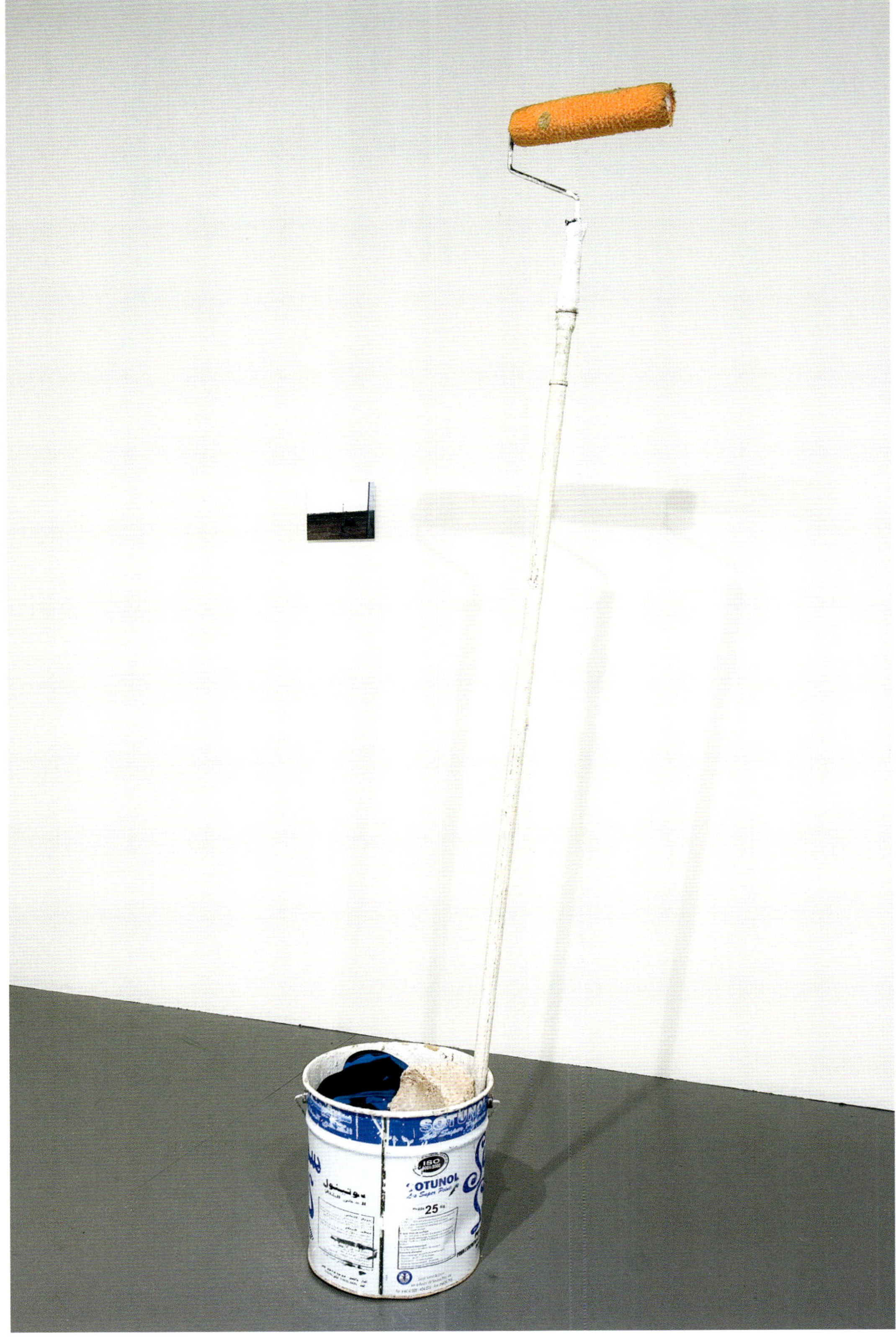

Tobias Arnell
Jørgen Craig Lello

Born 1978 Lund
Born 1978 Fredrikstad
Live and work in Oslo

We have collaborated on art projects since 2003. Our works take recourse in broken chains of logic, false explanations and fictional scenarios, in order to research how the world is interpreted and understood. We work primarily with sculpture, but allow the media to bleed into photography, painting and other pictorial genres. The works are characterized by a resigned, trash and DIY aesthetic, with pretensions of slickness. Although permeated with a strong material and sculptural approach, the works are fundamentally idea-based. They question the validity of basic social structures and methodologies. By using events and historical documents, objects, symbols and registered underlying structures, there arises a wide spectrum of connected themes. These are subjected to a deconstructive process, resulting in a skewed understanding of 'the whole picture'. The leitmotif running through our works has to do with the way themes have been treated. This constructs an interpretation which seems complete but is actually invalid, or even insane.

Lello//Arnell (Jørgen Craig Lello
& Tobias Arnell)
*Vice Admiral Francis Drake's
Expedition to the South
Pacific Aimed at the Disruption
of Spanish Exploration
and Conquest I,* 2007
Digital print on aluminium
70 x 100 cm
Astrup Fearnley Collection, Oslo

Lello//Arnell (Jørgen Craig Lello
& Tobias Arnell)
*Vice Admiral Francis Drake's
Expedition to the South Pacific
Aimed at the Disruption
of Spanish Exploration and
Conquest III,* 2007
Digital print on aluminium
70 x 100 cm
Astrup Fearnley Collection, Oslo

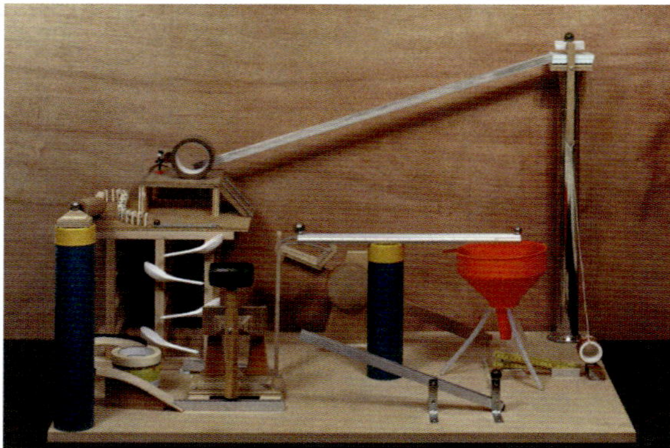

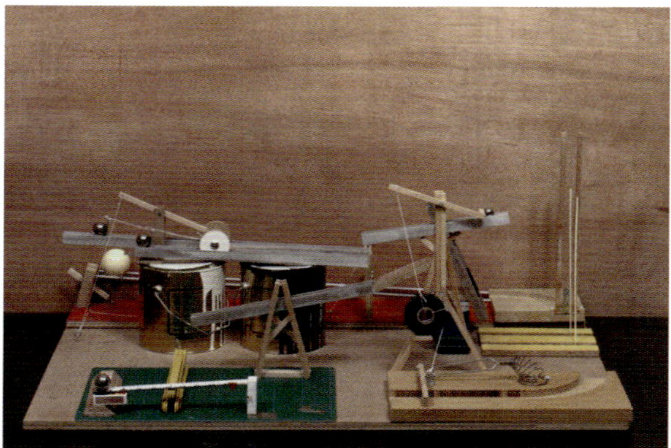

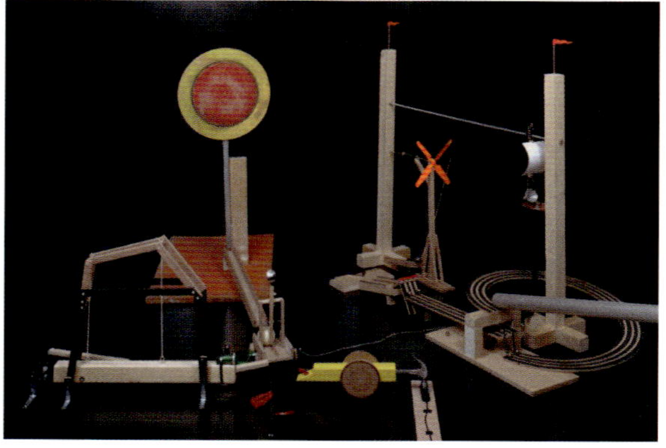

Lello//Arnell (Jørgen Craig Lello
& Tobias Arnell)
*Vice Admiral Francis Drake's
Expedition to the South Pacific
Aimed at the Disruption of Spanish
Exploration and Conquest II
(Self Portrait of an Explorer)*, 2007
Digital print on aluminium
70 x 100 cm
Astrup Fearnley Collection, Oslo

Lello//Arnell (Jørgen Craig Lello
& Tobias Arnell)
*Inflation, Interest & Investment
(To Infinity) I*, 2007
Digital print on aluminium
70 x 100 cm
Astrup Fearnley Collection, Oslo

Lello//Arnell (Jørgen Craig Lello
& Tobias Arnell)
*Inflation, Interest & Investment
(To Infinity) II*, 2007
Digital print on aluminium
70 x 100 cm
Astrup Fearnley Collection, Oslo

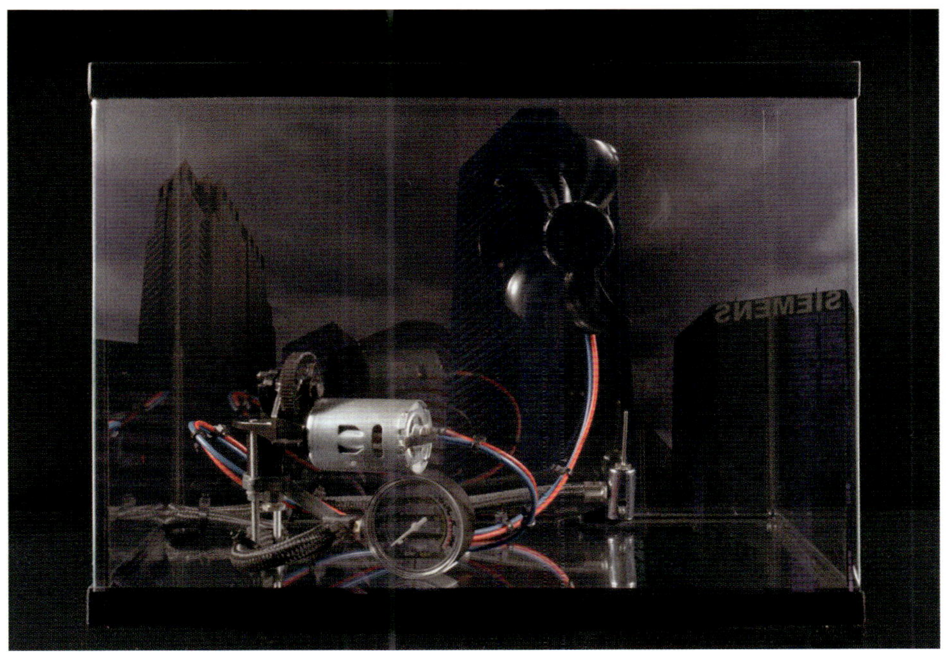

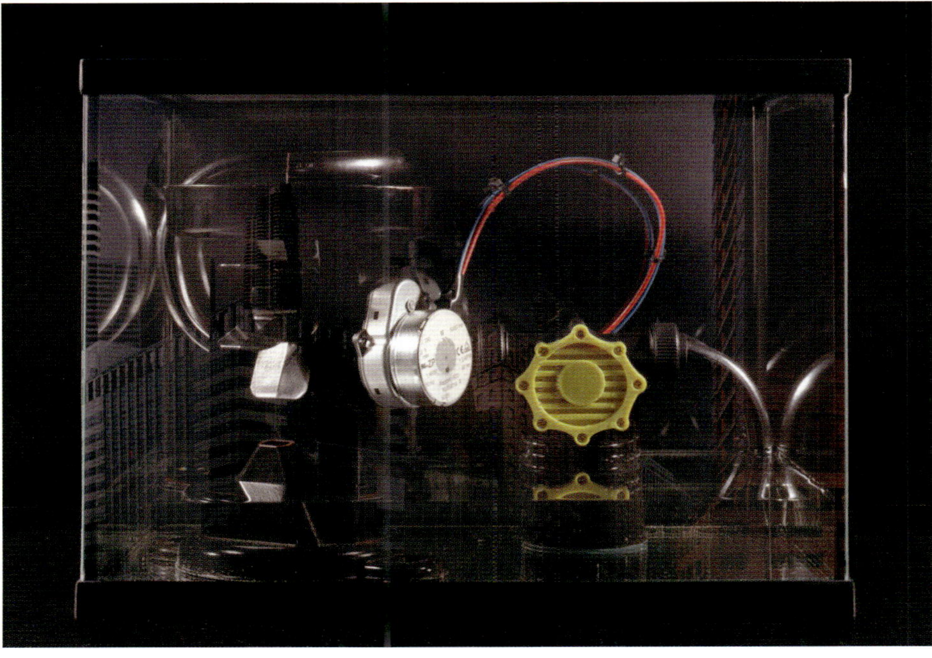

Lello//Arnell (Jørgen Craig Lello
& Tobias Arnell)
Knowing about the Universe, 2008
Powder varnished aluminium
125 x 125 x 5 cm
90 x 60 x 60 cm
Astrup Fearnley Collection, Oslo

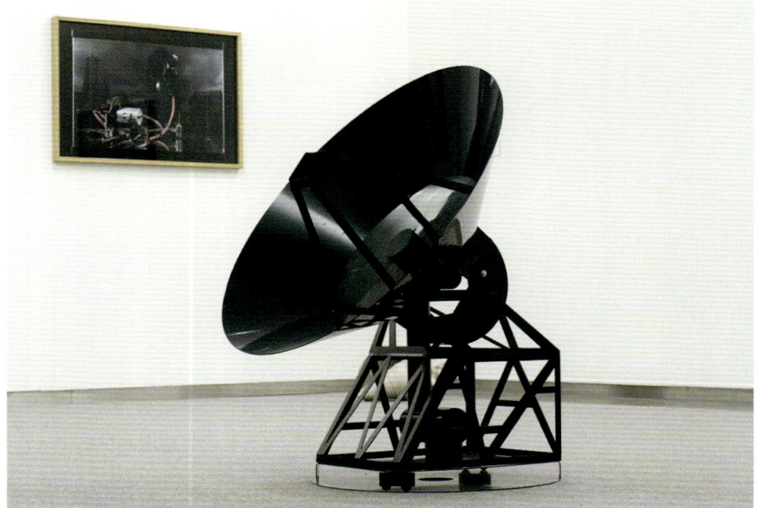

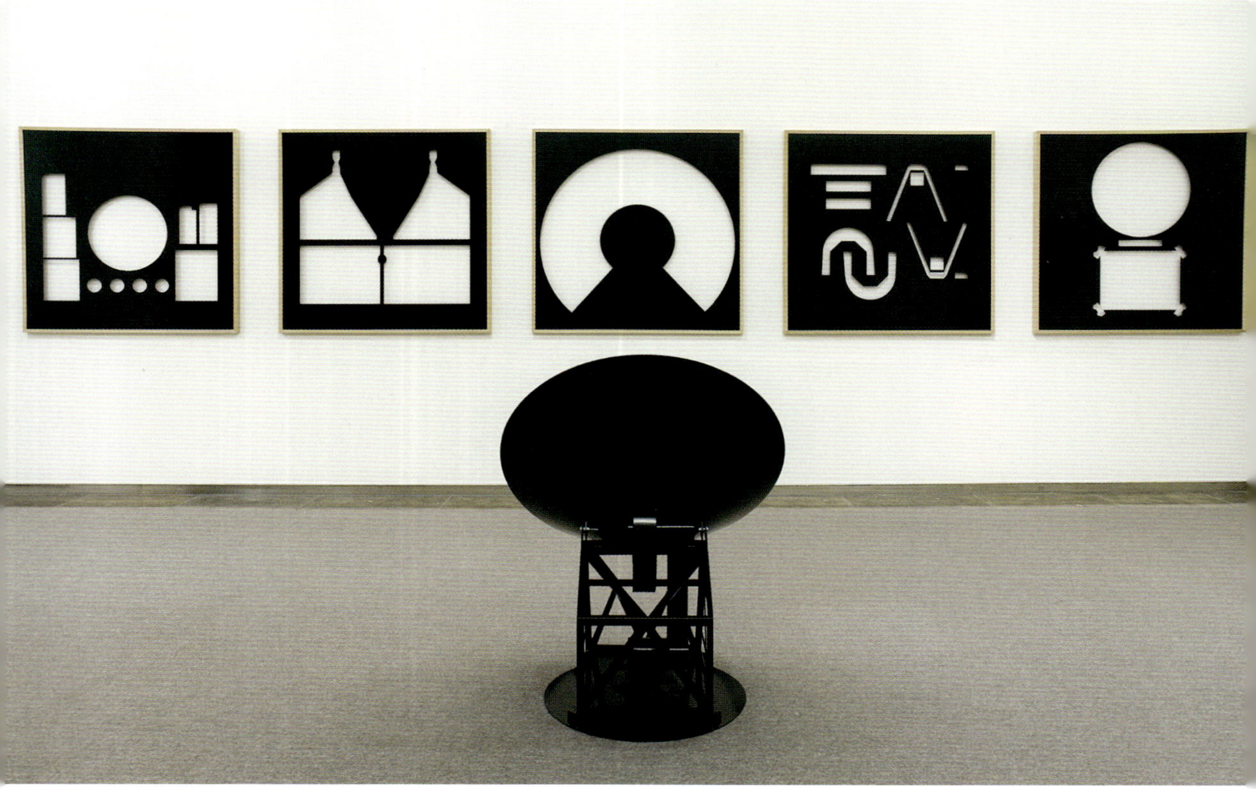

Lello//Arnell (Jørgen Craig Lello
& Tobias Arnell)
The Seer, 2008
Plywood
145 x 60 x 60 cm
Astrup Fearnley Collection, Oslo

Lello//Arnell (Jørgen Craig Lello
& Tobias Arnell)
The Oracle, 2008
Plywood
50 x 25 x 25 cm
Astrup Fearnley Collection, Oslo

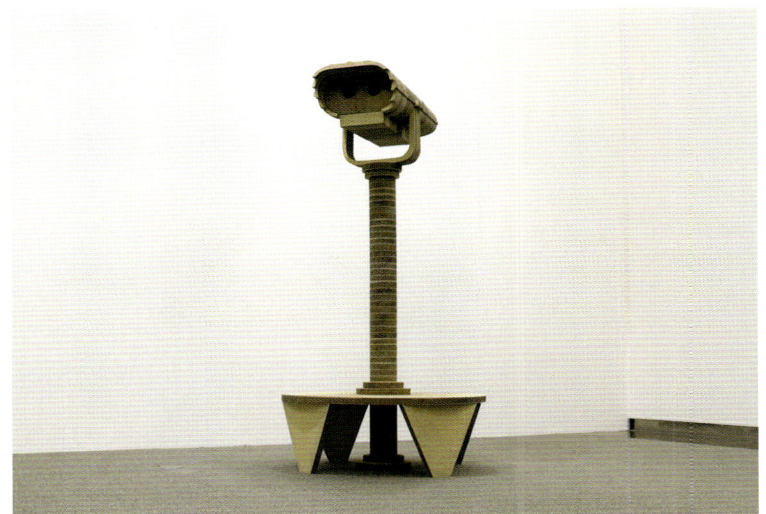

Lello//Arnell (Jørgen Craig Lello
& Tobias Arnell)
The Seer, 2008
Plywood
145 x 60 x 60 cm
Astrup Fearnley Collection, Oslo

Lello//Arnell (Jørgen Craig Lello
& Tobias Arnell)
The Oracle, 2008
Plywood
50 x 25 x 25 cm
Astrup Fearnley Collection, Oslo

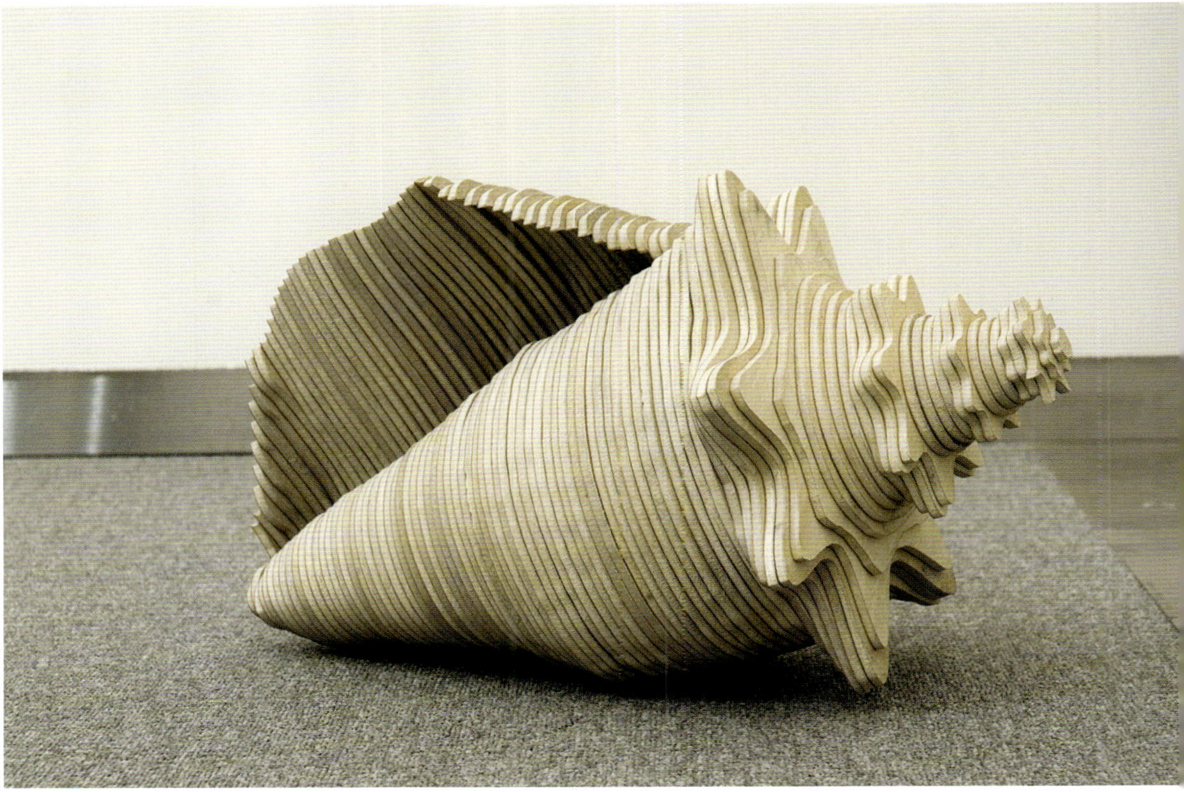

Thora Dolven Balke

**Born 1982 Oslo
Lives and works in Oslo**

'Be calm'
(Louise Bourgeois, b. 1911)

My works bring together absurd and mundane phenomena, and are impelled by the idea that the most real aspect of life – mankind's frailty and transience – is the most difficult to accept. I use fear as a construction in my works, a fear striven for in order to feel something fundamental, e.g. by watching horror films. I simultaneously refer to fear as genuine and unavoidable in contexts such as sickness and death. My works present aestheticized and intangible situations, through pictures, sound works or scenographic room-installations. Here the action is not necessarily shown directly, but only suggested as a 'before' or 'after' situation. Hollywood films and popular culture are dream and nightmare conjoined. Just as in real life, no one knows anymore who represents good or evil, but everyone refers to the same accepted truths. *Oh God No* is about sleep and the longing to forget, but also the fascination for death and terror. As with my other works, this piece deals with safety as being the most fragile of all constructions, and so-called normality as the most sinister.

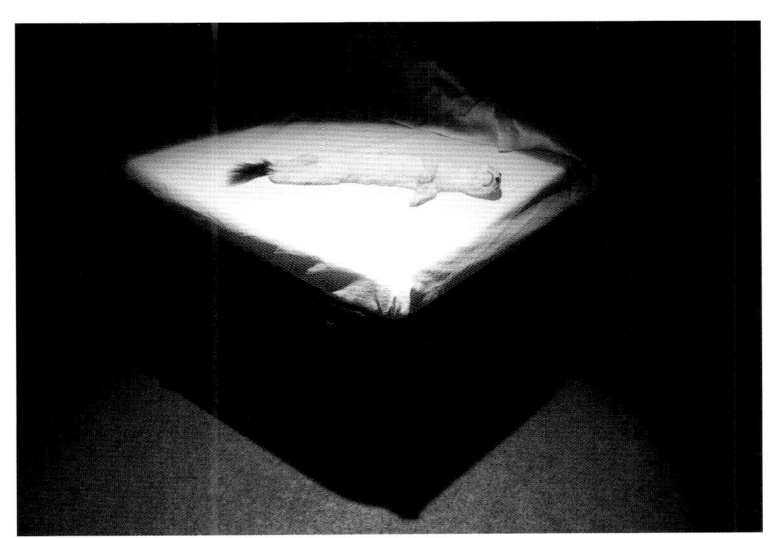

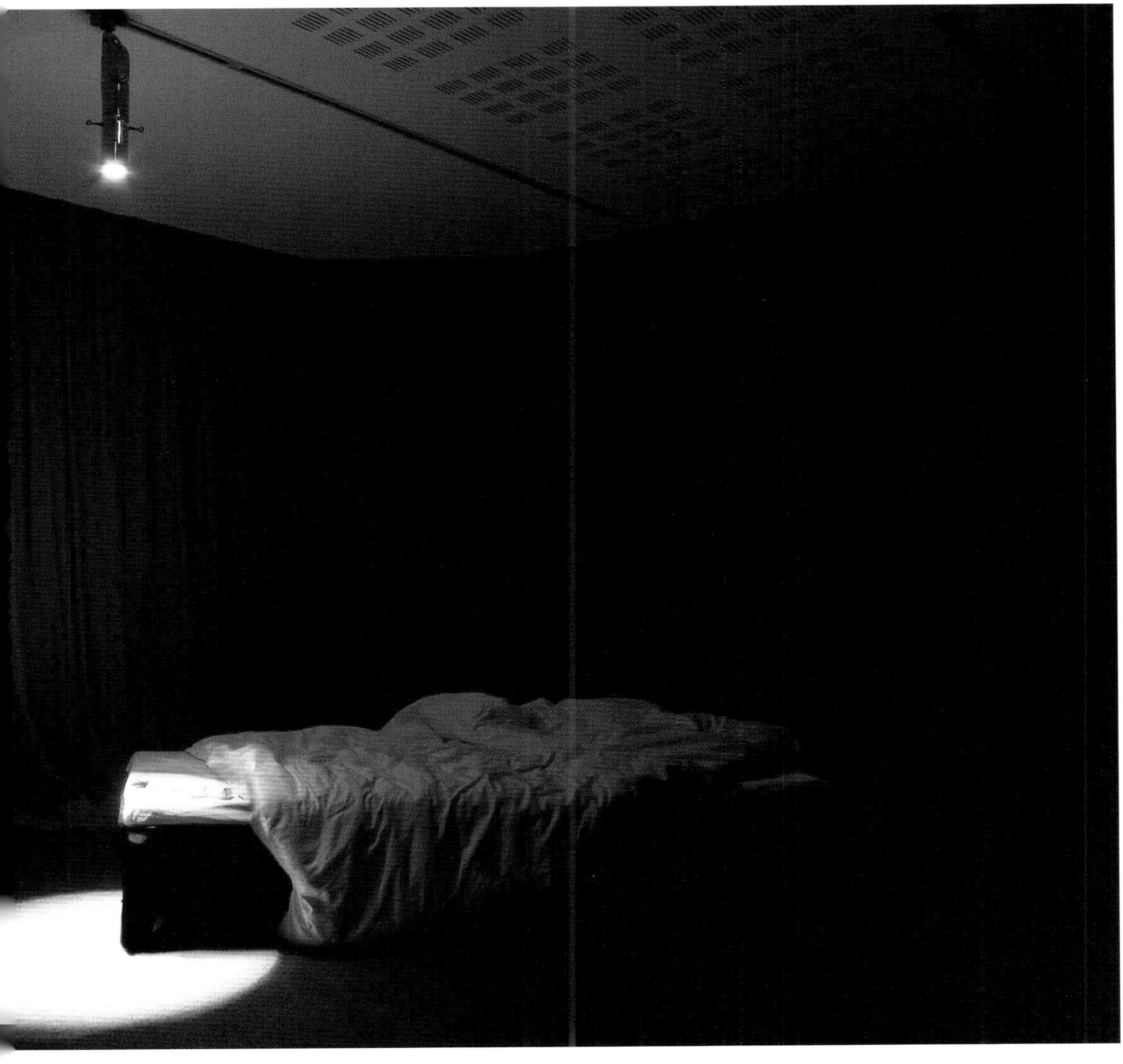

Siri Bergqvam

Born 1977 Skedsmo
Lives and works in Oslo

My works deal thematically with the 'everyday' motif, inasmuch as I create sculptural caricatures of reality. Typically mundane objects are the point of departure for my textile objects; they are immediately recognizable and both real and absolutely unreal. There is no connection between what one believes one sees and what a thing actually is. The soft textile character communicates a kind of uniformity. It is as if the things belong to a separate world in which everything that exists looks the same way: imprecise and uncanny. Ordinary objects have the potential to express human experience because of their obvious presence in our lives.

I am interested in the vulnerable world of children, how they view their surroundings with an open gaze. The child's mind archives secrets we grown-ups cannot understand. Their reality is mysterious in many respects, lost to us for all time. I want to emancipate things from the hard functional world, so that they can exist without the oppressive reason which comes to characterize us after we abandon the realms of childhood. Freud explains that children at play do not distinguish sharply between animate and inanimate things – they often treat their dolls or cuddly soft toys as living beings. Children talk to their dolls and teddy bears in a language grown-ups do not understand, and they project their own feeling onto them. I want to invite the viewer to empathize and identify with children, to explore the peculiarity of childhood experience through unique and vulnerable variants of everyday objects.

I imagine the things existing like feverish visions in which normally inanimate objects gain independent life. While this state can be quite threatening, it can also be open and promising. Now and then one can be shaken to the point where everything in the environment is perceived differently, as in a vacuum or muffled in cotton. The objects I use as my point of departure belong to our modern society and represent alienation in our lives. To buy and sell objects on an impersonal market causes us to forget that both the production and the distribution of commodities are social processes. We prefer effectiveness and profit more than human values. Mass consumption entails conformity of products, which does not allow the satisfaction of individual needs and tastes. Using slow techniques turns time into a visible factor. I am concerned with the value of this time in conjunction with modernity and the idea of the fastest way to a goal. In a capitalistic and commercialized society, I deem it important to take time to do 'meaningless things' in the non-functional sense. For me it is also a silent protest against the steadily increasing pressure for effectivity.

Siri Berqvam
2 hours and 15 minutes, 2007
Chrocheted, knitted
Life size
Courtesy of the artist

Siri Berqvam
Miele Exclusive, 2005
Sewing, embroidery
Life size
Courtesy of the artist

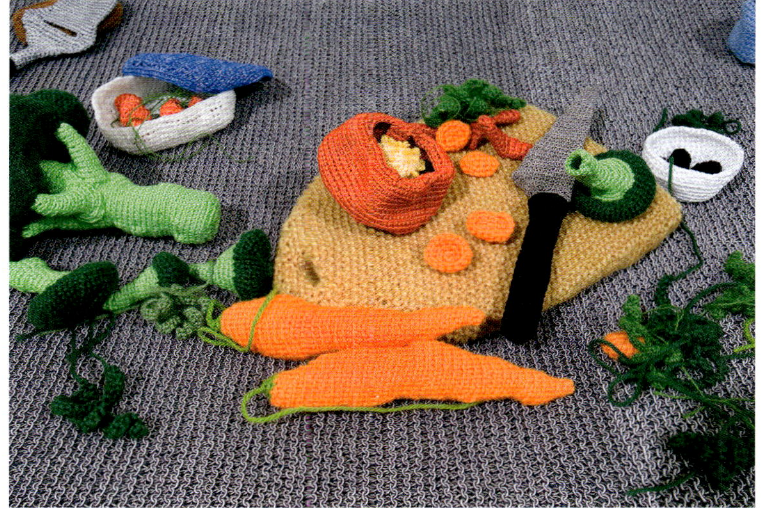

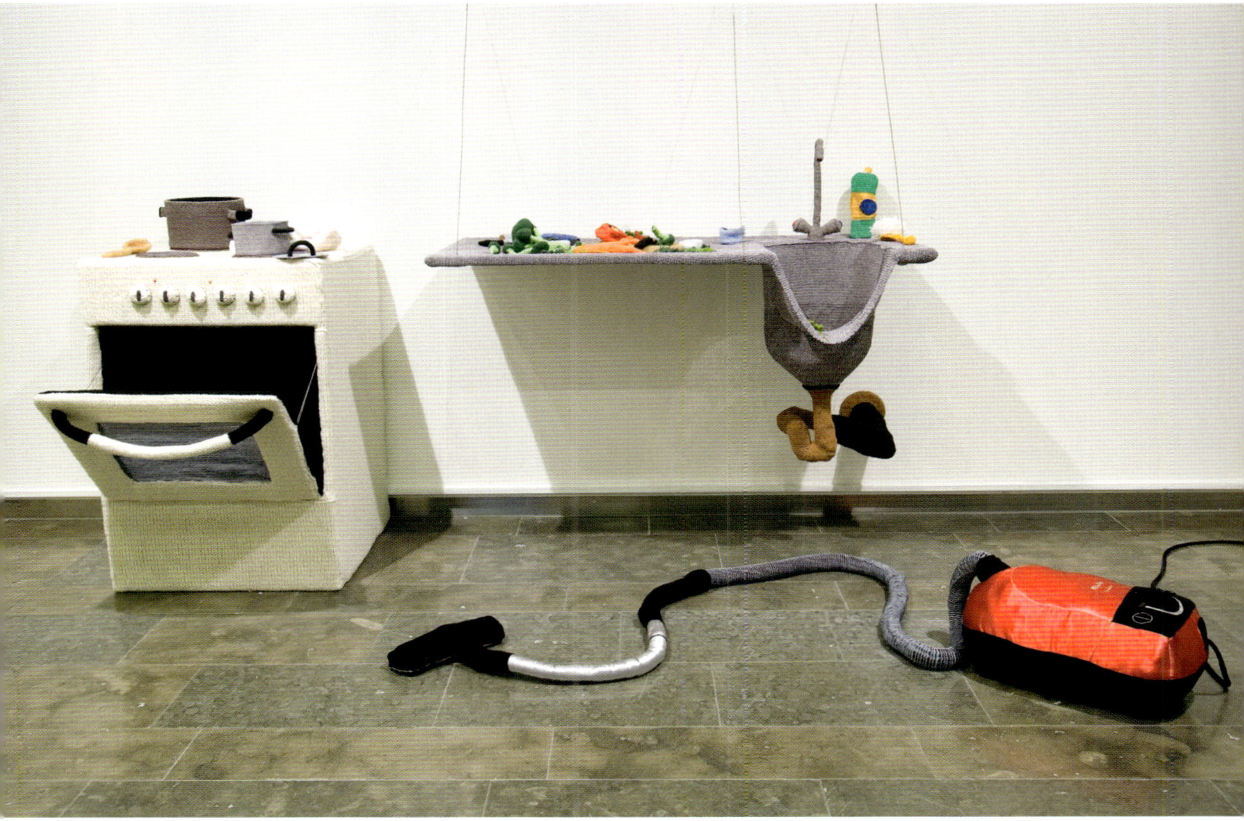

Kyrre Bjørkås
Rune Andreassen

Born 1979 Sandefjord
Born 1976 Tønsberg
Live and work in Oslo

The collaborative partnership Bjørkås/
Andreassen has existed since 2001. After
the graduate exhibition at the National
Academy of the Arts in 2004, we have
worked, together and individually, with
sound, video and sculpture, in the context
of art exhibitions, sound publications, music
video production and theatre set design.
An interest in perception and the language
of film undergirds our work. With pictorial
art and art history as leverage, we attempt to
do combat with the language we believe
comprises the backbone of our audio-visual
enculturation or socialization.
When we do projects in other fields than
that of pictorial art (e.g. our collaboration
with Transiteateret-Bergen), interesting
synergies usually arise between the fields,
and in this way pictorial art becomes one
of several possible forms of expression.
Many artists of our generation, we feel,
use similar strategies.
Bjørkås/Andreassen is inspired by old
men's avalanche poetry and the blood-red
sunsets of computer games.

Bjørkås/Andreassen
(Kyrre Bjørkås & Rune Andreassen)
Flat as a birdshit on a buick, 2006
Acrylic on glass and laminated
parquet
200 x 125 cm
Courtesy of the artists

Bjørkås/Andreassen
(Kyrre Bjørkås & Rune Andreassen)
It's all around you, 2007
Mixed media
160 x 160 cm
Courtesy of the artists

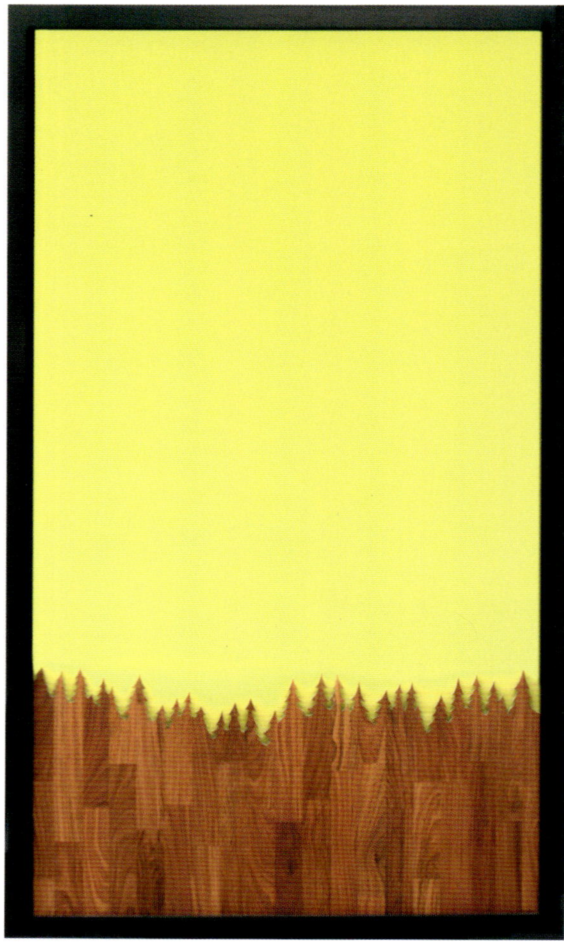

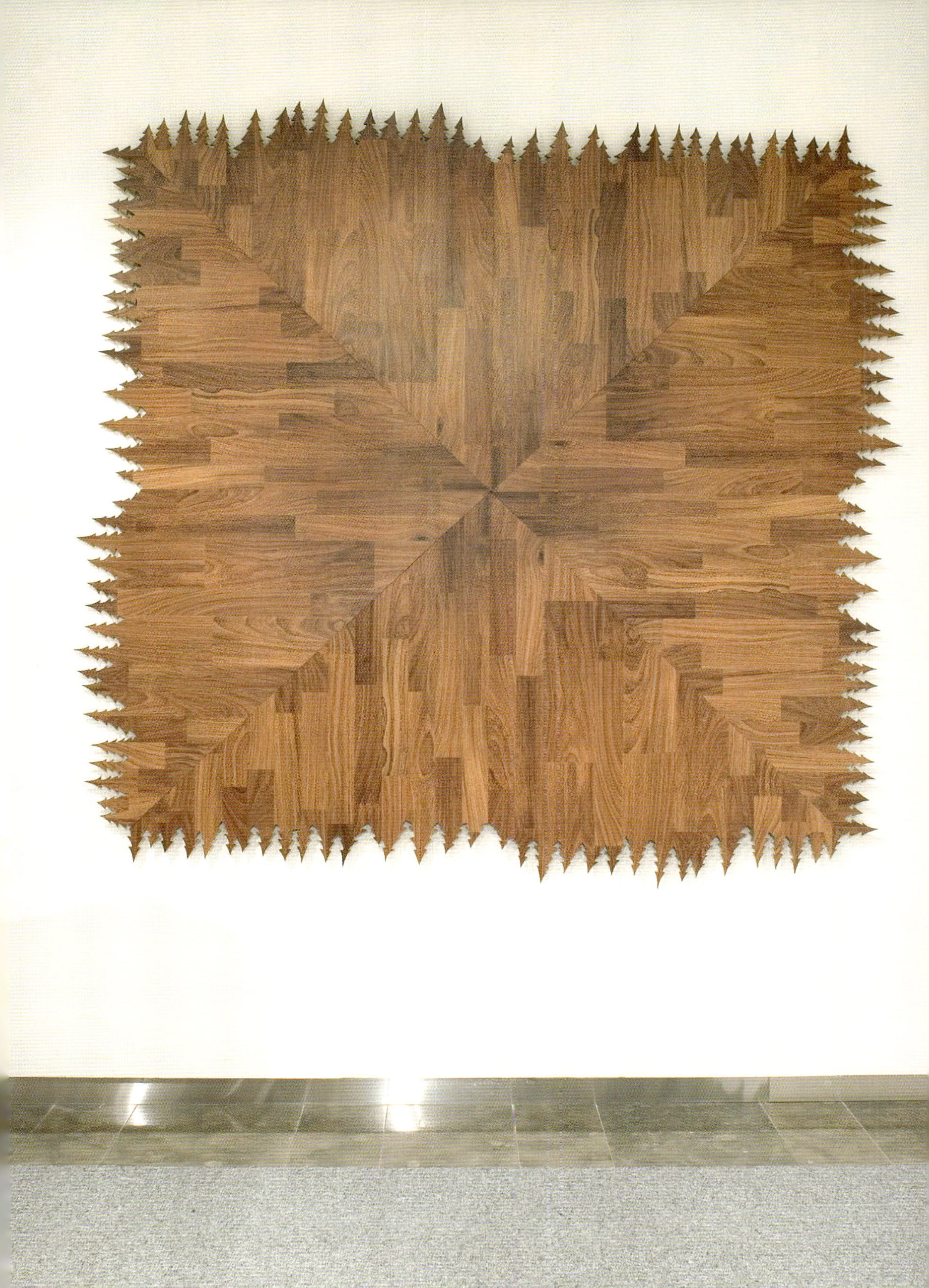

Ole Martin Lund Bø

**Born 1973 Stavanger
Lives and works in New York**

My art production thus far has dealt a great deal with the rhetoric of authoritarian power and the relation between contents and form. Architecture and design have consequently been central elements.

My works often focus on the architectural structure of contents, and on regulations, provisions and premises for a façade's construction.

In the work *(deceptive outward appearance)* I have used one of the definitions of 'façade' found in *Wiktionary* and projected it onto an assemblage of building materials, such that the text is only readable from one specific angle. When a façade is constructed, there are always certain angles from which it is best seen; these may be few or many. Yet regardless of how many prime angles there are, the purpose of a façade on a building/institution is to represent the contents to those standing outside it. This way of thinking about representation presupposes that the viewer dutifully follows the 'game rules' laid down as preconditions.

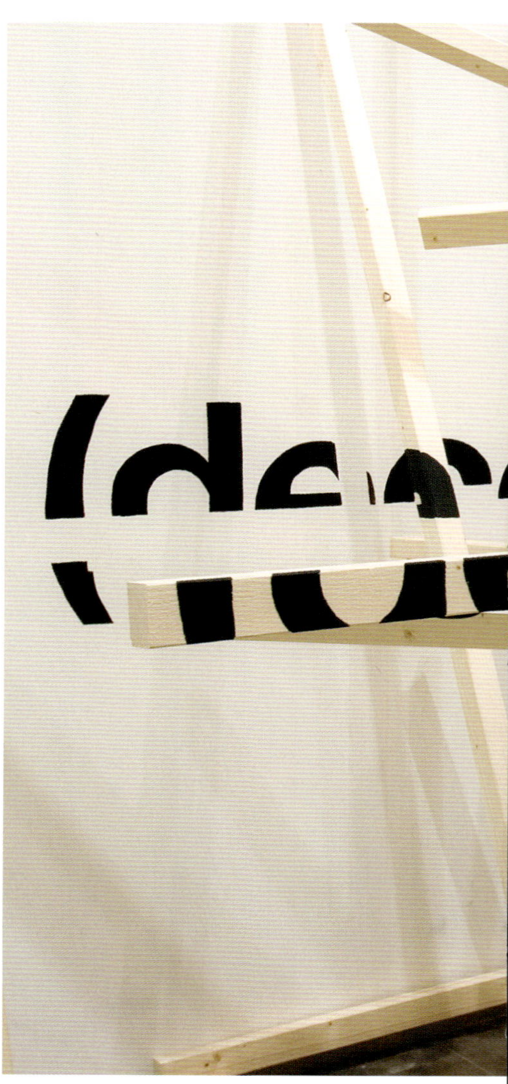

Ole Martin Lund Bø
(deceptive outward appearance),
2008
Wooden planks and paint
Dimensions vary
Courtesy of the artist

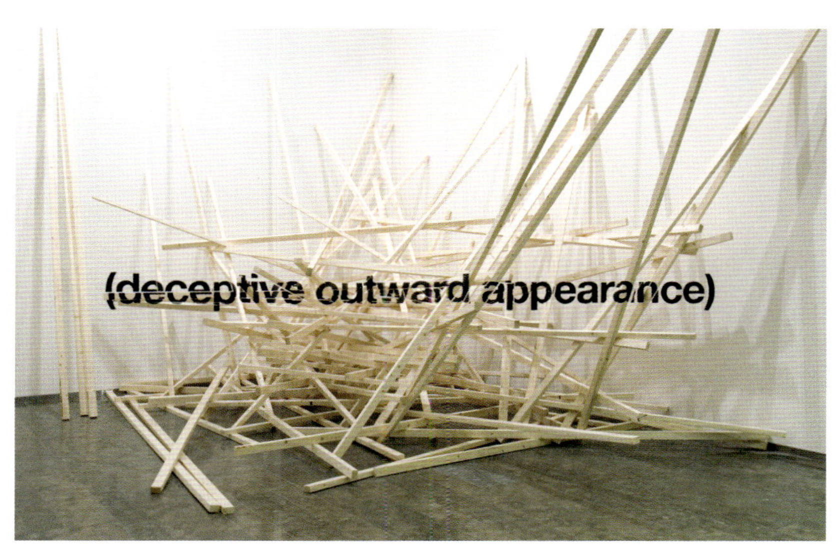
(deceptive outward appearance)

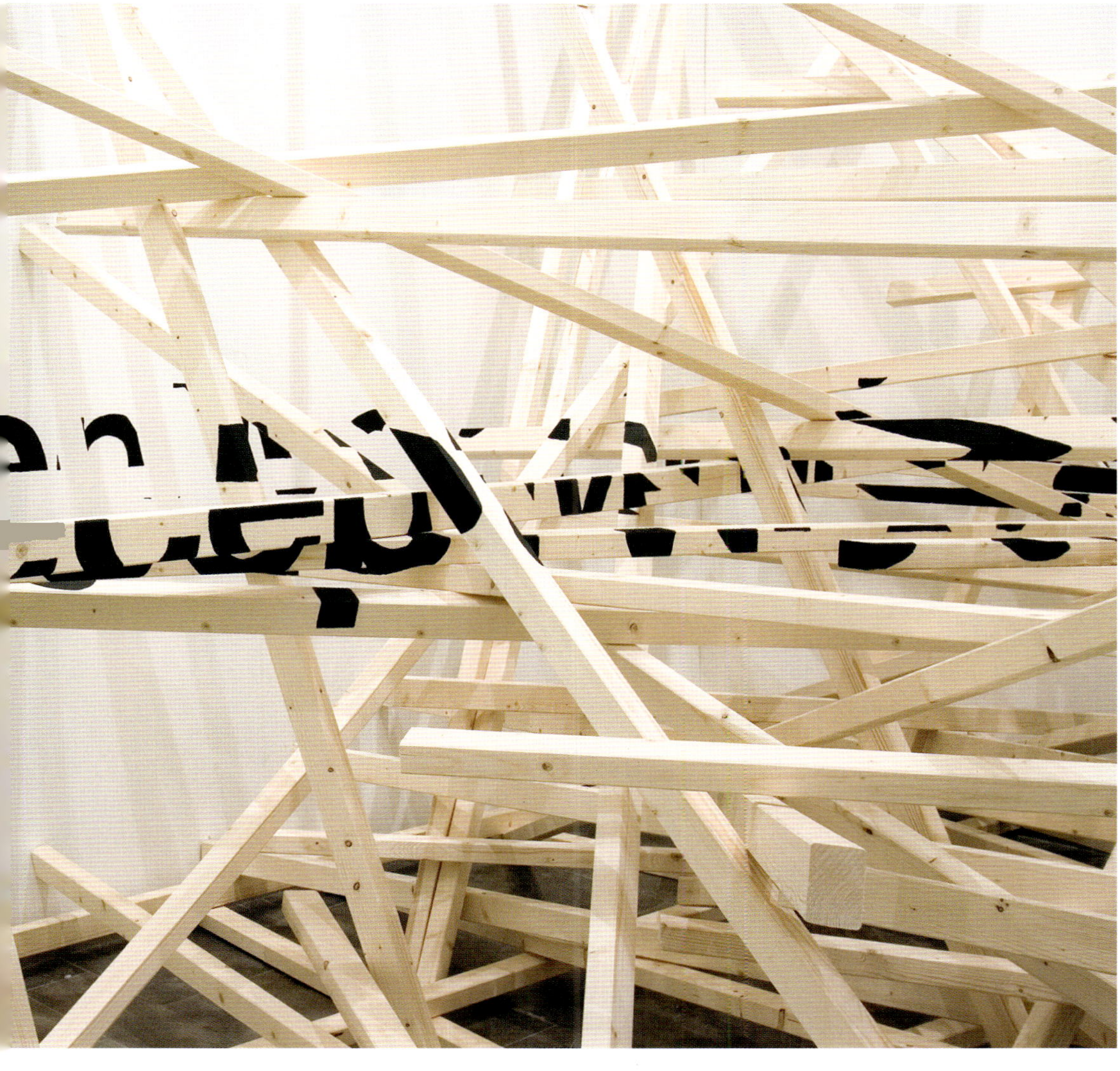

Bjørn Båsen
Termus, 2007
MDF, wood, gas, chalk, skin glue,
oil paint and gold leaves
80 x 35 x 45 cm
Astrup Fearnley Collection, Oslo

Bjørn Båsen

**Born 1981 Eggedal
Lives and works in Oslo and Eggedal**

My works revolve around a personal mythology I myself have construed over some years. This mythology is based on a dilapidated and decadent world. I use my works to shed light on art historical traditions or the pompous façades and ceremonies of the aristocracy and bourgeoisie.
I want to portray this through a hideous-beautiful aesthetics that has as much in common with the Japanese 'super cute' tradition as it does with Arnold Böcklin's paintings. The Manga style's perversion of sweetness can also be found in antique myths and Marquis de Sade's 'pastoral' descriptions. It is this effect I want to achieve in my works; a Wagnerian notion of luring people to the point where they can more easily swallow the burlesque content. The concept of kitsch is also conspicuous. For me, kitsch is not something I need to react against. Rather, it is a wellspring to be sampled and used for creating objects and pictures at the threshold between irony and sincerity. My paintings are atmospheric depictions of this mythology. The sculptures and pictures are character portrayals of originally functional structures in a distorted period style. Through clear references to handicraft traditions, I want to create a false legitimacy of the object's historical origin. In the same way as the aristocracy is a luxurious subculture suffused with internal ceremonies and etiquette, I think of my works as indefinable, functional or ceremonial objects. By giving the impression of having a historical or cultural origin, they appear to be authentic style-objects with an enigmatic function.
Termus is based on a fascination for the period when electricity was first installed in the homes of the nobility. As with everything else, the electrical apparatuses were subordinated to a decorative tradition in order to harmonize with oak panelling and plush furniture. *Termus* is an attempt to create an object that could have emerged from just such a 'borderland'. The title alludes to the object's supposed function, a thermostat or air filter. It was important that it should sound like a proper name in order to appear not only as an object but as a character. As sculpture, it has no actual electrical function. My intention was to investigate which function it could have had in this nearly-historical mythology, and what kind of burlesque object it reveals itself to be in a contemporary setting. As with everything else I create, *Termus* is a sampling and manipulation of known and unknown styles and manufactures, but situated in a dilapidated and naïve-aesthetic mythology.

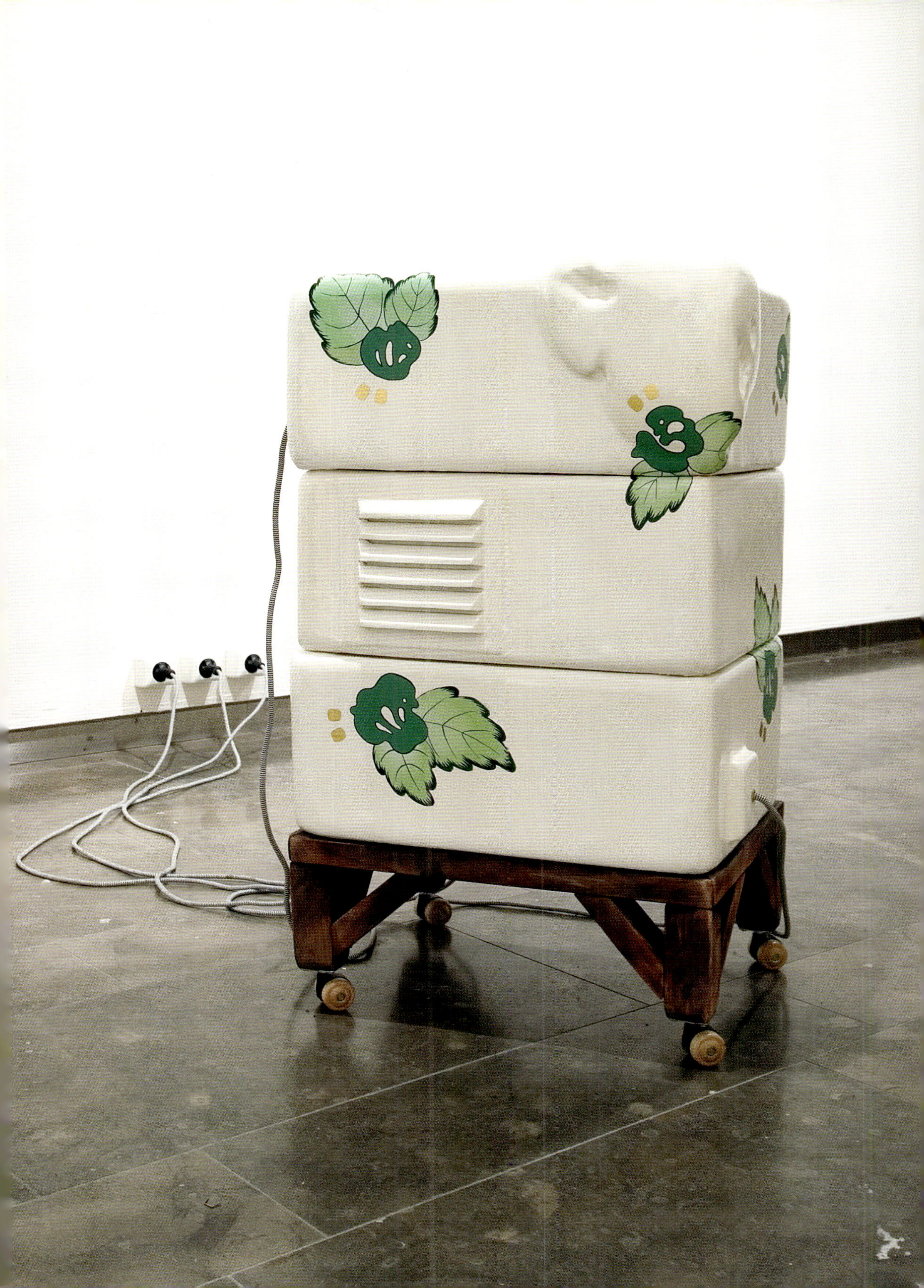

Jan Christensen

Born 1977 Copenhagen
Lives and works in Berlin

I created a design for the exhibition poster and invitation. The text is made to look like extremely diffuse handwriting, with the subtitle in Helvetica Neue. The vague, exhausted contrast gives the impression of something ambiguous, distant and undefined. It looks like a field of fog, unclear and indescribable, yet with some points of light lending it certain readability. Several of these descriptions should aptly apply to an exhibition that includes so many young artists from a new scene, where a great deal of them is not yet fully documented and artistic practices are hopefully still developing. I therefore hope this can function as a unifying logo for the exhibition.

It seems like Norway has a milieu of young artists, curators and critics who are on the verge of establishing themselves in the public discourse. For me, unfortunately, Norway seems too far away – mentally speaking – for the international art scene. This is possibly the greatest hindrance to Norwegian art, regardless of one's generation or artistic practice. As far as my own practice is concerned, using Berlin as a base gives me several opportunities, because many people travel to it, or through it, or come here to do projects and research. It provides the impetus for much of my own activity and I am able to experience a great deal of art at close range. In addition to the Berlin base, I maintain good contact with people in Oslo and Stockholm whom I met up to ten years ago. Without doubt, it takes several years to create the network and milieu necessary for clarifying a wider artistic expression – a so-called *zeitgeist*, if one dares to claim such a thing, and a contemporary discourse.

My own practice is characterized by a desire to keep many possibilities open, conceptually as well as technically. I have created a number of works critically examining my own role as an artist, or showing the limits of our expressive possibilities in relation to context, value and tradition. One could perhaps say that I cultivate a certain skepticism regarding my own role, the artist's role, and that I sometimes try to create works which almost undermine my own practice, or facilitate equivocal, indeterminate readings. Clearly, I express myself visually, often through larger graphic works and texts, and I admit I have numerous sources of inspiration – everything from art to popular culture. I see parallels, in many respects, between the artist and the ad designer, given that the focus of both is to sell a product through expressing a precise idea. Nevertheless, the art scene is still experienced as a sort of sanctuary where ambiguity and absurdity are allowed to come to expression.

Jan Christensen
Nonsense, 2007
Vinyl
Dimensions vary
c/o Atle Gerhardsen, Berlin and
Galleri MGM, Oslo

Jan Christensen
LIGHTS ON – norsk samtidskunst,
2008
Illustrated title / logo
Dimensions vary
c/o Atle Gerhardsen, Berlin and
Galleri MGM, Oslo

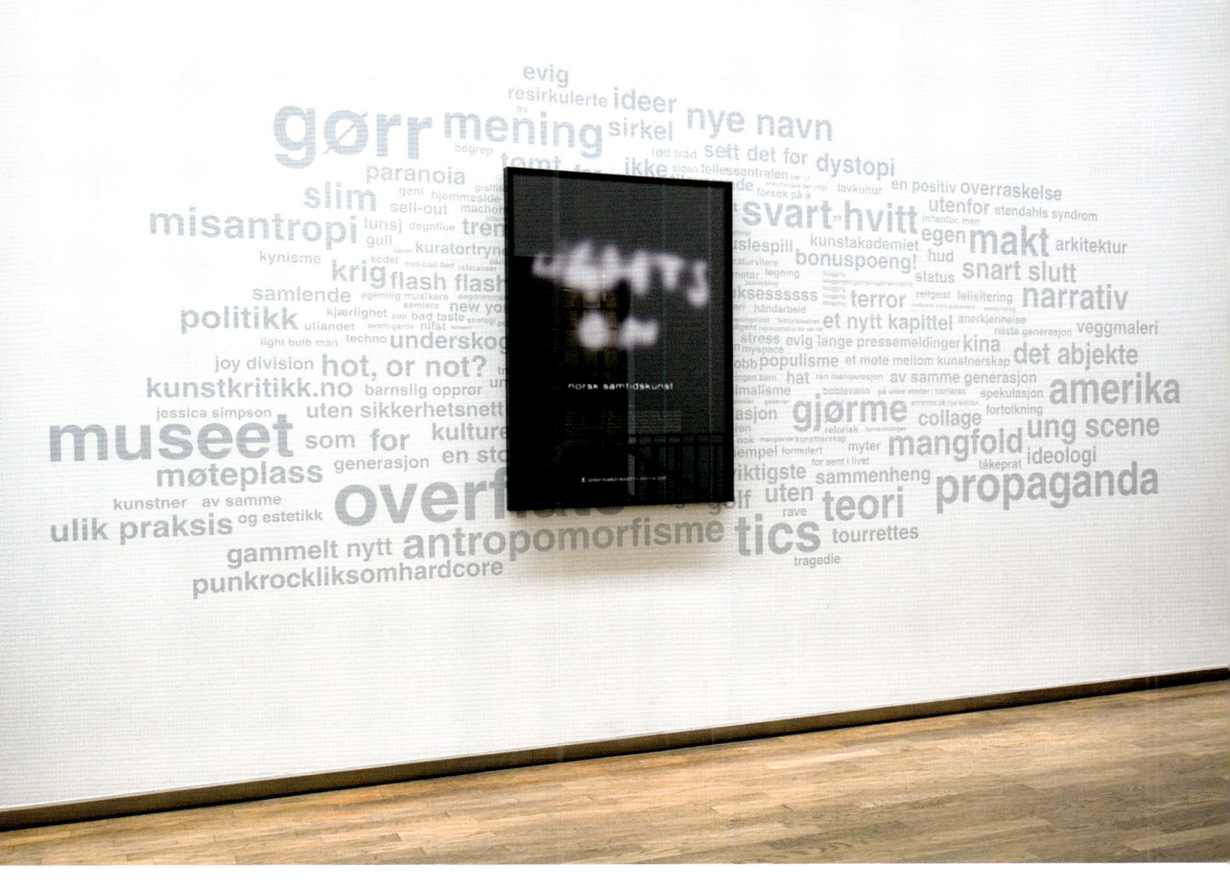

Jan Christensen
Nonsense, 2007
detail

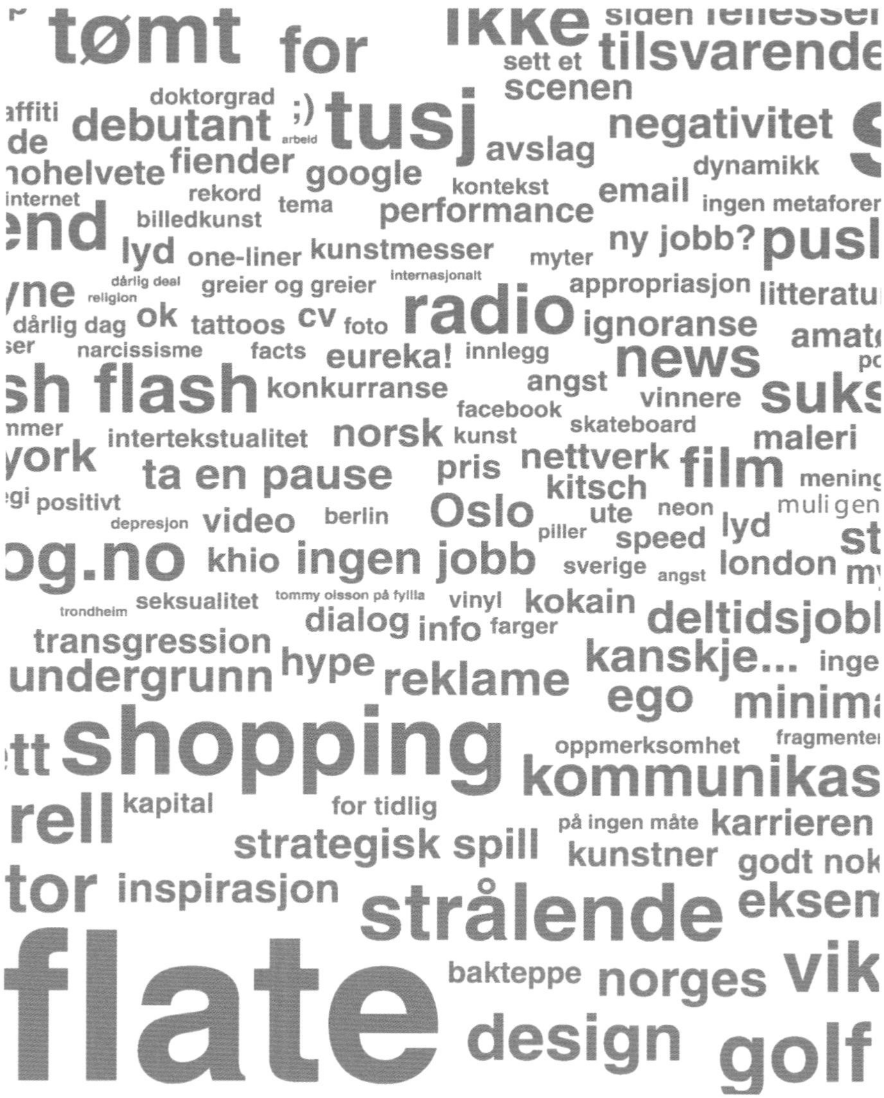

Jan Christensen
LIGHTS ON – norsk samtidskunst,
2008

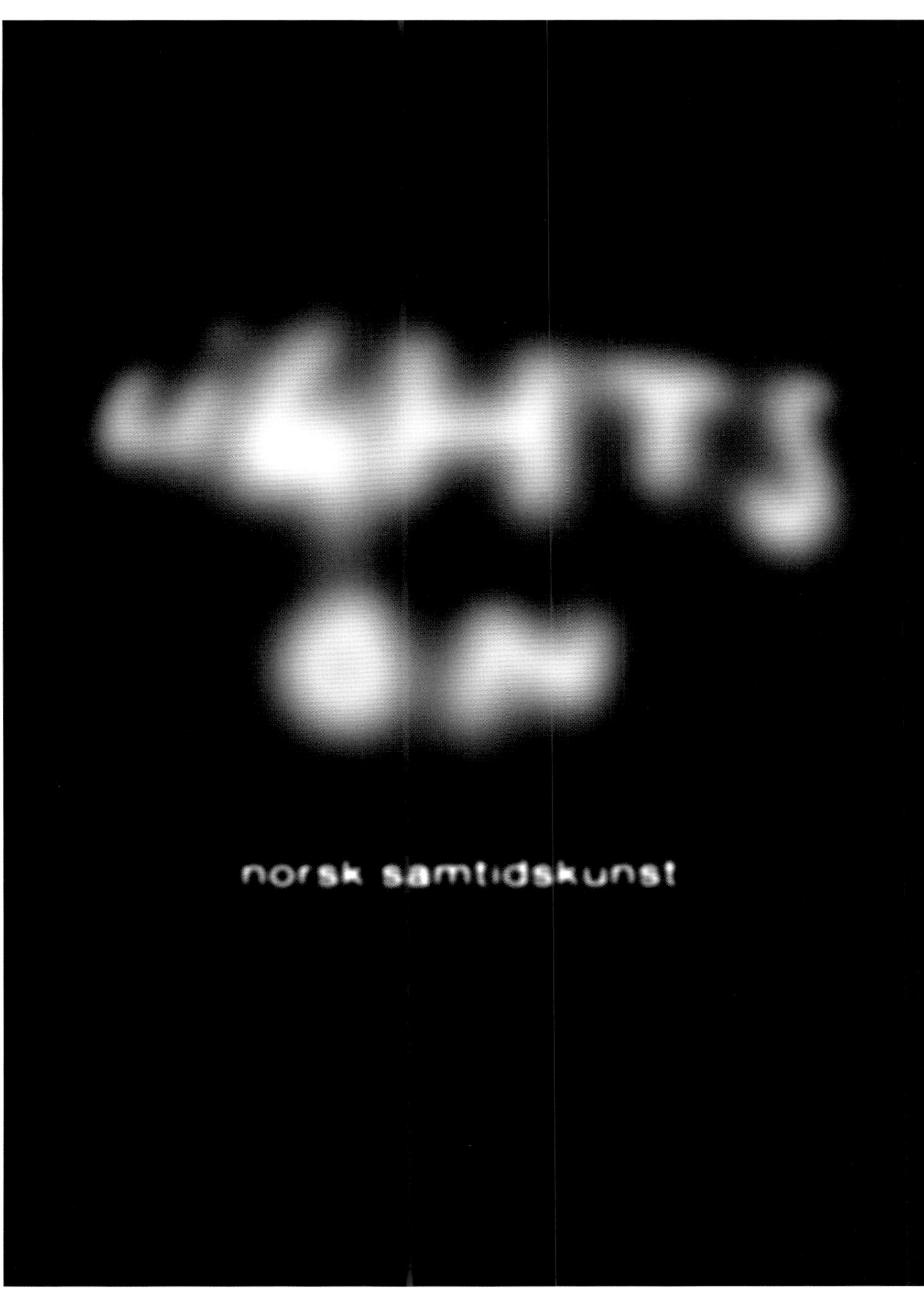

Gardar Eide Einarsson

**Born 1976 Oslo
Lives and works in New York**

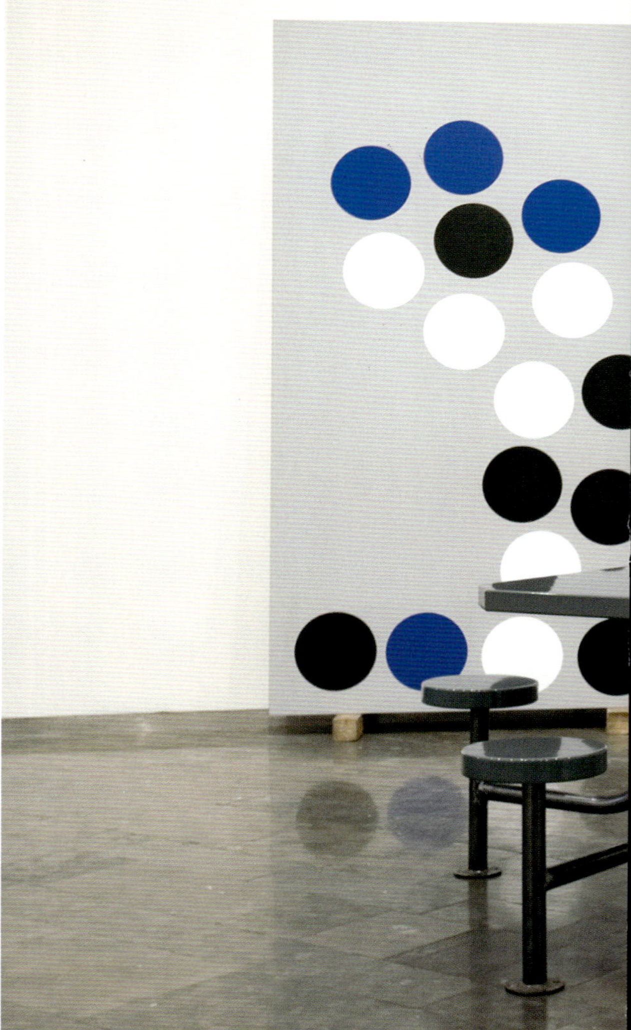

Gardar Eide Einarsson
Untitled (Dining Cluster), 2006
ed. 2/3 and 3/3
MDF, aluminium, steel
80 x 172.7 x 172.7 cm
Astrup Fearnley Collection, Oslo

Gardar Eide Einarsson
Untitled (Barrels), 2006
Enamel on aluminium
269.2 x 149.9 cm
Astrup Fearnley Collection, Oslo

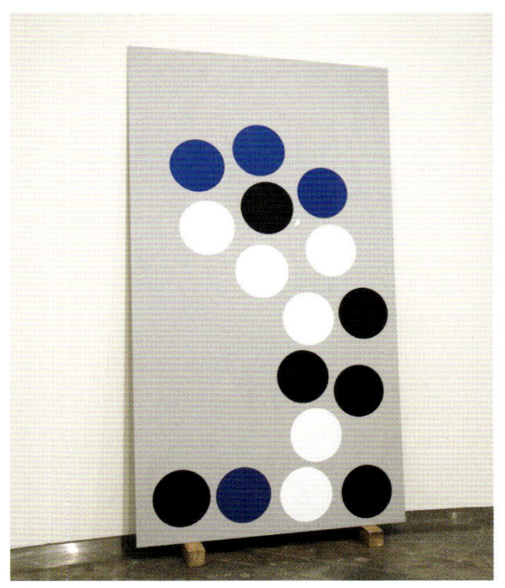

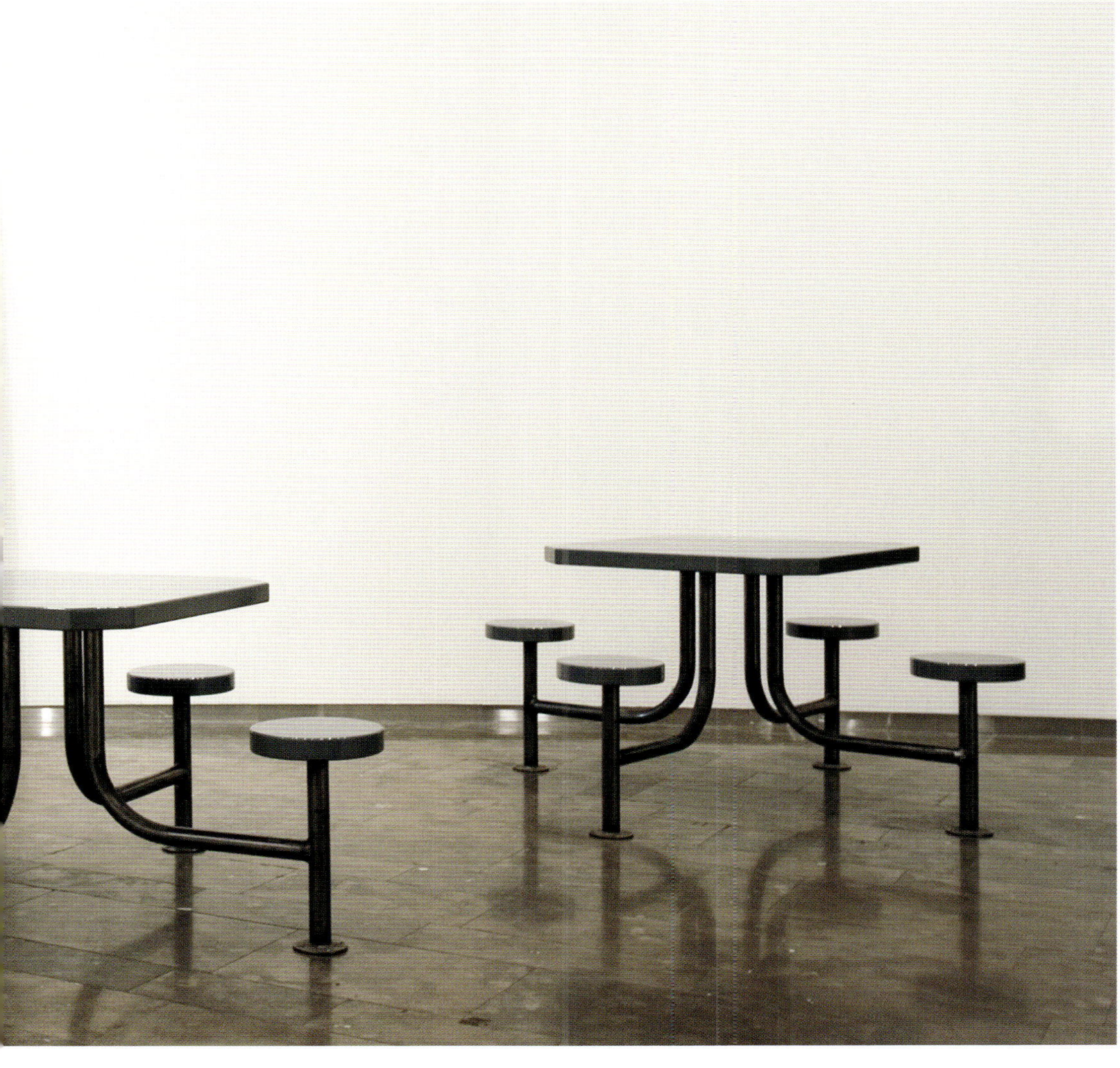

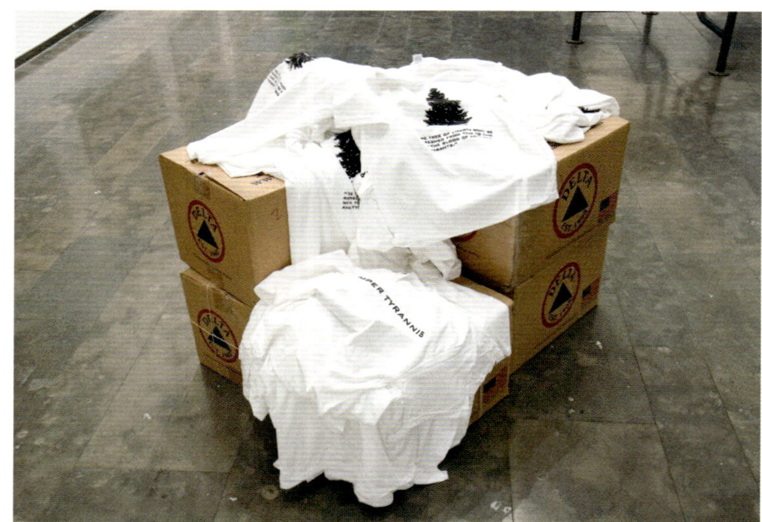

Gardar Eide Einarsson
Untitled (T shirts), 2006
500 silk-screened cotton T shirts
and 7 cardboard boxes
Dimensions vary
Astrup Fearnley Collection, Oslo

Gardar Eide Einarsson
installation view

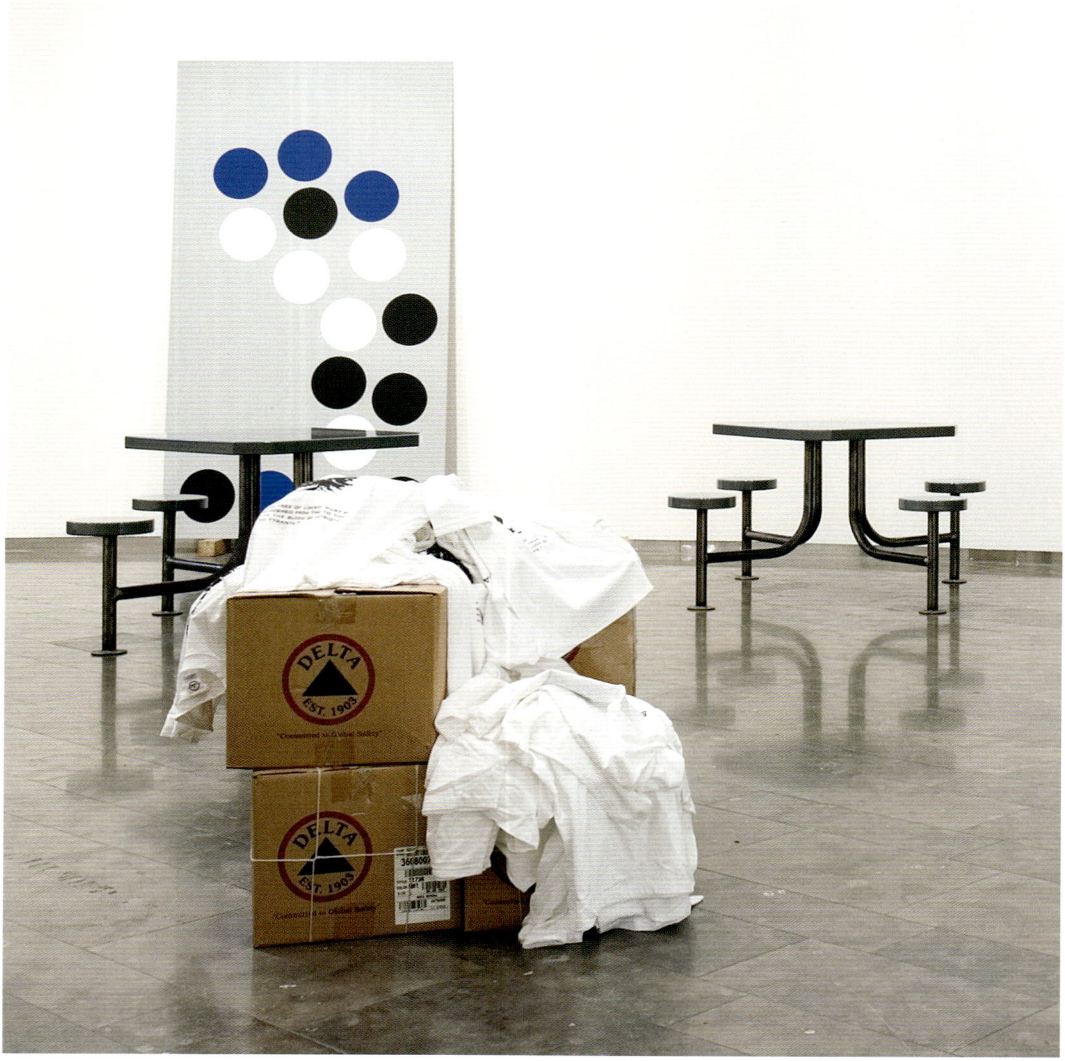

Gardar Eide Einarsson
Untitled (Greeting), 2008
Acrylic on canvas
183 x 213 cm
Private collection

Gardar Eide Einarsson
Untitled (No Collaboration), 2008
Acrylic on canvas
183 x 213 cm
Astrup Fearnley Collection, Oslo

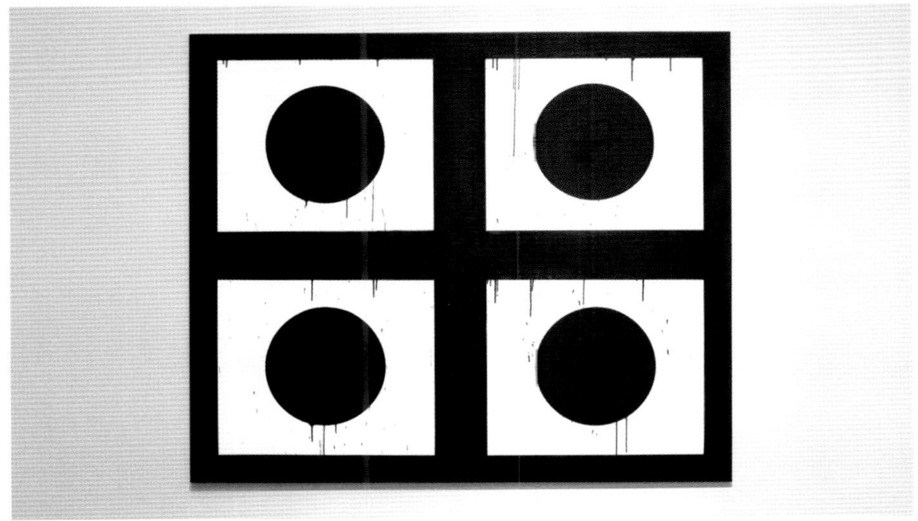

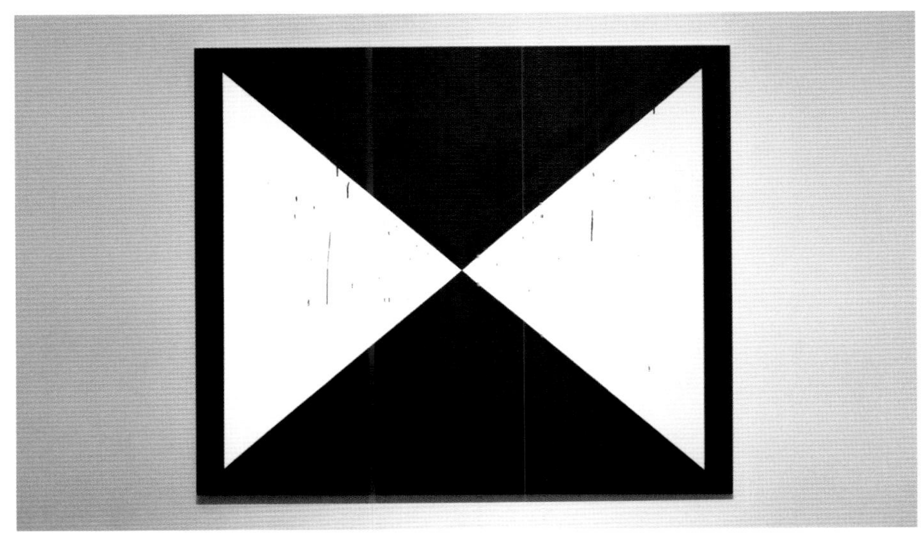

Ida Ekblad

**Born 1980 Oslo
Lives and works in Oslo**

I create art in order to get depressed, to misuse, to shame myself, to feel pain, to obtain financial problems, and for other scarcely desirous reasons.

Poetry Tomb (Death DEATH) and *Poetry Tomb (chase layers of time)*, 2008. This work is a dystopian, poetic *détournement*, consisting of texts, headlines and captions I have photographed from older editions of *National Geographic* magazine.

Political Song for Jessica Simpson to Sing, 2007. This is a bubblegum attack on a silkscreen print of the American pop singer Jessica Simpson, appropriated from the cover of *GQ* magazine, July 2005. In the reproduction, Simpson – clothed in unzipped camouflage trousers, an American flag bikini and a military dog-tag around her neck – flashes a smile while giving the peace&victory sign. She could be said to appear as a stereotypical emblem of American patriotism during the Iraq War and in the war against terror generally. The title alludes to The Minutemen's *Political Song for Michael Jackson to Sing*.

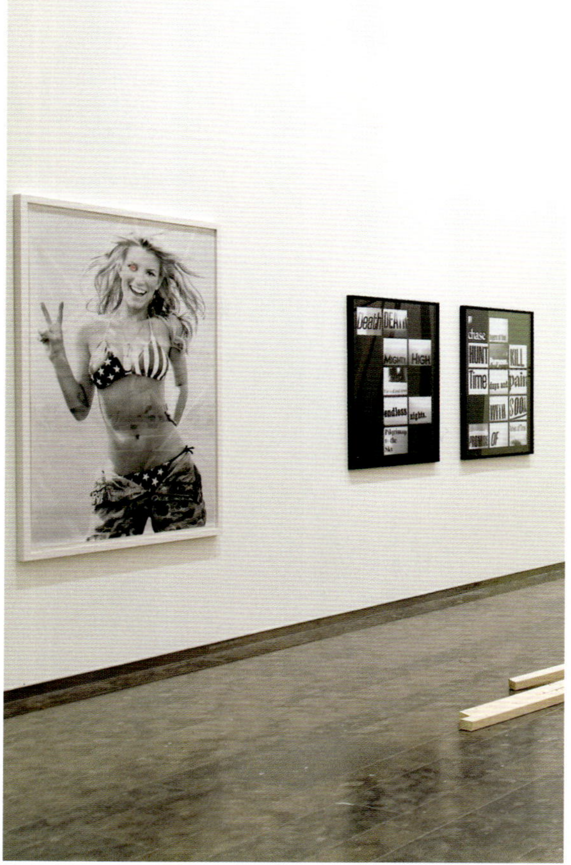

Ida Ekblad
installation view

Ida Ekblad
Political Song for Jessica Simpson to Sing, 2007
B/w print on paper, chewing gum
175 x 125 cm
Astrup Fearnley Collection, Oslo

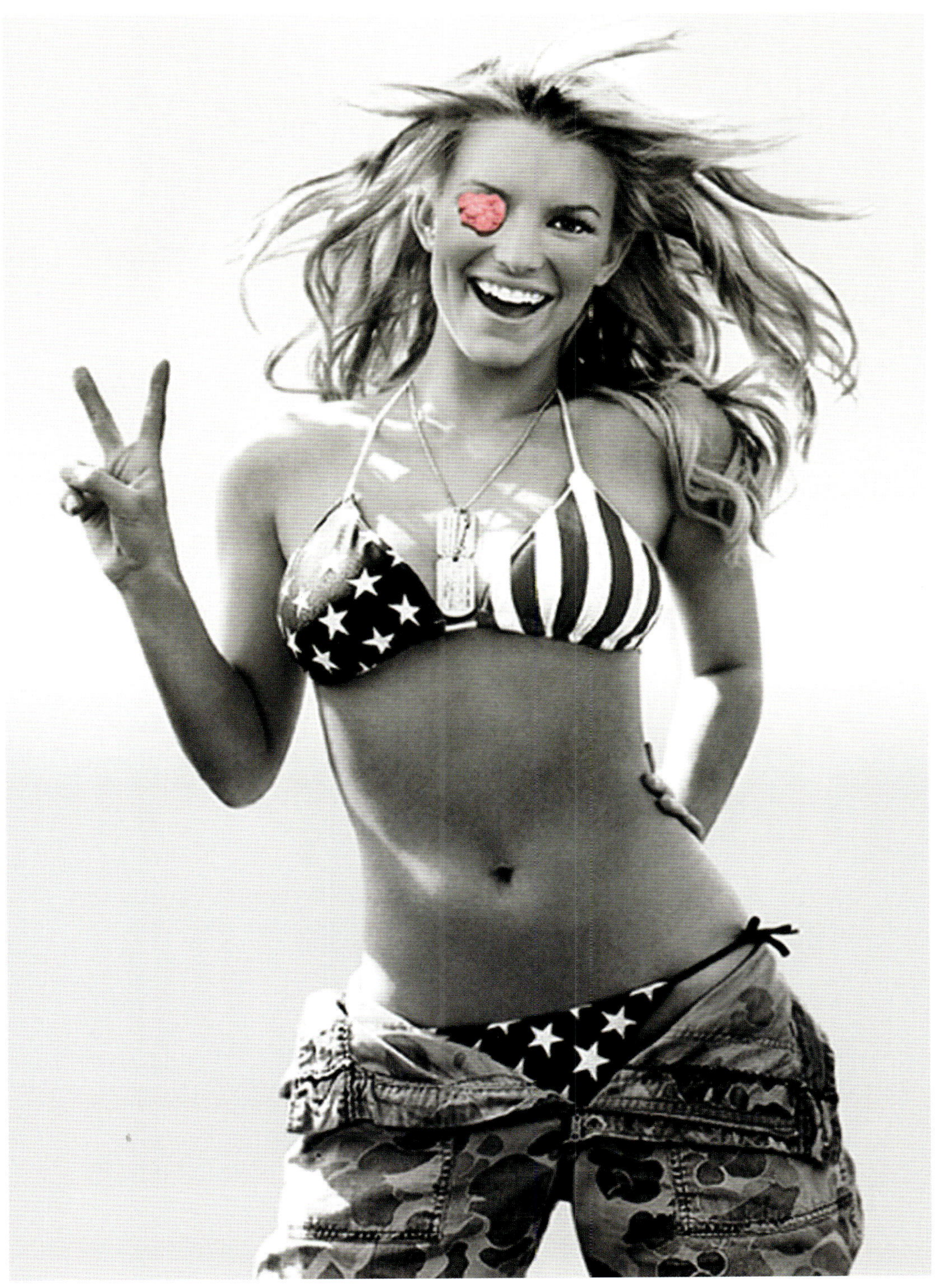

Ida Ekblad

Ida Ekblad
Poetry Tomb (chase layers of time),
2008
C-print
116 x 93 cm
Astrup Fearnley Collection, Oslo

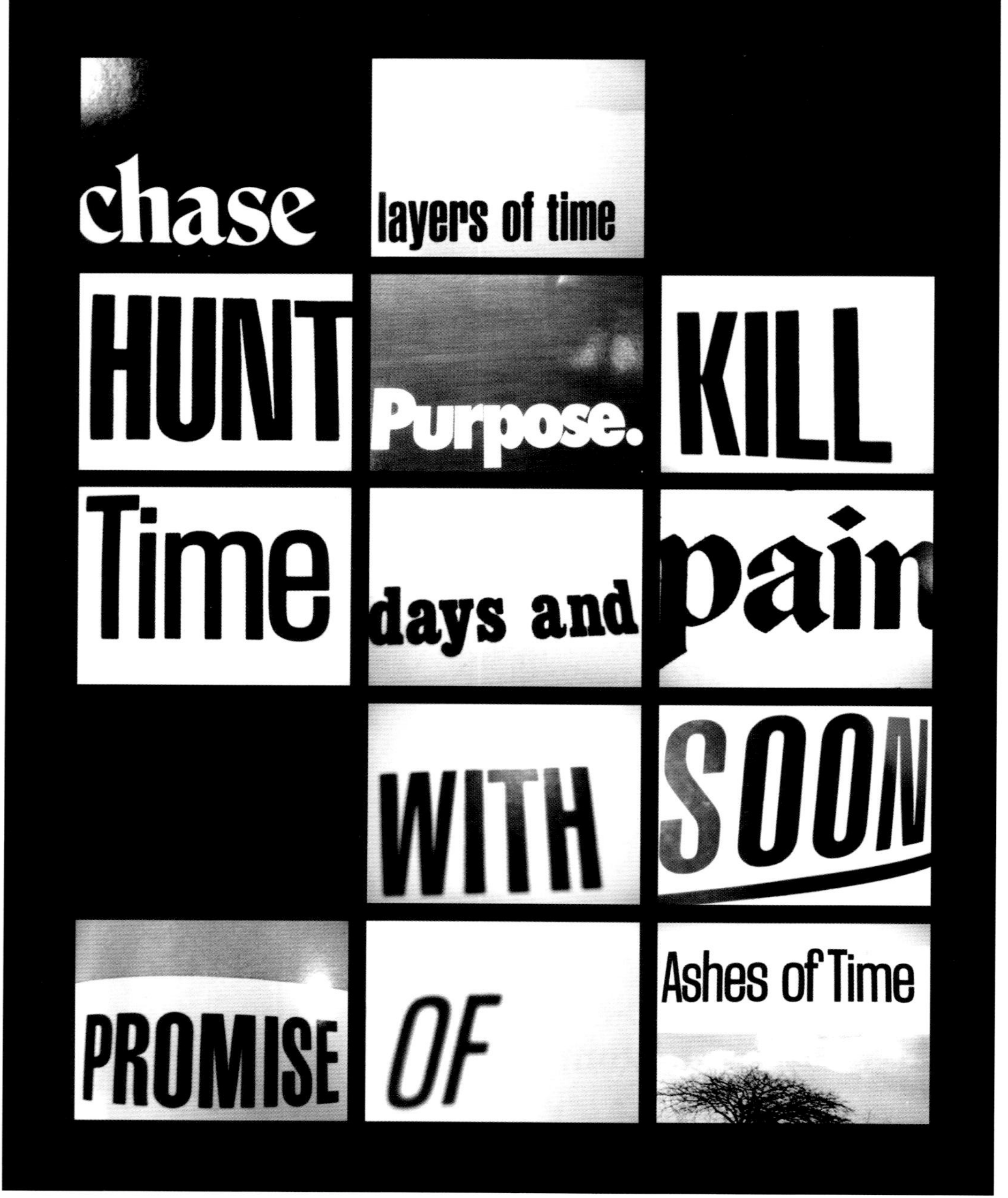

Ida Ekblad
Poetry Tomb (Death DEATH), 2008
C-print
116 x 93 cm
Astrup Fearnley Collection, Oslo

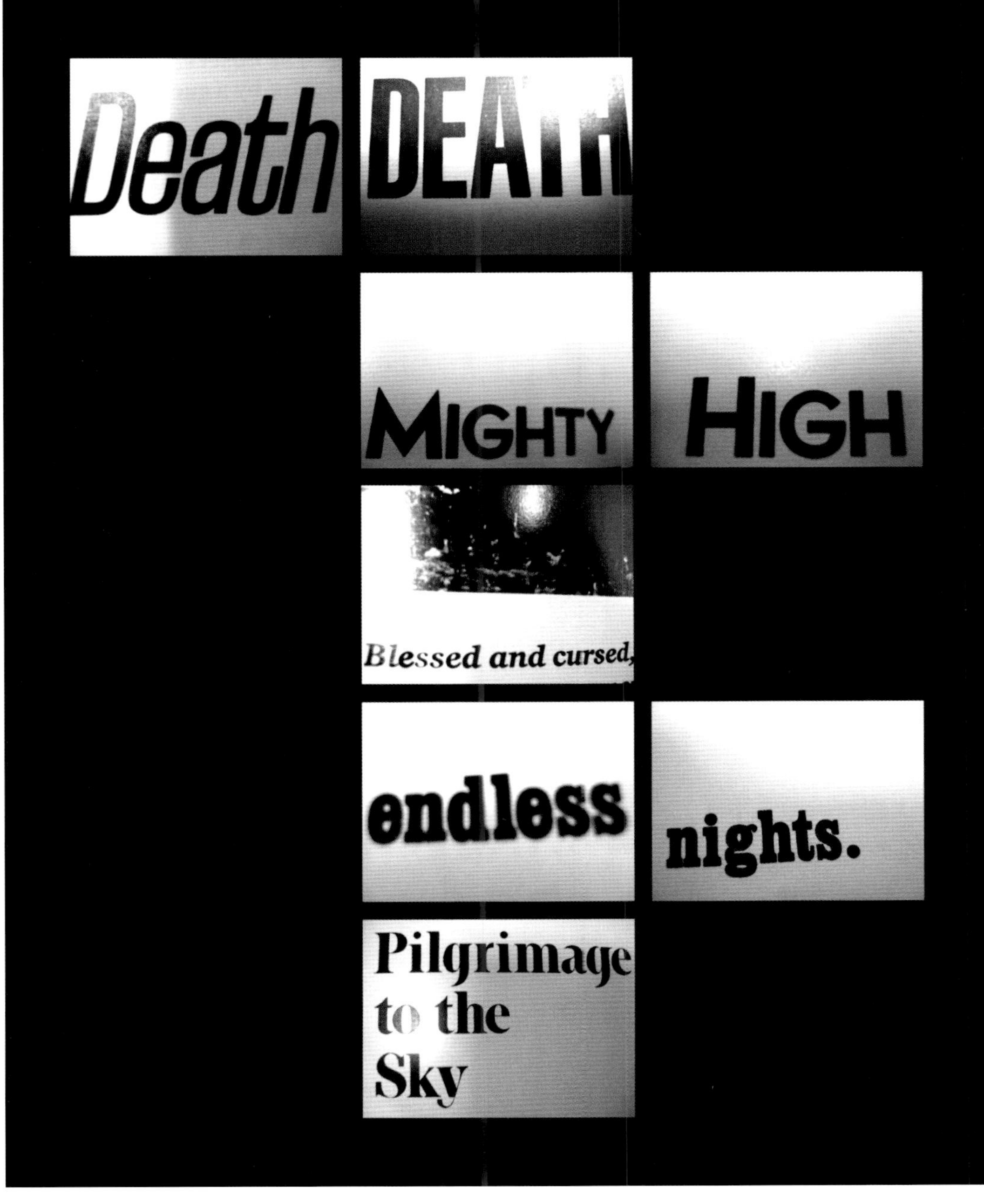

Jan Hakon Erichsen

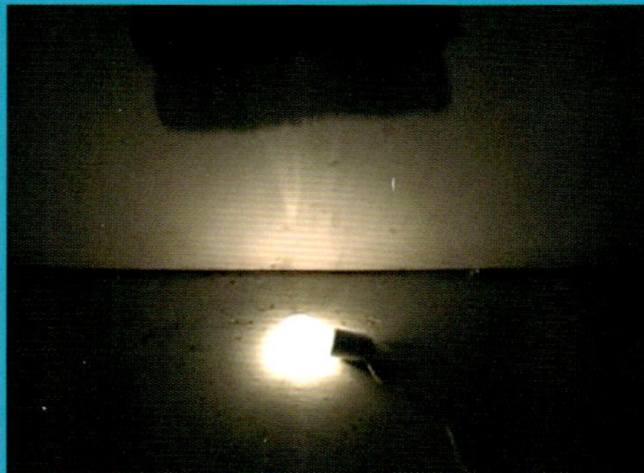

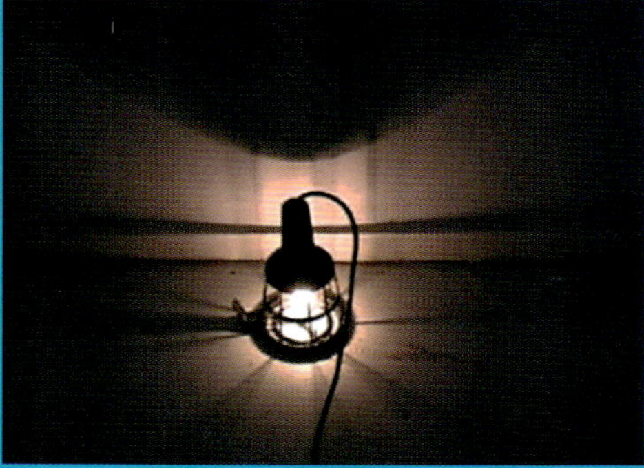

Born 1978 Oslo
Lives and works in Oslo

The starting point for most of my works is ordinary everyday frustration. The pathetic man who has problems tackling the challenges of modern life is a recurring figure, and rebuilt or destroyed everyday objects are another leitmotif. In the last two years I have mostly worked with videos, but with an aggressive approach.

Lights Out is an elaboration upon my degree work entitled *Running with Scissors*, in which a number of electronic apparatuses and cords were staged as potential accidents. From these 'almost accidents', it was natural for me to go a step further and create a video involving real destruction. I wanted to create a work that had destruction as its driving force.

For an artist working with digital media, a number of radical changes in how to present one's work have taken place. In order to show my films worldwide, I use contacts found on the Internet. This, I believe, is a common practice for young video artists. Since it has become easier to contact presentation venues, artists operate with an international profile at a far earlier stage in their careers.

My works generally start with a specific object I believe can give resonance to a mood or feeling from everyday life. I try to hold onto the small frustrations I meet in everyday life and use them actively in my works. The sense of powerlessness I can feel when, for example, I get more work than what I physically can manage, is given vent when I destroy a lamp or shatter a vase. I focus on the small dark moments in life and manipulate them through aggression, black humour and slapstick.

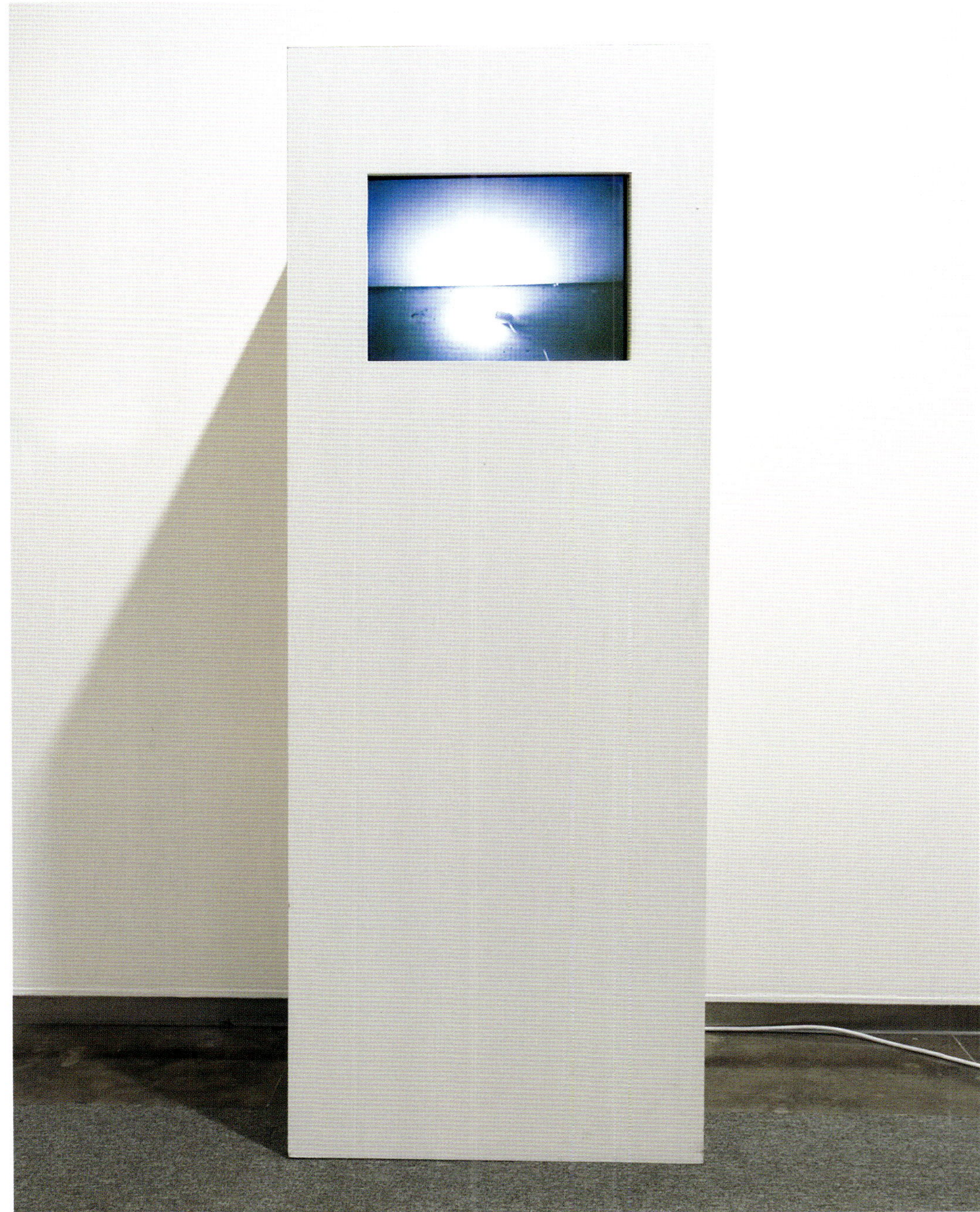

Matias Faldbakken

Born 1973 Hobro
Lives and works in Oslo

Matias Faldbakken
Untitled (canvas #15) – Untitled (canvas #19), 2008
Canvas tape on Belgian linen
and wooden stretcher
each 152.5 x 152.5 cm
Astrup Fearnley Collection, Oslo

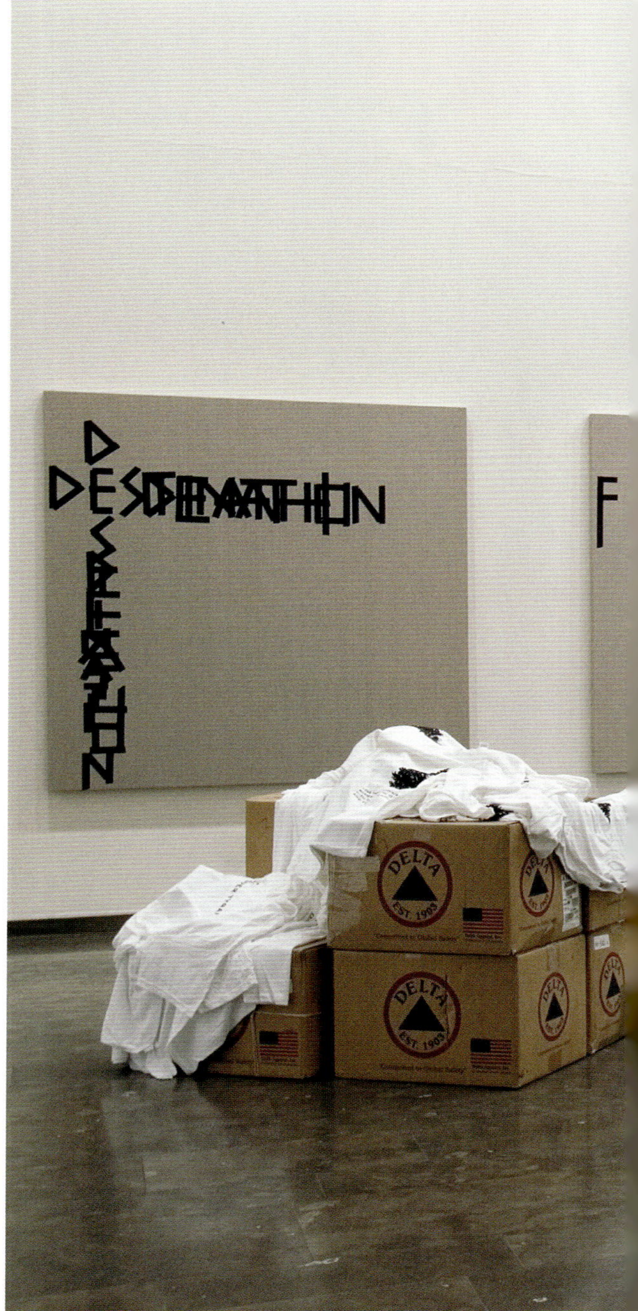

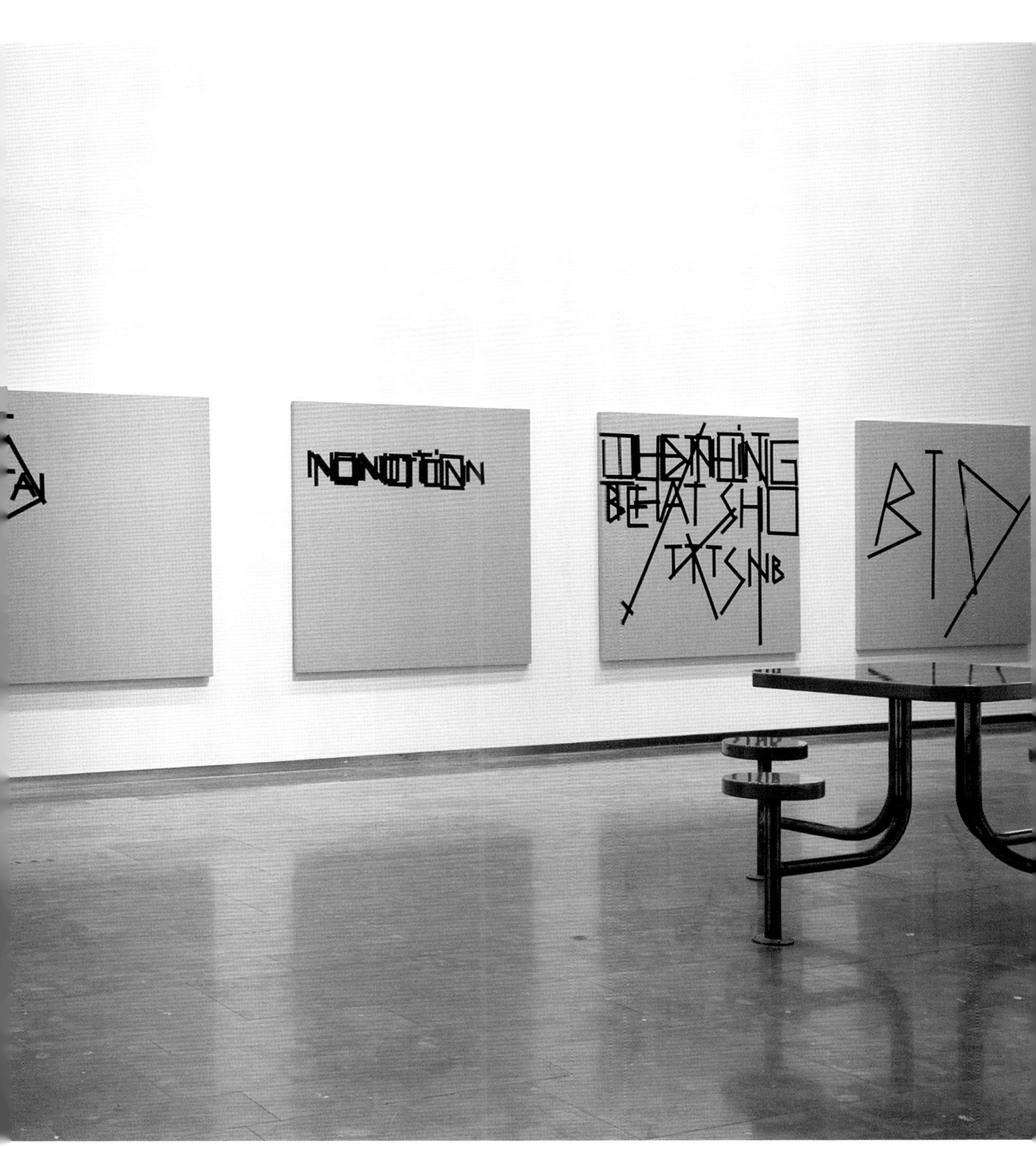

Matias Faldbakken
Newspaper Ad #17, 2007
Inkjet print on Billboard paper
STANDARD (OSLO)

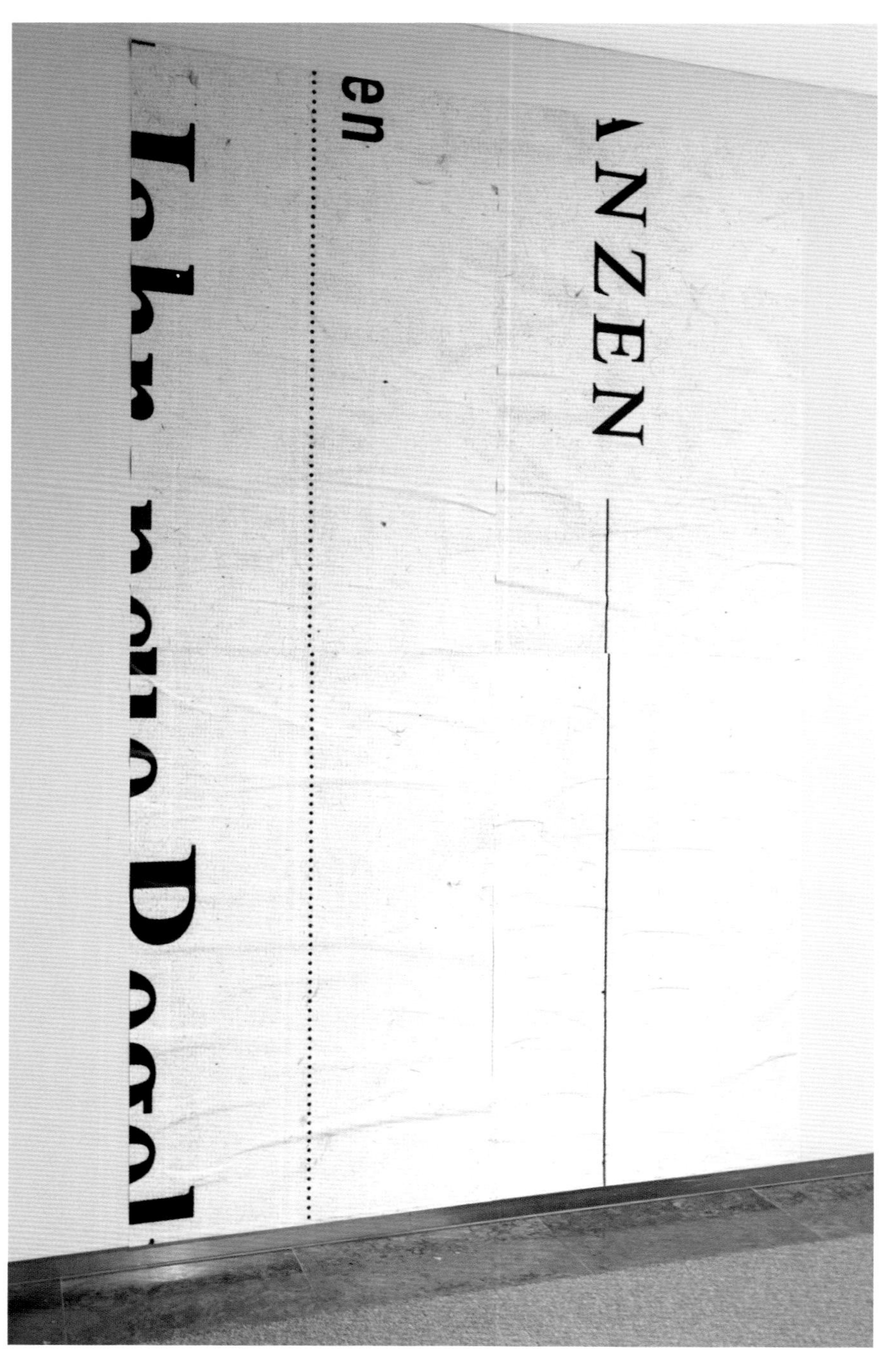

Matias Faldbakken
Newspaper Ad #16, 2007
Inkjet print on Billboard paper
321 x 200 cm
STANDARD (OSLO)

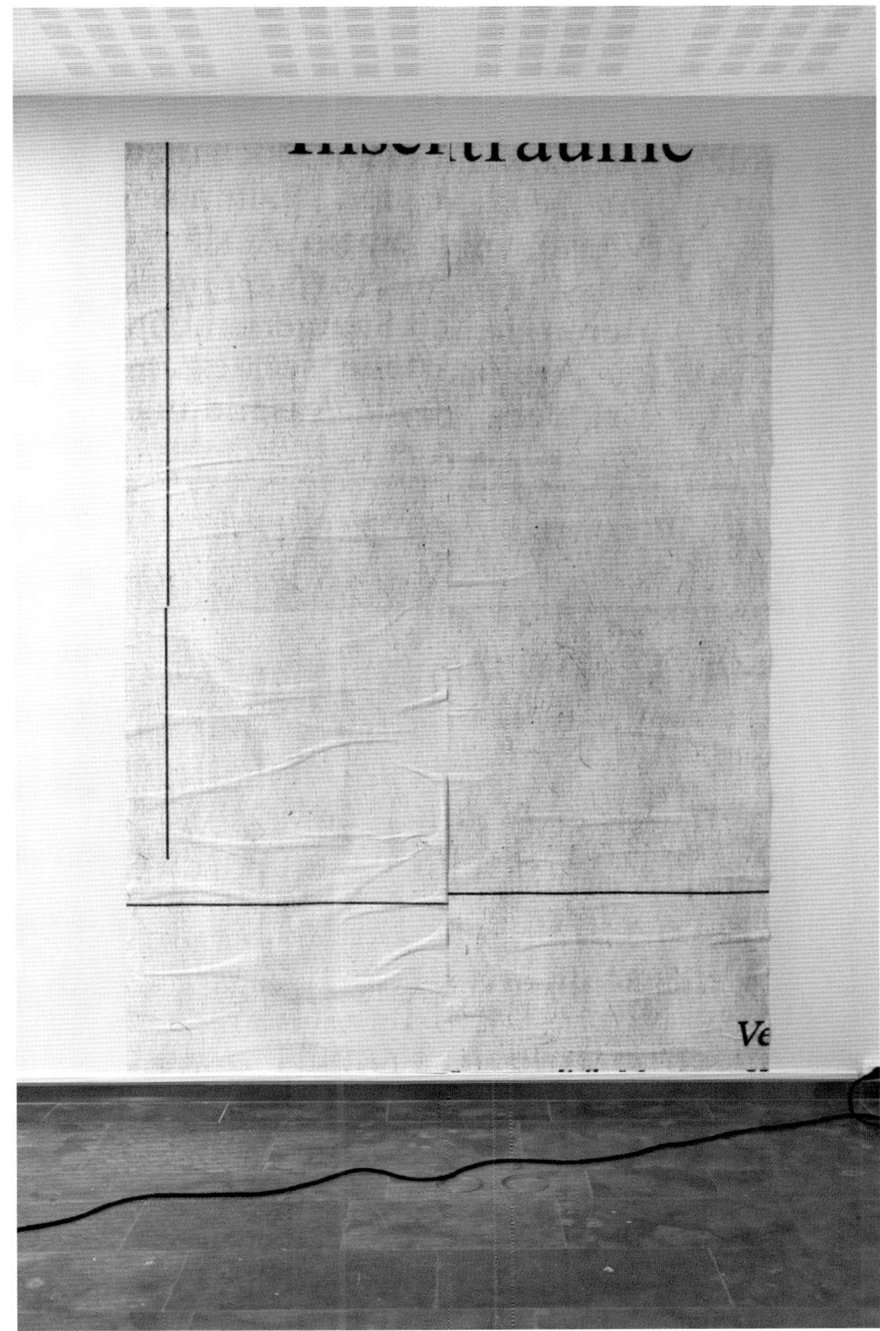

Jan Freuchen

**Born 1979 Stavanger
Lives and works in Oslo**

Expressivity and subjugation constitute a recurring dichotomy in my works. It involves the accumulation and manipulation of information happening within a closed system. This self-referential circuit is the core of *26 Gasoline Stations*. The T-shaped gasoline station is an architectural icon from the 1900s. It tumbled 45 degrees and took on the shape of a primitive lean-to.
In *26 Gasoline Stations* the motifs are structured according to a unique documentational typology in which the perspective (as in Ruschas' work from 1963) often derives from the rolled-down window of a passing car. There is a theatricality and transparency in these motifs: a sculpture consisting of the parts that keep it from collapsing.

Jan Freuchen
26 Gasoline Stations, 2007
26 C-prints on aluminium
each 57.5 x 46.5 cm
Courtesy of the artist
Galleri Erik Steen, Oslo

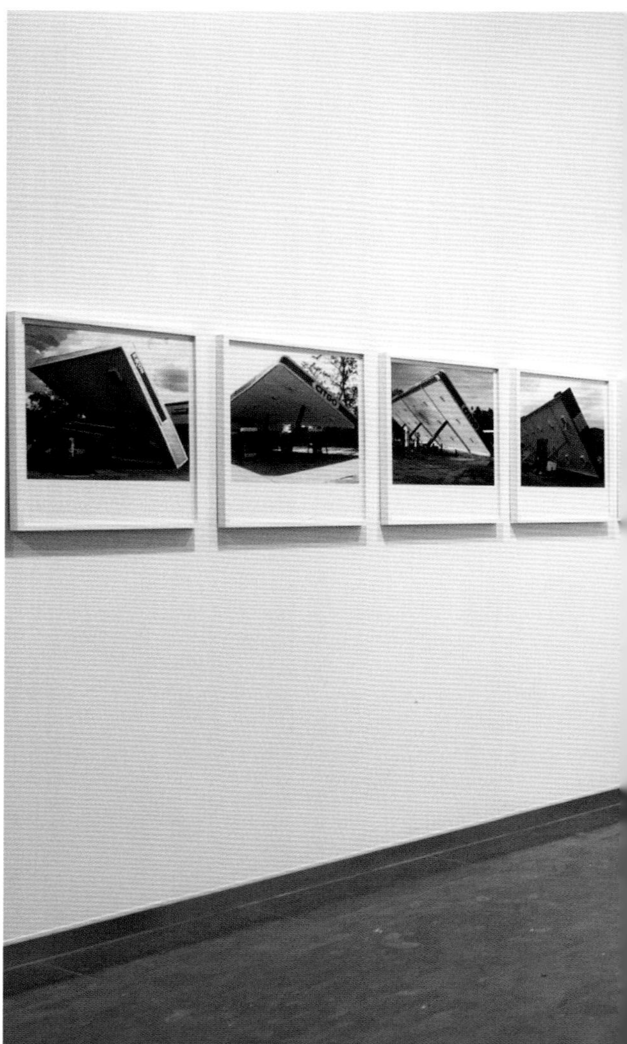

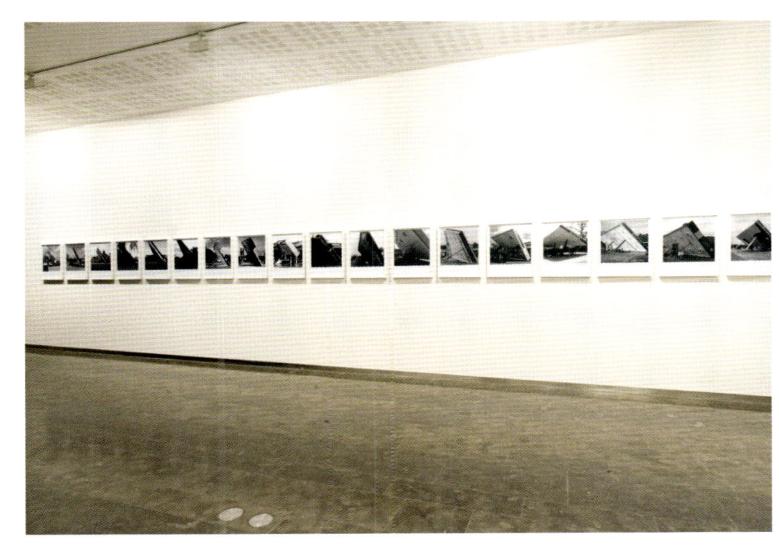

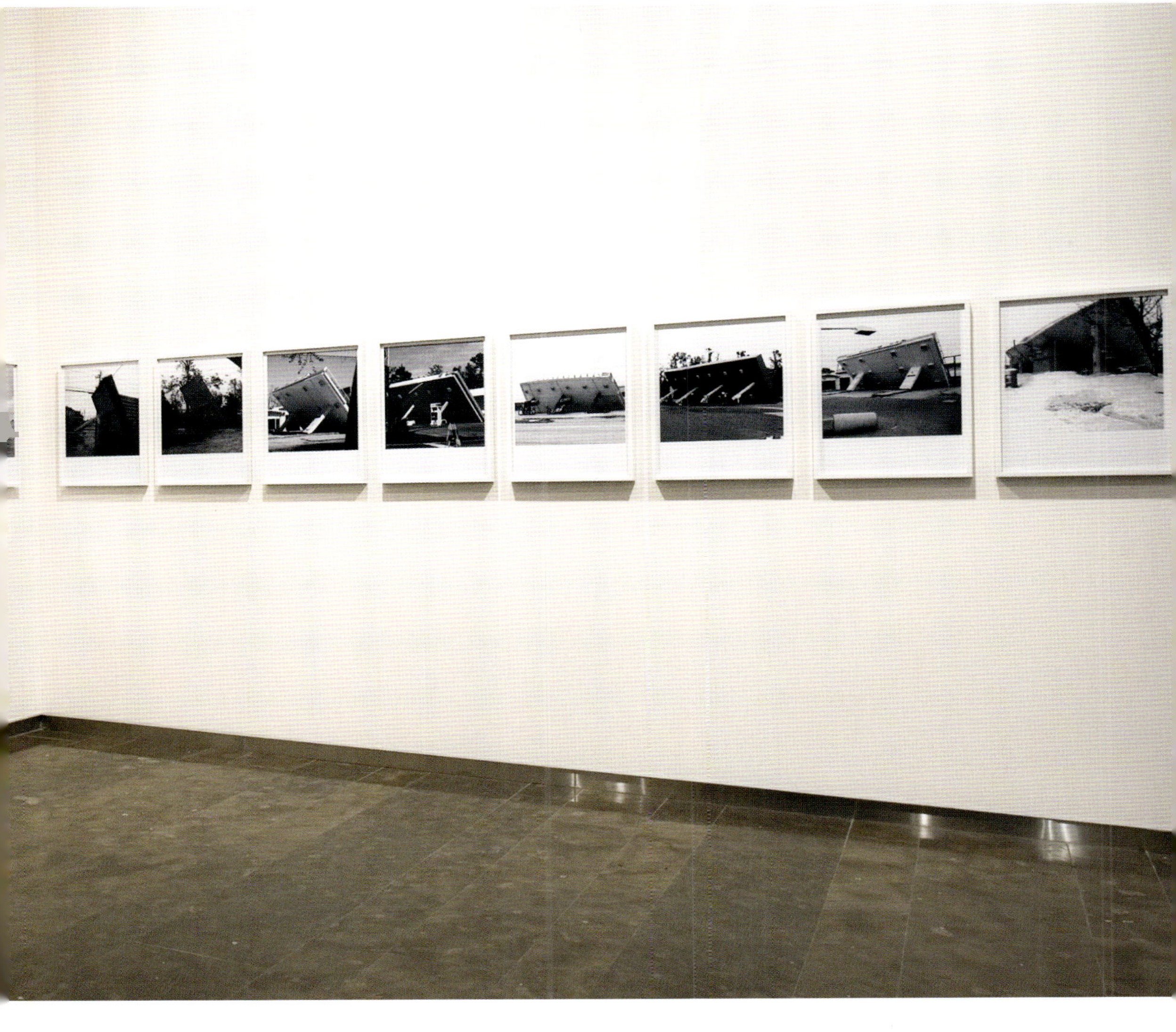

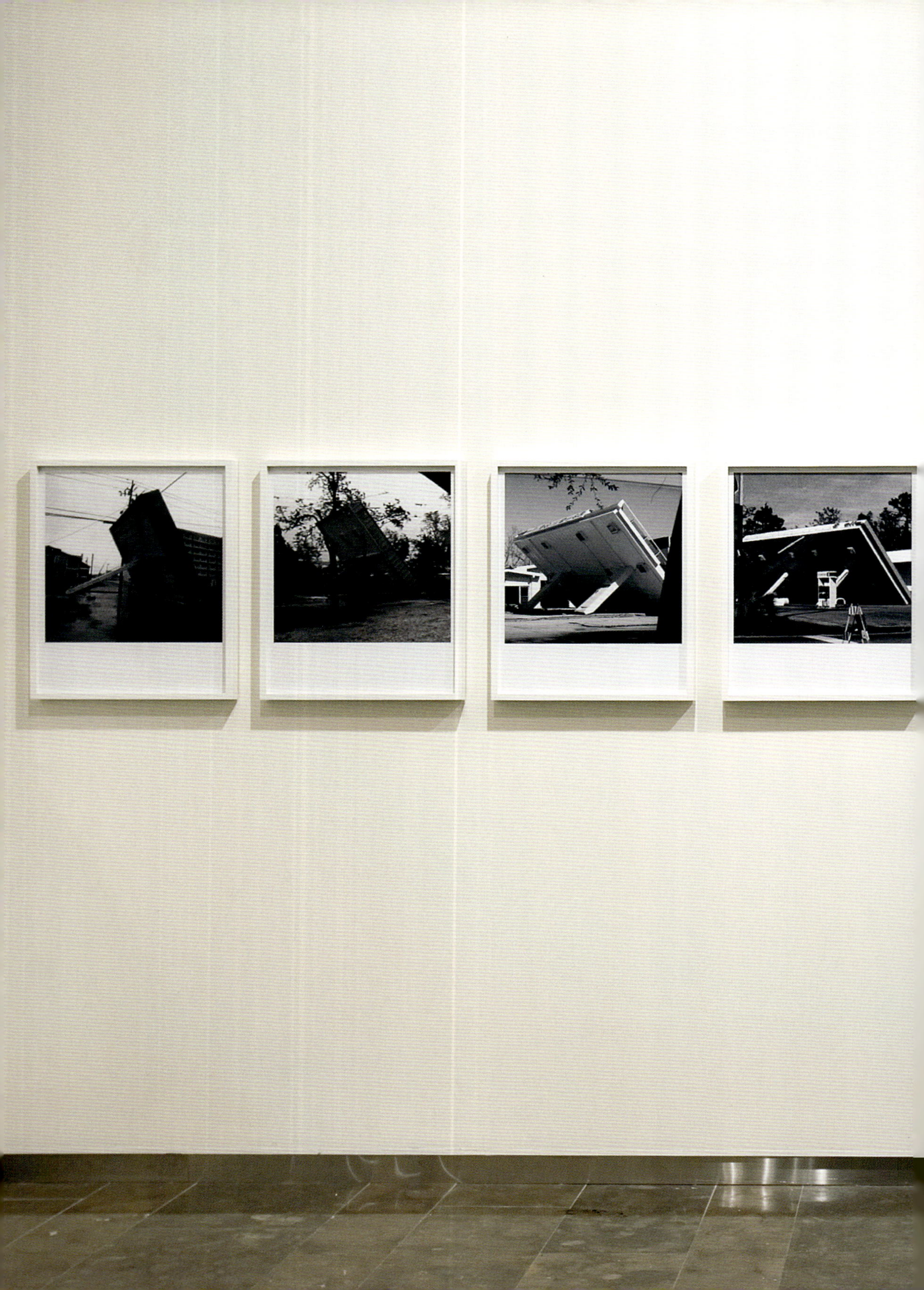

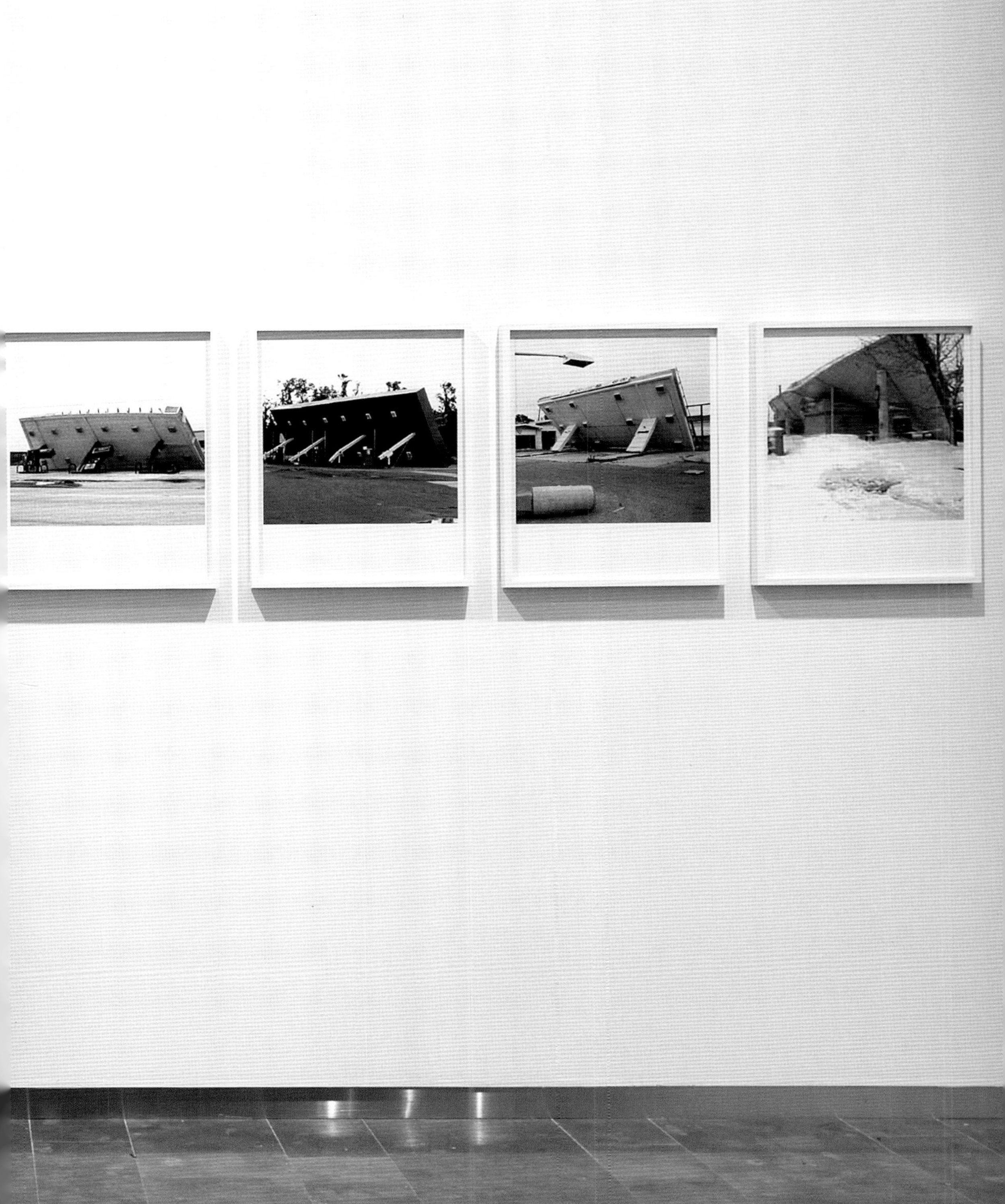

Ivan Galuzin

Born 1979 Groznyj
Lives and works in Vadsø

I've been out wandering, and don't say
much these days.
These days I think a lot about things I've
forgotten to do, and all the chances I had.
I've stopped joking around, I don't gamble
much. These days I think a lot about all the
changes that have come my way, and
wonder if I will see another highway soon.
I had a girlfriend – don't think I will risk
another these days, and if I seem afraid
to live the life I've laid in my songs, it's only
that I have lost battles for such a long time.
I've stopped dreaming, I'm not going to
do as much mischief these days.
These days I'll just sit on cornerstones
and tell time in the leaves on the ground.
Please, don't confront me with my
deficiencies and mistakes, I haven't
forgotten them.
These days.

Ivan Galuzin
Killed by Death, 2008
Collage, objects
Dimensions vary
Courtesy of the artist

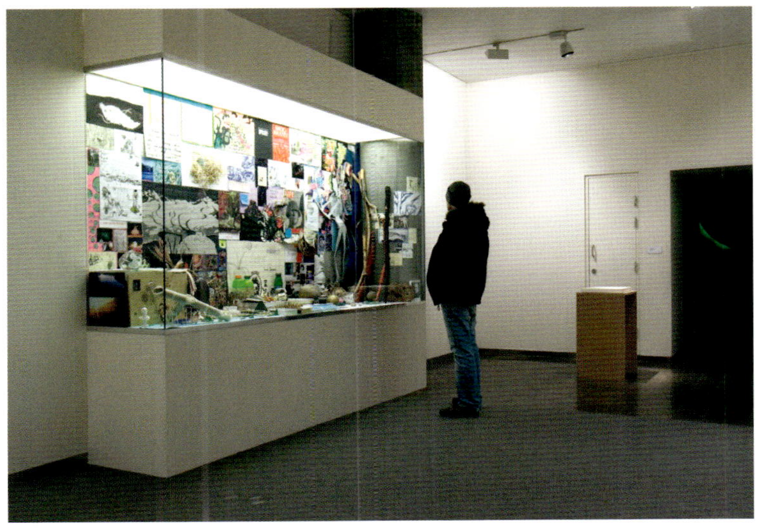

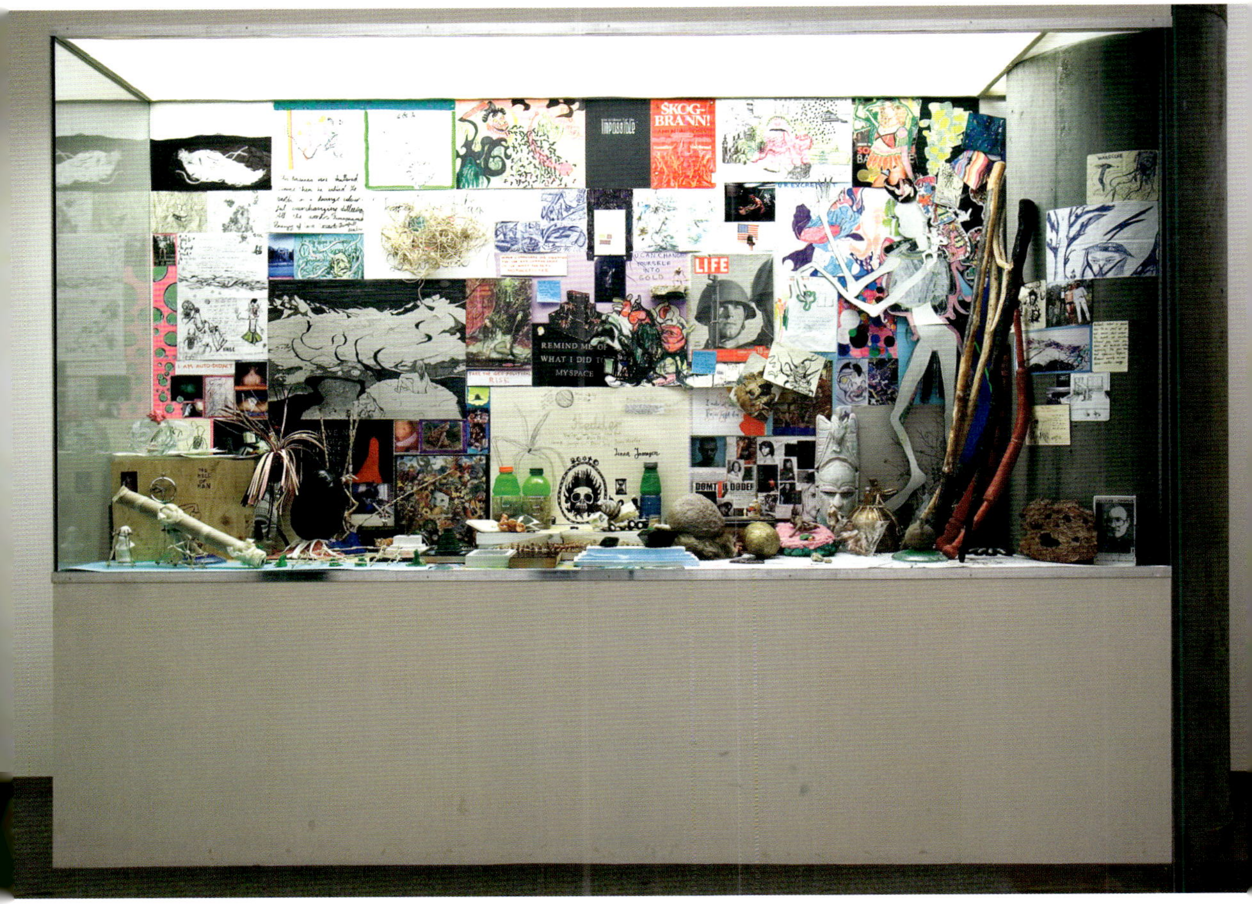

Ivan Galuzin
Killed by Death, 2008
details

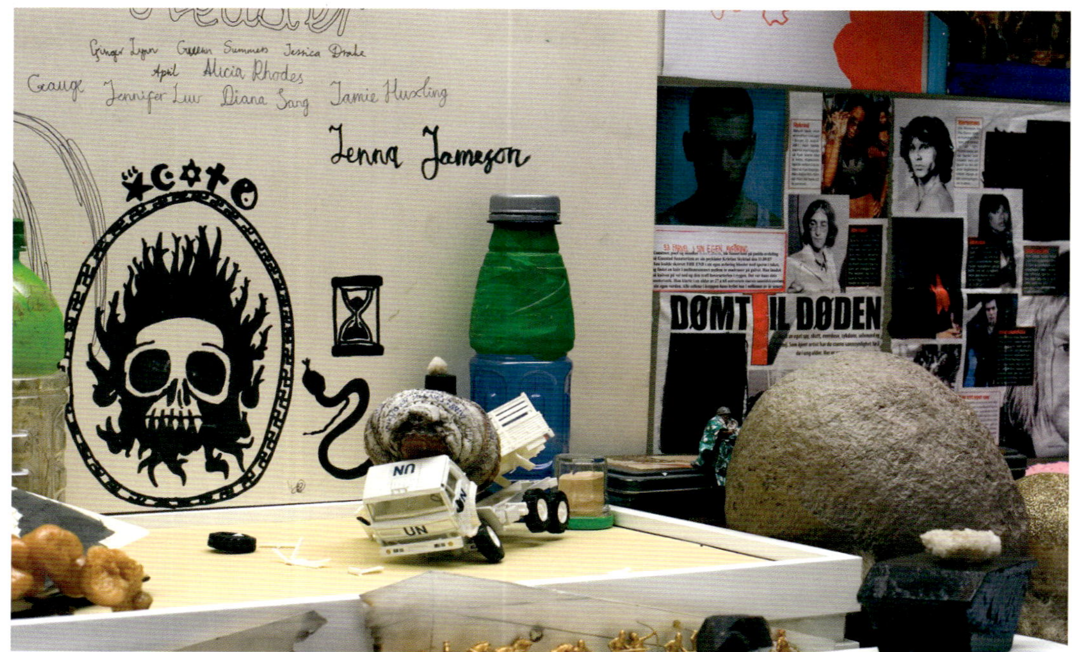

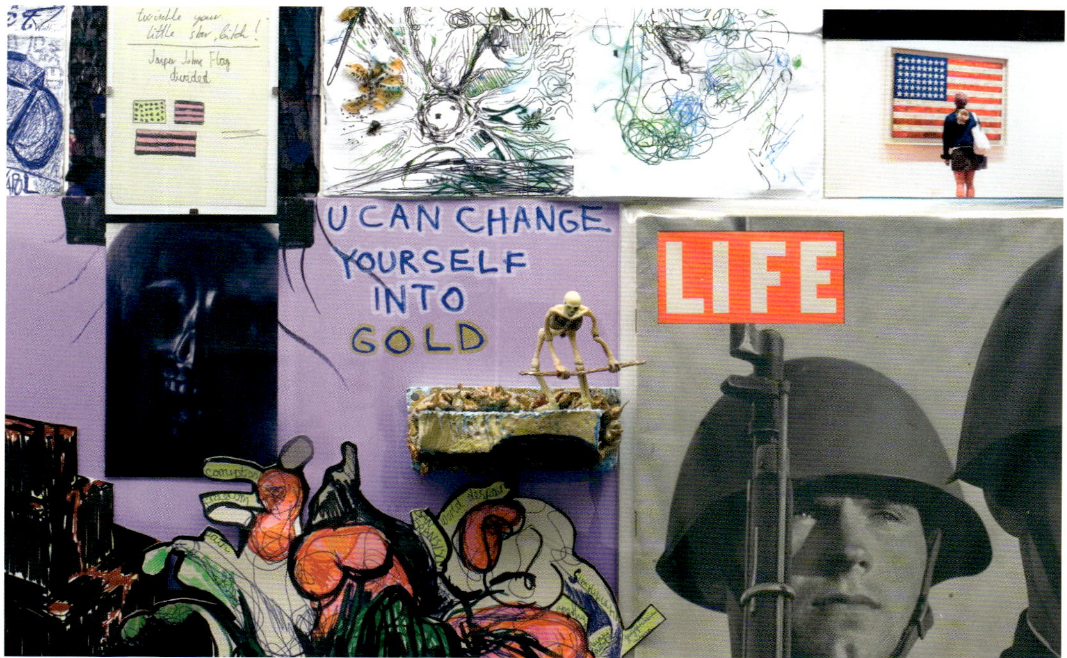

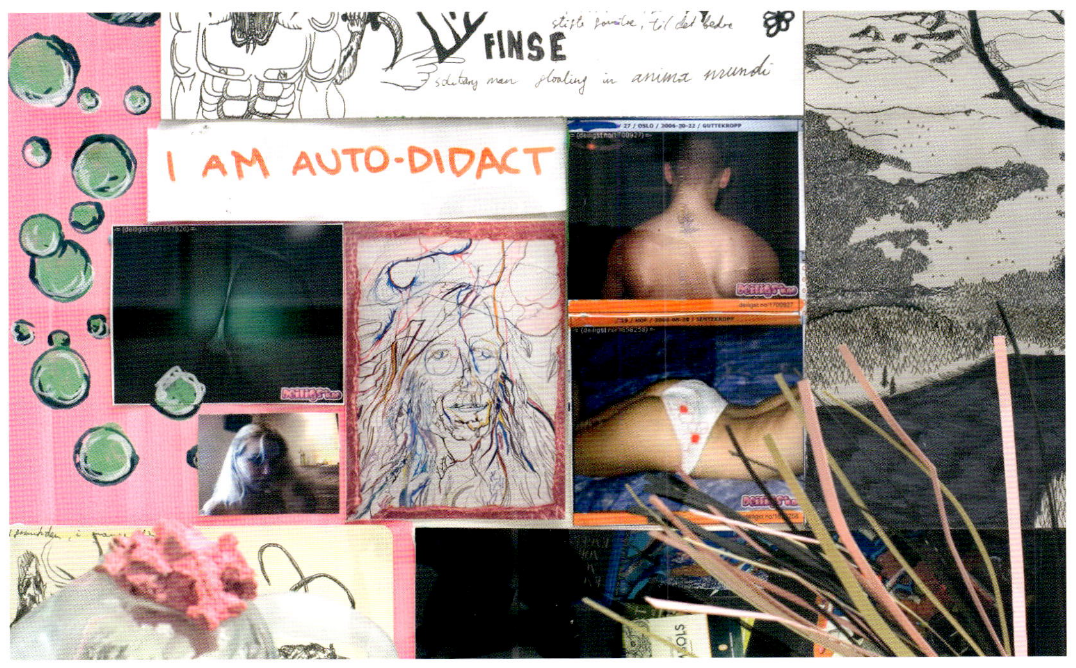
FINSE
I AM AUTO-DIDACT

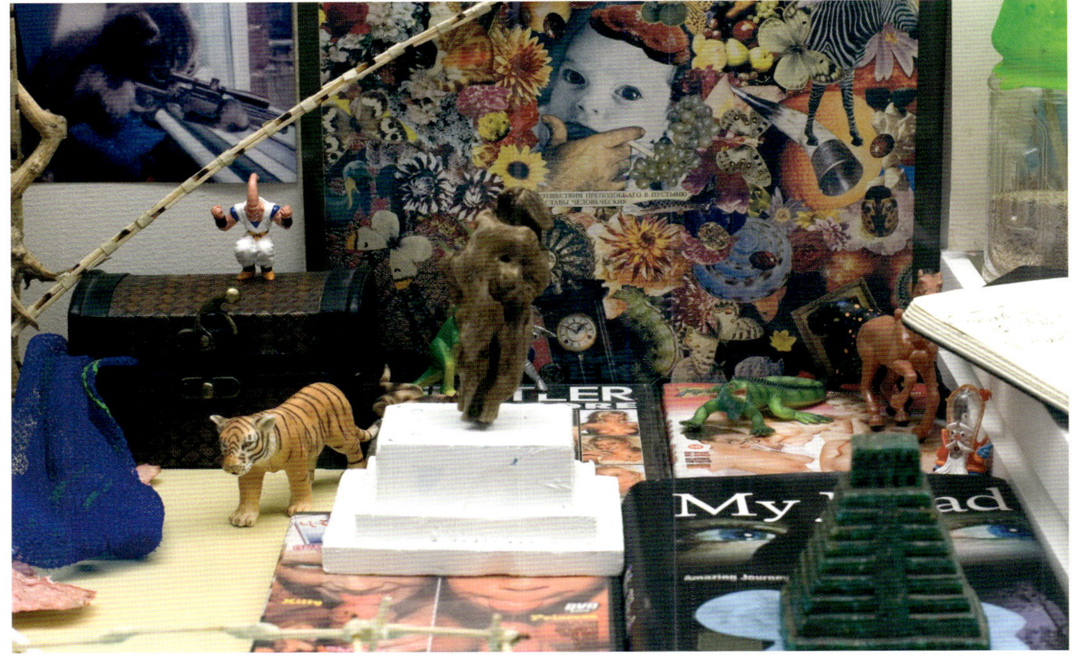
My Head

Anna Sigmond Gudmundsdottir

**Born 1974 Reykjavik
Lives and works in Oslo**

Be extremely careful what you are thinking and feeling, it affects everything.

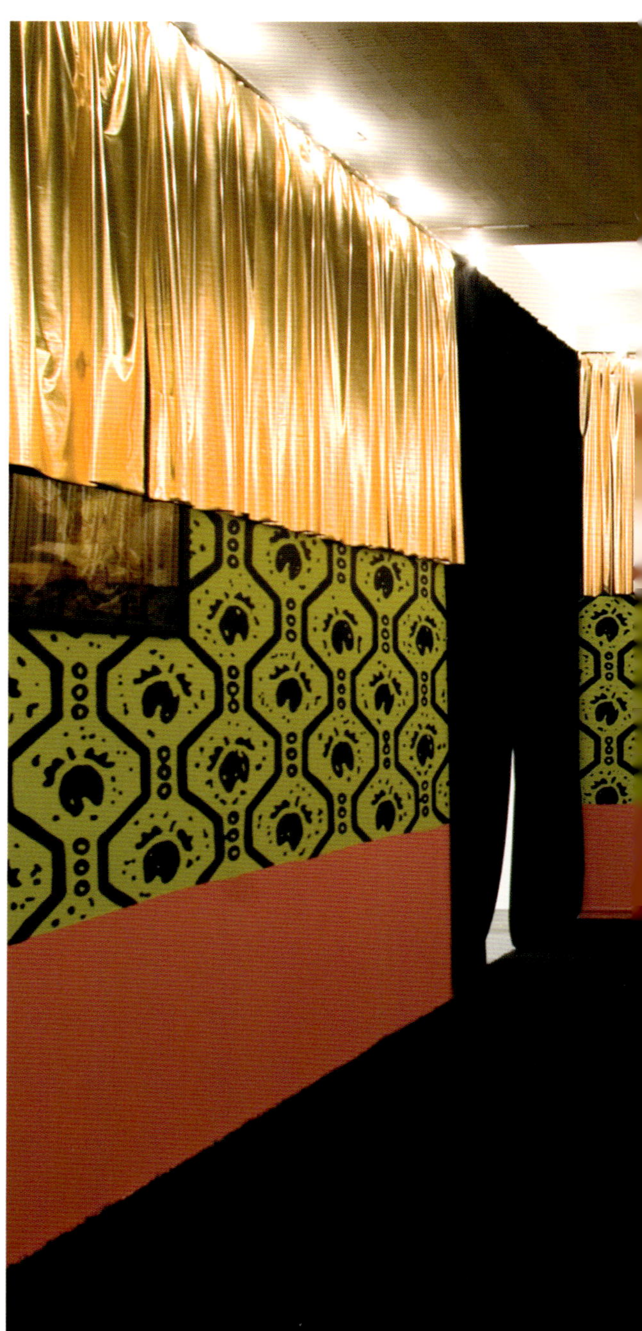

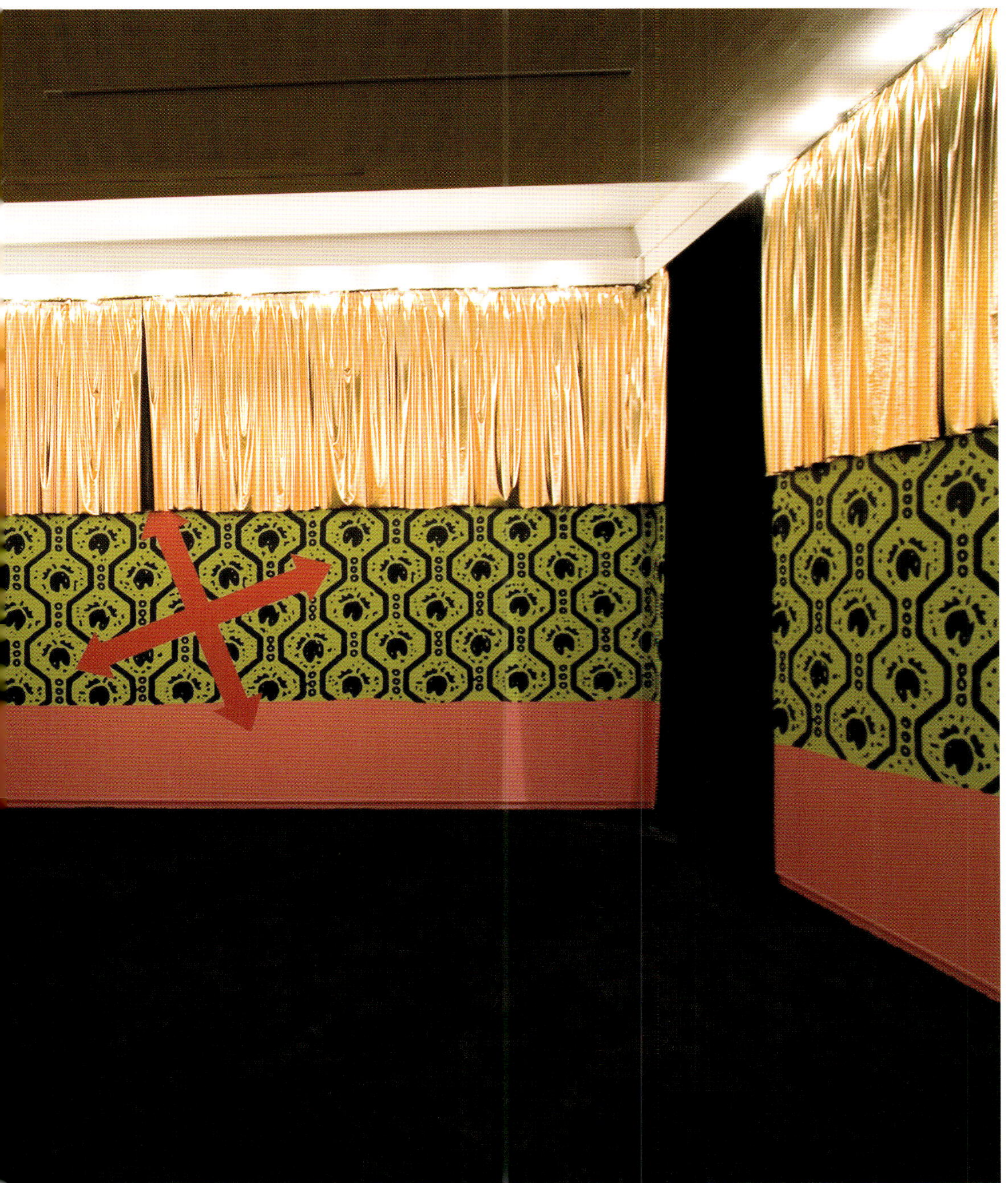

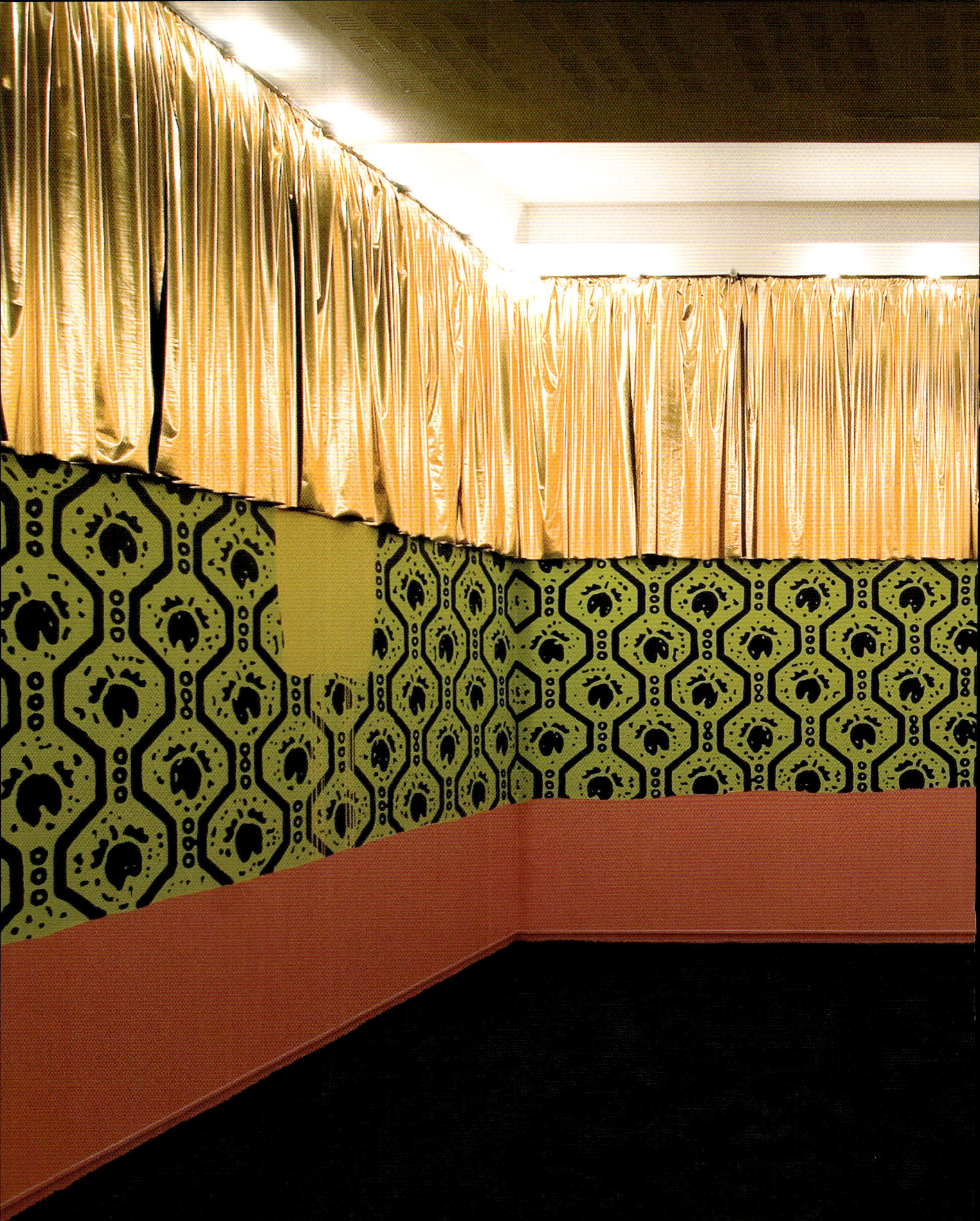

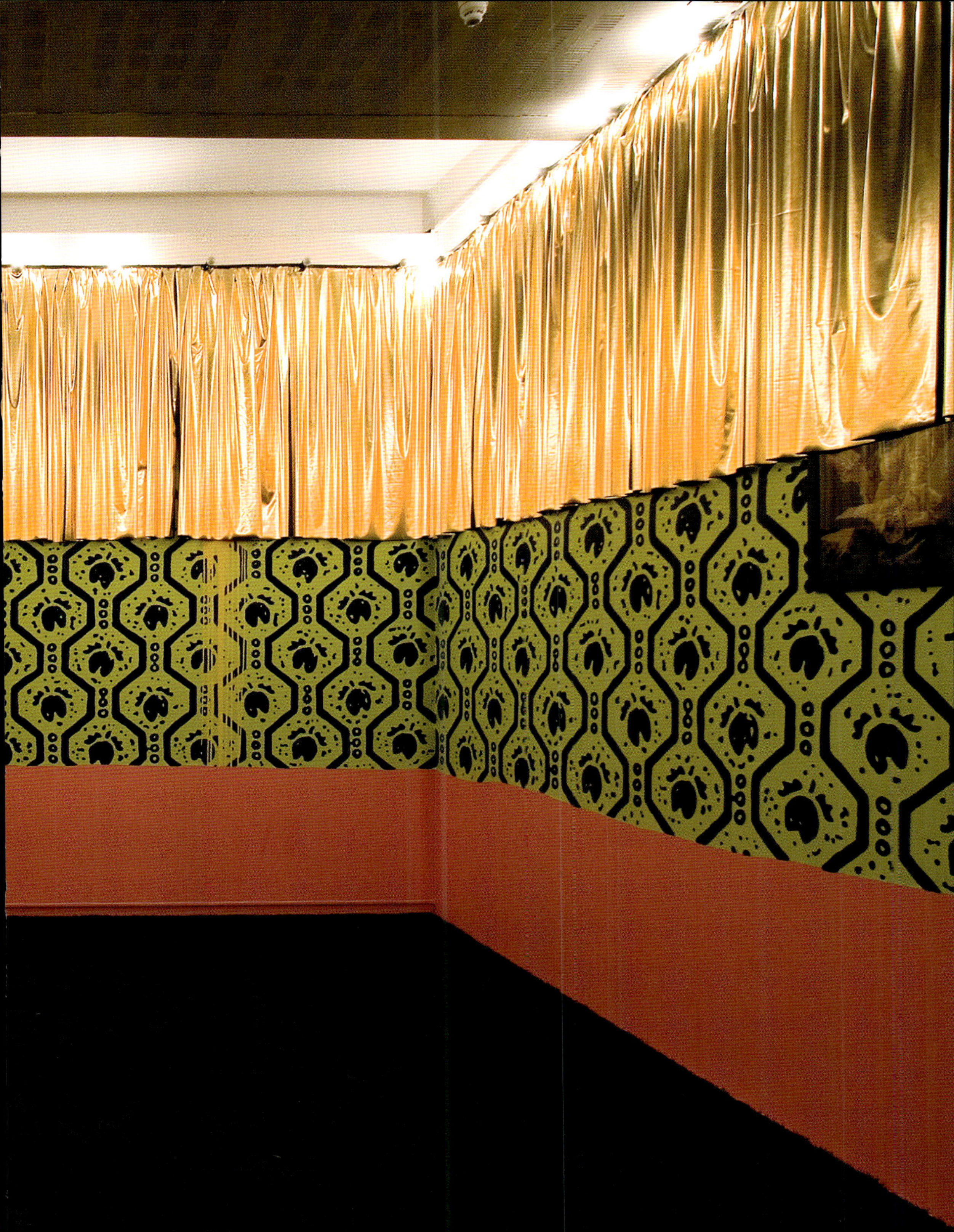

Ane Mette Hol

Born 1979 Bodø
Lives and works in Oslo

Duplication (After Xerox Untitled), nos. 1–9 consists of nine duplicates of photocopies in A4 which are reproduced as drawings. Each drawing is based on an original photocopy that originally was an incorrect copy. The project consists of found materials, thus the choice of number, size, form or picture is subordinate to the concept and the actual carrying out of the project.

One reproduction of a photocopy in A3 has a different and perhaps more well-known motif from art history: Sherrie Levine's *After Walker Evans:4*, 1981, from page 96 in Howard Singerman's essay *Sherrie Levine's Art History*. The pencil drawing *Untitled (After Sherrie Levine's Art History)* copies a photocopied page from an article in a journal. The drawing renders how the photocopy has gone through the copy machine, but it also depicts the photocopy's wear and tear after many years' use.

Ane Mette Hol
Duplication (After Xerox Untitled), 2007
nos. 1–9
Drawings, pencil
each 21 x 29.7 cm
Lautom Contemporary, Oslo
no. 5 private collection
no. 6 private collection
no. 9 private collection

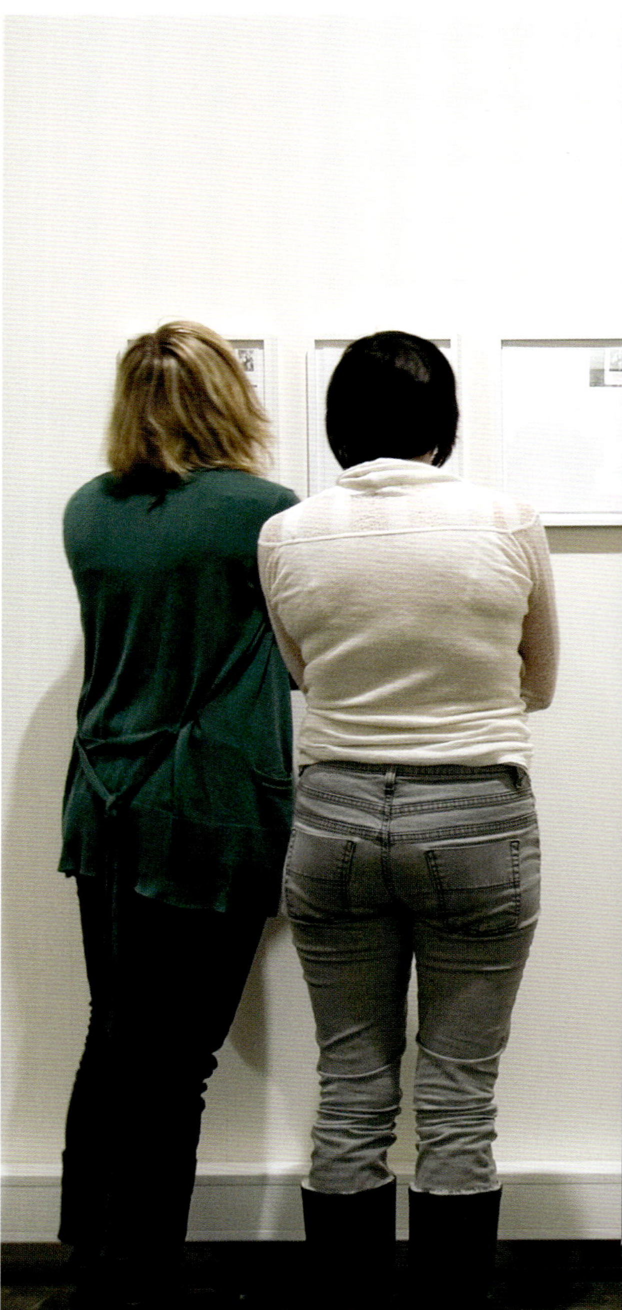

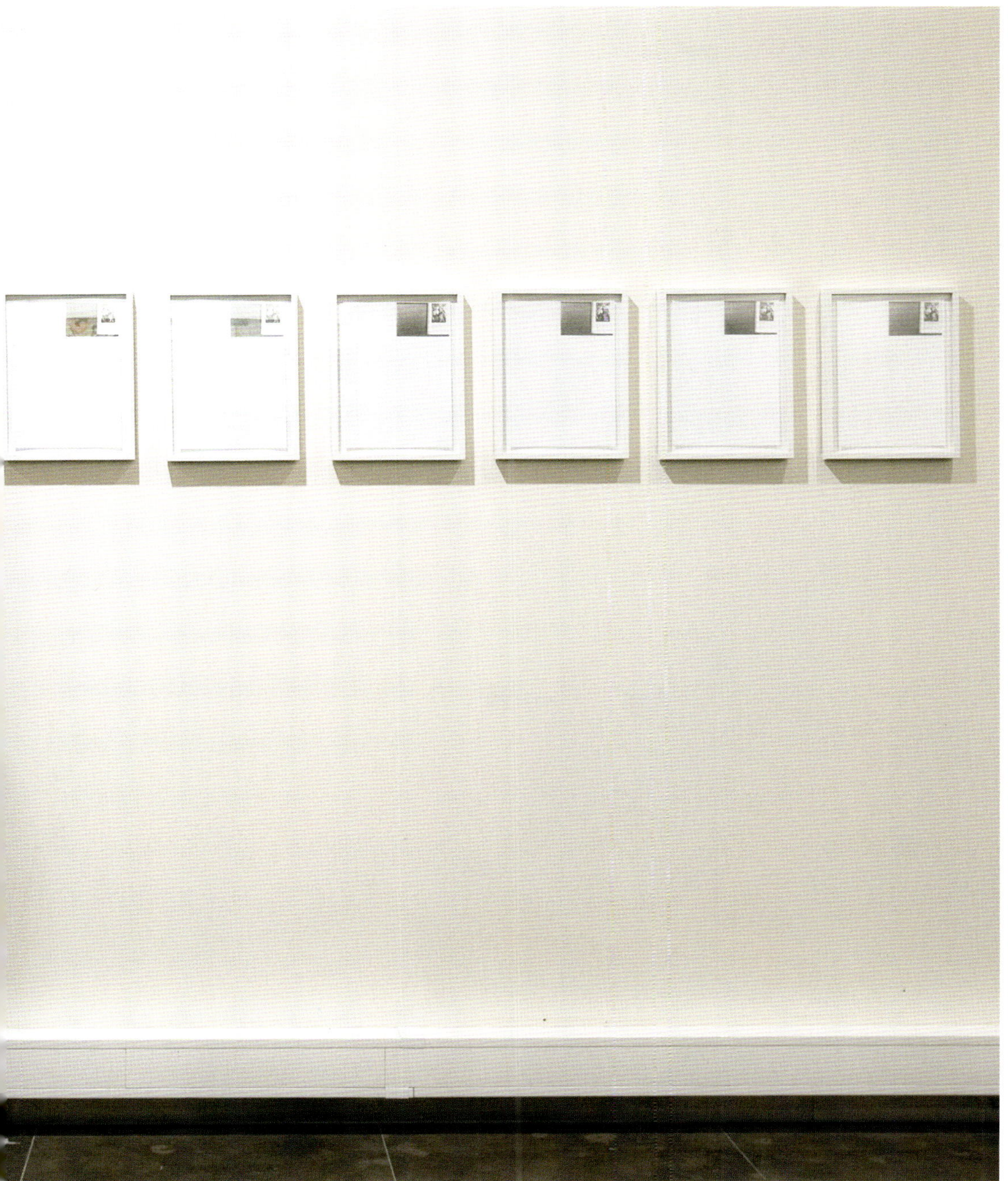

Ane Mette Hol
Duplication (After Xerox Untitled),
2007
no. 3

Ane Mette Hol
Untitled (Art History Essay), 2007
Drawing, pencil and pen
29.7 x 42 cm
Lautom Contemporary, Oslo

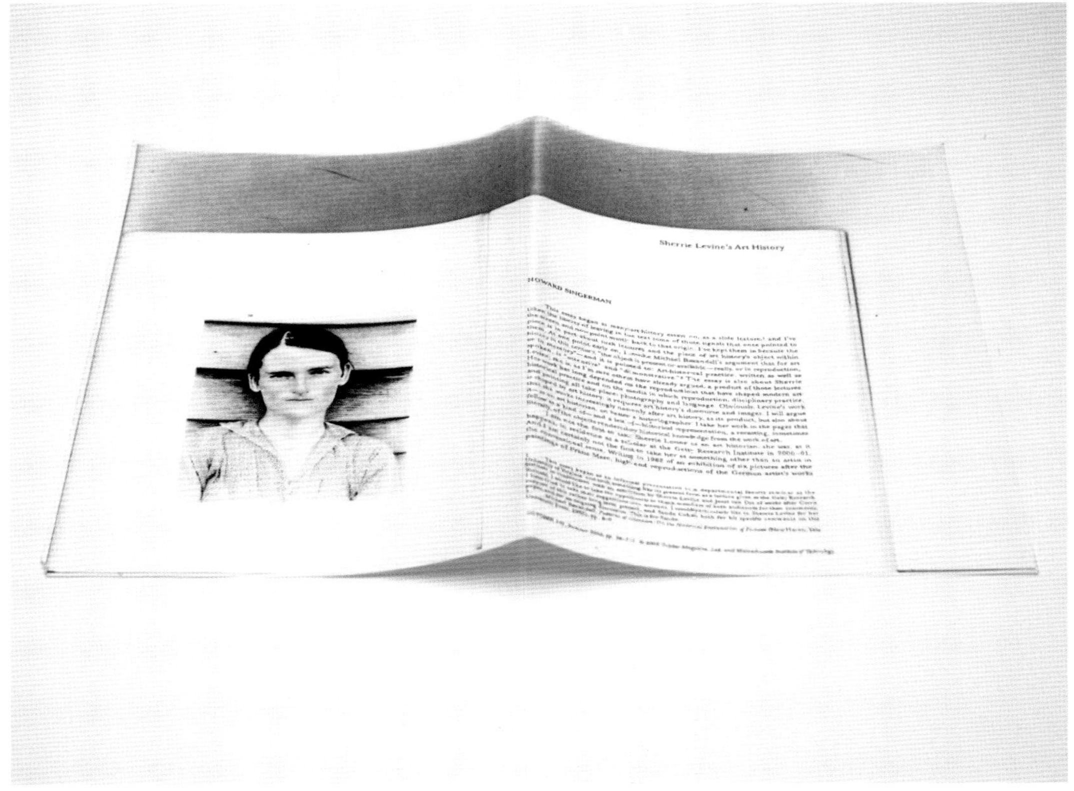

Håvard Homstvedt

Born 1976 Lørenskog
Lives and works in New York

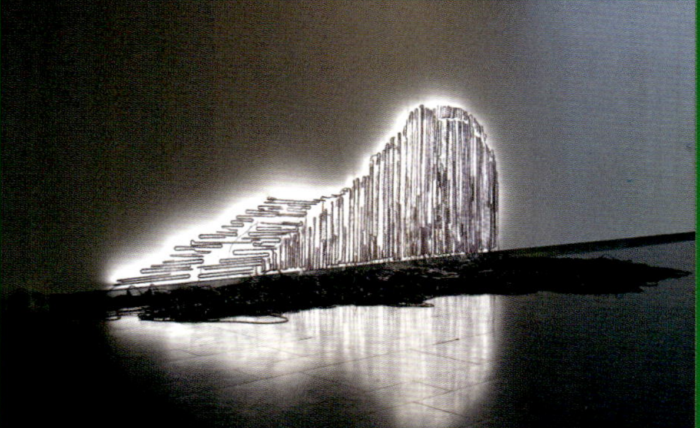

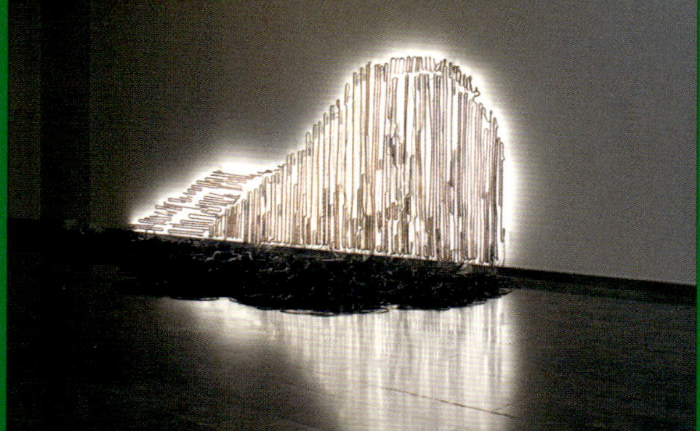

You will hardly know is a variant of a motif I previously used for a painting. It represents a kind of archetypical romantic picture of a female head on a watery surface. In this version I have tried to translate the motif into a neon line drawing. In a lighted, drawn sign the face is reflected on the floor's surface. The meeting or junction between the floor and the wall creates a horizon and a landscape in the motif. The title suggests an intimate message, as if from a pulp fiction story. Through my works I want to create stories. By constructing a theatrical scene created out of fragments – a scene inspired by everything from outmoded graphic reproduction methods to the making of pictures, home decor, knitting patterns, earlier avant-garde design or advertisements from women's magazines – I try to suggest a placeless narrative unity in the works. In the media and materials I choose to work with, an ocean of associations and stories already exists. Nevertheless, the materiality in them spawns the construction of new associations and stories. I relate my own work process to that of textiles and weaving, insofar as how they are constructed is often clearly apparent in the final result.

Håvard Homstvedt
You will hardly know, 2007
Neon and cables
147 x 412 x 6 cm
Cable installation on floor
Dimensions vary
Courtesy of the artist
Galleri Riis, Oslo

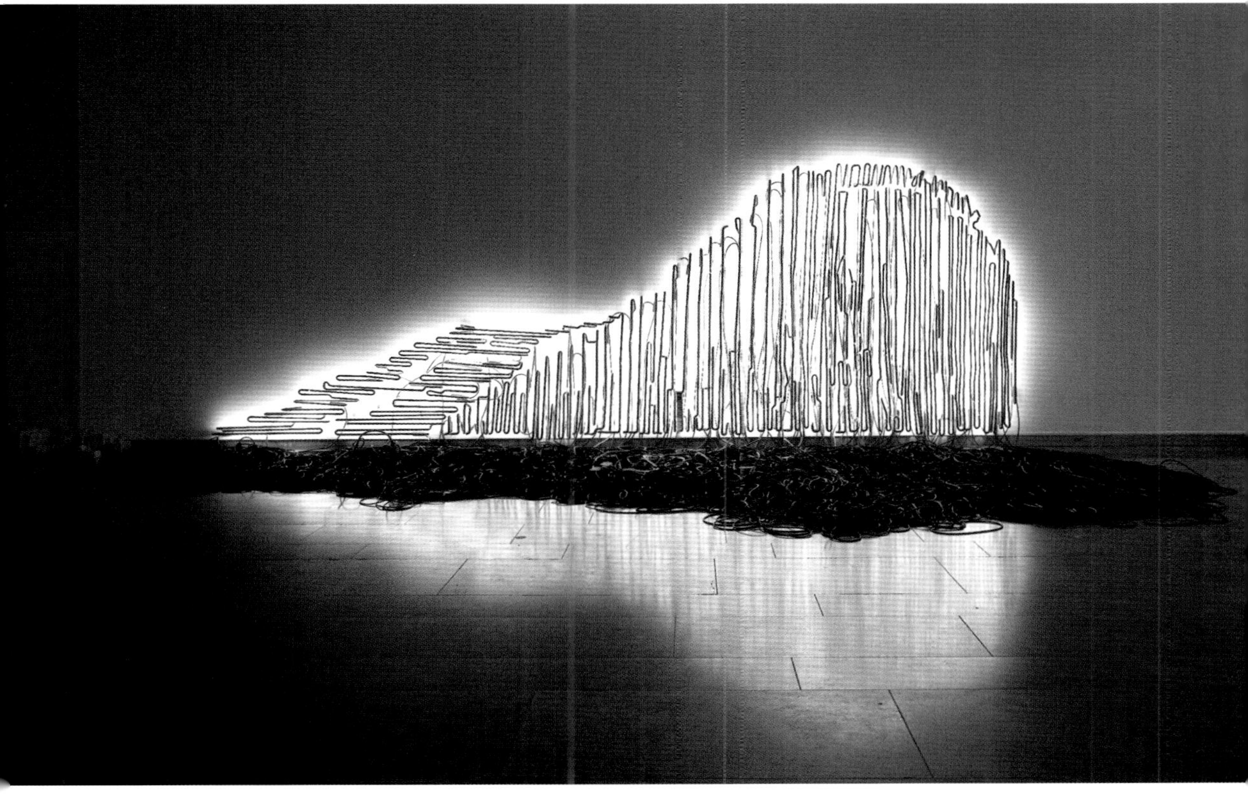

Lars Kjemphol & Espen Henningsen
Improvised Wall Piece, 2008
Mixed media
Dimensions vary
Courtesy of the artists

Lars Kjemphol
Espen Henningsen

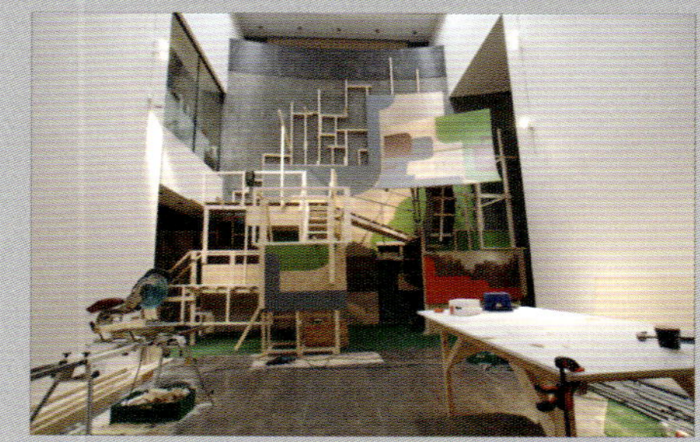

Born 1980 Oslo
Born 1981 Holmestrand
Live and work in Oslo

Å jobbe er å skape.
Å skape er å jobbe.
Der skal skapet stå. *

We often build our works on site. This way, the architecture of the location affects the work. It gives us a great sense of accomplishment to see a work gradually take shape, to build things as well as one can and take photographs during the process. Through the process the project takes shape and develops, both thematically and formally. When we build something we make it as large and comprehensive as possible. We believe the public needs and wants to be impressed when they go to an exhibition. All the pictures and impressions people are confronted with every day cause them to seldom get enthralled. Yet it is precisely this we want to try to achieve through this particular work. We want to surprise and engage the public. We hope the documentation of the work will be good to look at, but that actually seeing it will be an experience.

We feel somewhat on the sidelines of the 'art situation'. We create what we ourselves would have liked to see at an exhibition and hope others like it too.

Working in partnership is inspiring because it allows us to maintain a high level of energy. Collaboration is a process of give-and-take through which a new expression comes into being. We do not exactly know how the work will be when finished. Our common interests involve a fetishizing of the aesthetics found, for example, in military camps, on construction sites, skateboard ramps and in science fiction. Nevertheless, what is most important for us is that we immerse ourselves in what we do. This results in the best works.

* In Norwegian 'to create' is *å skape.*
Et skap is a cupboard. Thus the pun on words.

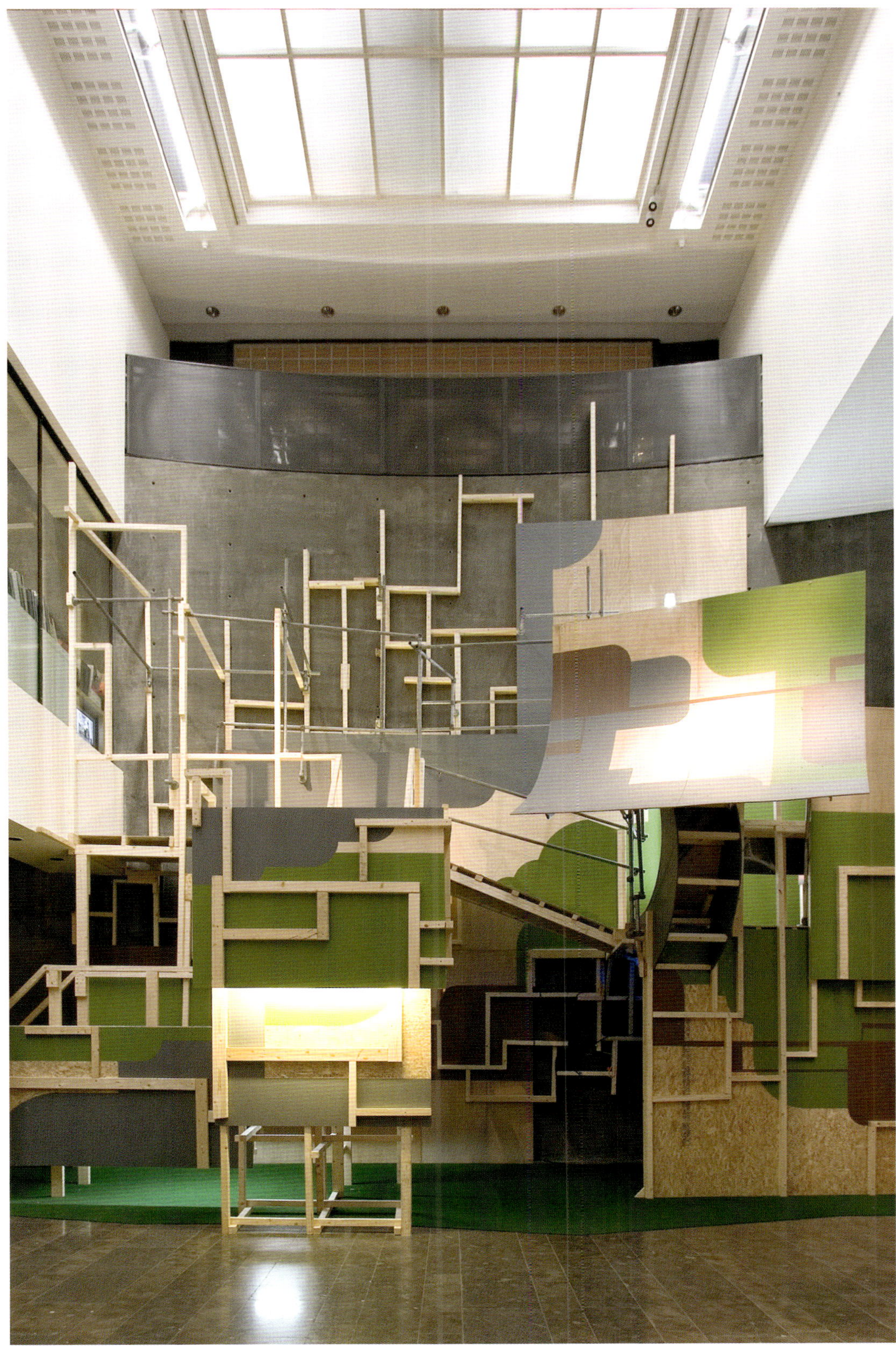

Lars Kjemphol & Espen Henningsen
Improvised Wall Piece, 2008
details

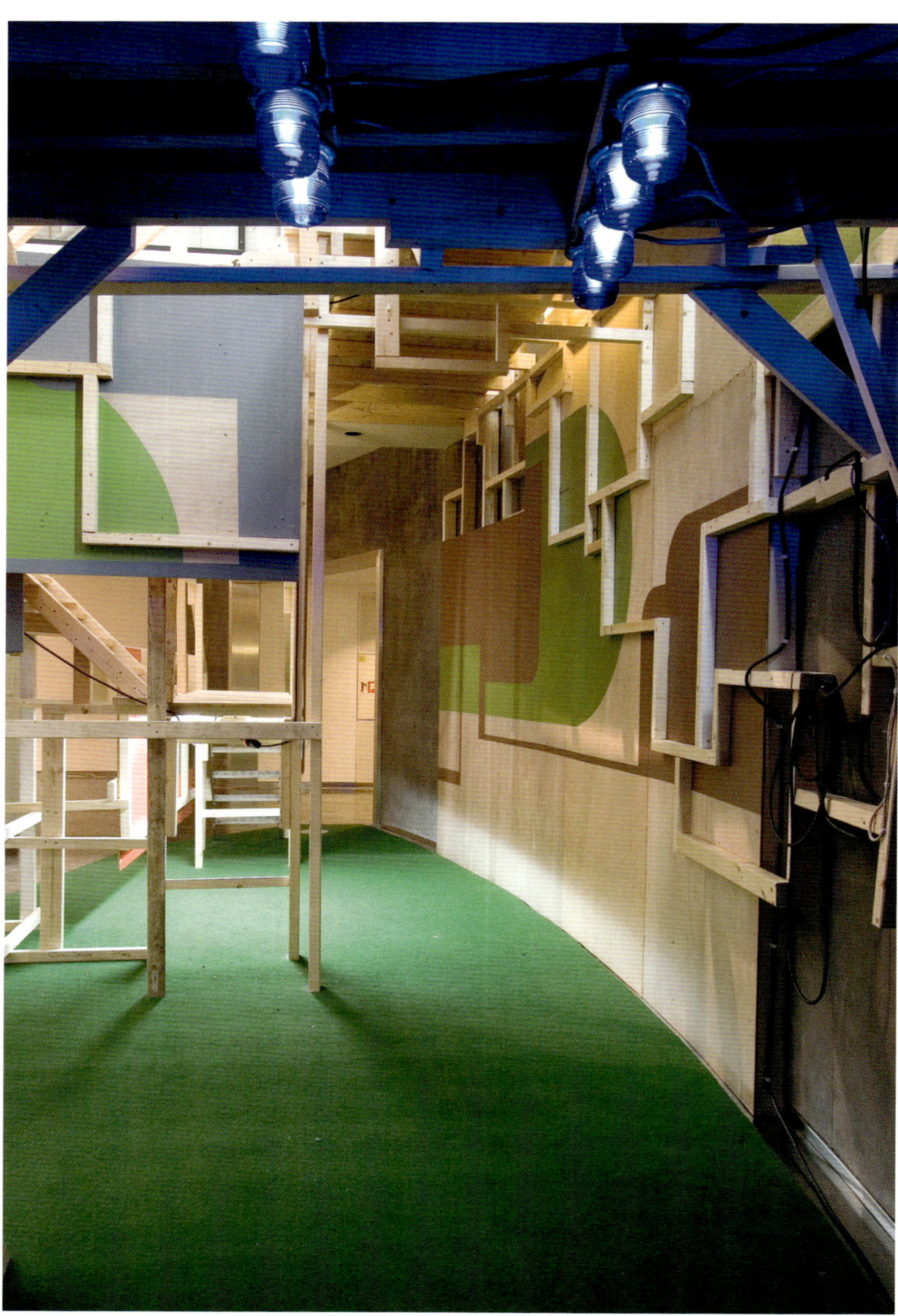

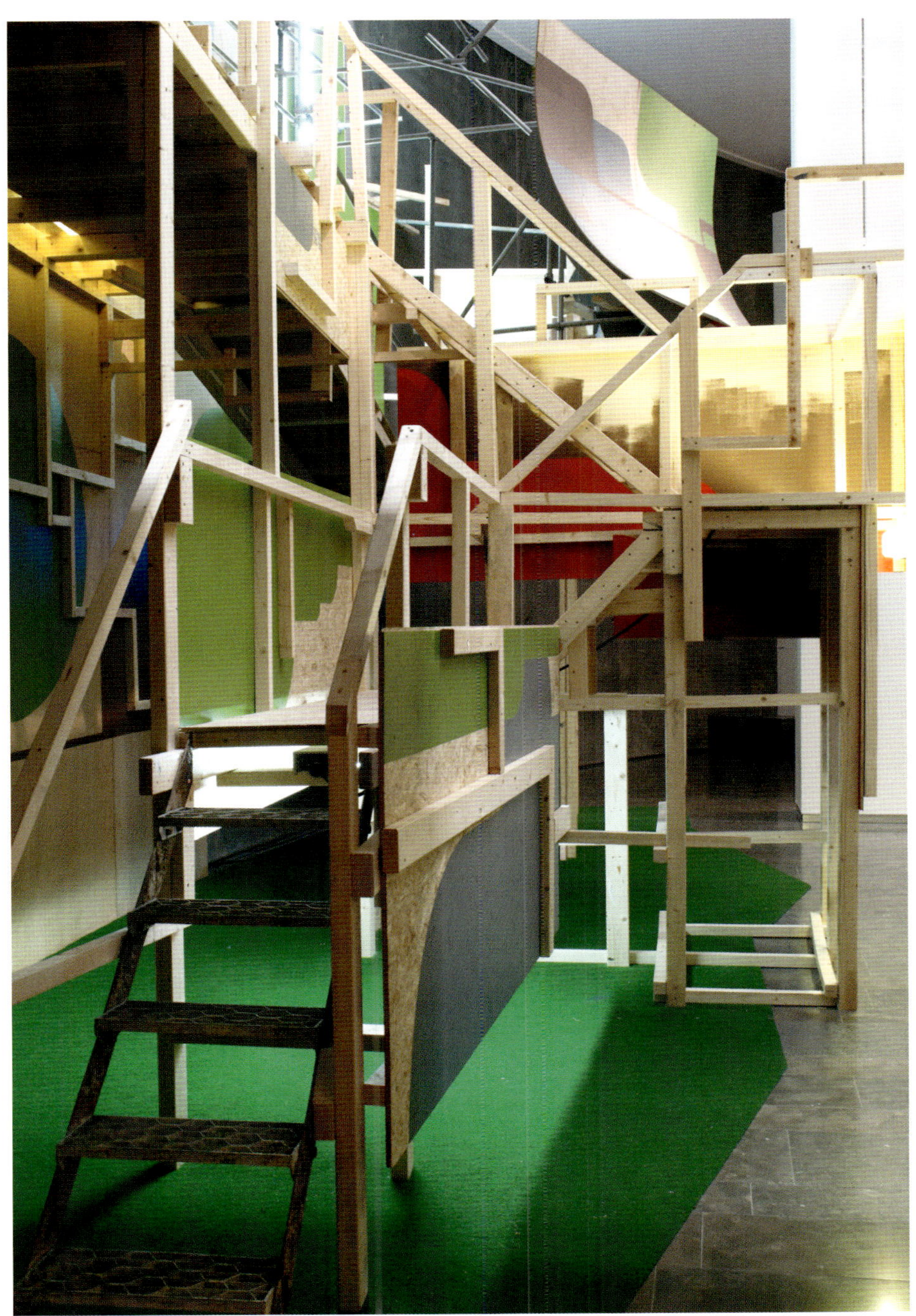

Maren Juell Kristensen

Born 1976 Oslo
Lives and works in Oslo

I work with video, both as a device for storytelling and as a physical presence of light. The dramaturgical and material composition of the video is usually an essential part of the concept. The works concern the balance between physical and imaginary entities, and the expectation of an explanation, a meaning or sense of belonging. Expectation is a key concept in my works: expectations about the meaning or function of a physical material, but also about how it is interpreted as having symbolic value, inside as well as outside the context of art. Expectation also exists on another level, namely as personal dreams and attitudes. How does one tell one's own life story – what can one expect of life? What does success mean and what does it actually mean to fail? Where does one belong? Are expectations about the history of myself and others realistic? Are they based on the American dream, reality TV, or perhaps Paulo Coelho's *Alchemist*? I am curious about the extent to which these expectations are created by my own will, or projected by mass media, or myths and folkloric traditions. I regularly use elements from mass media and the entertainment industry in my works, both referentially and by appropriating materials and symbols. These borrowings can consist of camera or clipping methods, objects, compositions or dramaturgy.

In addition, I am concerned with, and influenced by, a number of things: barriers – both physically and metaphorically, the dramaturgy of amusement parks, cruise ships and shopping centres. Then there are myths, idols and saints, CNN, Hollywood and television series like CSI, not to mention texts by Susan Sontag, Laura Mulvey, Martha Rosler, Jean Baudrillard and others.

Wish consists of the first or last phrase from well-known Hollywood musicals (*Pinocchio*, *The Wizard of Oz*, *Annie…*) animated as if by Disney's magic wand. This work also refers to Disney and Hollywood's propagandizing of an attitude: if you wish intensely enough and are good and kind, you will achieve your heart's desire. I would like to question the possibility for success. What is success? What is romantic hope? I studied in London and lived there for seven years. Those I studied with now live in many different countries. What we shared – and what I have in common now with artists in Norway – is difficult to describe. Networks, rapidity and a nomadic existence can characterize the community. This creates natural counter currents; things have to move fast, on every level. I would characterize today's art situation as fragmented – more so than what surfaces in Norway at any particular time. I see it as highly diversified, referential, playful and fearless, but also confused, stressed and worried. It is simultaneously global, peripheral and central, and thus difficult to characterize.

Maren Juell Kristensen
Wish, 2007
Animation
1:15 min.
Courtesy of the artist

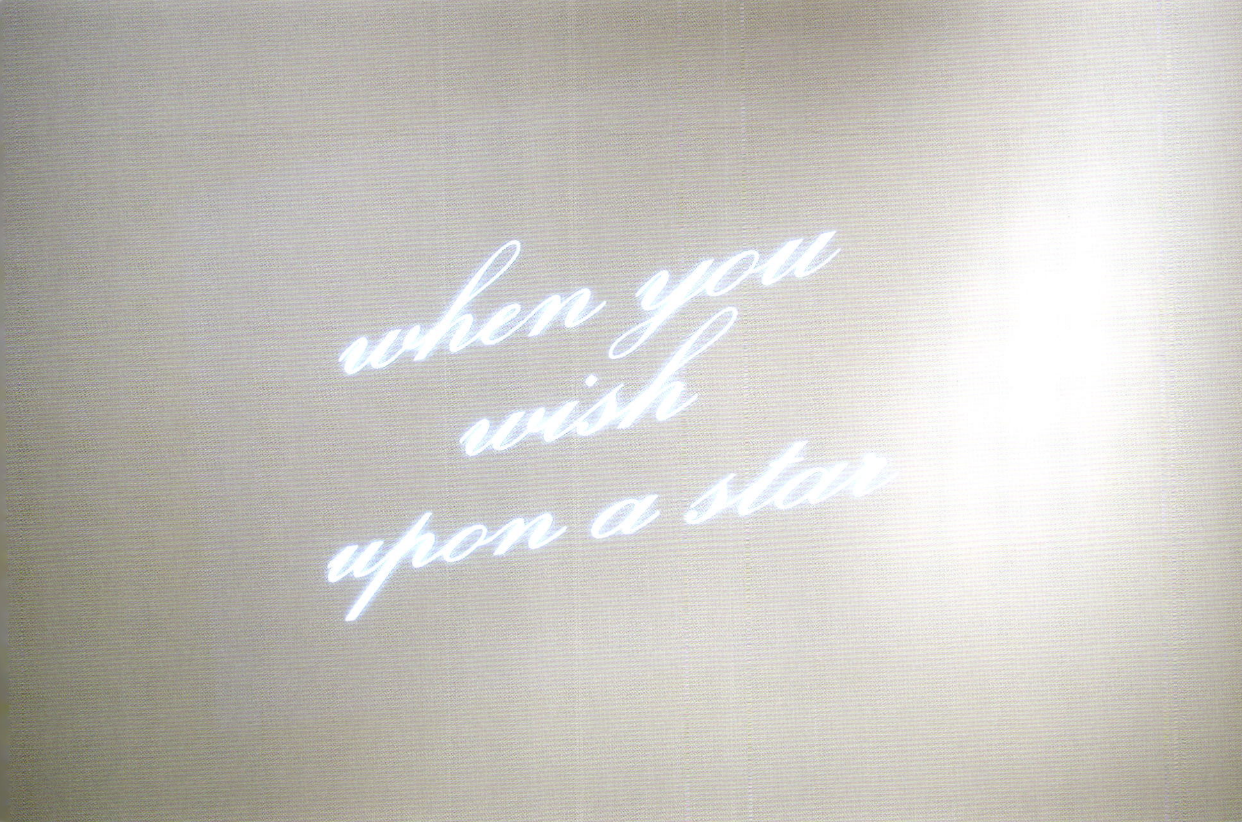

Hjørdis Kurås

Born 1974 Oslo
Lives and works in Oslo

In my works, I explore mechanisms that construct identity as reflected in mass media, new technology or my own environment. With the initial impetus of human relations and social contexts, my works show variations of figurative collages in installations including drawing, sculpture and video. They combine found materials with materials of my own, and alternate between fiction and reality. They are not necessarily founded on any explicit theory or dogma, but reflect fragments of divergent directions and tendencies, or details referring to contemporary themes.

• *Liminal Inception #1*, 2004
The Latin word *limes* was originally an expression used by land surveyors, and denotes the border between two areas. In anthropology, 'liminality' is theoretically discussed by Arnold van Gennep and Victor Turner, among others. Here the concept is used when accounting for transitions, e.g. rituals involving changes in participants, and the liminal state is characterized by ambiguity, openness and indeterminacy. The 8 mm film from the early 1970s shows my mother standing at the border of her property, along buildings belonging to her family since the early eighteenth century. The digital video recording, which shows me standing at the same places in 2004, is edited in layers. It has peepholes showing the time interval. Identity is linked to the environment one lives in, but also to areas divided into networks of overlapping patterns and transitions. Time is divided in the same way: in calendar-based celebrations. It is often used to mark a change or transition, but also marks individual milestones in life. With the 8 mm film as a reference and documentation of something that once was, and the digital video recording, *Liminal Inception #1* points to things vanished, changed, or in the process of changing. It explores the space between the subject and eternity. Liminality points to the expanse between generations, historical periods or cultural collectives, between politics and aesthetics, theory and practice.

• *Total Solar Eclipse*, 2007
In a total solar eclipse, the moon passes between the sun and the earth in such a way that the sun is completely blotted out. During the minutes the eclipse lasts, the sun's corona is clearly seen as a ring of glowing plasma streaming out over the solar surface from the sun's core, where combinations of hydrogen atoms form helium atoms. This fusion follows Einstein's equivalence, $E = mc^2$, and through it, the sun's hydrogen atoms are reduced. Hydrogen is the most essential element for life on earth and the mainspring of new stars and galaxies – a process of eternal creation and death in the development of the universe. And it was the pacifist Einstein's famous equivalence formula that was first corroborated by the atom bomb.
Hinode is an observation satellite equipped with a solar telescope. On 19 March 2007 it filmed a total eclipse not seen from the earth. The sound picture in *Total Solar Eclipse* consists of samples from diverse home video recordings, found on Google Video, of solar eclipses seen throughout the world.
One of the soundtracks repeats in a loop, and we hear someone commenting on an eclipse. A phrase repeats: 'Do you think it will be like this forever?' An excerpt from Roland Barthes' *Camera Lucida* speaks of the feeling or fear, of eternal darkness.
It is said that mourning, by its gradual labor, slowly erases pain. I could not, and I cannot believe this, because for me, time only eliminates the emotion of the loss (I do not weep), that is all. For the rest, everything has remained, motionless.

Hjørdis Kurås
Liminal Inception #1, 2004
Digital video
2:15 min.
Courtesy of the artist

Hjørdis Kurås
Total Solar Eclipse, 2007
Digital video installation
4 min. loop
Courtesy of the artist

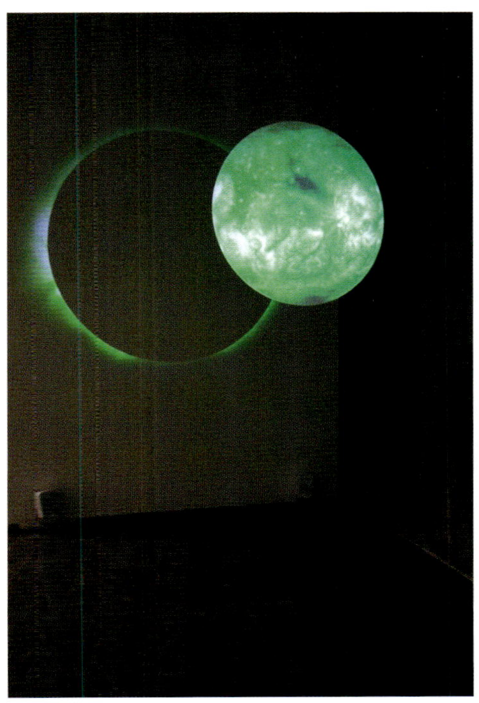

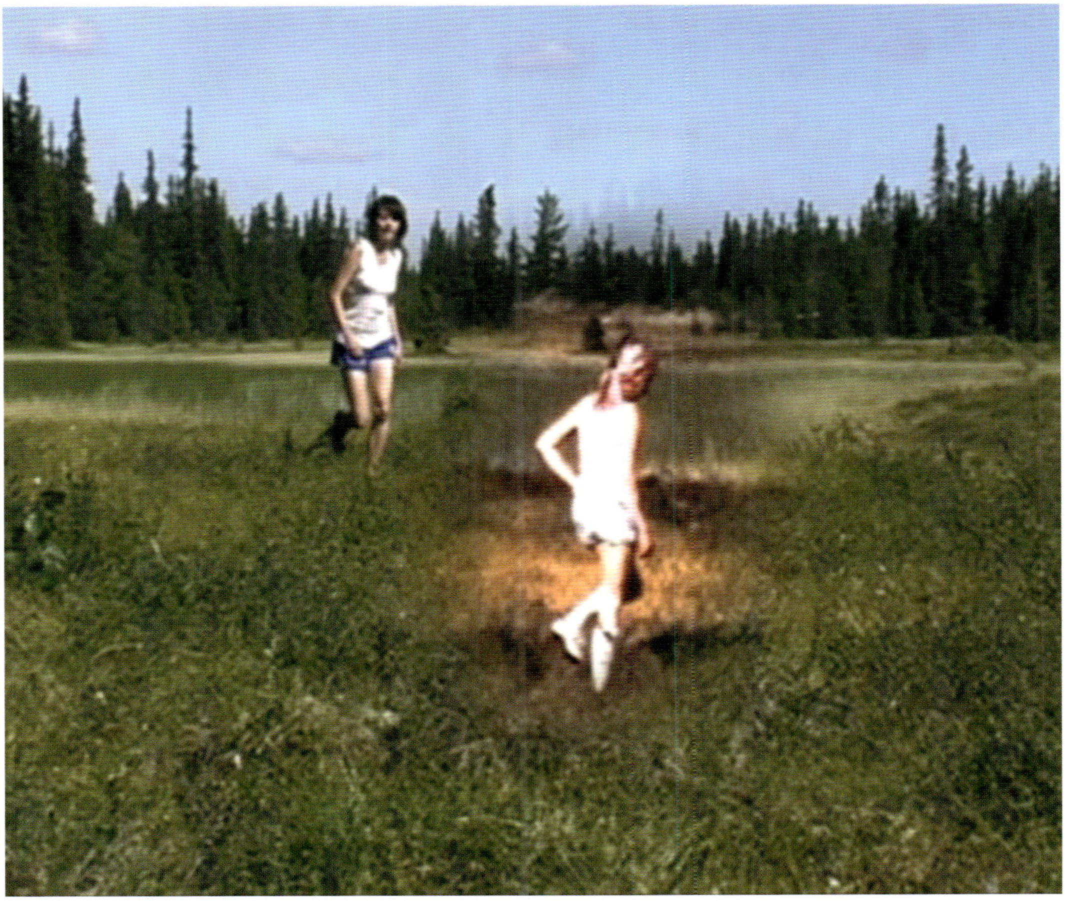

Ingvild Langgård

Born 1978 Fredrikstad
Lives and works in Oslo

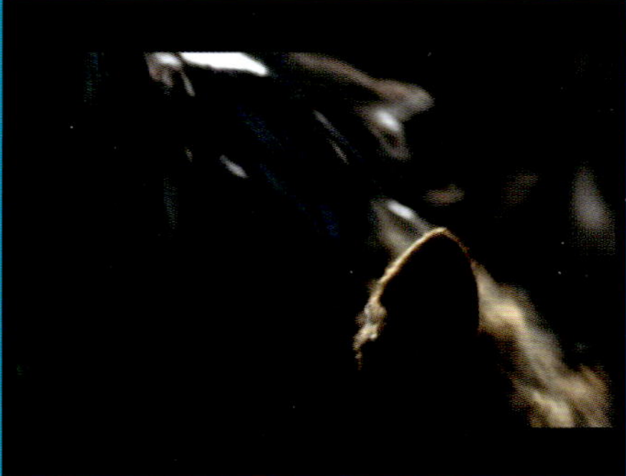

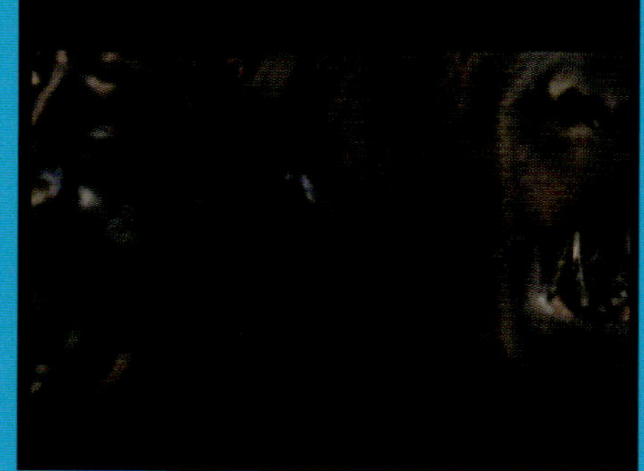

I work with music, sound and visual art in a way that causes contents, composition and rhythm to become equal parts of the process and the final piece. In constructing aesthetic tableaux, beauty slips into the Baroque or grotesque. Pleasure is transformed into discomfort, something dangerous and strange emerges. *The Beast* is an unrecognizable, constantly morphing nature, an ungraspable yet alluring creature. Faust meets a black dog who offers him a choice: beauty, wealth and eternal life can be gained in exchange for his soul. Religious ecstasy and meaning are traded for material luxury. Through ambition and greed, your own wishes may turn against you. Your perception may be altered when you enter the black box. You are in a cramped black room where claustrophobic, hellish heat changes into a limitless pit of darkness. The beast is yourself after you have sold your soul. When you look into the void, the void looks back into you.
"… but this beast, that is commonly called a Tyrant, I know not how many heads it has, nor if it be crooked of claw, and armed with horrible fangs. … And of wild beasts you cannot say that they were ever known to eat their own mother" (from Apollonius of Tyana).

Ingvild Langgård
The Beast, 2008
5.1 audio and 16 mm film transferred
to DVD, 3:33 min. loop
in black box, mixed media
244 x 308 x 244 cm
Courtesy of the artist

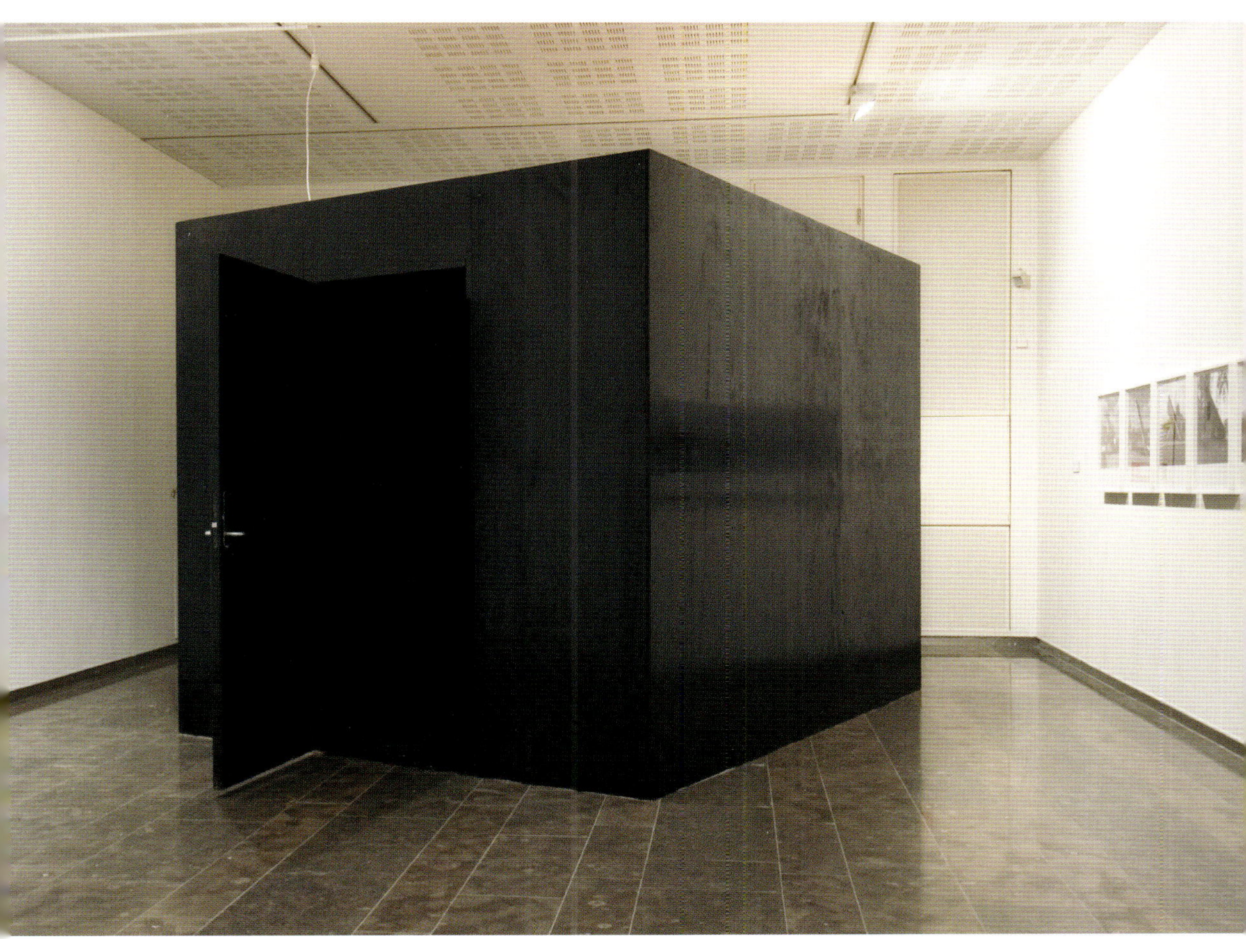

Trine Lise Nedreaas

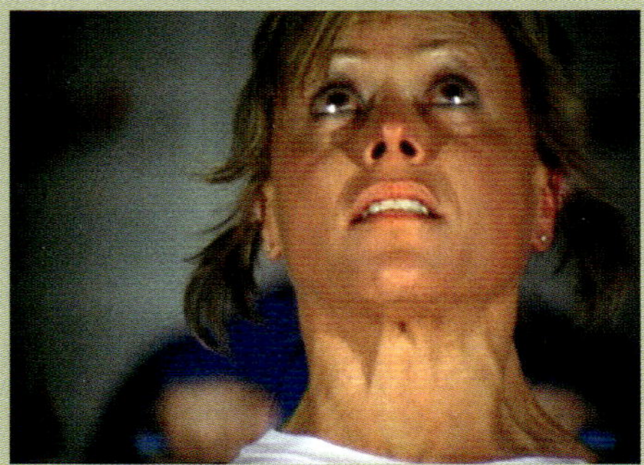

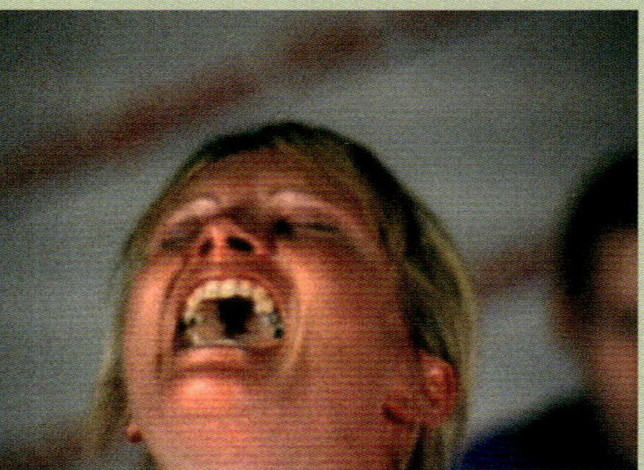

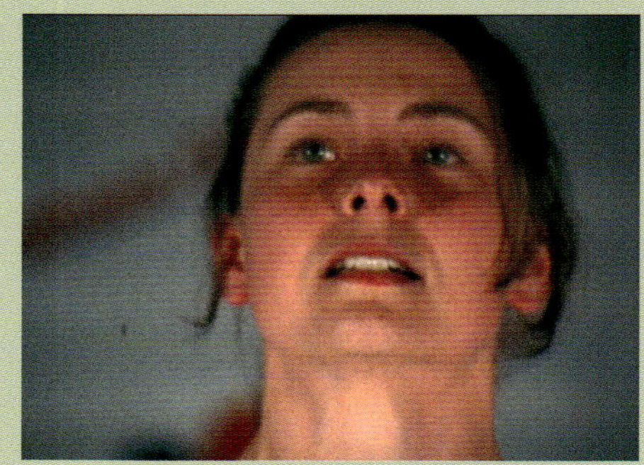

**Born 1972 Bergen
Lives and works in Berlin**

My work often revolves around the driving force in people. I am interested in the different ways people interpret existence and its meaning. I see the manifold of human existence, ambitions, philosophies of life, interests and activities, and gather inspiration from individuals I meet and hear about.
I use things that are personal and close at hand, banal and the simple things – for illumination, but also to stand as metaphors for larger and more universal issues.
What causes us to get up every morning?
What is the driving force that keeps us going?
What is the meaning of it all?
I try to question the roles we choose and present to each other, what we want to achieve in life, and whether what we leave behind means anything, or will be remembered after we are gone.
I often use humour to communicate my ideas.
Humour allows difficult themes to become accessible. It strengthens the viewer's ability to recognize and empathize with the filmed persons and their destinies, and makes the works more understandable and entertaining on several levels.
My films portray the individual, often alone, sometimes goal-directed, but always seeking, testing.
The focus of my artistic development has become clearer of late: it is about coming to understand, or becoming intimately familiar with, an ever-present frustration over existence, and to creatively and courageously use this in my work.

Trine Lise Nedreaas
Dead Lift #1, 2005
16 mm film transferred to DVD,
with sound
Dimensions vary
Courtesy of the artist
Galerie Eva Hober, Paris and Luxe
Gallery, New York

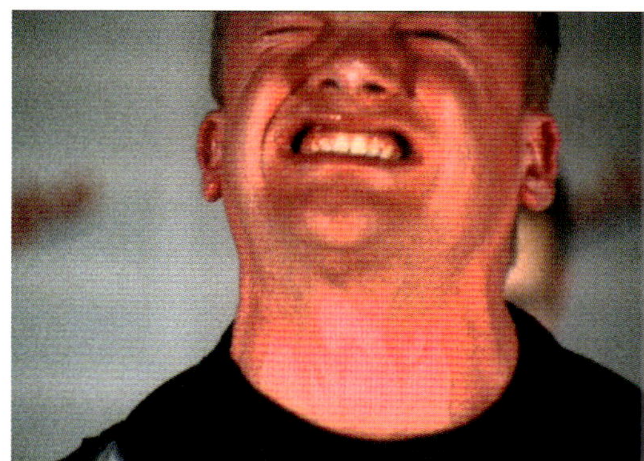
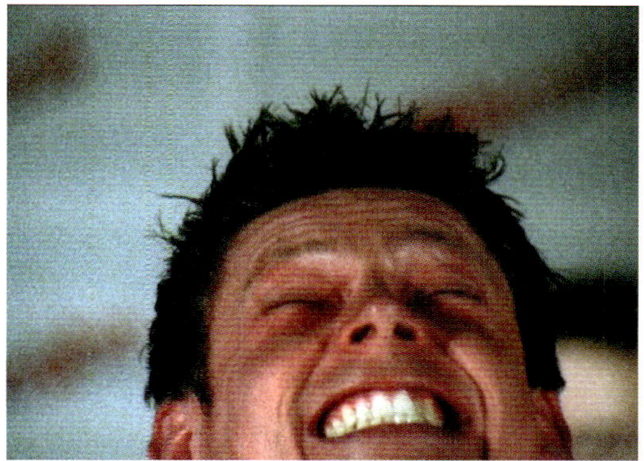

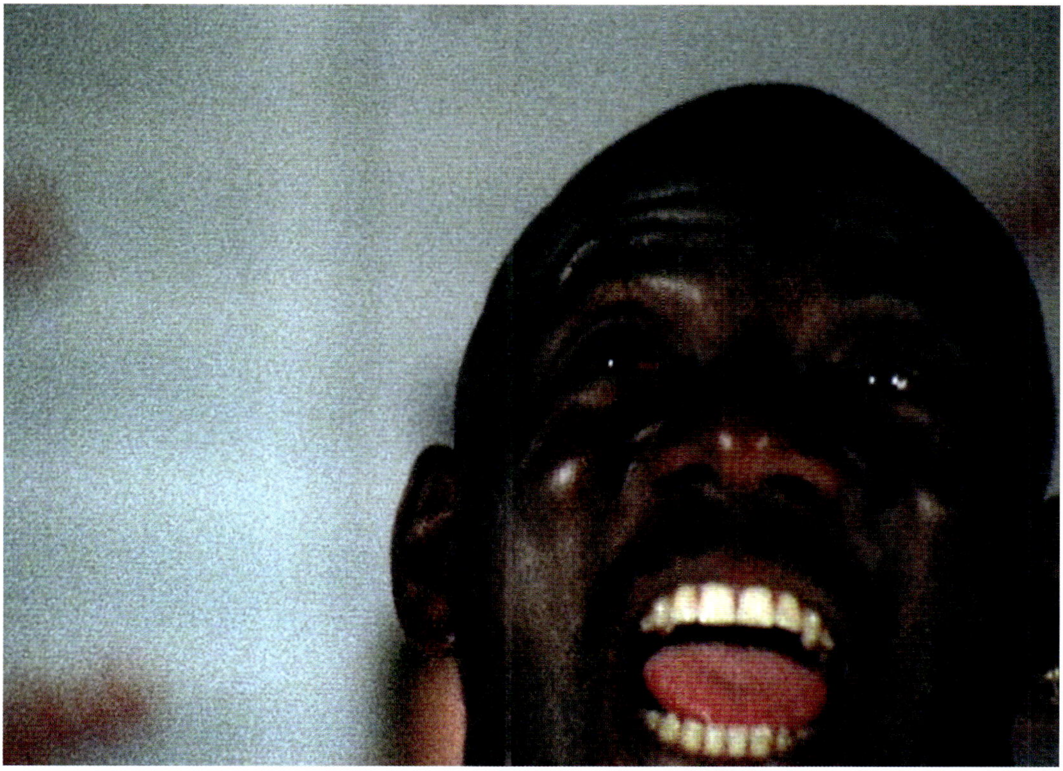

Martin Skauen

**Born 1975 Fredrikstad
Lives and works in Berlin**

In my works I explore human nature and society in relation to questions about faith, salvation, power and powerlessness.
Felix Culpa, A Handmade Massacre is a filmed drawing. It is perhaps best described by a quote from Marquis de Sade: 'There is no better way to know death than to link it with some licentious image.' Just now I live in Berlin, on a one-year stipend at Kunstlerhaus Bethanien. The working conditions are good and the level of activity high. An excellent situation. It is difficult to delimit the various sources from which I draw inspiration, or the themes that take up my attention, but the combination of *engagement, desire* and *weakness* is especially inspiring.

Martin Skauen
Felix Culpa, A Handmade Massacre, 2007
Video
5 min.
Galleri MGM, Oslo and Laura Bartlett
Gallery, London

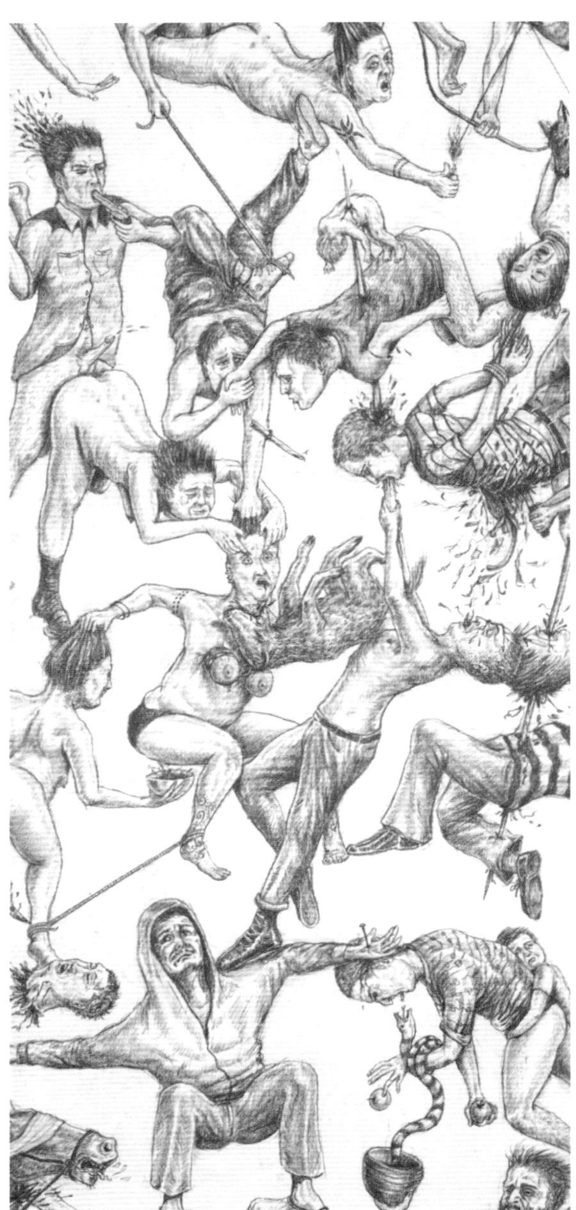

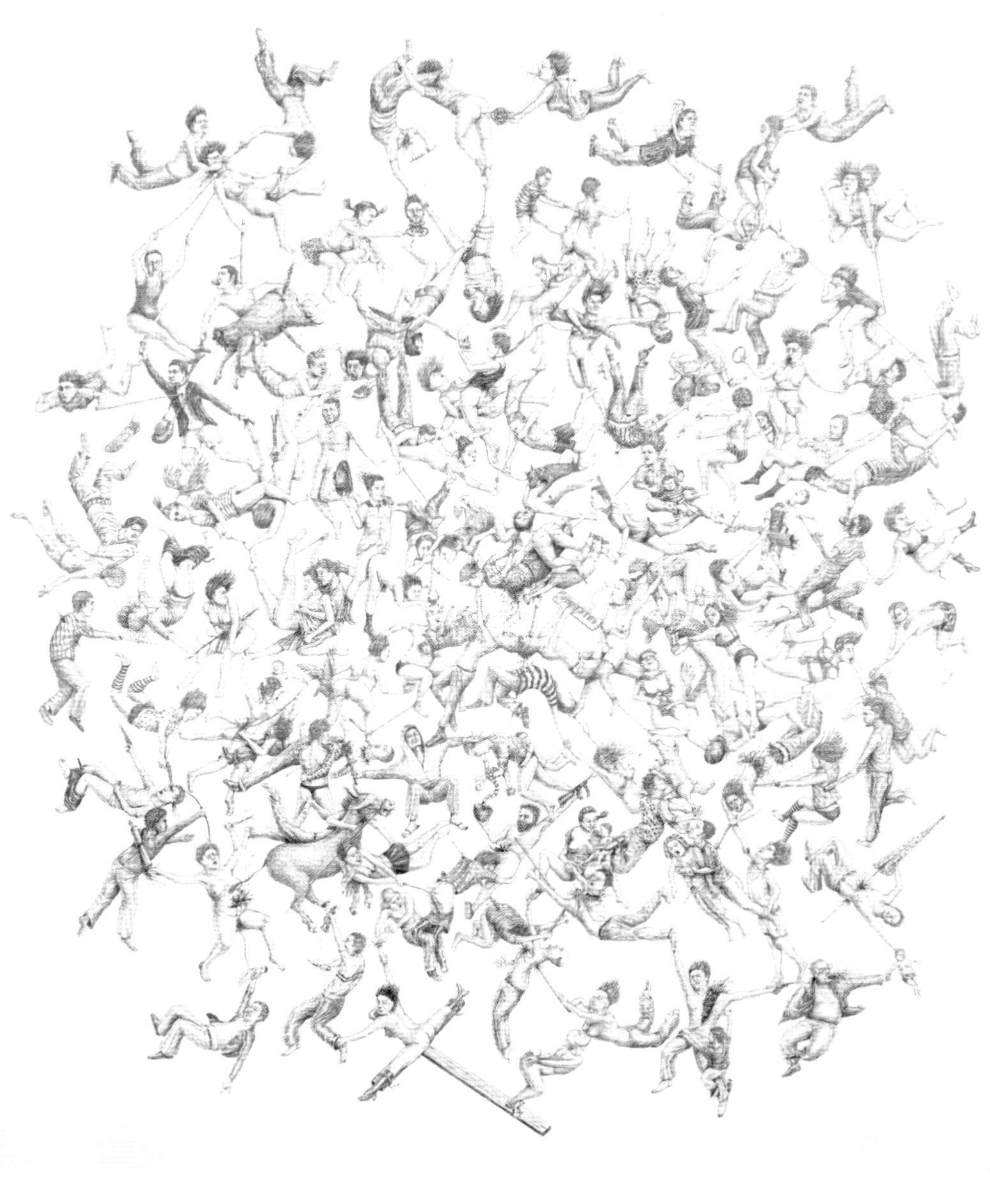

Eirin Støen

Born 1974 Oslo
Lives and works in Oslo

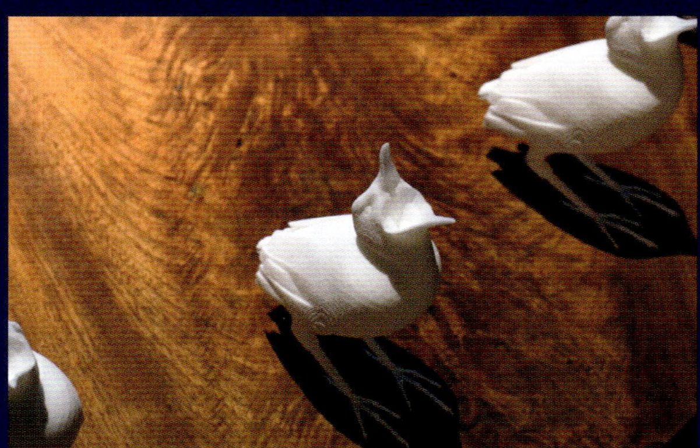

Eirin Støen
Black Cloud #2 (birds on table), 2008
Table (Rococo style) and Rapid
prototyping (3D print), nylon
117 x 88 cm
Courtesy of the artist

Eirin Støen
Black Cloud #1 (dog with bird), 2008
Projection
Dimensions vary
Courtesy of the artist

I work for the most part with photography and sculpture, and my projects often spring from a singular fear arising from more general social questions, problems and influences.

The catalyst for *Black Cloud* is the duality arising when the human being faces the future with fear and apathy, due to his or her own actions and strategies, but at the same time manipulates nature at an ever-increasing pace. Developing things to the point where we lose control over them, or to the point where we lack the preconditions for understanding the consequences, has, throughout history, shown itself to evolve into forces begetting fear rather than hope. If we are to believe climate researchers (who represent one extreme), complete chaos will result, anarchy will reign and human life will be obliterated.

The title *Black Cloud* is appropriated from astrophysicist Fred Hoyle's 1957 science fiction novel by the same name. In Hoyle's book, a tremendous gaseous black cloud has entered the solar system and threatens to block the sunlight, to the point where all life on earth will die.

The themes I address – climate change, gene manipulation and artificial intelligence – are complex. I therefore find inspiration in fragments, and scratch the surface to create a pictorial world relating to the individual subject's interpretations. I draw upon staged and symbolic means whereby objects, materials and techniques from divergent eras are amalgamated into a new unity with references, for instance, to the pictorial language of anti-realistic symbolism.

I am also interested in Romanticism's reaction against reason and the reverie of Nature Romanticism.

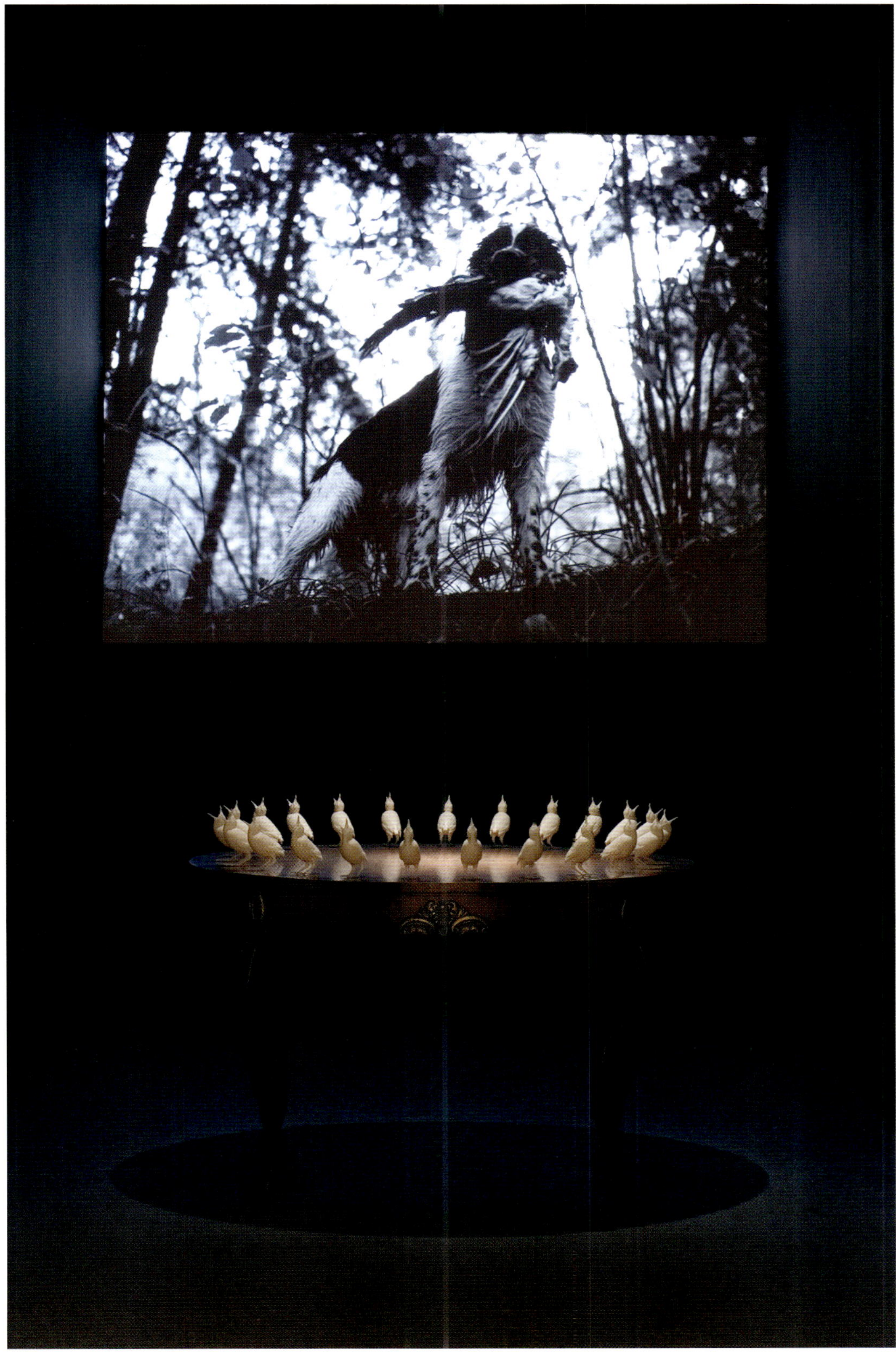

Stian Ådlandsvik

**Born 1981 Bergen
Lives and works in Oslo**

I often hunt for pictures or stories that describe the small in-between gaps in social development where logic has been suspended, or where development goes from being socially abstract to becoming a consequence of human initiative or failure. I try to uncover strange connections in the fast-paced, globalized world, and try to describe these in ways that also say something about how we as participants relate to this development and to the world around us.
Parallel to the development of digital photography, film photography naturally lost its foothold, especially 35 mm film. Its gradual reduction in use is easily noticed when trying to find film in regular photo shops in Oslo. The work entitled *Some Remarks on Discardedness* is a hybrid between a standard 'old fashioned' slide projector and bits of wood left behind after a remodelling project – both neglected remains after some sort of development. The work alludes to issues concerning the speed with which society develops. People have always found new and better solutions, and then neglected the old methods. The speed at which things are changing now is without parallel in history, and entails a transition from physically object-based development to virtual digitalized development. For example, pictures no longer exist as physical entities but merely as aggregates of pixels, and these actually only consist of a series of one and zero. Archaeologists of the future will not need to hack and dig in order to unearth our civilization's development, but they will need a lot of computer gear.

Stian Ådlandsvik
Some Remarks on
Discardedness, 2008
Plywood, Leitz Pradovit 150 dias
projector, dias
Dimensions vary
Astrup Fearnley Collection, Oslo

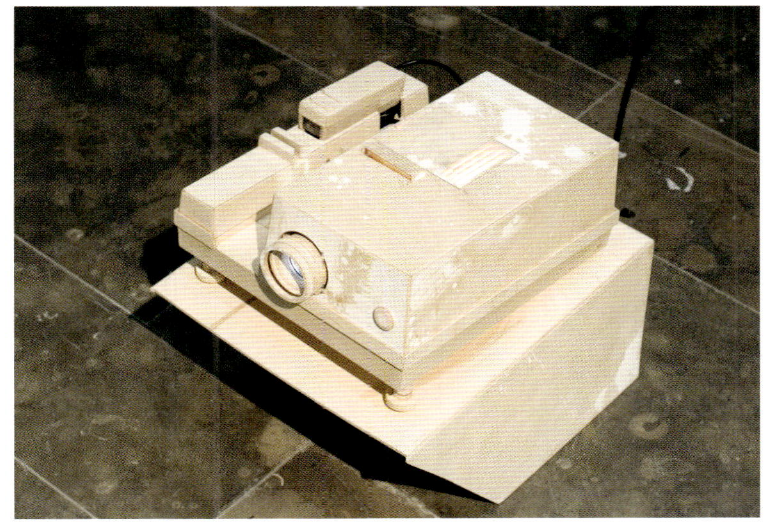

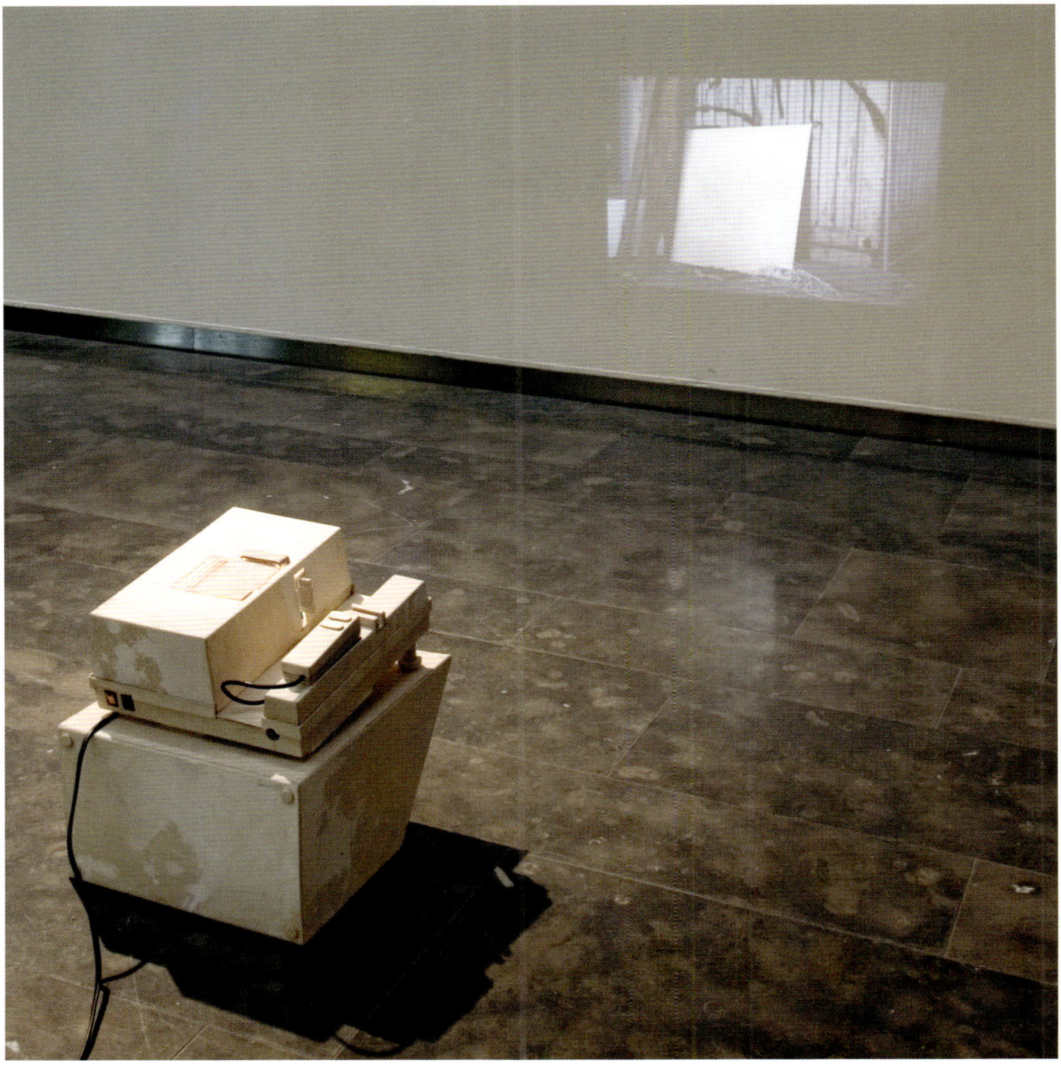

Øystein Aasan

Born 1977 Kristiansand
Lives and works in Berlin

The situation or context in which I work is what influences me the most. This is not primarily a matter of financial conditions, space, exhibitions, etc., but more a matter of what sort of information one consumes, how long it takes to find a use for it in one's work, and what happens in the meantime. My older sister is a literature theorist, and some years ago she and I discussed how one evaluates information from the first moment of exposure: how one, after a time, builds a network consisting of filters and systems that switch over to a control modus. It signals when various bits of information fit in with the pattern. It indicates whether the information harmonizes with what one is producing. This idea about information is central to my work in several respects, firstly because I regard what I do as a way of thinking (and not an expression), and also because I often work with memory and mnemonic techniques. When presenting what I work with, I often tell a story about ancient Roman oratory and the first known reference to mnemonic techniques. The great Roman orators spoke without relying on manuscripts. Instead they imagined themselves inside a long palace corridor with doors leading into different rooms. Each room represented a portion of the speech and had writing on the wall – key words and phrases for what they were planning to say. And *voilà*, they wandered down the imaginary corridor and found the paragraphs in correct order and with correct content. And so what? One key concept is the idea of memory, second is how text and architecture are inextricably interwoven, and third is representation: these three concepts function as categories or rooms into which many of my works can be placed. One of the problems I always return to is how I produce the works and what it actually means to produce. If I am going to explain what I do, and what I think about what I do, I usually deploy a graphic model of explanation. It starts with a little circle surrounded by a slightly larger circle, and then another and another. Each concentric ring is bigger than the last. The little circle is what I produce. The second ring holds an idea about art and perhaps art as an institution. The third is a discourse, possibly, and the next one holds a culture. Then follows a political circle, then society and so on. Each circle represents a distance away from what I myself am working with, and information bleeds in and out of the circles every day. Some bits of information are sent out into society and other bits are added to the discourse – from the institution or from some general cultural circle – and are glued into the innermost circle, before flowing out the other side. Etc. The logic arising from this way of thinking causes me to focus on secondary texts or descriptions of other kinds of productions. This is the case with the two works in the exhibition entitled *Display Unit*. I have worked towards this concept for several years. Initially, I was interested in a structure that had few inherent references to other kinds of production. It was rather like an empty structure, but could be determined through a given content. In language one can find a parallel in 'shifters': words that are largely devoid of content, but whose main function is to point to other words. The third exhibited work, *Echoplex*, is produced on the background of language-based ideas. It is a description of how an Echoplex machine functions. An Echoplex is a mechanical echo machine that came to prominence via dub music. It has a tape-loop and two sound-heads, one for recording and one for playing. It is the distance between these two heads that determines how much and what kind of echo is created. In the play-head there is also a delete function, such that the sound is always dubbed in real time. This description incited me to hunt for sound recordings with natural distortions that could be manipulated in this way. In this particular case, it is a wire-tap recording of a phone conversation. After Echoplex manipulation, there is a flattening of the background noise and an accentuation of all sounds that have 'peak'.

Øystein Aasan
Display Unit (Also by Tennessee Williams), 2007
MDF, book pages, paper and
mirror foil
186 x 143 x 35 cm
Lautom Contemporary, Oslo,
PSM, Berlin and Galerie Katharina
Bittel, Hamburg

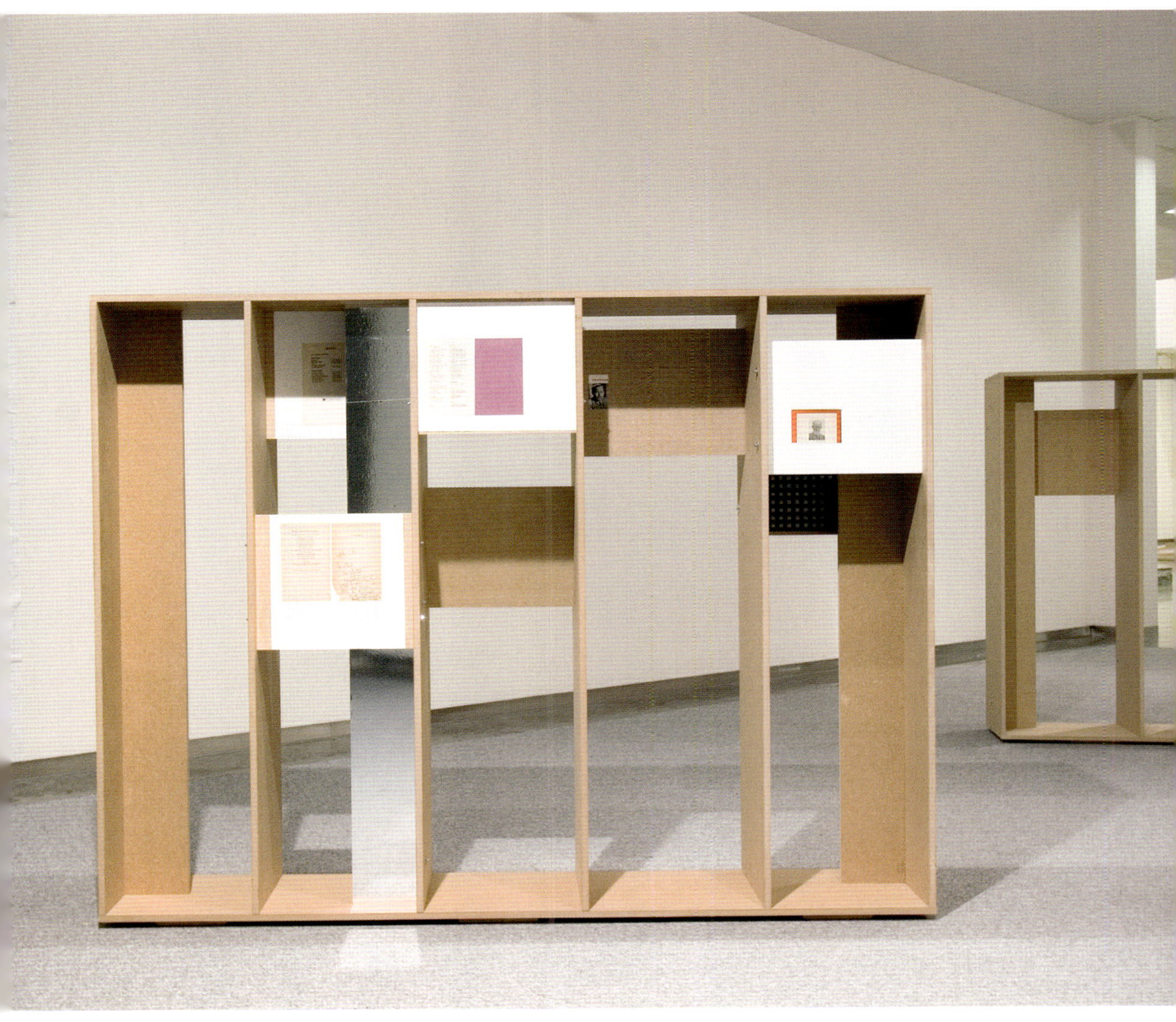

Øystein Aasan
Display Unit (Also by Tennessee Williams), 2007

Øystein Aasan
Display Unit (Meaning Death), 2007
MDF book pages, paper and mirror foil
186 x 143 x 35 cm
Lautom Contemporary, Oslo, PSM, Berlin and Galerie Katharina Bittel, Hamburg

Øystein Aasan
Echoplex 1, 2007
MDF, Celestion loud speaker, wires, wiretap recording, mirror foil and plywood
124 x 75 x 60 cm
Lautom Contemporary, Oslo, PSM, Berlin and Galerie Katharina Bittel, Hamburg

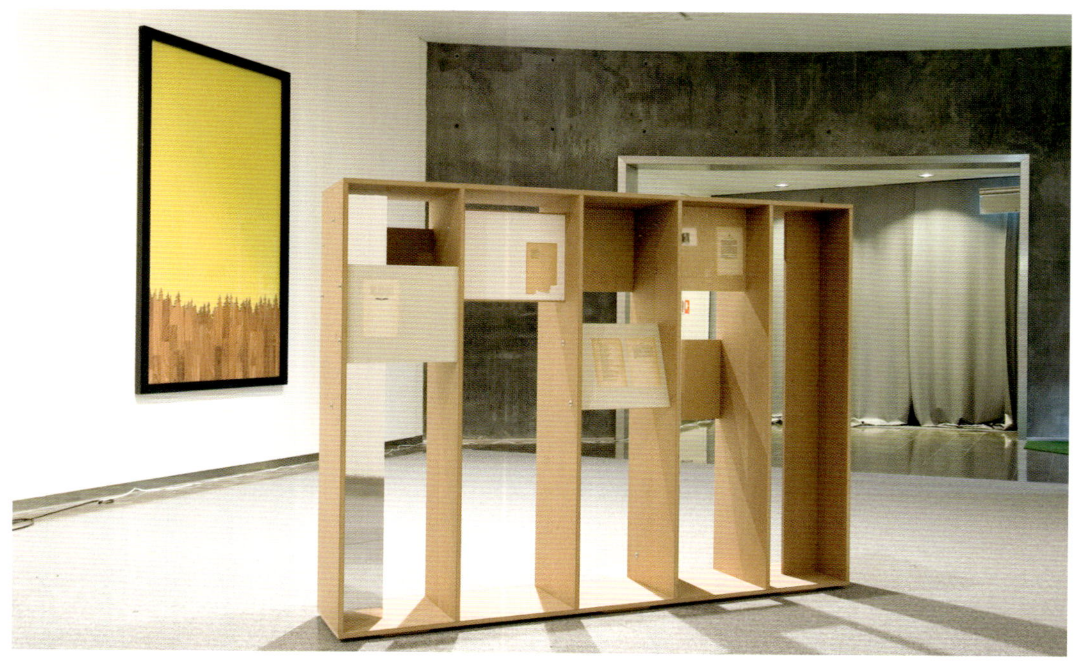

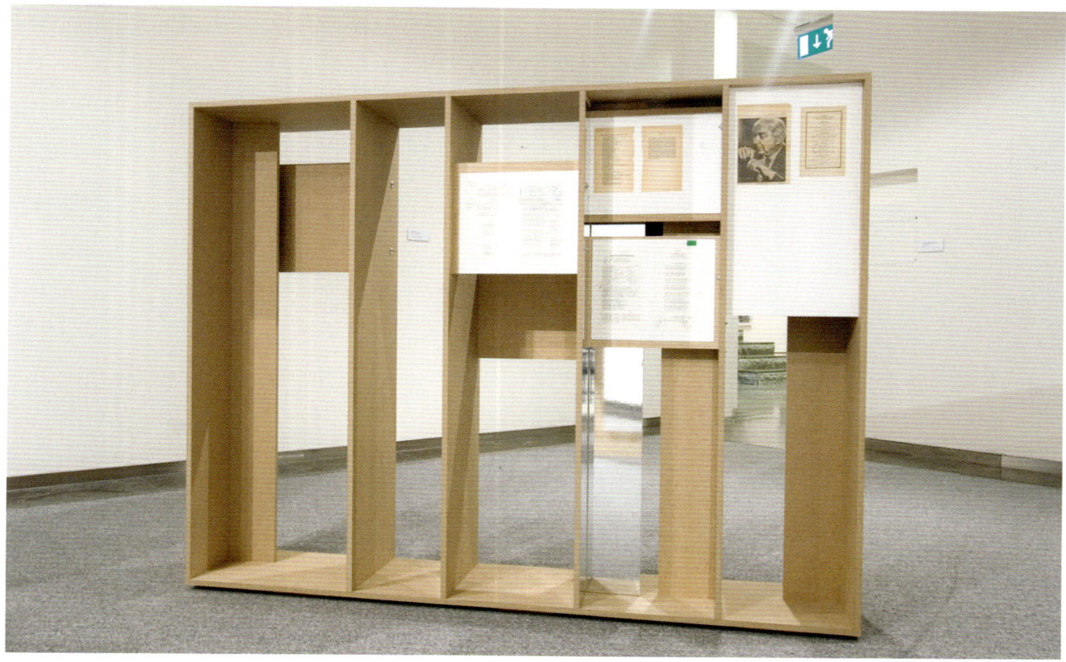

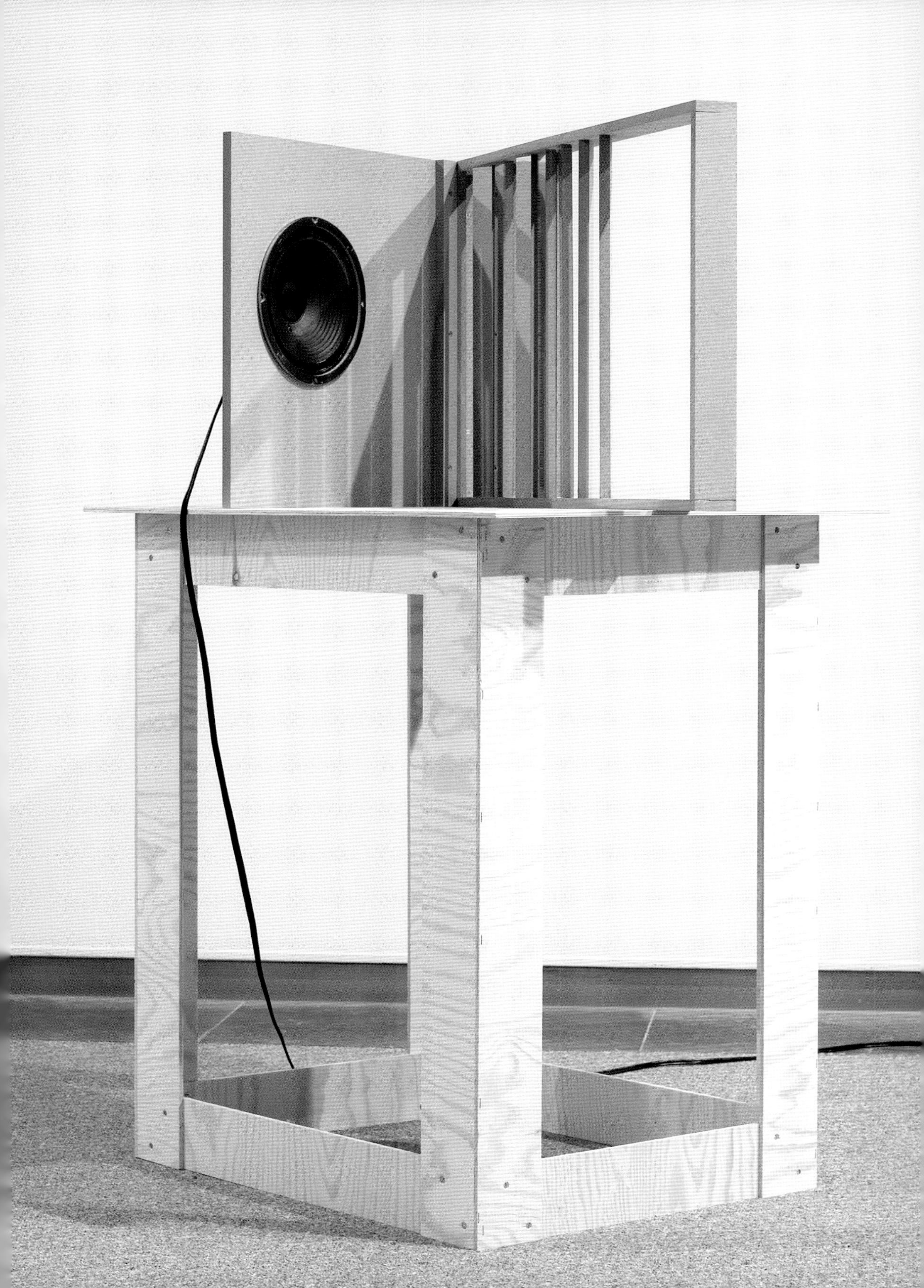

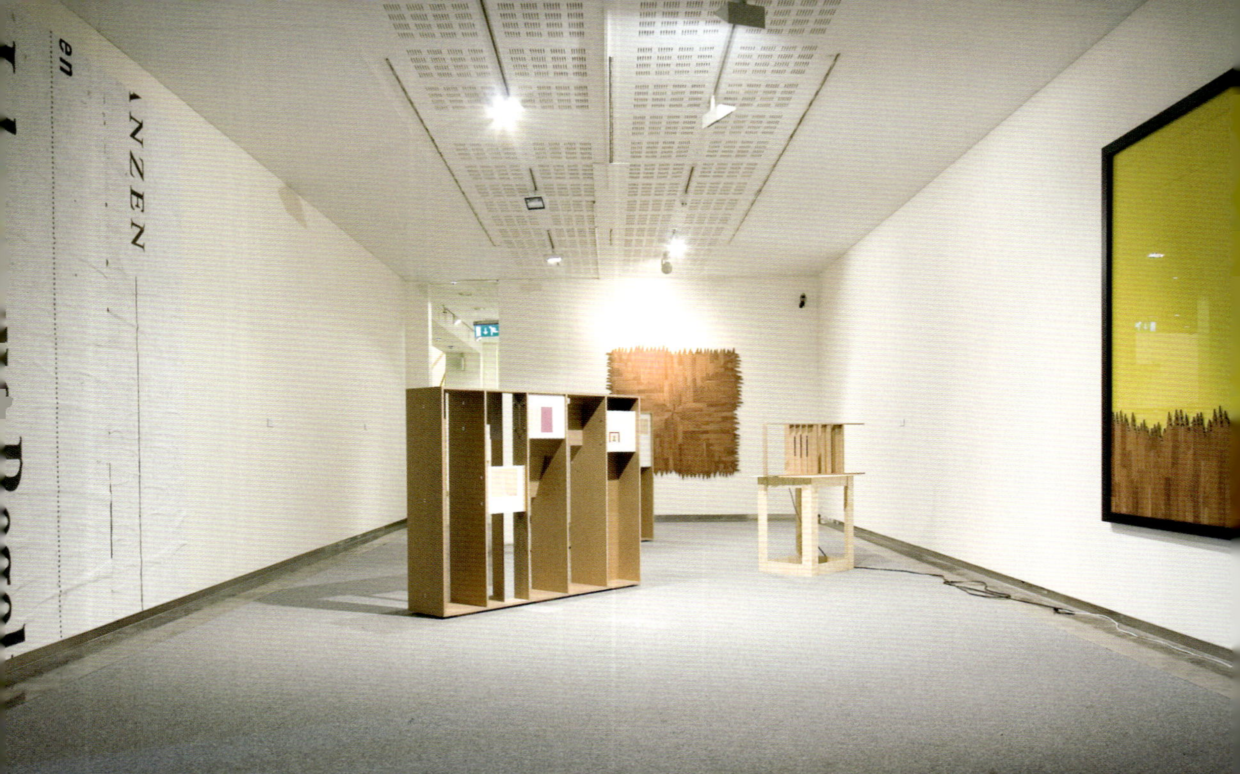

Pissing on the Nordic Miracle

Power Ekroth

A healthy art world contains not simply artists, but also critics, curators and collectors, as well as an infrastructure of institutions, which would include newspapers that take contemporary art seriously, magazines and journals, museums with competent and open-minded personnel, 'kunsthalles', initiatives showcasing private collections, along with all the other events that can boost the sort of exchange that takes place within these circles and beyond them. For at the end of the day, this is what it is all about: the exchange of ideas, and content. Art is one of the few meta-structures of our realities, if not the only meta-structure, and without exchange and communication everything is more or less futile. This goes for the reality the art reflects, not just the art that is trying to reflect reality.

The Norwegian art world has without question boomed within the last decade. This has to do with a local infrastructure that reflects, for the most part, how things work in the world at large, and which permits an international dialogue.

The art of the 1990s was generally speaking all about diversification and pluralistically dissolving genres, and also a return to the 'real' – to the everyday. It was about finding one's identity, about centre and periphery, the global vs. the local, and an opening up towards a 'global village'. Or, to put it in the language of Seinfeld, one of the most popular television series of the 1990s: loads of 'yada, yada, yada'. And while on the subject of yada, it is noteworthy that the best-seller of all times in art literature came out in 1998: *Relational Aesthetics* by Nicolas Bourriaud, which today still has an impact on everyone in the field of art. This was also when the curator stepped up and became the king of the art world for a decade, stealing the crown from the art critic.

One of the most talked about curators during the 1990s, and perhaps still today, is Hans Ulrich Obrist. For some, his words were gospel. Artists chosen by him could count on a bright future in the international circuit (or

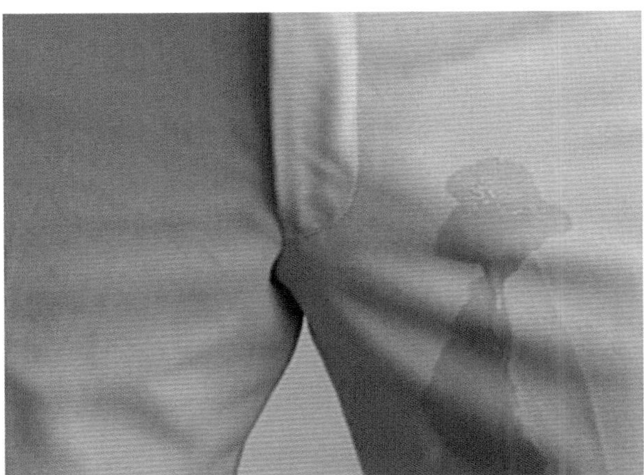

Knut Åsdam, *Untitled (Pissing)*, 1995

"

so they thought), which by itself was enough to make things spin upwards on their own, and collectors with big money were always sniffing around just one step behind Mr. Obrist. Right about when the Obrist frenzy was about to become *really* big, he wrote something which is now familiar to those in the Nordic art bubble, something that was quoted over and over again in the region in the following years because it gave us something to brag about. The most reproduced sentences were from the Nordic exhibition *Nuit Blanche* in Paris, in 1998: 'Periods when certain places claimed to be the centre of the artistic world have come and gone. Such an attitude is old-fashioned in an age in which we see a plethora of dynamic art centres emerging in Europe and elsewhere, centres which have their own special realities to investigate. In the 1990s we saw capital cities like Copenhagen, Helsinki, Oslo, Reykjavik and Stockholm contributing to this trend, along with Bergen, Malmö and Oulu, with an explosion of creativity which seems to signal a genuine "miracle". By being places for meetings and for transcending boundaries, these cities constitute a floating network that is at once compact and loose.'

The two words *Nordic Miracle* were singled out and were picked up by a number of prominent people in the business. For this was what it was all about: *business*. The words *Nordic Miracle* could be turned into green for everyone who had seen the rise of the phenomenon referred to as 'YBA', Young British Art, in the early 1990s – a group of artists with Damien Hirst in the foreground and Charles Saatchi as the man behind the scenes promoting the art, the artists, and its grand making in the market. About this time, NIFCA, the Nordic Institute For Contemporary Art (now defunct), decided to fund a magazine that would promote Nordic art to an international audience. The Finnish magazine *Siksi* and the Swedish magazine *Index* were merged into the new magazine *NU:* at the end of the 1990s. NIFCA gave *NU:* a considerable sum of money to start up a promotional machine for the art of the North. The *Nordic Miracle* of course became a useful tool because it was a catch-phrase that could be turned into a label, as was 'YBA'. This is part of the reason why one finds the label *Nordic Miracle* reproduced in so many articles and catalogues from the Nordic region during that time.

The reason the phenomenon of the *Nordic Miracle* occurred at that time, we have been told, is the oft-mentioned globalization of the art world, which meant that places previously considered to be at the geographic periphery – and the Nordic region had indeed been considered completely peripheral from the international perspective of New York, Paris, London and Cologne – could now compete on the same terms as the centres. Coinciding with this change was the curatorial hunt for 'newness' that had people 'shopping for art' in every remote corner of the world.

The North was far away from the centre: but maybe not far enough? Although *documenta 11*, in 2002, with its platforms and all, cited Antonio Negri & Michael Hardt's *Empire* and Frantz Fanon's *The Wretched of the Earth*, common knowledge about 'the periphery' never seemed to be about anything other than something exotic to most Westerners – which after all constituted the bulk of the target group of *documenta*. The Nordic region and its 'miracle' were quite simply not sufficiently exotic to make the cut from the standpoint of those dividing up reality like this. So, ironically, the most cited reason for the *Nordic Miracle* also became the ultimate reason for a diminishing role for Nordic art in the world at large shortly after its inception. Places that seemed to the Western 'centre' to be distant, such as China, were now the latest territory to be explored and exploited by an art world where the role of the curator was now taken over by the collector, who had emerged as the new diligent explorer of art and creator of the new. 'The curator is dead, long live the collector.'

But let's get back to the *Nordic Miracle* and its significance to the Norwegian climate, in particular by the time of the turn of millennium. In a Scandinavian context, even during the

Nordic Miracle boom, if one can call it a boom at all, Norway and its art seemed to be a bit of backwater. Of the artists most mentioned in connection with 'the miracle', most were Swedish; many of the hippest were Finnish (maybe due to the inclusion of quite a few Finnish artists in the Venice Biennial of 2001, curated by Harald Szeemann); and fewer were Norwegian or Danish. And oh, yes, we must not forget the one artist that quite often was erroneously referred to as Icelandic, the very same artist who gained the most international recognition during this period within the group. Frankly, the *Nordic Miracle* in retrospect was not *all that* Nordic, in fact it was not 'all that' at all because it had clung to a very small group of artists within a particular generation and no one tried to pin the label on the generation of artists that emerged immediately after, so it wasn't a very inclusive term. No one really cared about the miracle anywhere at all after a few years, aside from one or two of the most enthusiastic spin doctors.

To an outsider, it seemed that the Norwegian art world had been liberated from the ravages of modernism, at least more than Norway's Nordic neighbours had been. In point of fact, in the midst of a weird system that had been clinging to the structures of past centuries, lingering in its academies and museums, Norway all of a sudden woke up to a rupture of post-post-modernism. After what seemed like a wake-up call, quite a few Norwegian artists who emerged after 9/11 did not seem to be bothered to take part in the local or even the broader Nordic scene, even when they were both interested in, and up to date on, the local and the international art scene. Instead, many took a leap out of the local and moved ahead – to New York or Berlin or somewhere else, and found other ways of distributing their art, instead of using the local scene as their primary springboard. This seems to be an entirely natural and logical step to take for someone in the middle of antiquated local structures. By comparison, the Swedish situation looked quite different. In Sweden, artists seemed at the time to be steering towards the opposite pole, trying to take one or two influences from the outside world and implement them back home. During the very same period, the important scene for them seemed to be at the home base and not somewhere else. There are other reasons for this too. A significant incitement was the Norwegian centralization of numerous museums and institutions into *one*, the National Museum of Art. This was a drastic decision and things looked grim, and it might have been disastrous for the art scene, since the move made it in some ways increasingly impossible for young artists to come into the art world at large. Paradoxically enough, this turned out instead to be a positive thing for the art scene in Norway, even if the artists had to struggle even more. What happened was that a great many took things in their own hands; they started their own artist-run spaces, opened up shop and let the world know that they were there and they were not going to leave. Some, of course, instead chose to leave Norway for good, which also makes perfect sense.

The *Nordic Miracle* was a label, a brand without any real content, initially mentioned as one of many generous terms that were able to form a lasso that could capture an exhibition context. And as we all know, group exhibitions generally speaking all have themes that are often so loosely formulated that they do not really mean anything, but can be used to pin down at least some aspect of every one of the most disparate art works included in the show. This terminology took on a life of its own, into a brand pushing art and artists to an international market as a national export that could add flavour to another brand; the brand *Nordic*, and to Nordic heritage in general.

The miracle died out for the very same reasons it started. The Western concept of globalism has spread out to the corners of the Western World. What matters are the influences and friends one has – just like before, when a country or art academy had more relevance. Before, it was more reasonable to assume that most of one's influences and friends came pretty much from the same local place, had more or less the same cultural background, and teachers and other influential people in the more immediate environment had a huge impact on what one did and in what direction, or within which 'ism', one was working. Influences come about via networks and the networks are not really necessarily *local* any more. Neither are they completely global of course. The larger population of this 'global' world still does not have access to a computer, much less to the Internet, if they can even read and write at all. The gap between who is connected to a network and who is not, no matter the network, is quite wide indeed, and it keeps widening every second the technology takes 'a leap forward'.

The brand quite soon lost its allure in 'the global village' and couldn't fool anyone – being Nordic or coming from the region was not really that different from coming from any other Western region. What seemed to be the final blow to the brand was the rather large travelling survey, shown first at Moderna Museet in Stockholm in 2000, called *Organizing Freedom*, which included the Nordic art that emerged during the 1990s. It was maybe in the very same instant that it became clear that the lounge-style, with designer furniture in light, bright and icy colours, and birch and pine, was part of the Wallpaper hype, and was completely and utterly dead, or was at most a cul-de-sac.

It should thus come as no surprise that to an artist from the region born around 1980, the concept *Nordic Miracle* makes no sense today. No one claims that a unique and distinctive trait in the art coming from Scandinavia exists, that there is a special 'spiritual quality' to it. Nevertheless, some of the things that happened during this time had what can only be called 'sustainability', and were of great importance in the creation of the field of art today of course.

The machinery of the *Nordic Miracle*, including the Nordic Council, the cultural policies of the Nordic countries' central governments and institutions like the Finnish FRAME, Swedish IASPIS (International Artist Studio Program in Sweden) and Norwegian OCA (Office for Contemporary Art) were thus initiated in its wake. The main objective of these organizations is still to promote their national artists in an international arena via an exchange of studios and grants for artists. The programmes were indeed helpful in initiating a larger network for both national and international artists within the larger system of art production and consumption. All of the Nordic countries have also been very generous with state grants for artists. This fact makes some artists from less generous nations jealous, and others are instead astonished to see that even with generous state support for artists the average result does not really differ from that of other regions.

In Norway, regional investments like the biennial Momentum, in Moss, were initiated. *Nordic Miracle* was mentioned in the first paragraph of the curatorial statement in the first catalogue. The initial biennial took place in the summer of 1998 and included most of the artists often mentioned in the *Nordic Miracle*. The show was curated by Danish curator Lars Bang Larsen, the Swede Daniel Birnbaum, at the time director of IASPIS, and the Norwegian Atle Gerhardsen of the gallery c/o Atle Gerhardsen. Initially the biennial was named 'festival' and it was a *Nordic* festival of contemporary art. The festival is now a biennial (though the schedule is slightly irregular, it does not happen every second year always, but it is supposed to) and it is not a solely Nordic matter but instead an event with international artists.

A biennial is generally considered something to be proud of locally, and during the 1990s a plethora of biennials sprouted up to boost national credibility and to brand cities – and eventually to get the best goodies a government can imagine: gentrification with more taxes coming into the system and a prosperous urban culture. Nowadays, cities do not seek primarily to initiate new biennials – today the rage is art or design fairs, and every major city is looking to get one of their own, in pace with the ferocious market for art (and design).

Coinciding with the international art market's extraordinary expansion during the past five years, the Norwegian art world can no longer be considered to be solely Norwegian – it is extremely up to date about international occurrences, partly because the artists are spread out in places far away from Norwegian soil – and it has become much more integrated in an international art circuit than ever before. One name that should be mentioned in particular in this context is of course Atle Gerhardsen, who has initiated an influx of international artists to Norway and an 'out-flux' of Norwegian artists into an international market through his gallery, expanding his territory hand-in-hand with the market's expansion. Other galleries should be mentioned as well, in particular Standard (Oslo) Gallery. Unfortunately not many critics have emerged on the international circuit from the region, even if art criticism in Norway itself is extremely vibrant – it is most likely just a matter of time. Some Norwegian institutions, museums and 'kunsthalles' have also been important factors simply by doing their job and exhibiting a wide variety of international artists, thereby providing a rich input to the dialogue on art. Of course, the most important factor however is the artists, working hard and within an international context just as well as in the national context. The network of artists is large and complex; it transcends national borders, aesthetic interests, theoretical discourses and other boundaries – all factors that can readily become obstacles to exchange or dialogue. Dropping the names of artists, à la Easton Ellis, would be entirely superfluous in this context, where we are already 'sliding down the surface of things' – suffice it to say that there are many artists who could be mentioned here.

So, getting down to the nitty-gritty: does it mean anything in particular to be a *Norwegian* artist today, in contrast to being a Swedish, Caribbean, Iranian, Ukrainian or Nigerian artist? Maybe it does, but it might be more interesting to ask whether this question is at all relevant in the first place – and if so, in what ways? – rather than trying to grasp any answer about what it means for an artist to originate from within a particular national border. Most answers to that question are empty or ad hoc. Cultural heritage is of course not unimportant – on the contrary – but a common cultural background is not equivalent to commonality of national borders. That might seem like stating the obvious, but this is not the perspective manifest in most national governments' cultural policies. Instead, the governments address the same issues in a different way: by including policies about 'integration' and 'minority inclusion' – whatever that means. It certainly goes without saying that it is still good business for a government to brand a group of artists from within its borders as important or interesting since it increases GNP in a multitude of ways. And there is indeed a great deal of artists with a Norwegian passport out there, visible in an increasingly international art world, both in the commercial world and in the 'high brow' regular world of biennials and art fairs. But let's get real; as soon as *region* replaces thematic context and content as a category we should hear a little warning bell.

As long as it is human nature both to collect and to systematize there will be regional categories like this. It makes life easier, since complex things become less difficult to grasp. 'Isms' and movements were created this way, and still are. One of the attempts to put a label on one direction within Norwegian contemporary art is worth mentioning, since it not only had a deep impact on the local debate but it also reflects a larger international phenomenon; moreover, it is a locally constructed label: 'new conceptualism'. The Norwegian so-called new conceptualism is strongly associated with a close-knit group of artists who pinpoint subjects in society at large and comment on various structures (of power) in a critical way. Others may call it institutional critique. When this is incorporated into a structure that is part of, and supports, the very same structures that are criticized in the art works, another label is more commonly used, internationally, about the institutions: 'new institutionalism'. 'New institutionalism' is often linked to some of the leading curators from the 1990s like Charles Esche, Nicolaus Schafhausen, Jérôme Sans, Nicolas Bourriaud, Catherine David, Maria Lind, Vasif Kortun, the aforementioned Hans Ulrich Obrist and Ute Meta Bauer, the first director of OCA; all of whom in turn used to be headstrong independent curators, but have now been working for a couple of years *within* the institutions instead of 'outside' as freelance curators.

Back in the days when it first occurred, institutional critique was considered unable to incorporate itself within the institution it criticized without loosing its impact. Cheerleaders of the *new* institutionalism however claim that the institutional critique indeed works, as currently implemented, within the very same structures by emphasizing *other* functions than the exhibition itself and the objects of display (and power). Instead it focuses on seminars, the artist as a 'researcher', and investigates the production of works through 'processes' in conferences and through the new institutionalism's residency programs that focus on all aspects of production, aside from the results. Value is measured in its discursive and participatory elements. One of the problems with this approach, which is increasingly being used within quite a number of institutions, is that the discursivity is only directed towards a narrow *inner* circle, a choir that has already been converted, and while everyone involved pats one another on the back, there seems to be a disconnect with any wider audience. Another problem is that the new institutionalism seems to manifest no interest in true competence and knowledge, and praise is unthinkingly given to any artist with an interest in working within another field, like sociology or biology, even though the results are both poor and uninteresting, artistically, and also as seen by the lights of the other field (as in the 'used car syndrome', as Hal Foster calls it: 'you buy my used car and I buy your used car and we both end up with two shitty cars'). One simply eschews any kind of critical standards in both art and whatever other genre or area the artists are moving into.

Additionally, working as an artist in the context of institutional critique, new institutionalism and relational aesthetics as well, if you wish, can itself become quite a cynical tool used to gain artistic recognition and international success in terms of both artistic credibility (exhibiting in the very same institutions, biennials and shows the curators that support new institutionalism arrange) as well as, ironically enough, artistic viability in an economic market. But this is merely one outline of many in the increasing internationalization of artists and the infrastructure of art. All labels or trends lose their impact and interest sooner or later. Content and originality does not – content that has something to say to someone outside the tiniest group of people within the art bubble. Everything else is a lot of yada, yada, yada, and thankfully many of the Norwegian artists today have learned this lesson and are fully liberated from the national or regional labelling, which is more about branding and business than art.

New Ways to Work Together
Pragmatism, Quality and Relational Aesthetics

Erlend Hammer

In a strange and distant land

During the summer of 2007, I travelled to Seoul, South Korea, with the Norwegian artists Jan Christensen and Bjørn Kowalski-Hansen and the Swedish critic and curator Power Ekroth. Along with a group of young Korean artists, we spent three weeks creating a workshop/exhibition in an area far from the city's art world. Both the project and the trip were funded by the Korean Arts Council and the Royal Norwegian Embassy in Seoul, and came about in a fairly typical way: Christensen had been to Korea a couple of times before, and during a residency at Changdong had met the Korean artist Jooyoung Lee, who later invited him back for a project she was doing. He, in turn, invited the rest of us. The project had no fixed curatorship and was an experiment in flattening the power structures normally found in any exhibition situation. It was the kind of thing that look great on paper, and on one's CV: a meeting between artists from two very different countries on the periphery of the art world. We set up some interesting social relationships and generally had a wonderful time. We did not, however, produce much art of any particular value.

I was recently reminded of this when I read an essay by Taiwanese art historian Chin-tao Wu.[1] Wu questions whether Norwegian artists generally produce art of sufficiently high quality and critical value to merit the lavish government grants and project support awarded to them from the plentiful public funds available within the arts sector. In a lecture organized by the Office for Contemporary Art Norway, a publicly funded, semi-private organization that gives financial aid to Norwegian art projects abroad and brings foreign art professionals to Norway, Wu hesitantly suggested that Norwegian artists are perhaps simply too comfortable and thereby may be lured into a sort of complacency that cannot be found in less hospitable financial situations.

This is interesting because the question of quality is something we hardly ever talk about anymore. Art critics sometimes write that work is either good or bad, but not very often. It is more common for a critic simply to describe a work and attempt to place it within a context where it makes some kind of sense in its relationship to other similar, or different, artworks. In addition, a critic might discuss whether an exhibition is well put together and similar questions related to the tricks of the trade. It is usually possible to detect whether the critic likes a work or an exhibition, but very rarely will he or she go out on a limb and plainly state 'This is Bad' or 'This is Good'. This is especially true if the artist is young and there is a certain amount of critical hype surrounding his or her work. Nobody wants to be the guy who told the world that the next Sophie Calle would never make it. Another reason is surely the shift in power that has taken place over the last couple of decades. Perhaps critics don't talk about quality because they know that no one cares what they think anymore; the power structures have shifted. For a while, the curators were in charge, and today the dealers and collectors run the show. In this highly market-driven art world, the idea of a critic either making or breaking an artist's career is nearly unimaginable. Careers are made at fairs these days, not in reviews.

At the same time, there exists another section of the art world in which the market is much less a factor, but where we still rarely hear talk about artistic quality. This is the part of the art world that is currently coming to terms with (or, depending on your opinion, recovering from) a decade and a half of relational aesthetics. This is the part of the art world where it is perfectly acceptable to travel to the other side of the world and spend 20,000 Euros worth of public funding on three weeks of 'work shopping' that results in a few new friendships and a blog.[2]

Relational post-aesthetics
Since the late 1990s, the most talked-about concept within art theory has been so-called 're-lational aesthetics'. The term was first used by the French curator and critic Nicolas Bourriaud in a book of that name published in 1996. Subsequently, it has been put to much confused use, both as a tool and as a target. Some see it is a valuable guide for creating interesting work within an art environment where primarily studio-based practice is understood as insufficient; others see it as having carried on certain questionable tendencies of conceptual art so that the art world has deteriorated into a field of mere discourse.

One of the most interesting discussions of relational aesthetics took place in the pages of the American art journal *October* after the British critic Claire Bishop suggested that many of those artists who have been celebrated as important figures within the 'movement' of relational aesthetics, such as Rirkrit Tiravanija and Liam Gillick, were not as worthy of praise as many had assumed. The works of these artists, Bishop wrote, were not in fact the politically benign, democratic projects that they had often been deemed. Rather, they should be considered examples of an almost Romantic, and highly bourgeois, kind of fake utopianism, whose makeshift collectivist yearnings could not make up for their lack of genuine critical potential. From Bishop's perspective, a reconsideration of art-world relationships only gains value if the power dynamics that dominate them are significantly changed. And only such a shift could truly justify Bourriaud's claim that relational works might be considered more politically 'radical' than conventionally exhibited studio work.

Although Bishop does not discuss this, it is clear that Bourriaud's idea of the politics of relational aesthetics is closely related to certain elements of pragmatist philosophy, particularly in the notion that one needs neither principles nor clearly defined end goals to create change. Progress is seen as being achieved one adjustment at a time. Thus neither grand utopian statements nor ideologically funded critique are seen as pertinent to the development of social change. This way of thinking is very well suited to the methods of those artists associated with so-called 'new institutionalism' which, incidentally, also includes many of those artists who are associated with Bourriaud's idea of relational aesthetics. Within this way of working, critique is formulated not through seeking conflict, nor even necessarily through exposing the power dynamics, but through continuous attempts to engage with these established structures in shifting ways.

To Bishop, however, this is far from enough. Relational aesthetics does not criticize the structures of late, global capitalism, she says; it merely reproduces them. And to her, this has no critical value. Instead, she asks for work that is less ambiguous and more explicitly critical. She finds this in the projects of, for example, Santiago Sierra and Thomas Hirschhorn, artists who just like Tiravanija and Gillick create work that is highly context-sensitive and whose meaning depends completely on the potential involvement of the spectator. What makes it more 'critical' in Bishop's view is the uncomfortable feeling that is created when we are faced with a work like Hirschhorn's *Bataille–Monument* (2002). Here, the artist created a library of texts by the French philosopher Georges Bataille in a predominantly working-class, Turkish area outside Kassel, an area in which, it is safe to assume, the locals would not put the reading material to much use. This created a tension in the work that Bishop finds lacking in, for example, Gillick's architectural backdrops for thinking about the work of Gilles Deleuze.

This discussion mirrors the question of what is the better form of dissent: confrontational critique of the establishment or the creation of an alternative, quasi-autonomous practice on the outside? Much of the most interesting work carried out by young Norwegian artists over the last few years has attempted to come to terms with this question in new ways that don't necessarily tackle it head-on. This has proved frustrating for those who prefer their art to be critical in more explicit ways, in much the same way as Bishop positions herself in opposition to a certain tendency within relational aesthetics.

An example of this is the artist-run project space that began life as Gallery Galuzin and then turned itself into TAFKAG – The Artspace Formerly Known As Galuzin. Galuzin opened in Oslo in 2005 and quickly became one of the most talked-about art spaces in town. Although the talk was less centred on the actual art than on the openings and parties hosted at the gallery, Galuzin/TAFKAG became both a social playground and a place to see the work of young, emerging artists presented within a context that felt genuinely fresh compared to the rest of Oslo's galleries and project spaces. The gallery never showed any even remotely 'relational' work. In fact, the exhibited work was frequently highly conventional, sometimes downright romantic and unfashionable. There was, however, a 'relational' quality to the project, since the space was run with, even driven by, a kind of group mentality that is only possible when there is no feeling of obligation towards a general public. This also added a level of context-sensitivity that is rarely found in more conventional exhibition spaces, probably because the artists always knew, more or less, who their audience would be. This, in turn, meant that work always gained a certain aura by being presented in this particular environment.

The critic Johanne Nordby Wernø criticized TAFKAG's way of presenting exhibitions on the grounds that it did little to favour either the work or the visitor's experience.[3] Instead, the focus was primarily on partying and even the press releases rarely made much sense, adding nothing to the appreciation or understanding of the exhibited work. To Wernø, TAFKAG failed as both a regular exhibition space, and as an alternative space, because it did none of the things exhibition spaces are supposed to do. It neither presented work in idealized conditions nor in a way that was expressly institutional critique. Even worse, Wernø argued, its lack of both professionalism and a valid alternative exhibition practice meant that it did not attract spectators from outside its own fairly closed art-world circles. It did not occur to her that not attempting to reach a wider audience might in itself be part of the intention or meaning of the work. This seems based on the standard way of thinking about art as inherently both a public and a critical form of activity. Here, Wernø echoes Bishop's critique of Bourriaud in the sense that they both raise the question of what can be considered a critical act.

Wernø expected the people behind TAFKAG, as a non-institutional underground art space, to be critical in a different way, or at least to acknowledge that the space was intended as a critical practice. But perhaps TAFKAG was instead an experiment in non-institutional non-critique. For example, the people behind TAFKAG were not sceptical of the art market in the way underground, non-profit artist-run spaces are often expected to be. Rather, when faced with Wernø's criticism, the gallerists hit back, saying that the artists who had shown their work at TAFKAG had in fact frequently made sales from their exhibitions. The market is no longer something to escape from, but can be used even by the most underground exhibition space as a way to legitimize one's activity in terms of quality.

Relational neo-aesthetics

Galuzin opened around the same time as the Oslo art world was talking about a conflict at the Oslo National Academy of the Arts. Here, a process of consolidating the school's different departments into one big institution had led many students from the previously quite autonomous Academy departments to establish a new, unofficial and independent Academy under its original name Statens kunstakademi.[4] In parallel, the discontinued Institute of Colour, a former part of the painting department, was re-launched as a student-run, group-project school.[5] Both groups worked in a way that resembled the collective processes at work in much 1990s art, but a high percentage of their work is still studio-based. This focus among younger artists represents a slight, but important, shift away from some of the most important tendencies of relational aesthetics, such as open-endedness, 'post-production', the artwork as 'intervention' or 'platform' and so on. The artwork does not necessarily attempt to enter into dialogue with other social dimensions outside the art world; nor does it usually seek to engage the spectator in a way that differs much from a normal white-cube environment.

As such, the work of galleries like TAFKAG does not necessarily differ much from the way a commercial gallery is run. In fact, the most successful new gallery in Norway over the last few years, Standard (Oslo), has many similarities with a kind of collective or family into which the entrance of newcomers is not readily welcomed, and which is in fact something that must be earned. Its director talks openly[6] about how the gallery will evaluate a potential buyer before making a sale, and many of the gallery's artists work with structures that mimic, reference or generate semi-closed social networks. It seems clear that the strategies of Standard have influenced the younger artists in Oslo much more than any of the artist-run spaces that were prominent throughout Norway in the 1990s. So while there is still a strong element of a good old DIY ethic at work in many artist-run exhibition projects today, this has to some extent been detached from its formerly obligatory idealism. It is no longer necessarily a matter of 'dropping out' of the established system. This means that such seemingly idealistic and 'underground' galleries as TAFKAG can just as easily be utilized as (what some would call) cynical strategies to generate a maximum amount of credibility using only a minimum of means.

At the same time, the ever-present quest for what's cool is an important reason why so-called relational practices have never really caught on among young artists in Norway. Because of its close ties to the political ideals that have dominated Norwegian society for the last fifty years, relational aesthetics has to some extent become state policy when it comes to art in Norway. While there are certainly critics of this approach, especially among those who prefer their art to be more experience- and object-based, any project description founded on concepts, or rather keywords, such as 'democracy', 'public space' or 'reaching new audiences' will likely be looked upon with much political favour, and will be heavily funded. Projects such as *Kunstneriske forstyrrelser* (artistic disturbances), where artists are invited to 'interfere' with various local contexts in northern Norway, are based on a kind of democratic ambition that feels almost as well suited to the political climate in Norway as Social Realism did in a propaganda-hungry Soviet Union. The work is 'democratic' in its attempted outreach to a non-art-world audience as well as in its near-complete lack of focus on quality. The latter is important, because in Norway the

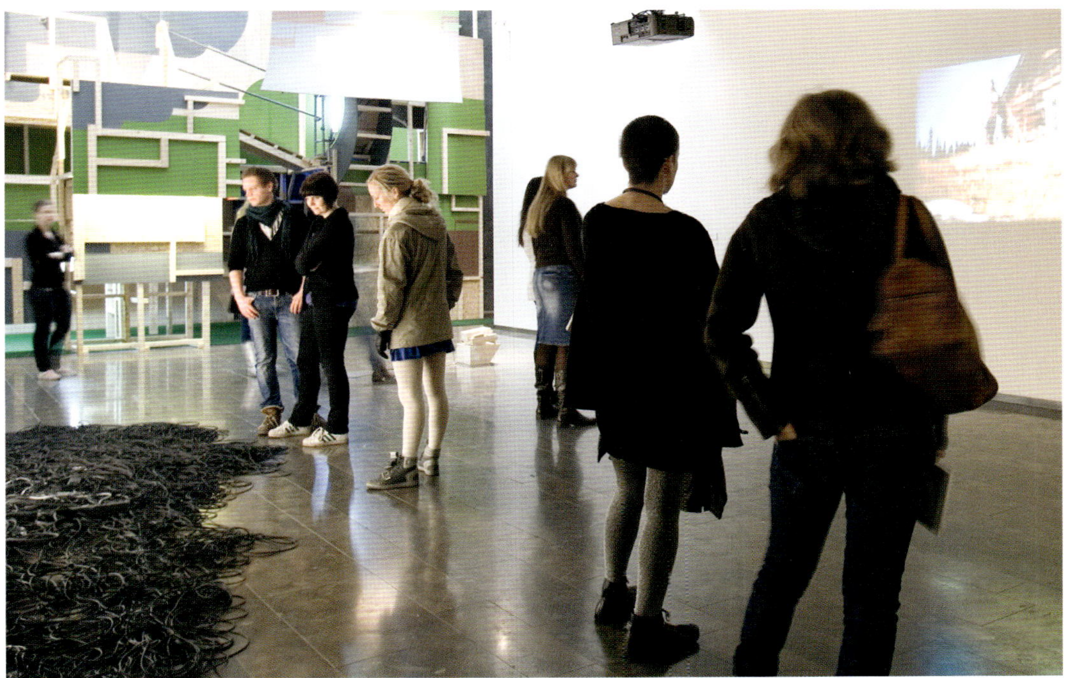

historical lack of anything resembling a class system or a cultural elite (we're all farmers and fishermen as one long forgotten pop singer once famously complained) means that the concept of quality as a means of distinction is usually met with distrust and hostility. By saying that something is good, it feels as if we're saying that another thing is bad, and if someone else likes those things we say are bad, aren't we then saying something negative about that person? So, best not to talk about quality. This means that relational artworks are perfectly suited to the kind of cultural logic that dominates the public sector in Norway. And naturally enough, this has led to a situation where the strategies of relational aesthetics (as a style) have become decidedly, and probably irrevocably, uncool.

Instead, the lessons learned from artists like Tiravanija or Gillick are based on exactly those aspects of their work that Bishop found lacking in critical value: the emphasis on local, short-term social relationships, or the ability to enter into undefined relationships within larger structures where it becomes difficult to tell whether the artist is making a critique or giving cultural legitimacy to an international corporation of possibly questionable ethical repute. Still, these lessons mean that it can be more interesting to do a small, independent show that is seen by twenty people than to stage an exhibition in a publicly funded space where perhaps eighty people see the work. This is not only because the sense of temporary community is stronger, but because this feeling of temporary community in itself can be reason enough to do the work in the first place; as the artist Douglas Gordon says: 'I make [art] so that I can go to the bar and talk about it.'[7] The real potential of relational aesthetics was never in its overtly political agenda of a radically democratized kind of art; it was in a renewed focus on social context as a primary component of both the artist's and the spectator's relationship to the art experience.

The importance of context is impossible to ignore after relational aesthetics. Whether the audience is eating soup in a gallery or watching paintings in the woods, our awareness of context has been sharpened. This also explains why it can be more interesting to carry out a corporate commission than another gallery show. Once the context changes, so too does the meaning, and with it how artists need to think about their work.

Go small!

So while it has been assumed that the main importance, and therefore influence, of relational aesthetics was a broad political potential or an attempt to destabilize certain well-established power structures, perhaps the nature of this destabilization has been misunderstood. It could be that it does not have so much to do with questions about the relationship between art and the outside world, or the old distinction between art and life. It seems increasingly possible that we should instead focus on exactly the kind of smaller units represented by both artist-run project spaces and commercial galleries. Relational aesthetics then becomes more like an argument for re-fracturing the public sphere into many, separate sectors. This is necessary in order to avoid the political ideals that have previously argued for the necessity of one, consensus-based, public sphere.

It will be especially interesting to see how these already growing tendencies will develop after *documenta 12* (2007), an exhibition that seemed to operate within a similar theoretical terrain. Here too, the focus shifted from a large and coherent unity to scattered and unmanageable segments. It was an attempt to get away from the grand statements typically expected from the giant exhibition within a cultural climate that fuels the world's ever-growing number of biennials with an event-based logic. More and more such large-scale events function as pawns in politically motivated chess games where taking the king amounts to some new level of city branding, often through 'putting the local in touch with the global', i.e. cultural tourism. In response, the truly local is simply inspired to go smaller.

From the perspective of the youngest generation of artists, therefore, the question is primarily the same as that of the previous generation of relational aesthetics proper: what kind of relationship are we able to set up within which to create our work in a satisfying way? Relational aesthetics in Norway, where it has been picked up by younger artists at all, often mimics corporate strategies and business models. Today, the use of an art project to create a business is just as relevant as creating a business to realize an art project.

The recent rise of artist-run galleries and independent project spaces is important because it suggests a willingness to work on a more moderate scale. It also suggests a desire to escape the public sphere as art's primary environment. These spaces haven't necessarily popped up because there aren't enough galleries to accommodate all the artists coming out of the Norwegian art schools, although this too is a problem since the government seems intent on educating people into art-world 'freelancing' rather than facing the fact that there are no longer enough real jobs for them to do. If someone is registered as an artist, this keeps them off the unemployment statistics. So the fact that more artists are able to get exhibitions as a result of more galleries is a by-product at best, and not necessarily a positive one since it disguises the fact that there are simply too many artists around these days. What's truly important, however, is that the existence of independent galleries within the art world creates spaces where there is neither the expectation nor the existence of a non-specialized audience. The most important thing about these galleries is that so few people know they exist. Without the bureaucracy and time-wasting elements that often follow the need to cater to a general audience, we get the kind of social environment that is needed to produce not only interesting work but also rewarding relationships. We might even find a new way to work together.

[1] Chin-tao Wu, 'Konsernenes inngrep i kunstverdenen: noen problemer til debatt', *Kunstjournalen B-post*, January 2007.

[2] http://www.195seoul.blogspot.com.

[3] Johanne Nordby Wernø, 'Persona angrep', http://www.kunstkritikk.no/article/16425

[4] http://www.statenskunstakademi.com/

[5] http://www.institutforfarge.net/

[6] Mona Gjessing, 'Situasjonen i det norske kunstmarkedet', *Billedkunst*, no. 4, 2007.

[7] Hans Ulrich Obrist, '(P)ARS PRO TOTO. Conversation with Douglas Gordon', http://www.mip.at/en/dokumente/506-content.html

Institutional Critique's Knowledge and Interest

Trude Schjelderup Iversen

Contemporary artists working in a conceptual tradition, who gather inspiration from a specific political sub-genre of it, namely the so-called 'institutional critique' (IC), and have an aesthetic interest in it, are well represented at international biennials. They are also represented in the commercial gallery system, albeit to a lesser degree. This renewed interest in art-institutional conditions has been characterized as a third generation or phase of institutional critique,[1] and is marked by a focus on institutional conditions as an aspect to be appropriated, manipulated, occupied and changed – not merely criticized.

An artistic practice based on positive cooperation is often associated with the relational 1990s, with its orientation towards social meals, seminars and events. It has been argued that today's artists, in contrast to the two previous generations, not only see the art institution as a problem, but also as a part of the solution. This does not mean artistic strategies involving activism no longer exist – the kind wanting to stand outside art institutional frameworks. Yet in this particular context, what needs exploring are questions about what exactly has caused these changed conditions for the exercise of a *critical practice*, and how such a practice comes to expression.

It is difficult to make one claim about Norwegian art and artists that would apply to the various generations of IC. To do so would presuppose IC has become a field about which one can lecture, with its own cannon of artworks, texts and artists. It would have narratives constituting high points, in the form of artworks, important exhibitions and key texts. These would in turn congeal into a nascent history of reception. Yet what if the field is in a constant state of flux and attempts to conceptualize it are necessarily reductive?

This was art historian Julia Bryan-Wilson's concern when she was asked to write a 'Curriculum for Institutional Critique' in 2003.[2] There is neither a consensus of opinion for evaluating IC as an artistic phenomenon, nor can it be described as a historical period or genre within art history, claims Wilson. Instead, disagreement and critique of one another's positions are what characterize this early research. This is problematic, especially if one is interested in writing a linear history of IC's origin and provenance.

Research on IC must also grapple with methodological problems: should texts about artworks be the research object, or should the art itself be the focus? This becomes important when writing about the relation between academic and artistic IC. Up until now, research has focused

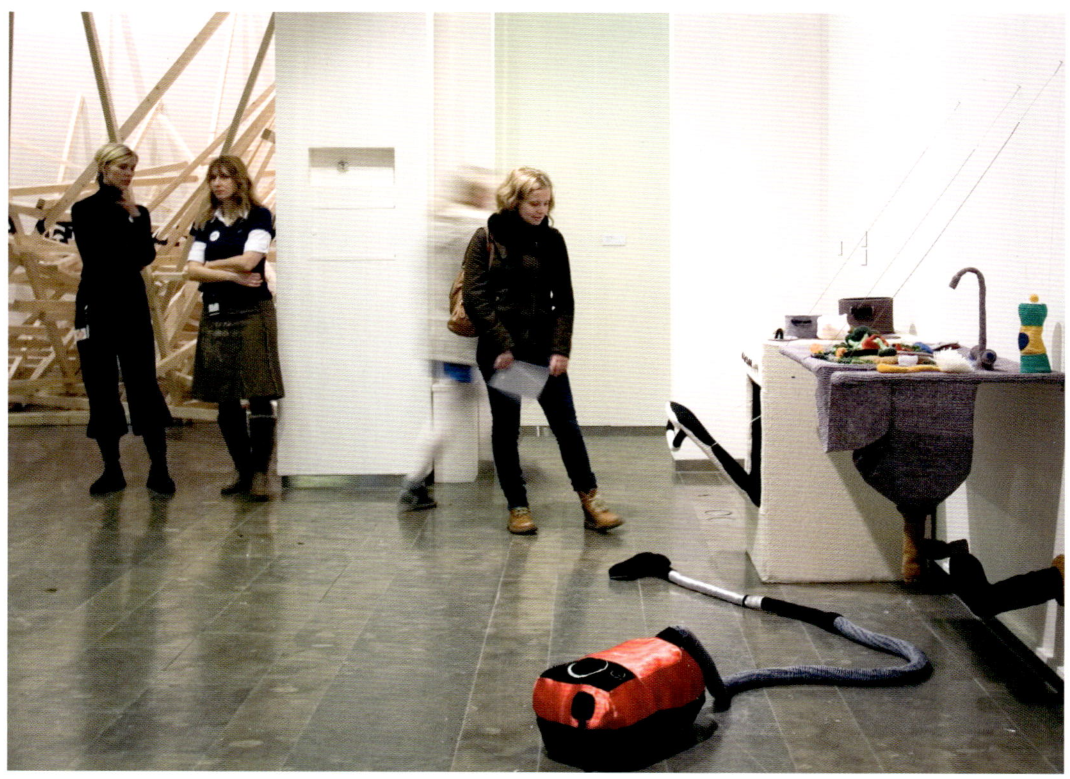

more on a history of reception (indeed, a critical one) than on the works themselves. With such an approach there is the danger of reproducing an unintentional mechanism of selection as far as which works and exhibitions should be classified under the IC concept. One also risks communicating the idea that IC is a phenomenon first materializing itself in the form of artworks, thereafter as curated exhibitions; it is thereafter addressed by critics and finally turned into an object for theoretical and academic research.

From my point of view this is not a successful method. To begin with, it presupposes a stagnated belief in a homogeneous field of art with clearly differentiated figures: the artist, the curator, the critic, the academic – and an axis from the most creative point (the artist) to the most reflective (the theorist). This assumption is now challenged by cross-over structures, e.g., when a curator is placed in the most creative position (the master-mind), or when artists derive inspiration from leading theorists. Artists also write influential theoretical works (e.g. Donald Judd, Adrian Piper), which in turn inspire other artists and theorists.

The most fruitful approach to the phenomenon seems to be to conceive of art projects, artworks, exhibitions and theoretical works as 'thinkers' of equal value, where the thinking, despite its various materializations, is not hierarchically ordered. One common criticism levelled against IC has to do with its complexity: it is an artistic practice only theoretically advanced artists, theoreticians, historians and critics can appreciate. Given its highly specialized field of knowledge, which is based on a sophisticated understanding of modern art, contemporary art and society, it is criticized for establishing a privileged discourse reserved for the enlightened few. The democratic ambitions some of these artistic practices articulate are imputed to stand in sharp contrast to their marginal catchment area. Such accusations have shadowed the art of every age, and have proven to be more or less legitimate. What is intriguing in this particular context is the extent to which the works manage to bring about interesting processes of realization and understanding, and whether they allow themselves to communicate aesthetically, above and beyond the theoretical level from which they themselves are informed.

A common conception is that to be an artist after Duchamp, one must examine the nature of art: art turns to its own origin and explores the various preconditions for its production, distribution, reception, collection and archiving. To this end, even the name 'institutional critique' is highly debatable, although some definitions are quite specific: IC is a critical artistic method for criticizing art institutions, first and foremost art museums, but also the commercial gallery system. It is customary to associate this definition, which is concrete and focused on an 'aesthetics of content', with the early phase of IC, and to names like Marcel Broodthaers, Hans Hacke, Michael Asher, Robert Smithson and Daniel Buren. IC is also often associated with artistic practices from the politically explicit 1960s, and to artists directly involved in protesting the Vietnam War.

The second IC phase is linked to artists such as Renee Green, Christian Philipp Müller, Fred Wilson and Andrea Fraser, all of whom came to prominence in the late 1980s and were active throughout the 1990s. Pierre Bourdieu's *The Field of Cultural Production* (1993) is a key text in this context, and the understanding of the art world as a 'field of struggles', in which diverse agents – artists, curators, critics, gallerists, collectors and academics – battle to control their respective interests and resources. The artwork is conceived as a manifestation 'in which all the powers of the field, and all the determinisms inherent in its structure and functioning, are concentrated'.[3]

The first and second phases are similar insofar as the art institution, with its ideologies, representatives and social practices, is the primary object for criticism. According to Robert Smithson, art institutions were seen as things to attack aesthetically, politically and theoretically. They were posed as problems (for artists).

Artistic criticism as pure negation seems less interesting today, and one can see the beginnings of an orientation away from what Foucault characterizes as a question about 'how not to be governed *at all*', to an interest in 'how not to be governed *like that*'.[4] Art theorist Simon Sheikh believes it no longer seems as interesting to straightforwardly criticize the institution – criticism has migrated inside the institution and become a part of it. As Foucault says, there is a shift from complete negation towards manoeuvring, in order to avoid a dualism between the criticism and its object. One gives up fighting windmills. This characterizes today's institutional critique and results in an affirmative and 'constructive' approach.

Contemporary artists are obviously more concerned to see art institutions not only as tools for change and betterment, but also as platforms and possible channels for distributing the critical message usually launched *at* the art institution. In addition, art production is marked by new alliances between curators, artists and institution leaders: 'In contrast, the current institutional-critical discussions seem predominantly propagated by curators and directors of the very same institutions, and they are usually opting *for* rather than against them. That is, they [the criticisms] are not an effort to oppose or even destroy the institution, but rather to modify and solidify it'.[5]

Although IC has never been the sole prerogative of artists – critical writing and theoretical/academic research are also associated with IC – we now find curators and institution leaders joining the company of artists. Key museum directors such as Jérôme Sans and Nicolas Bourriaud (Palais de Tokyo), Charles Esche (Rooseum / Van Abbemuseum) and Maria Lind (Kunstverein Munich / IASPIS), along with prominent curators such as Hans Ulrich

Obrist, Molly Nesbit, Anton Vidokle and others, now use their institutional positions in an institution-critical way. So-called 'critical institutions' have garnered respect and recognition for this orientation, but at great cost: a flagging public and reductions in private and public funding.

It is less interesting today, I argue, to see IC as a historical period, or as a genre within art history, than to conceive it as a method or analytical tool; IC can be an aesthetic articulation not only within the art world, but also vis-à-vis institutions generally – there where new control forms arise and the exercise of power takes place.

New alliances in the art system also require new analytical tools. The curator's rise to prominence has, in many instances, led to direct alliances with artists (in IC-oriented art projects). This contrasts with the first phase, in which artists worked in immediate opposition to the institution, with all its habits, ideologies and practices that were manifested through staff as well as museum directors. The exhibition *Opacity* curated by Nina Möntmann and the undersigned in 2005, examined today's new forms of collaboration and explored how critical art practices focusing on current art systems in fact (and empirically) function. Characteristically enough, the artists were not only interested in the *art*-institutional conditions. Kajsa Dahlberg's film *20 Minutes (Female Fist)* is an interview with a member of a feminist activist group who speaks about the need for 'opaque' and separate rooms in order to build an individual identity. Non-dialogue as a strategy is deemed necessary for fragile groups outside the dominant culture. Dahlberg deals with this complex of problems by leaving the lens cap on while filming the interviewee.

Danger Museum has, for several years, worked with so-called 'concept illustrations', which present imaginary situations from various art institutions (e.g. vernissages) and focuses on the particular institution's self-understanding as a purveyor of 'markers of belonging'. For its exhibition at UKS (Young Artists' Society), Danger Museum thematized the institution's new ambitions, among other ways, by installing an elegant Vico Magistretti lamp – reminiscent of industrial chic – in the gallery's reception area. The lamp blended with the thoroughly designed room. Meanwhile, for UKS's longstanding public, this 1970s designer object represented a non-professional 'make-over' of the institution. The lamp had, along with three other lamps, been a peculiar element in the gallery's old bar for several decades.

Marianne Heier's interventionist project *Crew*, from 2005, represents a slightly different approach to the 'use' mentality characterizing an affirmative institutional critique. Here the artist offered to refurbish the dilapidated lunch room used by museum hosts at the National Museum in Oslo. The prestigious architect firm Snøhetta was engaged to design the room and its furnishings, and the museum itself finally saw fit to pay for the materials. In this way, Heier's project was able to interact with, and disrupt, the low status these solidly educated museum hosts have within the museum system. Heier, who herself previously worked as a museum host, also made a video about the overly qualified personnel.

One kind of objection often recurs: institution-critical artworks are too internally directed. Increasingly voiced from within the art system itself, this sort of complaint can express both legitimate and populist attitudes. Even so, it has sharpened the focus on the extent to which criticism functions incisively, or whether it is tolerated, permitted and even sought after. This is relevant with regard to discussions about the quality of relations in relational artworks, and the quality of criticism in institution-critical artworks.

An artist donating her own significant savings to a heavily funded public institution like the National Museum, can, at first glance, seem futile. Yet the gift is incisive. The knowledge society's demand for a highly educated and qualified work force exposes its soft underbelly;

after completing one's education, there are not enough relevant positions in the cultural field. Investment in higher education does not yield expected dividends, and the fact that the National Museum knows how to take advantage of this situation is worthy of critique, and far from being an 'internal' problem.

Confirming and affirmative, or negating and radical – IC is not always *critical* in the traditional (French-theoretical) sense of the word. As artistic practice, neither is it a homogeneous description under which a 'generation' of artist names can be subsumed. The sustained interest in institutional and political conditions out of which art is created causes IC to be a recurring phenomenon. The fact that Nordic artists now articulate this interest speaks for the current relevance of examining the structural preconditions for institutional critique.

[1] Gerald Raunig and Simon Sheikh both claim that one can now see the contours of IC's third phase. They are less interested in mapping which artists are working within this phase than in recommending what such a third phase should reflect. See, for example, Gerald Raunig, 'Instituent Practices and the New Administration of Aesthetics', in Trude Iversen and Tone Hansen (eds), *The New Administration of Aesthetics* (Oslo: Torpedo Forlag 2007). Andrea Fraser also believes we have entered a third phase in IC. See *Artforum*, September 2005.

[2] 'Curriculum for Institutional Critique', in Jonas Ekeberg (ed.), *New Institutionalism* (Oslo: Office for Contemporary Art Norway, 2003).

[3] Pierre Bourdieu, *The Field of Cultural Production: Essays on Art and Literature* (New York: Columbia University Press, 1993).

[4] See Gerald Raunig, 'Fleeing the Art of Governing', in *The New Administration of Aesthetics*, in Iversen and Hansen 2007.

[5] Sheikh Simon, 'Notes on Institutional Critique', 2006, http:// transform.eipcp.net/transversal/0106/sheikh/en

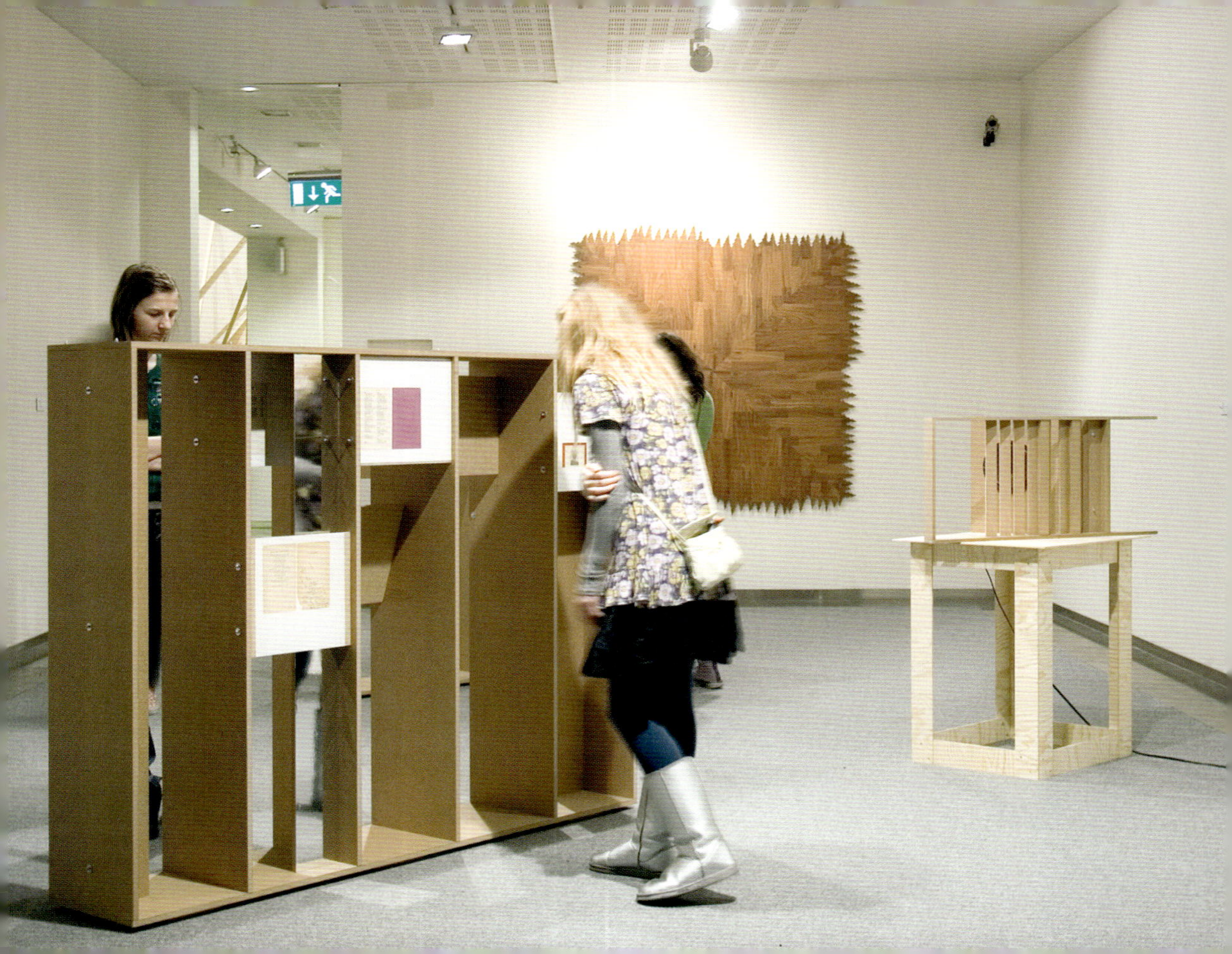

Art Criticism: A Picture

Kjetil Røed

The role of artworks is no longer to form imaginary or utopian realities,
but to actually be ways of living and models of action within the existing real
(Bourriaud 1999, 13)

The point would then be, not to find some other term to replace criticism,
while continuing the same kind of activity, but to get rid of the habit, which depends,
fundamentally, on the abstraction of response from its real situation and circumstances
(Williams 1985, 86)

1

In the film *Ein Bild* (A Picture) by Czech artist Harun Farocki, a photo shoot of a nude model (for *Playboy*) is documented with extreme richness of detail: the body is arranged repeatedly, stage scenes are built up and torn down, make-up is applied to the face and skin. Removed again, applied again. Beauty or the naked body as an object of desire is not, Farocki claims, anything immediate. Rather, it is the result of a long and laborious staging process.

What is it one actually sees? Where is the body in relation to the stage setting? The body is already seen before one sees; the arrangement is part of the gaze that is directed towards it. A common platform exists for both body and gaze and springs from certain concepts about desire and beauty. What Farocki reveals is the drama behind the natural, the directions for the *mise en scène*. Just as the woman's body is arranged and dramatized in front of the camera lens in *Ein Bild*, so also the art object is arranged and dramatized on a stage. Just as the female body is not naturally 'beautiful', neither is the art object: the object is neither 'good' nor 'bad'. The situation is rather more complex: it is a matter of a use or gaze one already finds oneself in. As viewers, we are already on stage *with* the object. We are part of the same drama: there is no outside.

What then is art criticism? What is its function in this context? These are questions one never tires of asking, at least as far as critics themselves are concerned. In the closing text of the anthology *Critical Mess*, critic Peter Plagens writes that we must simply accept that 'art as a historical phenomenon has ended: [that] the Duchamp-Beuys-Sekula revolution has succeeded and that you're now making "postart"' (Rubinstein 2006, 205). Inferring from *Ein Bild*, the 'quality' concept's loss of naturalness – its staginess – has come to define what art is. In extension of Plagens's view, criticism has, we must conclude, also become 'post-criticism'. Plagens is on to something. 'Criticism' understood as a judgement of taste, and 'professional art experience' understood as viewing an object with a measurable value, which exists within a pure aesthetic domain separated from the viewer who stands outside that domain, is on the verge of becoming (or already has become) an anachronism. The critic does not, or rather cannot, judge art in the same way as before. In the age of post-criticism, one must scrounge for new categories to describe art experience, for judging art.

More art critics exist in Norway today than ever before. There is also a tremendous interest in criticism. We see the rudiments of several distinct critic personae. First, the performative, biographically oriented critic has burgeoned, through writers such as Jon Refsdahl Moe, Tommy Olsson, Grethe Melby and others. We also find the nascent beginnings of a kind of critic who, through his or her writings, latches onto local research problems. Let us call this site-specific criticism, such as we find in Tone Hansen (who approaches Antonio Gramsci's concept of 'organic intellectual' in an interesting way. This we can discuss in another context). Thirdly, in conjunction with newspapers such as *Klassekampen* and *Morgenbladet* and websites such as kunstkritikk.no, a culture-critical, essayistic current of criticism has developed (where the undersigned finds himself). Here there are also young, promising voices such as Miriam Prestøy and Johanne Nordby Wernø. Nevertheless, the landscape is still dominated by classic taste-oriented critics who, allowing their own subject to rest in the background, are motivated by art historical methods – examples are Truls Ramberg and Arve Rød. I will not use this as an opportunity to sketch the contours of art criticism in Norway; the task would require a great deal more space. Notwithstanding, in diverging from taste-criticism, I will offer some reminders about what post-criticism can, and perhaps should, be.

One crucial element of post-criticism is how we have learned to actively use or consume the world. Consumers are increasingly admonished to design their own consumption, to produce their own taste. New media underscore the increase of interface-thinking: it is an intensification of the degree of interactivity and dialogue between object and viewer. Art migrates into an aesthetic in which the viewer's participation, in one form or another, defines the art and the judgement thereof. Parallel to this trend, we find a new softening of criticism as a profession. Journalism and Internet-based democracy, where anyone and everyone can become critics, has made its definitive entry into the public square. For this reason some believe the critic's traditional function is about to disappear. If one wants to know what others think about a specific artwork or film, there are usually a number of opinions available via Internet-culture and blogs.

For me, criticism is not a diminished form. Quite the contrary. Yet we must redefine what criticism is, we must look more closely at the critic as a figure or character, and what sort of function this character has: we must look at what the critic in fact does within participatory aesthetics and the framework of active consumption, and sketch what that role can be. We must look at which picture the critic finds himself or herself in. Here again I am thinking of Farocki.

One way of starting such a sketch is to conceive of criticism as *theatre*, an art form in which the stage-instructions point more directly to the public sphere, to reality, our lives, you and me as persons on stage. A play such as this will always be rewritten; many competing versions will exist, contemporary as well as historical, but crucial at this first stage is to learn to follow the critic's contours as a staged persona.

In today's situation criticism is open for stronger integration between a writer and his or her project; the interface between criticism and the object is already culturally determined as being defined by use. There is no longer anything external, everyone is a consumer, everyone is woven into the product or consumed commodity. On the path to post-criticism, neutrality and the judgement of taste are exchanged with theatre, drama and a fictional framework that writes narrative modules (roles) for criticism and art. These are glued in-between individual experience and abstract reflection.

This is an immanently pragmatic situation, perhaps the kind of situation John Dewey dreamt about in *Art as Experience*: criticism can become a more productive practice in which the art object is defined more precisely by being situated in a culture of use. Critic Robert Rosenblum migrates towards this position from a slightly different angle when he says, 'What you're really trying to do is to educate yourself, and educate the audience that's going to read about how you're going to educate yourself' (Barrett 1999, 8). By moving about in a field defined by a culture of use, criticism is not only opened to biographical content, but also, and perhaps more so, to an everyday realm previously excluded from art and the experience of it. Key elements here are specific practices whereby the critic finds himself or herself in a certain milieu, and uses his or her own subject actively rather than taking on the role of 'classic, distanced critic'.

I will say more about this shortly, but first, some words about tasks that perhaps are more important than anything else: to create a consciousness of *aesthetic quality* and *value* as being two distinct things, and, *summa summarum*, to convey that when it comes to art, nothing is natural, nothing can be presupposed as given.

2

We can easily imagine the field of art as *mise en scène*, staging *per se*. Initially, it was by means of a capitalistic form of production that literature and pictorial art emancipated themselves from the Church and other authorities and became products on an open mark: as such, capitalism is the foundational stage setting for modern art and modern literature. Yet it was with Marcel Duchamp, about two hundred years later, that staging became an integral part of the artwork. The readymade is a mapping of the stage setting, an indexing of the stage directions. Duchamp made us aware that nothing is *inherently* art. Or: that everything can be art. In *Kant after Duchamp*, Thierry de Duve points out that with Duchamp, evaluation of aesthetic objects changed from being judgements of taste about what is beautiful – or (we can imagine), judgements about qualities belonging to an object's essence – to stipulatory naming: 'This is art'. Art became an idea, and the material available for being named 'art' became, in principle, unlimited. This formal determination of art has its advantages, inasmuch as it reveals the scenic backdrop or preconditions for the entire aesthetic field. The conceptual turn in twentieth-century art, along with its attendant vocabulary, orients itself towards just such a technical and functional organization and reading of aesthetics.

Therefore: nothing inherently 'is' art, or 'art in itself'; there are only constructions of art in the form of works, discussions, criticism and attitudes to other constructions. One may object to this claim by countering that a lot of things 'are' art, e.g. what we find in galleries, art history, etc. Many of these material entities are repeated, over and over again. Montages of well-known materializations are the most prevalent stage productions at present. Nevertheless, the origin of art is always an action, even when it reproduces or appropriates well-known themes from earlier productions.

One of the key figures in the drama called 'art' is the critic. Each and every criticism (reading) is a performance of the art – directly or indirectly, in one form or another. I long for a greater degree of performativity in criticism: actors who criticize, and in so doing, manifest their scenographic rootedness, stage themselves as scenic personae in the drama in which they act. At this juncture the discussion about 'quality' is interesting: to speak of an artwork as undoubtedly good, to mention this as an essential characteristic of an object, can be compared with reintroducing illusion into the art drama. In talking about literature or artworks as 'good' or 'bad' we discuss qualities about the art we rub shoulders with; we forget the scenographics from which the artwork arises, the drama it plays a role in. Here Marx's concept of the evolution of labour can also be instructive. When commerce received its now so dominant capitalistic form in the mid-eighteenth century, the commodity or product, as a reflection of this new form of commerce, became an abstract entity whose worth was determined according to its trading value rather than its use value.[1] The production of goods, the labour itself, also became abstracted as a value, in line with the transformation of the commodity form. Labour became something to buy and sell, independent of its specific character. Art criticism as labour can be seen as a comparable process of abstraction; it becomes a generalizeable ability or capacity, and the concrete reading situation becomes written over by formally oriented modes.[2] The actual effort of art criticism is concrete labour, and its results will be related to the situation in which it takes place, the material's re-forming through the laborious process. Seen from this angle, criticism's work is a reading in which the artwork *as drama* is involved in the action: the coordinates for the labour are stage directions. Abstract labour is, however, a product and sign for the organization of the social space where the concrete task takes place. The abstract reading is criticism that treats *quality* as a natural characteristic of the object and deals with it accordingly. In other words: abstract criticism leads to a model of reading in which certain characters and sequences of action in the drama are identified *with* the object.

In keeping with the commodity form's abstraction, the product also becomes a fetish. With Marx, we could say that the critic's abstracting jargon carries an implicit claim about the artwork's value being part of its fetish character. That artworks appear 'to be independent beings that stand in relation to one another and to people' (Marx 2006, 87) has its roots in different types of labour – the author's, the editor's and the advertiser's. These figures are all dramatic personae. The art object understood as a carrier of inherent value is – if we continue to read with Marx – a legitimization of just such a context; it is a manifestation of a network of relations *around* the artwork.

Roland Barthes describes this claimed identity between value judgements and the object as *naturalization*. The naturalized version of, in Barthes' context, 'the work', transforms art into myth: 'the very principle of myth: it transforms history into nature' (Barthes 1972, 129). In our context we could say that the naturalization of aesthetic quality *de-theatricalizes* the drama of criticism and art.

Let us now return to this essay's beginning theme: participation. Here we find a model for reading and criticism that expands a theatrical concept of art.

3

If we shadows have offended
Think but this, and all is mended,
That you have but slumber'd here,
While these visions did appear
(Puck, from the close of *A Midsummer Night's Dream*)

The French multi-theoretician Michel de Certeau, in *The Practice of Everyday Life*, compares reading with being in a borrowed room, or sneaking inside another person's property. As literature's 'renter', one would redefine the borrowed room according to one's own preferences: e.g., one reads one's own childhood through the evening news broadcast (Certeau 1984, XXI), or one's marital break-up through the relationship between Tristan and Isolde. The same could apply for the art object: it establishes a fictive area we can live in or rent for a short period. The point here is not the work's 'actual meaning', nor whether it is 'good or bad' art. The matter is rather that users make their own montage of the 'borrowed room' through their own associations and needs.

This is a banal point; it should go without saying. The consequences of just such a everyday use of art seldom lead to any consequences. Yet if we read further into the outer-lying circle of such use, the montage artwork can be seen as a synthetic practice, a cross between divergent conceptual fields, e.g. 'artist', 'work' and 'reader', or between institutional fields, e.g. 'art' and 'literature'. This, again, leads us back to the staged scene.

In participation-aesthetics the world (or social relations) does not become the artwork – instead the artwork becomes a part of the world. Said differently: the sensibility that is effective when one interacts with artworks is expanded to include the world at large as well as our private lives – and conversely, the social everyday life bleeds into the space of art. Nicolas Bourriaud defines relational aesthetics as 'a set of artistic practices which take as their theoretical and practical point of departure the whole of human relations and their social context, rather than an independent and private space'. When the work is opened to the surrounding social relations, the work itself and the reading merge with the social room, which usually is conceived as external to the object. Using Bourriaud to extrapolate further, we can say that the relational aesthetics also establishes a scene sharing affinities with Marx's commodity concept: Rirkrit Tirvanija's work can readily be seen as a staging of the production-relations surrounding the artwork, but the problem arises when the relations gain the same status as the artwork. The participants in Tirvanija's works are more like a blueprint of a social layer of artists, critics and curators, rather than people who act out art as theatre, or as art's relations of production. In this sense, Bourriaud illustrates a point rather than realizing its potential. Nevertheless, there is a direction in the 'commodity' concept that points towards a staging of what Marx calls the 'magical' qualities of the artwork. That said, it is important to underscore that of course, one will never be able to trace the object back through all its stages of production and give an exhaustive picture of its social origin. Yet when the relations surrounding the object are integrated into its use, a scene is staged in which this aspect of the artwork can in fact have free rein.

Matias Faldbakken's practice is interesting in this respect. His books refer to the field of art and his art refers to the field of literature; through this interplay he illuminates characteristics of both. He alludes to a common scenic platform for both literature and art in the interaction between the fields. In this sense he also invites the reader to participate in 'the works': they cut across pre-defined conceptions about what literature is and what art is. We can of course ignore the scenic or staged bias in his projects, 'that we have but slumber'd here, while these visions did appear', to quote Shakespeare, but in so doing, we loose sight of the project's own momentum. Literature's 'external side' applies pressure and external factors can compel us to do a re-reading. Inter-institutional beings are conceptual personae. They are fictionalized, staged persons who disrupt our concepts about boundaries between genres, but who also invite us to actively participate and re-think the categories 'work', 'author', 'reader' and 'viewer'.

The point here is that each and every use establishes a role in the artwork or literature's staging.

4

Even the history is completely without interest if it does not undertake to awaken a dormant concept and to play it again on a new stage, even if this comes at the price of turning it against itself (Gilles Deleuze and Félix Guattari, *What is Philosophy?*)

With regard to the manifold variety of stagings of literature and artworks, I tend to side with Ernesto Laclau and Chantal Mouffe,[3] who claim that a political model – which follows a rational consensus and holds the goal to be conflict-free agreement – misunderstands what democracy actually entails. If we read literature or criticize art through their concept of democracy, it becomes clear that 'art' is formed through social collaboration: it is the disagreement that is articulated and comprises the liminal threshold in the battle over what art is. Through the recognition that art, at its core, is an object for battle, and that one never will come to clarity about what exactly exists outside the perimeters of this battle or strife, two radically different positions join together into one common concern. This concern is perhaps the most basic interaction with art that we have: a kind of meta-relational literary concept. From this perspective, 'art' as such is not satisfactorily stage-directed through *some* (or one) stage production, but through *all* its stage-productions. The social relations constituting the institution of art, which establish a stage setting for it and battle over who will be allowed to define it, are just as finite in relation to their object as literary quality is in relation to the book. It is this lack of identity that nurtures criticism, energizes it and sets it in motion. The diverse stage productions are 'sparring partners' who, rather than viewing each other as enemies, should see each other as opponents who rightfully belong in the same symbolic arena. The *sensus communis*, which should develop in relation to the art object, is therefore a culture of use in which the art object becomes a tool and a building block in the most important narrative: its own life. In this way, this essay preaches a form of utopianism, yet not one rooted in a pre-determined method or a universally valid or conflict-free condition. Instead it is micro-utopianism, here and now, one envisioning the art object's enchantment breaking and the work being installed in its own life-story. In this way, perhaps criticism can return to its source: us.

Literature
Terry Barrett, *Criticizing Art: Understanding the Contemporary* (McGraw-Hill Humanities, second edition, 2000).
Roland Barthes, *Mythologies* (New York: Hill and Wang, 1972).
Nicolas Bourriaud, *Relational Aesthetics* (Paris: Les Presse Du Reel, 1999).
Michel de Certeau, *The Practice of Everyday Life* (Berkeley and Los Angeles: University of California Press, 1984).
Thierry de Duve, *Kant after Duchamp* (Cambridge MA: MIT Press, 1998).
Ernesto Laclau and Chantal Mouffe, *Hegemony and Socialist Strategy: Towards a Radical Democratic Politics* (London: Verso, 2001).
Georg Lukács, *History and Class Consciousness* (Cambridge MA: MIT Press, 1972).
Karl Marx, *Kapitalen* (Oslo: Oktober, 2006).
Peter Plagens, 'At the crossroads', in Raphael Rubinstein (ed.), *Critical Mess* (Lenox MA: Hard Press Editions, 2006).
Raymond Williams, *Keywords* (Oxford: Oxford University Press, 1985).

[1] 'So that [...] the commodity form [shall] come to be [a culturally constitutive form], it must [...] permeate expressions in all layers of societal life, forming them in its own image. It [the commodity form] must not only be connected to an external form with processes that are directed towards producing use value, and which are independent of the commodity form' (Lukács 1972, 83).

[2] To clarify: I do not mean that reading or art criticism have never been concrete in the sense I am going to describe here. This practice has never had a 'golden age' or a history of 'rise and fall'. Relational critique is conditioned upon a capitalistic form of production.

[3] See Laclau and Mouffe 2001.

Untitled (Rendering Things from Memory due to a Lack of Facts and Other Sources)

Leif Magne Tangen

Part One: Background

Writing is a way of finding out what you think
(Jerry Saltz)

I come from a long line of farmers and fishermen; on my father's side, the farmers of the deep forests of Trysil, north-east of Oslo; on my mother's side, the fish-farmers of the northern coast of Norway. I grew up on the same island as my mother and her father, namely Moskenes in Lofoten, off the coast of mainland Norway. For the avid readers amongst us, Moskenes would be known through Edgar Allan Poe's dramatic short story *A Descent Into The Maelström*.[1]

This is a remote part of the European world, a place where the local boys traditionally walked in their fathers' paths. That was the way it had been for centuries. But then Norway struck oil. We started to earn money.[2] What will happen when the oil runs out, no-one knows, but as a British art dealer once said to me, by that time Norway would be so 'stinking rich' that it would not matter anyway. Maybe he was right. At any rate, the result of all this was that I could choose to get an education without having to worry about my parents being able to afford it.[3]

Part Two: The Beginning

In the midst of everything, in the centre of nothing
(Hans Ulrich Obrist)

When I came to Oslo to study in 1999, the 1990s were over.

Most of those famous and infamous artist-run spaces were closed down or were well on their way. Some of the places I remember which retained an aura of the decade past were Anders Eiebakke's[4] Samtidskunstforum,[5] which had solo as well as group exhibitions with his friends, demonstrating a penchant for social-political tendencies. The legendary Zoolounge (a bar which had exhibitions as well as a video archive, an incredible source to learn from) was still going strong. But not for long: the air was somehow not as radiant as it had seemed to be in articles, stories and catalogue essays I had read.[6]

During the time I was there, the experimentally-inclined commercial gallery c/o Atle

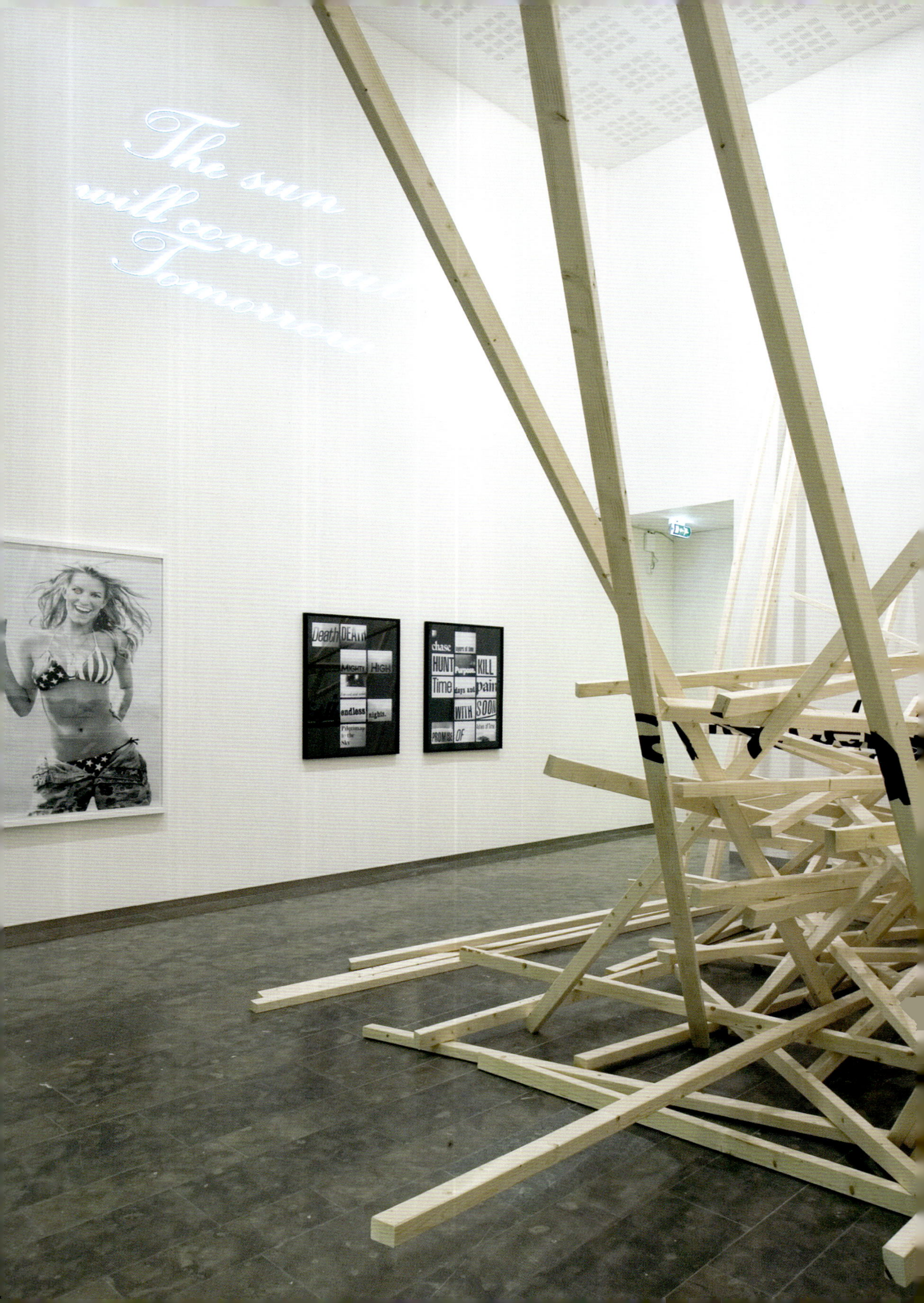

The sun
will come out
Tomorrow

Gerhardsen moved to Berlin. The gallery appeared to have been accepted into the international scene, but still retained its playful attitude, offering its space to younger artists. Kalle Runeson's solo exhibition in the summer of 1999 and Aphex Twin's show the following year are two good examples of this.[7]

Photographer/artist/curator/critic/editor[8] Jonas Ekeberg[9] opened the Oslo Kunsthall[10] in the fall of 2000. It seemed like a major breakthrough for the scene: Ekeberg opening Oslo Kunsthall, Bo Krister Wallström starting his tenure at Bergen Kunsthall, and Per Gunnar Tverbakk starting to work for Kunstnernes Hus in Oslo. Ekeberg quit his job in 2001 and so did Tverbakk. So the big structural and programming changes at the Oslo institutions never really happened. Oslo Kunsthall, however, went on for a few more years with many good shows, before losing its space and finally closing down in 2004.

It felt like an interim period indeed. These, and other driving forces of the 1990s – artists and curators-to-be – had completed their education as well as the above-mentioned projects. However, they had yet to attain more prominent roles in the hierarchies of the Oslo scene.

Part Three: Remembering

In September 1978, the New York-based artist
XXXX accepted an invitation to take part in a group
exhibition at Artists Space.
His contribution consisted in rigorously deleting
all references to his person. This removal of his name
left gaps on invitation cards and in catalogues.
Since then his trace has been lost
(Famed, Untitled, 2007)

I have the distinct feeling that the younger art crowd and workers in Oslo (myself included) were sitting on the fence, waiting for… what. Maybe there is always a need for a gap between movements.

The first manifestation of what I would call the '2000 generation' (what do you call a gap between two generations?) was Elna Hagemann and Martin Skauen's brilliant space, Subcomandante.[11] Inspired by the artist-run spaces from the generation before them, and, in my opinion, particularly by the way Bjarne Melgaard[12] and Ole Jørgen Ness ran their gallery. Subcomandante had a mix of local and international artists. I remember well Brian DeGraw's exhibition.[13] A video of a burning house (a church?) was projected on a wall, partly covered by torn out book pages. This very… *raw* way of displaying art was different from that of the Oslo scene as I knew it. Quite the opposite was Børre Sæthre's show at the Astrup Fearnley Museet for Moderne Kunst around the same time: an almost perfectly built architectonic installation that stretched over several rooms and depicted another world. DeGraw was said to have attended the opening, and wryly comment: 'We went to this furniture exhibit around the corner'.

But if Sæthre's *My Private Sky* did not impress a Connecticut-born, it certainly did impress one born in Lofoten. Another exhibition that had a major impact on me was Anders Smebye's first solo exhibition in Oslo at the Galleri 21:24 in 2001. The small L-shaped gallery space, owned by the Academy, was filled almost floor to ceiling by a large crate. One could barely squeeze around it. The crate was covered with stamps declaring it to contain art, arrows indicating 'up' and other markings that belong on a crate. It depicted, as the title of the show – *Transporter* – indicated, a transport crate. Only two things gave the crate away as an installation: the autobiographical reference through a deep bass sound emanating from the box, and the black and yellow striped corners. This is something usually found on one, maybe two corners, showing how to put the crate together. Smebye painted all four top corners, transforming the utilitarian markings into formalistic design.[14]

These shows, together with the screening of Matthew Barney's films *Cremaster 4* and *Cremaster 5* in Oslo[15] a year and a half earlier, marked the change in my perception of art. Those experiences impacted me at different levels, but what they all shared was the use of mythology, dreams and the artist's body as an explicit starting point for their production. Basically, they made it clear that anything was possible.

Part Four: The End

I don't like Helvetica. It stands for a kind of modernism that I don't believe in. It stands for an optimism that led us to World War II. The Museum of Modern Art uses Helvetica
(Lawrence Weiner in an interview with Jonas Ekeberg)

A number of exhibitions impressed me during this time in Oslo, both on a gallery as well as on an institutional level.[16] As stated, however, there were not that many artist-run initiatives around anymore. Maybe my generation was not interested in building our own playgrounds. It seemed like the *esprit du temps* was more about being accepted into the more established parts of the art scene, to be allowed into the various galleries and institutions – something the 1990s scene would have regarded as outrageous.[17]

A clear indication of this was given in January 2002. Rirkrit Tiravanija was invited to take part in the show *Passenger – The Viewer as Participant*.[18] His contribution was the extension of his exhibition at Oslo Kunsthall six months earlier,[19] a show that gave many of us a crash course in 'relational aesthetics' with a dash of 'institutional critique'. Tiravanija was not the only one to hang out with the younger artists. Liam Gillick, Jason Rhoades, Patrick Bateman and Jane & Louise Wilson, to name a few, also visited or worked in Oslo around this time, and thus had an impact on 'us'.

And this is the core of what I came to realize in my time in Oslo. I think my generation, which was still studying in 2000, was not as interested in building up a local art scene. 'We' were not as interested in Oslo's social infrastructures and political struggles as the 1990s art scene had been.

It is clear that the world has changed in many ways in the last decade or so. There are no clean breaks, no revolution at the gates, just slow and illuminating changes. The world has become more globalized – a clear indication of which is the fact there are more Norwegian artists living abroad today than ever before. Some of them have far less contact with the Norwegian art scene than with the local art scene where they live: Gardar Eide Einarsson and Øystein Aasan are two good examples, Jan Christensen and curator Hanne Mugaas are two more.[20]

That being said, it is a fact that some Norwegian artists of the 1990s had the same experience and approach. Two prime examples are Knut Åsdam and Ingar Dragset (of Elmgreen & Dragset). Elmgreen & Dragset were an insider's tip for a number of years, unknown to the general art public in Norway whilst doing both gallery and institutional solo shows in the rest of the world.[21] Dragset was never a part of the Norwegian art scene and lived in Copenhagen and Berlin. Åsdam only had a solo exhibition at Galleri Riis in 1994 before his big show at Museet for samtidskunst in 2001.[22] Åsdam also has an all-international education[23] and lived abroad.

I cannot claim to be intimately familiar with the current Oslo art scene, but once more it seems to be driven by the initiatives of young artists. TAFKAG, Bastard, Rekord, The G.U.N. Ladies, No. 9 and Barbara Hansen[24] are all artist-run spaces. What they have in common with the previous generation is that most of them graduated from the National Academy of the Arts in Oslo and that this institution – as in the mid-1990s – is trying to force a new structure over the heads of its students. Then as now, the students are fighting back.[25] Another equally significant factor is the establishment of a new major art institution. The National Museum of Art, Architecture and Design was created in 2003 by merging four large museums into one mega-institution. It seems to be struggling to find its place within the Norwegian art scene, and how much contact it should and could have with the grassroots movements in Norway. This is reminiscent of the late 1980s, when Museet for samtidskunst was established and was not able to give enough support to the local art scene.[26]

The difference between then and now lies mainly in how the art scene has become more pluralistic and compartmentalized. We have, for instance, more and more so-called independent curators, working and studying both in Norway and abroad. Thanks to the online magazine kunstkritikk.no we now have a fleet of young art critics. Furthermore, the commercial scene is stronger today than ever before.[27] And I have not even started with the Office for Contemporary Art Norway (OCA), the main sponsor of all Norwegian activities abroad as well as THE catalyst for international art workers' presence in Norway (by bringing them there).

[1] The maelström of the island of Moskenes has been written about for the past two millennia, but Poe is the first modern fiction-writer to have dealt with it. Anyone with even a vague knowledge of the geography of the islands and their tidal flow knows Poe never visited them and only used the legend of the maelström as a backdrop for an action-driven story about stoic fishermen.

[2] Finding oil combined with the social democratic welfare and the Norwegian tradition of travelling around the world stirred some things up – from then on, most people had a chance to choose for themselves what to do, where to be and how to do this.

[3] My mother never got an education as her family couldn't afford it, and neither did my father.

[4] Eiebakke seemed like a pivotal figure in Oslo around that time. Although he had given up his fanzine magazine *Kunstinnsikt* (1996–98) he

was still running Samtidskunstforum, was the chairman of Unge Kunstneres Samfund (UKS) (The Young Artists Society) where he curated a number of exhibitions, and for a short while in 2000 had a bar named Ingenmannsland – No Man's Land.

[5] Eiebakke's partner at the gallery was Jan Egil Nordvik.

[6] Galleri G.U.N. was also still around, although I cannot remember any of the shows they put up around that time.

[7] Both shows were curated by c/o assistant Jan Christensen. He asked Aphex Twin if he could use his video, photo and music material to make a solo show. This was the first time I saw a curator using his own personal visual aesthetic, mixed with that of the artist, to make an exhibition.

[8] Ekeberg was once accused of having too many nominal roles in the Norwegian art scene, something he had in common with Anders Eiebakke.

[9] He was in the first class to ever study photography as fine art in Norway (1990–93). After that he founded and edited the magazine *Hyperfoto* (1994–97). Later he re-formed *Billedkunst* magazine. He also co-curated the Momentum Park Biennial in 2000. Throughout this time Ekeberg was also an active art critic.

[10] The Kunsthall opened with a bang. *Pumper kunst til folket*, as one newspaper article claimed. An ad in an international magazine stated 'Yes, we're open' – but as critic Lotte Sandberg noted in the *Aftenposten* paper, the 'fresh' art they brought for the opening was a five-year-old piece by Monica Bonvicini.

[11] First named Subcomandante Marcos, it was shortened to Subcomandante after a while.

[12] For a short time Melgaard ran, together with Frode Saugestad, Norsk Anarkistisk Fraksjon (NAF for short), the gallery which gave the Oslo art scene a few lessons about painting,

photography and installation. After a while NAF closed down only to re-open under the name Institutt for Sivil Ulydighet. I remember best Terry Richardson's photographs of Batman and Robin giving each other blow jobs. Other exhibitions included Fabrice Hybert and a show curated by Bart de Baere, to mention a few. Unfortunately the gallery closed for good after a terrible fire burned down the whole building, full of artists' studios on New Year's Eve of 2001. No one was injured, but many artists lost both their studio space and, in some cases, whole life-spans of art production.

[13] Invited by Bjarne Melgaard to do a solo show at UKS, Subcomandante invited him to do a show at their space as well.

[14] Dealing with art-handling myself at the time, my initial reaction was shock: HOW DID HE GET THE CRATE THROUGH THE DOOR? See a review of the show at: http://www.barokkminimalist.com/aarg1/nr1/BM01.pdf – something called *Barokkminimalist*, that, together with *ArtAround*, must be seen as the forerunners for www.kunstkritikk.no. Both magazines are now defunct.

[15] Also by Astrup Fearnley Museet for Moderne Kunst, in the Art-House cinema Cinemateket, next door to the museum.

[16] A small and incomplete list of important exhibitions: Momentum Park; *Illumination* at Museet for samtidskunst; *Museum* at Astrup Fearnley Museet; Tom Sandberg at Astrup Fearnley Museet; *Sincerely Yours* at Astrup Fearnley Museet; *Composite* at Museet for samtidskunst; *Eksenter*, Lofoten Art Festival; Bjarne Melgaard at Museet for samtidskunst and Galleri Riis; Hamish Fulton at Galleri Riis; Børre Sæthre at Galleri Wang; Erikka Fyrand at Galleri 21:25; Louisa Lambri at Fotogalleriet; all the shows at Subcomandante; Thomas Struth at Galleri K; Talleiv Taro Manum at Fotogalleriet; Barbara Wien Gallery and Bookshop at Oslo Kunsthall; Heli Rekula at Fotogalleriet; Rirkrit Tiravanija at Oslo Kunsthall; Tom Sandberg at Galleri Riis; Steinar Jakobsen at Galleri K; *Schpaa: du har ikke en sjans! – Ta'n!* at UKS; *Pave the earth* at Museet for samtidskunst; *Modellmakerne* at Kunstnernes Hus; *Body Matters* at Museet for samtidskunst; Ingrid Book and Carina Hedén at Fotogalleriet; Per Christian Brown at Galleri MGM; Eline Mugaas at Galleri Riis; Victor Lind at Samtidskunstforum; Victor Lind's video projection onto the façade of the Building of Fremskrittspartiet; Terje Nicolaisen at Tegnerforbundet; Knut Åsdam at Museet for samtidskunst; Oslo Open, 2000; *Samfunnsengasjement, Politikk og Hverdag 1970/90* at Museet for samtidskunst; *Forbundet Frie Fotografers (FFF) 25 års jubileum* at Fotogalleriet, Astrup Fearnley Museet, RAM and other places; *Just what is it that makes the internet so different, so appealing* at Galleri F15 (an online project); Mikkel McAlinden at Galleri K; Fotogalleriet's *25 års jubileum* at Fotogalleriet.

[17] Or, as a young Norwegian artist declared in a lecture he gave, 'I will not waste my time running an "off" space [...] instead of making shows for galleries and institutions.'

[18] The exhibition was at the Astrup Fearnley Museet, curated by Øystein Ustvedt. It was by far the most important show in Oslo that year.

[19] The logo was made by Lars Morell, the wall painting by Jan Christensen and the carpet chosen by Josefine Lyche and Hjørdis Kurås. Øystein Aasan designed the bar, and the lamps were made by Jorge Pardo. There were numerous activities happening in the space; it was used as a kindergarten, Fia is Famous held a spiritual workshop, an artist group named OK Tokyo had a presentation and street poets used the space to recite poems, to mention only some of the going-ons at this exhibition. Documentation of the project is to be found on artist Aksel Høgenhaug's home page http://ah.vitakuben.org/oVERstation/index.html

[20] Christensen's first institutional solo show was in Switzerland, not Norway. He lives in Berlin; Einarsson recently had a solo show that gained attention at TEAM Gallery in New York, where he lives. Hanne Mugaas is curating shows for Art in General and MoMA. She got her MA in curatorial practice in London. She lives in New York; Øystein Aasan, who resides in Berlin, had never been shown in Norway before he was invited by Henry M. Hughes to be a part of the show *BoundLess* at Stenersenmuseet in Oslo in 2005. As for myself, my first experiences in both writing (for magazines, for institutions) and curating were abroad. The reason was very simple: more interest was shown in my writing and my alleged curatorial skills outside Norway. Why this is so, is as diffuse as it is clear: I have been living in Leipzig for the greater part of this decade, and although I was well in touch with – especially – the Oslo art scene, the people I met and talked to were more often Germans, Americans or from other countries than Norway. It was never an intentional, meditated tactic of mine: it just happened that way.

[21] It should be mentioned that Elmgreen & Dragset took part in a few projects in Oslo in the 1990s; most notably their solo show *To Ken Ishii...* at Galleri Struts in 1997 and their bar turned inside out at Momentum Pakkhus the following year. After that, no manifestation of the artists was to be seen for half a dozen years in Norway.

[22] But Åsdam was in close dialogue with the Oslo art scene through the magazine *UKS Forum* and he participated in two of the most influential self-initiated projects in the 1990s, DIXI, and Prosjekt i Gamlebyen (PiG) as well as the first UKS Biennial in 1996 – and the first Momentum Biennial in 1998.

[23] London's Goldsmiths College, Maastricht's Jan van Eyck Akademie and finally, New York's Independent Study Program at the Whitney Museum.

[24] The Artspace Formerly Known As Galuzin, started under the name Gallery Galuzin by Kristian Skylstad and Ivan Galuzin, renowned for their

day-long parties and bad-boy attitude. Bastard started in the studios of Marius Engh and Anders Smebye, and is now run on half-year intervals with Smebye on his own, helped it seems by freelance curator Marianne Zamecznik. Rekord is run by the three young artists Ingvild Langgård, Eirin Støen and Thora Dolven Balke. It feels less of a temporary artist-run space and more like a small institution. The White Tube, also called The G.U.N. Ladies, is a reincarnation of G.U.N., the longest running space from the 1990s. The ladies are Sabina Jacobsson, Mariken Kramer, Madeleine Park, Hanne Rangul and Camilla Øyhus. They are, for the time being, using a poster display at the Tøyen metro station to do shows. No. 9 in Exile (it is said that they were thrown out of their permanent space after an opening that lasted several days) is run by Vilde von Krogh. Hjørdis Kurås opened her Gallery Barbara Hansen with a Tommy Olsson retrospective video show in 2005.

[25] The difference is that while in the mid-1990s the students were fighting over internal changes at the academy, there is now a reform changing the whole structure of art studies in Oslo, effectively cancelling out the concept of "the Academy". It is now the "MFA program within the dance/music/craft/design/whatever Academy".

[26] Arkitekturmuseet, Kunstindustrimuseet, Museet for samtidskunst, Nasjonalgalleriet and Riksutstillinger became Nasjonalmuseet for kunst, arkitektur og design.

[27] Although they showed the pivotal piece *Opus Osiris* by Ole Jørgen Ness in 1994, they failed to recognize its importance and did not buy it until 2006.

[28] The last three years we have seen the birth of Galleri Erik Steen, owned by former co-owner and director of Galleri Wang, who went bankrupt in 2005. Although he brought some of his artists with him to his new gallery, there are a number of very young artists that have been given shows. Also, GAD seems to show exclusively younger artists, and STANDARD (OSLO) has taught us a lesson in how to become part of the international art circuit in record-breaking time. And this year we have seen the birth of Lautom Contemporary, which also set a very ambitious agenda regarding programming at a commercial art gallery. And these are just the newcomers. The oldest Oslo galleries Galleri Riis and Galleri K also make an impact both at home and abroad.

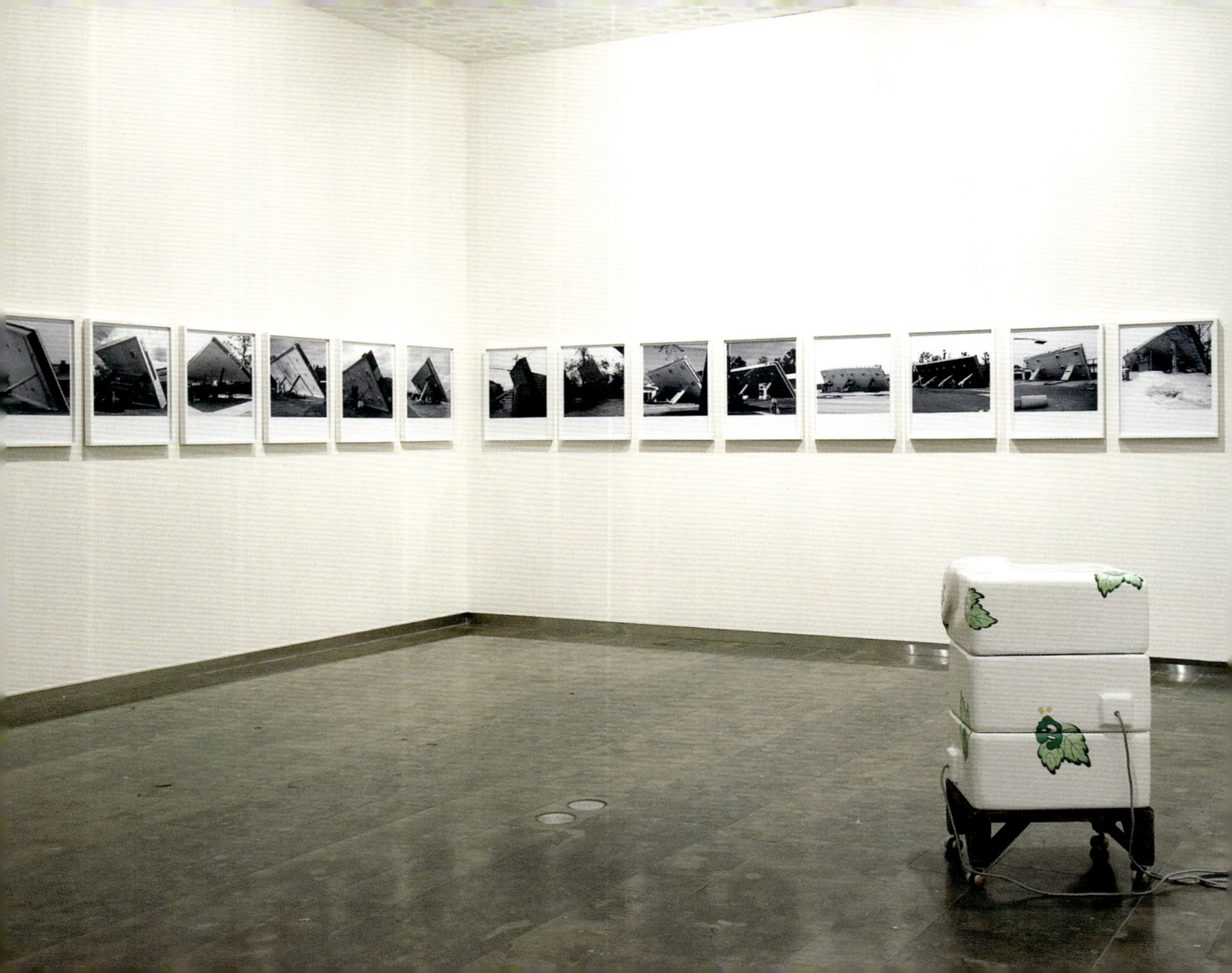

The Spirit that Returns

Line Ulekleiv

Metaphysical ambitions in culture have begun surfacing, also amongst young Norwegian artists. In recent years a burgeoning attraction to irrational phenomena has been noticeable, and certain parts of the art scene are showing conspicuous interest in spirituality and metaphysics, often dystopically shaded. This is also reflected in commercial culture. Such an approach to art stands in stark contrast to the focus on everyday and real-life experiences, which has been a longstanding art world activity, in the form of documental and socially involving strategies. In these new practices, institution-critical and theoretical approaches fall in the shadow of more subjective, escapist visions and personal and cultural mythologies. In many respects, mysticism as a cultural element represents the antithesis to a modern Western consciousness oriented towards palpability, capital gains and concrete utilitarian values. Perhaps this new metaphysics is akin to Surrealism's excesses and exploration of the unconscious, paired with a romantic sincerity that incorporates the possibility of magic and paranormal experience in a forcefully turbulent world.

The exhibition as a spiritual arena

The tendency we draw attention to here does not necessarily establish a comprehensive vision or any inner connection between apparently related phenomena. Rather, it appears as an autonomous characteristic of an art scene marked by complex interests. A number of international exhibitions seen in the last four to five years have just as fully reflected a mystical aspect. Spiritual and mystical themes can be traced in certain artworks from *documenta 12*, e.g. works reflecting romantic codes. Nevertheless, it was the staging of the works that most expressed the tendency. Mountings were in opposition to the 'white cube', emotional and narratively intoned, with an atmospheric use of dark colours, light and shadow. There had clearly been a more naked technological character to *documenta 11*. The use of symbols in viewing art is another recurring motif in several recent curations. When Douglas Gordon put together the exhibition *The Vanity of Allegory* at the Deutsche Guggenheim Berlin, in the summer of 2005, he used *vanitas* motifs as portals into an allegorical and artist-mythologizing thinking. Here the mirror, the symbol and the Baroque pictorial world grasped hold of a series of newer artworks and imbued them with dense meaning.

A number of exhibitions in recent years have explored the theme more directly, not least *Spiritus*, produced by Swedish Riksutställningar, in collaboration with Magasin 3 in

Stockholm, and later shown at Bomuldsfabriken Kunsthall in Arendal, Southern Norway, in the summer of 2003. This exhibition focused on states of consciousness, ecstatic states, parallel worlds and rituals. In works by Doug Aitken, Carsten Höller, Ann Veronica Janssens and others, these marginalized experiences were explored both tactilely and mentally, in modes ranging from meditative to aggressive. The exhibition also included a collection of early twentieth-century photographs showing spiritist séances with attendant ectoplasm, a materialized substance emanating, for the most part, from female mediums in contact with a spirit world. This linkage between contemporary art and an early manipulative use of photography was interesting and inspired when seen against the more general backdrop of art's ability to transcend the everyday – it becomes an alternative space in which art can act.

A telepathic turn?
Lars Bang Larsen has pointed out how what he calls 'occult art' has changed character since manipulation of photographs and paintings was used to present the spirit world:

> *Many contemporary artists are turning to the unseen to evoke a sense of historical space. […] Its new forms renegotiate the visible world through what is felt and intuited, rather than through what is seen and interpreted, and even if their position on the veracity of paranormal phenomena is often elusive, most contemporary artists are not ironic or nostalgic in their use of the occult in art; rather, they see it as a means by which to opt for new ways to communicate and make things happen. […] Through the occult, it seems that art can take a position at the fringes of society, and yet at the same time communicate broadly in ways that go beyond the scope of artistic codes.*[1]

What triggers this special attraction for artists today? Is it rooted in a widespread dismal view of contemporary life? A reluctance and resignation in relation to one's own era and its pressing challenges can surely be part of the answer, yet perhaps one could just as easily localize a need for creating individual shadowy 'pockets' torn from a logical timeline. By producing genuine references to Baroque *vanitas* art or Victorian spiritist mania, an open and utopian course is established, which is non-committal as regards strict cause-and-effect relations. It can seem rather escapist.

Although the growing interest in esoterics, magic and the occult can no longer be shrugged off as obscure underground phenomena, they are nevertheless barely discussed or theorized. The lack may perhaps lie in the matter's inherent nature: 'We have heard of "the linguistic turn" and even of "the social turn", but which theorist would announce a "telepathic turn" in contemporary art?'[2] The allergic reaction to veiled spirituality sits in many a professional's backbone, not without reason. The English art theorist Marina Warner is however an exception; for several decades she has studied mystical frameworks such as cults, fairytales and metamorphoses, insofar as they come to expression in various kinds of artistic production. In *The Reenchantment of Art* (1991), Suzi Gablik calls for a return of spirit and soul in art, which she claims is in a sorrowful state after Modernism's so-called cold, autonomous formalism and post-modern deconstructivism. Gablik sees the solution as being in art's possibility to express a life-giving principle, and its taking recourse in rituals in order to find a way back to a mystical sphere presently lost to view, as a consequence of empiricism, materialism, rationalism and science – all of which are Enlightenment values and intellectual baggage.

In trying to establish a possible perspective on the new and darker art discussed here, it is difficult to avoid obliquely glancing at the politicized art scene and relational aesthetics, whose defining text has been Nicolas Bourriaud's *Esthétique relationelle* from 1998, for it has exercised influence on an entire generation of artists:

> *The possibility of a relational art (an art that takes as its theoretical horizon*
> *the sphere of human interactions and its social context, rather than the assertion*
> *of an autonomous and private symbolic space) is testimony to the radical upheaval*
> *in aesthetic, cultural and political objectives brought about by modern art.*[3]

Subjective vision and a more reserved activity therefore stand in strong contrast to the relational art discourse. Art as a form of engaged activism and a carrier of democratic ideals has perhaps promised more than it manages to deliver. The theorist Stephen Wright claims that simultaneously as art's factual influence in public affairs steadily wanes and its actual social role is undermined, the art world continues to make demands on art's political possibilities – as if artistic practice were political *in itself.* This potential force, Wright points out, should have been visible today if it indeed proved itself to be real.[4] He continues by again dystopically confirming that art either has become fully grafted into a mainstream production of symbols, or else has become completely marginalized by it. If Wright's standpoint is about to become more widespread, development towards a more solitary expression and a longing for fictive parallel realities seems quite plausible.

Norwegian mysticism

Also in Norway, irrationality, mysticism and the occult can be identified as a 'rising star' of interest for a number of artists, particularly amongst the younger guard or the newly educated. This observation can also be linked to the exhibition programmes of specific galleries, especially young, un-established, non-profit galleries, e.g. the now-defunct Galuzin, later known as TAFKAG (The Artspace Formerly Known As Galuzin), Prosjekt 0047, Rakett and UKS (Young Artists Society). In addition to these gallery spaces, one can also point to certain curatorial dispositions. Examples are legion: for instance, in several exhibitions and performances, TAFKAG has dedicated itself to an aesthetic tailored towards black masses, visionary romantic mythologizing and heathen rituals. The exhibition *Vodou* at 0047 (curated by Lina Selander and Marianne Zamecznik, opened in late 2007) typically aims to circle in on stories about the spirit world with roots in Nordic fairytales. In bygone years these stories had a more pronounced moralizing and entertaining function, with accounts of horror, death and suffering. Today's interest in trans-personal and supernatural myths and stories, in contrast to the personal and private history of identity, has once again returned centre stage. This revitalized narrative construction returns to us tales of epic proportion for which there seems to be a certain need.

The kind of art under discussion here can be characterized as neo-romantic, inspired by magic and the occult, and therefore comprising a wide field. In particular, figurative and narrative drawing has come into its own, and represents a return to artworks whose execution is hand-based. In the following paragraphs, I present a handful of representative exhibitions produced in Norway in recent years, focusing on Norwegian artists who engage in drawing. That drawings are well suited to this ongoing neo-mysticism is not surprising, since atmospheric accents often tend to supervene on line drawings. Meanwhile, drawing *per se* goes back to shamanism and primitivism, as a mystical trace of creativity. After the 1990s dominance of video and photography in most large exhibitions and biennials, both internationally and in Norway, drawing has now received a more prominent position, partly on account of artists such as Marcel Dzama and Ryoko Aoki. Drawing as a medium offers artists a practical freedom, an anti-monumentality and lightness over and above the heavier theoretical discourses on the complexity of representation and similar things. While an emotional aesthetics has burgeoned – rich in associations and irrational undertones – it has largely remained unexplored and un-discussed in an art-theoretical setting, for drawing has historically been conceived as a preliminary stage of the real artwork. The activity of pencil or pen on paper is also easily linked with literature and storytelling, not least to the tradition for drawn illustrations (e.g. Theodor Kittelsen and Louis Moe) and cartoon series. During Romanticism, in the late eighteenth century and throughout the nineteenth, drawing was the medium of spontaneity and intimacy and a well-suited tool for expressing uproar, fear and visionary ideals of freedom. One can interpret the return of drawing in the contemporary era as a post-romantic outcome of more or less the same sentiment, and a desire to explore dreams, automatism, myths and legends.[5]

Crystal/Rhythm
As part of the fringe program to Momentum – Nordic Festival of Contemporary Art, summer 2006, Ida Kierulf and Helga-Marie Nordby curated the exhibition *Imagine the Universe Burst into Song*, in which seven young Norwegian artists presented works with an irrational and spiritual character. Excerpts were also shown at Laura Bartlett Gallery in London the same year. The exhibition title – an allusion to the late romantic composer Gustav Mahler and choral music's striving towards ever new heights – is one possible approach to the works, which are outgrowths from an immediate and graspable world.

For *Imagine the Universe Burst into Song*, Sofie Berntsen made a large wall composition consisting of colour pencil drawings, collages and abstract details painted directly on the wall. With various elements reflecting each other's contents, the work is an elaboration upon her earlier production – a code-conscious and personal 'visual juggling' with myths and desire. The different components cover a wide range; from intimate fragility to a more enveloping monumentality. The work has total experience as its goal, achieved through gradual, sequential movement experienced over time. Seen from the context of art history, the intensely personal and romantic landscape painting is a resonating ground, and its intensity is both stimulating and disturbing. Meanwhile, Berntsen's landscape is treated with a cool know-how, for beating waves in the finely tuned colour spectrum break against lightning-stiff lines.

Energy and the visual attraction of crystals are also present in Berntsen's motifs. The prism effect – facets splitting light into optical fields – is a frequent motif in newer contemporary art, e.g. in works by Josefine Lyche, Ane Graff, Mikkel Wettre and Ann Lislegaard. The mineral's status in alternative New Age contexts is beyond question, a fact Benjamin Alexander Huseby drew on for his exhibition at Fotogalleriet in the winter of 2006. Among other things, he presented a series of light-filter sculptures inspired by Rudolf Steiner and natural crystal formations. Historically, the German romantics were interested in the crystal's 'will to form' in spite of its lifeless matter, for the mineral kingdom was not actually dead, but strove towards pure spirit. Or so it was claimed. The crystal phenomenon has been interpreted by romantic poets as a mineral movement in the direction of fully perfected spirit, but also as cultural stagnation – for example, by the dystopic Paul Klee, who believed abstraction contained a fundamental estrangement, an inhuman form.

Martin Skauen's production is tuned to a darker scale. He works with pencil drawings in large formats. These describe a world out of kilter, immensely grotesque and flamboyant, yet not without humour. The style of drawing is captivatingly detailed. Scenes of raving decadence can remind us of Hieronymus Bosch's intricate visions of Hell, with bodies enduring torment and enslaved to pleasure, as summed up in *The Garden of Earthly Delights* (1505–10). Skauen deploys an unusual technique when he films the drawings with a moving hand-held camera. The camera dwells on specific areas, creating the illusion of movement and an infinite yet claustrophobic room. Skauen gives voice to absurd worlds anchored in the unconscious, and throughout his works he conveys a conjuring forth of prehistoric forces, shamanism, violence and sexuality found in the world's earliest inhabitants as well as in so-called modern human beings. Speculative sadism and an inclination towards ritual group-behaviour follow civilization like a shadow. *The Polar Bear Split* (2006), his work from *Imagine the Universe Burst into Song*, focuses on worship and fanaticism in religion, sexuality and youth culture. The camera pans mechanical and hybrid characters engrossed in an ongoing drama that follows its own inherent logic. An electrical circuit seems to load the film with a movement the speed of syrup – interrupted by more volatile camera swings over violent and ecstatic scenes. A religious worship, in the form of a group stretching its hands in the air, is attended by hallelujahs and clapping hands.

The pendulation between ecstasy and drunkenness, violence and uproar, shares an affinity with Dan Graham's famous film *Rock My Religion* (1982–84). Through ecstatic experience, Graham binds together Puritan religious movements, e.g. the Shakers, with rock music and youth culture development since the 1950s. The film shows religious sects' methods of rhythmically reciting Bible texts, speaking in tongues, removing clothes and shaking and rolling on the ground in collective attempts to expel Satan. These recordings are cross-clipped with rock concert scenes in which ecstatic frenzy is achieved by similar means. Shake, rattle and roll.

In April–May 2007, Martin Skauen presented the video *Felix Culpa – A Handmade Massacre*, in connection with the exhibition *Future Primitive* at UKS. The exhibition aimed to point out connections between science, mysticism and a fascination for other-worldly and esoteric phenomena. The works took their point of departure in contemporary myths and esoteric tradition – an undercurrent in European spiritual life with roots in antiquity. Etymologically speaking, 'esoteric' derives from the Greek *esoterikós*, indicating 'the select few' or 'belonging to an inner circle'. In esoteric tradition, those joining such groups underwent ritualized initiation rites. Several works in *Future Primitive* explored ritual mechanisms of sects and closed brotherhoods. Skauen's video was located at the exhibition's entryway, and its pitch-black temperament swarming with primitive and destructive forces, stabbings and obscenities, cast a pall over all the other works. The idea of evil, visualized with Old Testament dimensions, was deployed for all its worth. Skauen also presented a six-drawing series entitled *Scent of a Woman*, through which he explored historical representations of the woman as a gestalt that activates superstition.

Mysterious botany

In February–March 2007, Gallery Haaken presented drawings by Sverre Malling, whose art many had noticed at Oslo National Academy of the Art's graduate exhibition in 2004. There he showed works permeated with dark, gothic death-romanticism, deep night forests replete with occult scenes of reptiles, devils and pursued adolescent girls. This consummate fantasy world was carried further in his 2007 solo exhibition, which suggested the feeling of trying to negotiate one's way through a dense, tangled wilderness. Malling's motifs are richly detailed – their surfaces crawl with death and muddy botanical culture.

The sugar-sweet character of illustrated children's books and beautifully rendered botanical drawings in the spirit of Carl von Linné provide a fresh backdrop for apparently innocent actions suggesting more explicitly decadent scenes. In several drawings we spy strange miniscule flower children with hidden faces; naked but with unidentifiable sex, they crawl on the stalks and leaves of plants and carry burnt matches. Crawling upwards, they stretch towards something out of sight, in a kind of perverse divine yearning. The thematic focus on children's potential for unfathomable cruelty is reflected in skewered flies, wasps and ladybugs lashed to plants. The mood recalls horror films, the evil mental motor of which is a child's mind (a phenomenon the artist Susan Hiller has successfully explored). The idyll breaks into occult undercurrents with visual references lodged in black magic and Hippiedom. Nature and remnants of a wrecked culture amalgamate into almost Baroque tableaux with insects, amphibians and gnarly tongued toads, all hinting at transitory life. Nature's ruin is underscored in a drawing showing a gloomy, half-dead Cappelenesque coniferous forest, amputated by a bombastic black circle. Malling takes recourse in a wide range of references: for example, he points to the use of hallucinogenic substances and the overstepping of time zones, dissolution of historical chronology insofar as lost time is juxtaposed with the present. This effect is also achieved by devoting attention to conspiracy theory literature, the occult and insights into hidden worlds.

At the brink of horror
In November 2007, Tegnerforbundet (Drawing Association of Norway) opened Vanna Bowles' solo exhibition *Prudent, Vain and Devoted.* In addition to drawings, on show were individual mechanical sculptures in paper. Bowles' works are characterized by a material fragility, the motifs turn in the direction of burlesque scenes, vaudeville and film noir, in which murder and shadowy sexuality play key roles. Magritte-like psychotics, nineteenth-century props and an inter-war patina allude to dramatic film stills – the knife is at the throat and innocence is no more. Perhaps most eye-catching were technically impressive drawings combined with three-dimensional reliefs, their papier-mâché figures about to fall from flat fictional space. A male figure in pinstripe suit clings tightly to a woman encased in a tight, claustrophobic pictorial room. Bowles masters the dramatic and formal tension between fictive depth, real depth and flatness. The theatre's classic 'peep box' illusionism is an important precursor, just as are entertaining effects and the technical contrivances of movable pictures predating film.

Art historical *trompe l'œil* compositions run through our heads at the sight of these precise motifs, encased in drawn frames with overwhelming floral ornamentation and references to Victorian and Historicist visual language. These frames sometimes transcend the imaginary capacity of narrative figuration, underscoring that in this case, the presentation and the work are of equal weight. Through her illusions, Bowles establishes history as a fictional precursor. This is a selective retro style found in works by several young contemporary artists. Bowles' control of the pencil point and her historical popular-cultural anchoring perhaps first of all demonstrate Romanticism's strong, enduring influence on the art scene and consequently, drawing as a medium both for caricatured desire and nostalgic longing.

Concurrent with Bowles' show at Tegnerforbundet, Oslo Kunstforening (Oslo Fine Art Society) presented a solo exhibition of Liv Tandrevold Eriksen's precise drawings in ink and acrylic paint. Thematically, their point of departure was cinematization of intermediate states between dream and reality, and the young girl's transition from child to adult, situated in a terrifying fictive universe. Here popular culture's references assume deeper relevance. The iconic

American musical *The Wizard of Oz* establishes one outermost point; horror films such as *Poltergeist*, *The Exorcist* and *Ringu* establish another. Insofar as drawing is seen as the most authentic and personal artistic medium, leaving direct traces of the hand, it comments on commercial mass media. Tandrevold Eriksen recreates the characteristic television flicker, with the screen's fuzzy grain and stripes seen at close range. The horror films referred to all concern victimized young girls in close encounter with supernatural forces. Characteristic portraits of main protagonists, such as *Caron Anne* and *Regan Teresa*, appear rather like movie stills exuding a kind of perverted innocence, yet it is most of all the two *Ringu* works that crystallize discomfort. Through an almost three-dimensional black thickness, iconic long black hair becomes a horrifying imaginary emblem of hidden horror – with the frame as a container for demonized visuality. A thin stripe of black paint runs down the inside of the glass. The *Ringu* films' plots revolve around the assumption that seeing is more than a passive, innocent act; seeing entails a kind of death – merely by watching a video, one signs one's own death warrant. Vision's fatalities cause the eyes to become the most powerful and sinister of film segments, as witnessed in *Poltergeist*. Living pictures are ascribed evil powers by virtue of their own medium. Thus the screen, Tandrevold Eriksen suggests, is merely a membrane between our world and the other side, a boundary that could rupture at any time.

[1] Lars Bang Larsen, 'The Other Side', in *Frieze*, no. 106, April 2007.
[2] Ibid.
[3] Quoted in Claire Bishop (ed.), *Participation* (Cambridge MA: Whitechapel / The MIT Press, 2005), 160.
[4] Stephen Wright, 'Tid uten egenskaper, kunst utenfor *radaren*', in *TXT* (KORO), no. 1, 2007, 27–28.
[5] This link to Romanticism is developed in Emma Dexter (ed.), *Vitamin D – New Perspectives in Drawing* (London: Phaidon Press, 2005).

Bookshop

With the project 'One for the Books', we aim to spotlight Norwegian artists' book production and other printed material produced by Norwegian artists. We will present artist's book publishers, independent publishers, exhibition catalogues, sound works and other material about, and by, young Norwegian artists. In this way, the public will have the opportunity to learn about these various artistic practices and will have the chance to buy limited edition artworks.

Curator: Marte Johnslien

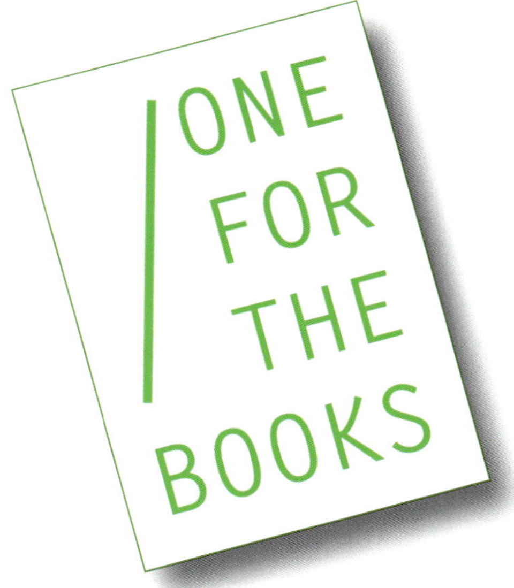

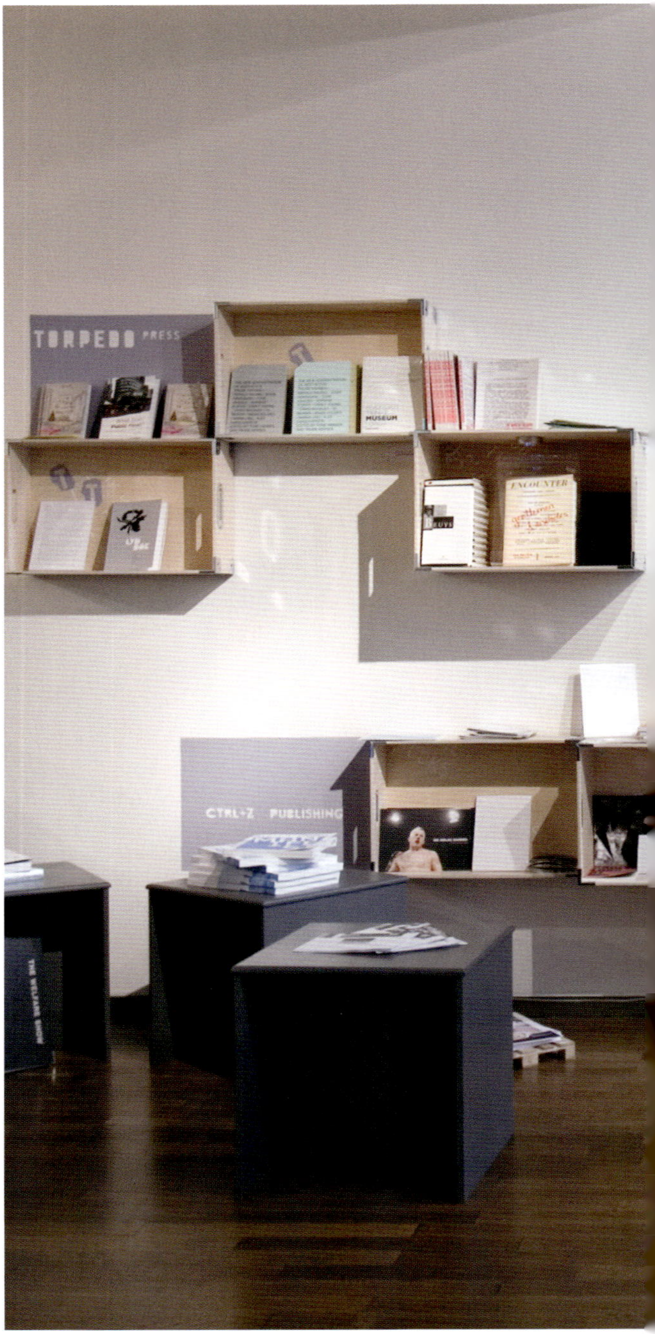

Marte Johnslien
One for the Books, 2008
Temporary bookshop with various
dimensions

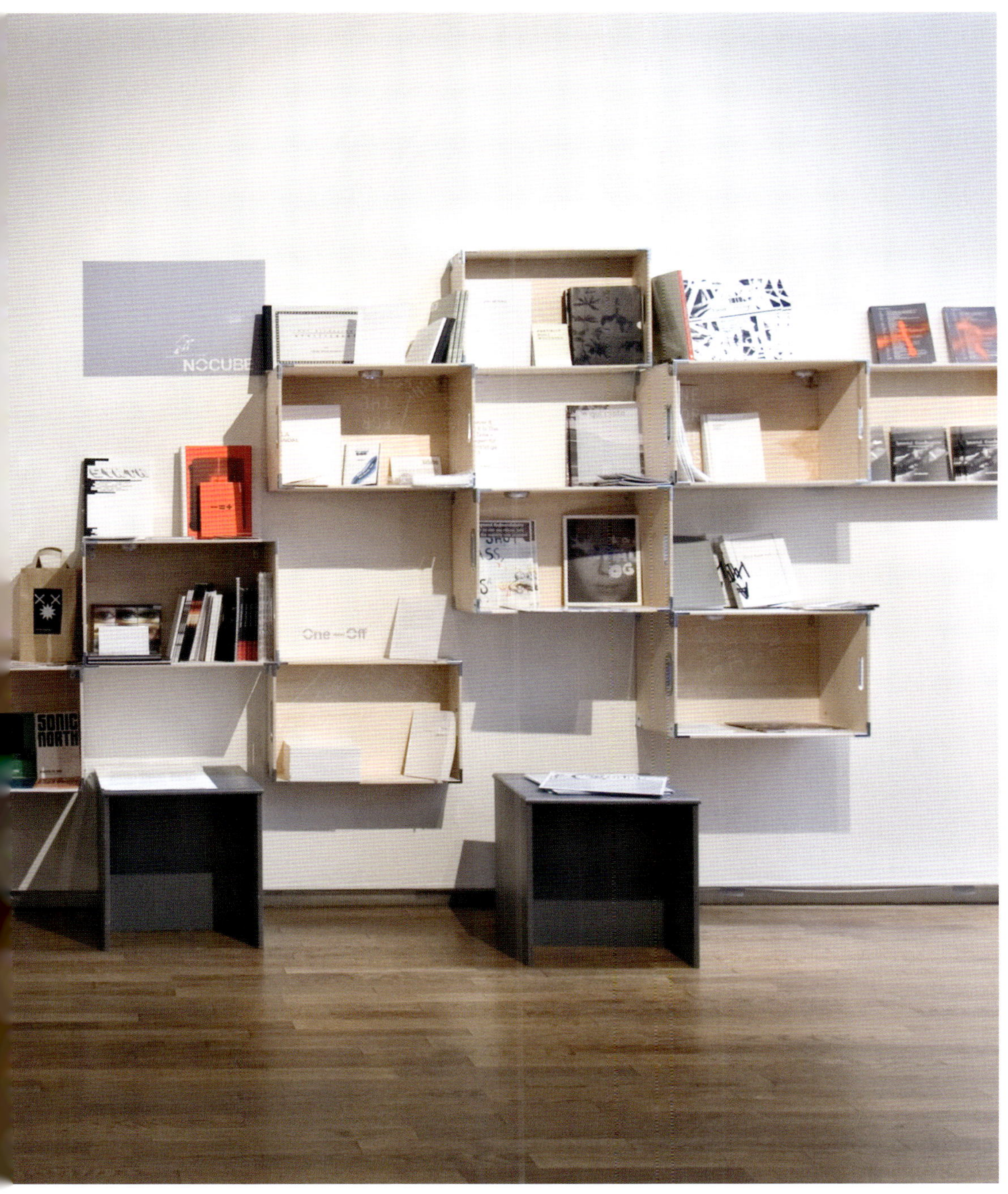

131

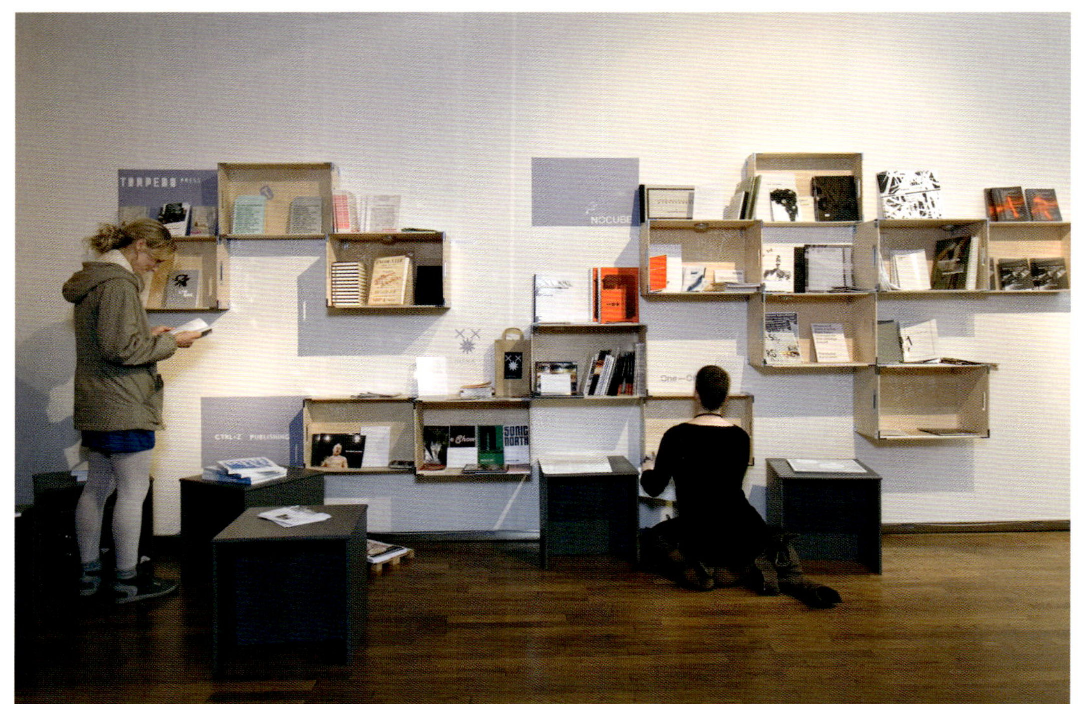

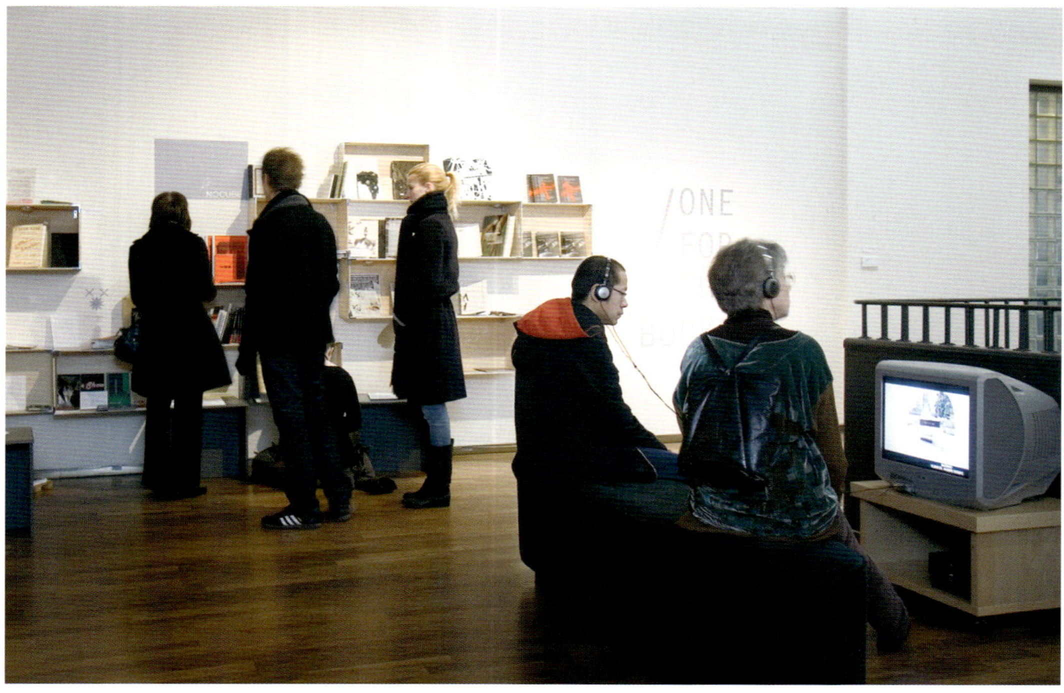

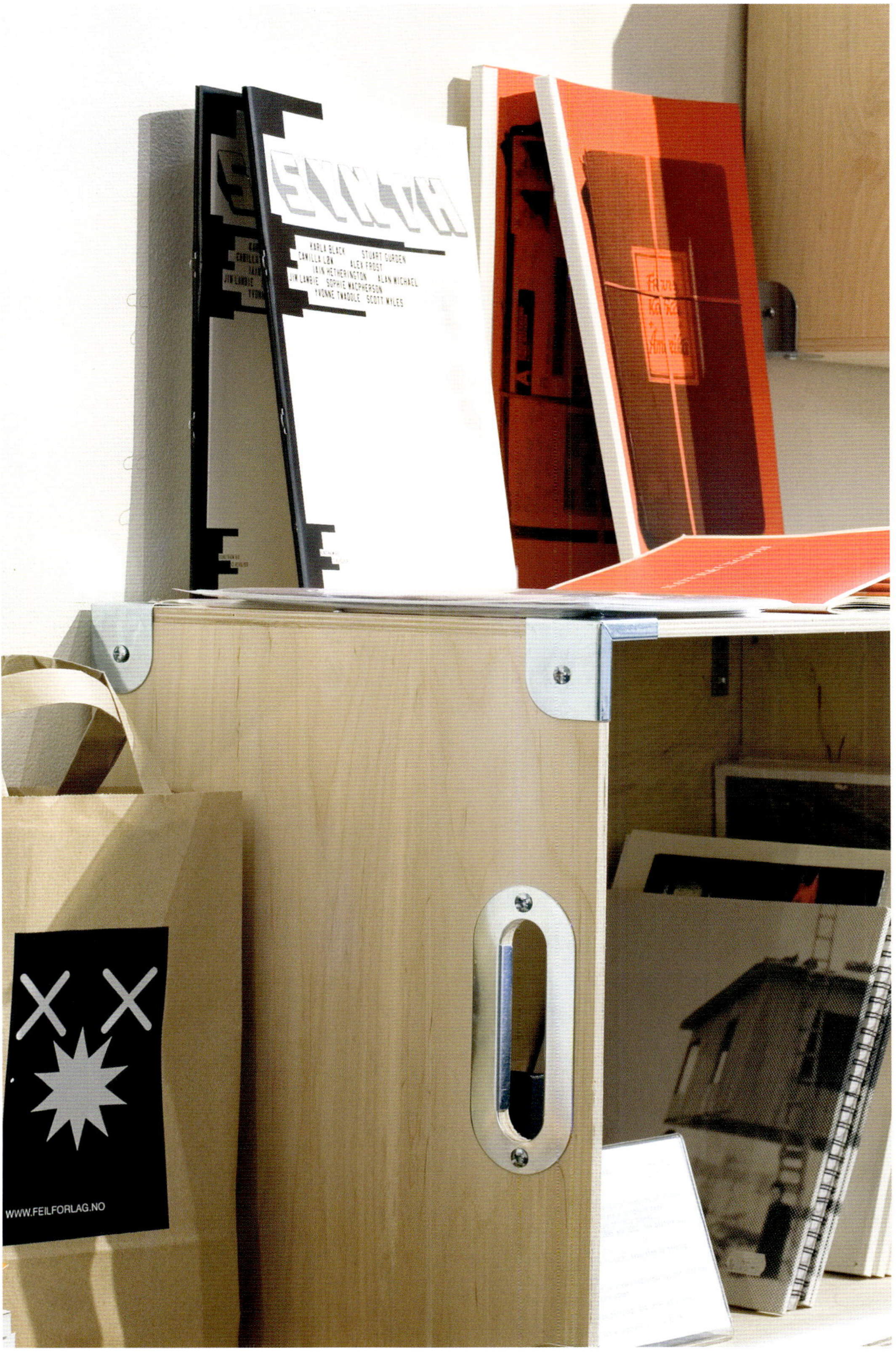
KARLA BLACK   STUART GURDEN
CAMILLA LØW   ALEX FROST
IAIN HETHERINGTON   ALAN MICHAEL
JIM LAMBIE   SOPHIE MACPHERSON
YVONNE TWADDLE   SCOTT MYLES
WWW.FEILFORLAG.NO

Artist Spaces

Baſtard

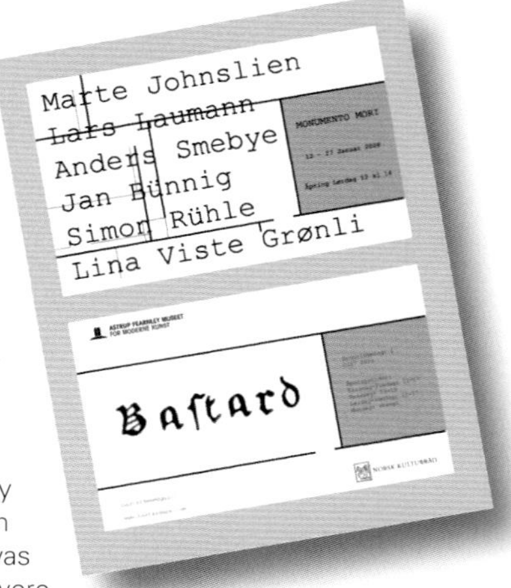

Bastard
12–27 January
Monumento Mori
Curator Anders Smebye

Noun
1. A person born of unmarried parents.
2. Something irregular, inferior, or of doubtful origin.
3. A person, especially one deemed to be a simpleton or thoroughly disliked.

Adjective
4. Born of unmarried parents; illegitimate.
5. Spurious; not genuine: a bastardized form.
6. Resembling a known art or species but not truly such.

Bastard is an Oslo-based project room run by Anders Smebye.

Momumento Mori
The exhibition addresses the themes of monumental change: death, rebirth and metamorphosis.

• Marte Johnslien's two works, *Untitled (Pink)* and *Untitled (Blue)*, are photographs of eclectic pavilion architecture from Lusaka, Zambia. The pictures appear as documentation of schizophrenic objects at the frontier between architecture and sculpture. The objects can be seen as hybrids (elastic monuments) that have gone from being representations of Imperialism's picture of 'the other', to being annexed symbols of the independent Zambia. Thus they are resurrected as anti-monuments, negations of their earlier lives.

• Lina Viste Grønli presents *The Conclusion*, a modified rendition of Henry David Thoreau's classic work *Walden; or, Life in the Woods*, with a number of worthless objects (buttons, small coins, etc.) imbedded in the pages. The objects, which one usually finds on the forest floor or in trouser pockets, surface in the book's first chapter, 'Economy', and thus allude to an 'alternative' currency or economy. The title refers to a kind of abridged reading of the book's essence, simultaneously as it addresses itself to the reader on a more spiritual, ideological level.

• Anders Smebye shows the textile work *Hunter's Funeral*. Its motif is from the funeral of Hunter S. Thompson. The legendary author took his own life in 2005, and his last wish was fulfilled when his ashes were fired from cannon, followed by a gigantic fireworks display. Smebye also exhibits *Sculpture Kills Top Ten*, a top-ten list over actual deaths either caused by, perpetrated with, or in the proximity of sculptures.

• Lars Laumann presents the film *La Reine est Morte* and the fanzine *Morrissey Foretelling the Death of Diana*. The film is a drunken taxi ride and a decadent pilgrimage following in the footsteps of Princess Diana, from the Hotel Ritz to the scene of the fatal accident in the Pont d'Alma tunnel. This is accompanied by the tune of Morrissey's *The Queen is Dead* on car stereo. Laumann also exhibits a fanzine listing the various conspiracy theories speculating over whether Morrissey's lyrics contain hidden divinations foretelling Diana's death.

• Jan Bünnig and Simon Rühle's work *Fountain of Youth* is a movable fountain consisting of a plastic swimming pool, a pump and three thousand litres of healing mud from the Bad Freienwalde spa in Germany. The idea of a 'fountain of youth' was originally Baroque; an epoch possessed by the notion of eternal life. Fear of death is a symbol of human tragedy – our limited time, the weakness of flesh and the end of a cycle. *Fountain of Youth* is a reminder that we all will turn to dust sooner or later.

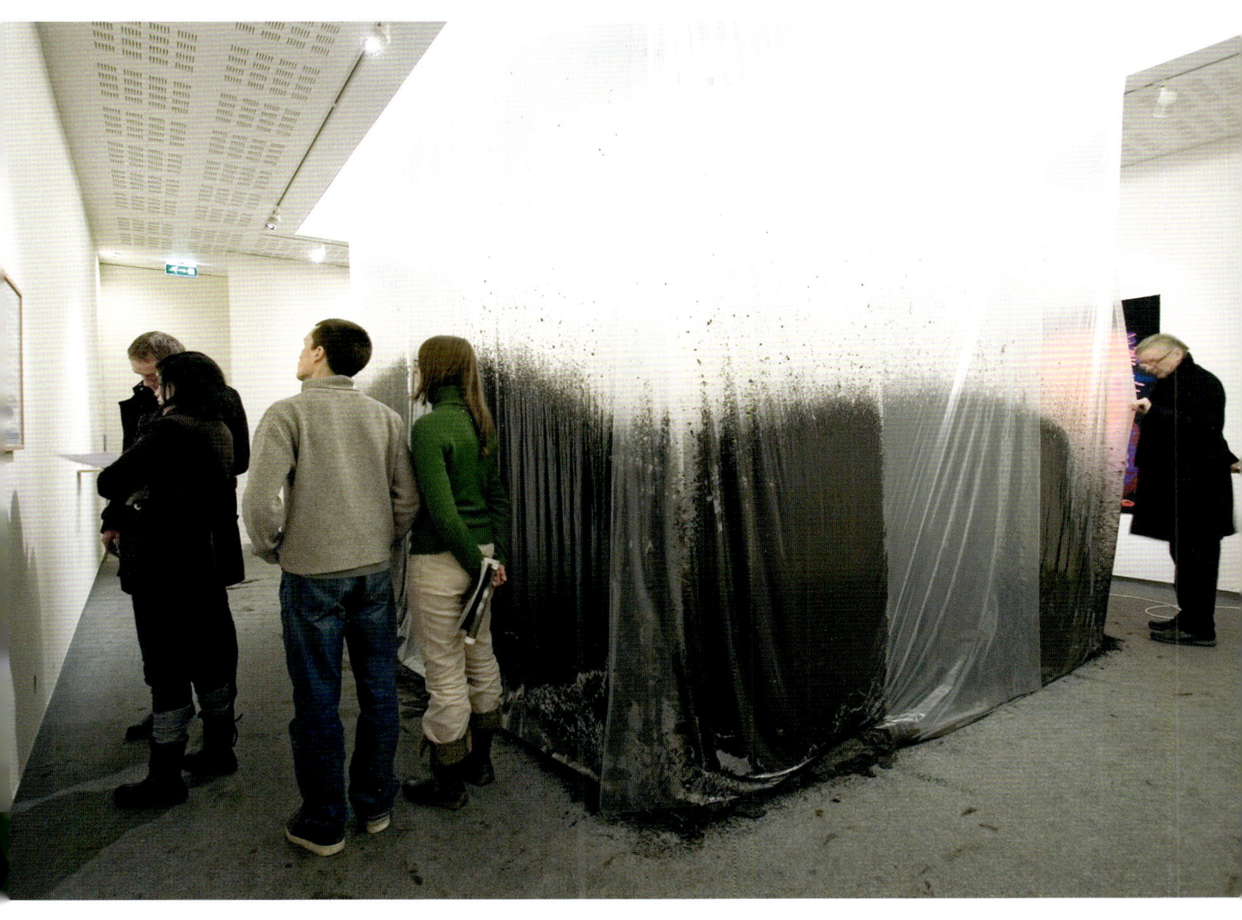

Lars Laumann
La Reine est Morte, 2006
Video
5:18 min. loop

Marte Johnslien
Untitled (Pink), 2007
Digital print
180 x 110 cm

Lars Laumann
*Morrissey Foretelling the Death
of Diana*, 2006
16 pages, A4-format
Fanzine (edition: 250)

Marte Johnslien
Untitled (Blue), 2007
Digital print
180 x 110 cm

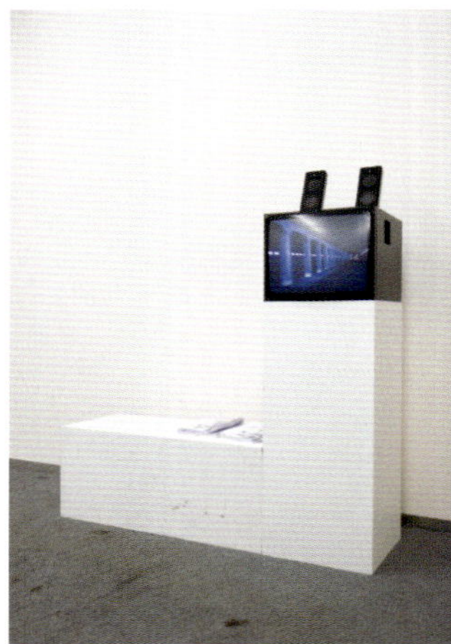

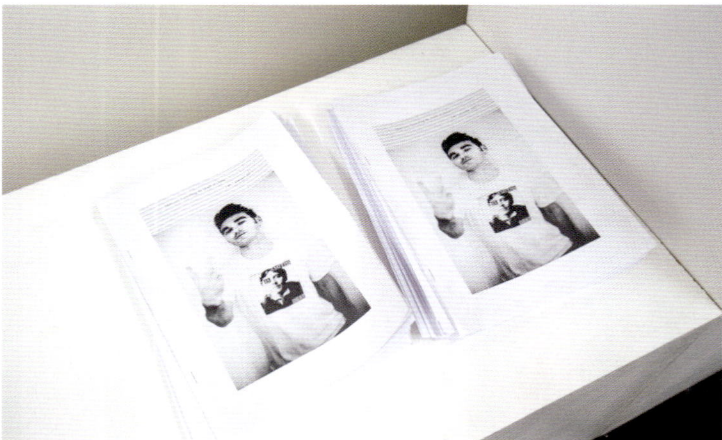

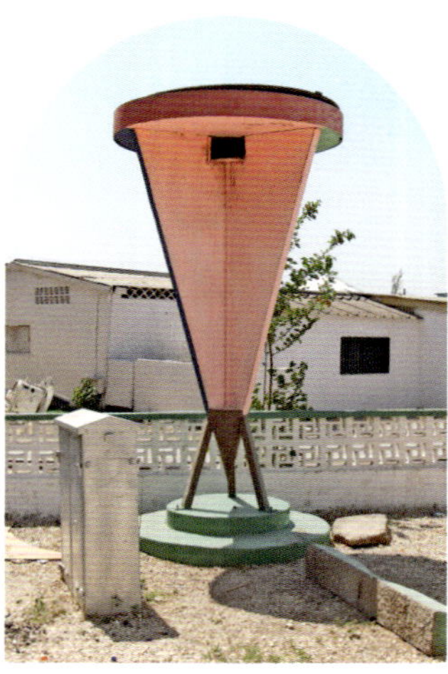

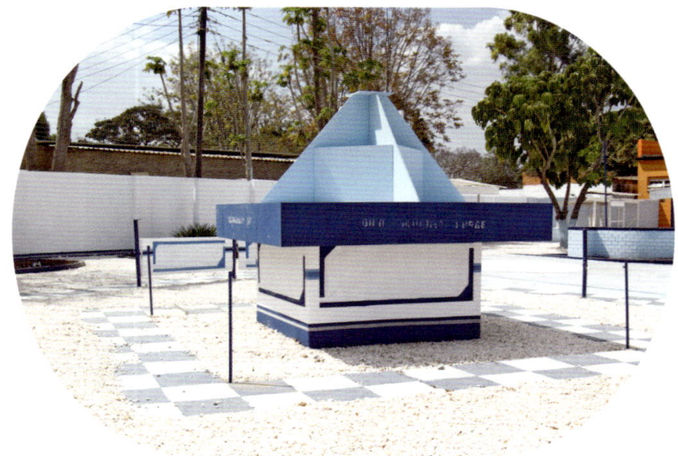

Anders Smebye
Hunter's Funeral, 2007
Felt, vlieseline, thread
180 x 120 cm

Lina Viste Grønli
The Conclusion, 2006
Paperback, plastic pearl, buttons,
coin, raisin, piece of glass, match
7 x 11 x 18 cm

Anders Smebye
Sculpture Kills Top Ten, 2006
Framed A2 poster
60 x 40 cm

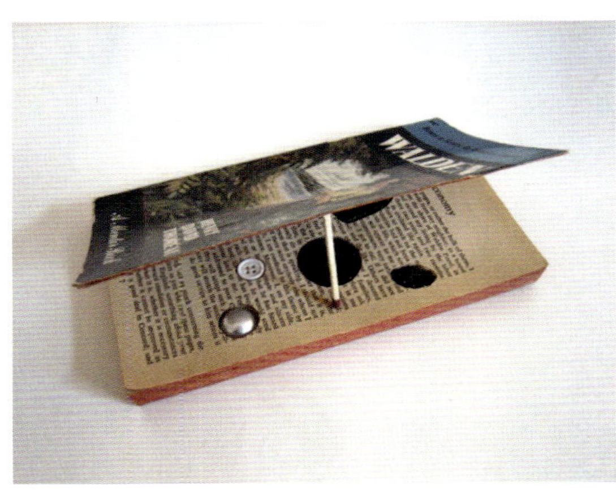

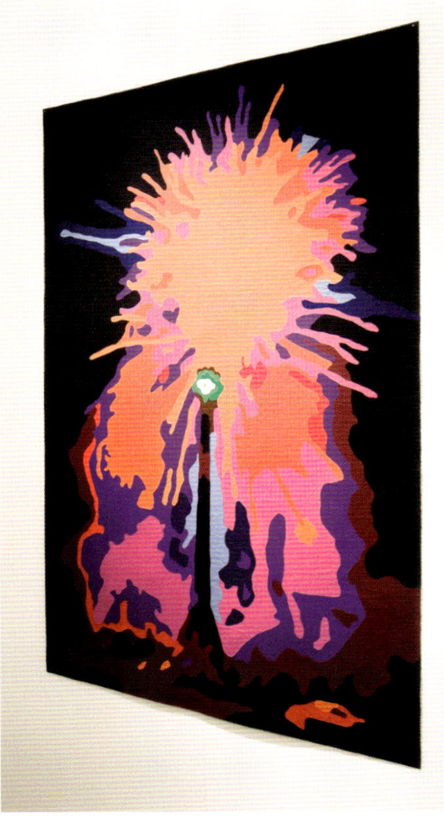

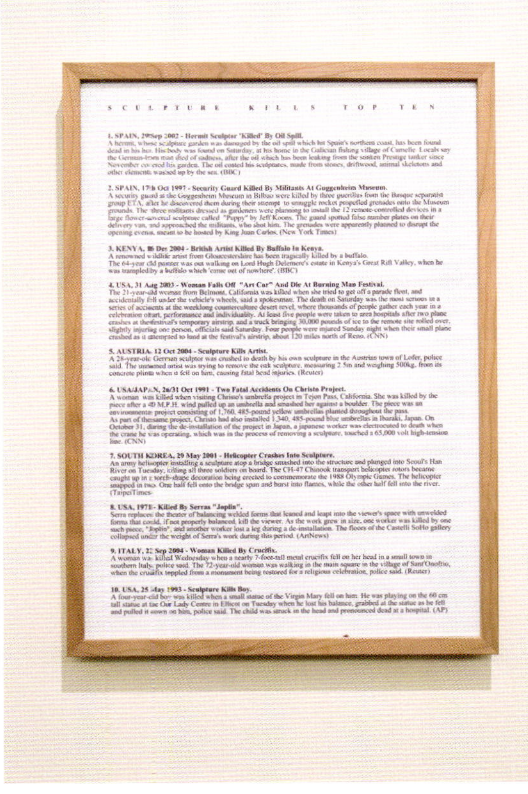

SCULPTURE KILLS TOP TEN

1. SPAIN, 29 Sep 2002 - Hermit Sculptor 'Killed' By Oil Spill.
A hermit, whose sculpture garden was damaged by the oil spill which hit Spain's northern coast, has been found dead in his hut. His body was found on Saturday, at his home in the Galician fishing village of Camelle. Locals say the German-born man died of sadness, after the oil which has been leaking from the sunken Prestige tanker since November covered his garden. The oil coated his sculptures, made from stones, driftwood, animal skeletons and other elements washed up by the sea. (BBC)

2. SPAIN, 17th Oct 1997 - Security Guard Killed By Militants At Guggenheim Museum.
A security guard at the Guggenheim Museum in Bilbao were killed by three guerillas from the Basque separatist group ETA, after he discovered them during their attempt to smuggle rocket propelled grenades onto the Museum grounds. The three militants dressed as gardeners were planning to install the 12 remote-controlled devices in a large flower-covered sculpture called "Puppy" by Jeff Koons. The guard spotted false number plates on their delivery van, and approached the militants, who shot him. The grenades were apparently planned to disrupt the opening events, meant to be hosted by King Juan Carlos. (New York Times)

3. KENYA, 8 Dec 2004 - British Artist Killed By Buffalo In Kenya.
A renowned wildlife artist from Gloucestershire has been tragically killed by a buffalo.
The 64-year old painter was out walking on Lord Hugh Delemere's estate in Kenya's Great Rift Valley, when he was trampled by a buffalo which 'came out of nowhere'. (BBC)

4. USA, 31 Aug 2003 - Woman Falls Off "Art Car" And Die At Burning Man Festival.
The 21-year-old woman from Belmont, California was killed when she tried to get off a parade float, and accidentally fell under the vehicle's wheels, said a spokesman. The death on Saturday was the most serious in a series of accidents at the weeklong counterculture desert revel, where thousands of people gather each year in a celebration of art, performance and individuality. At least five people were taken to area hospitals after two plane crashes at the festival's temporary airstrip, and a truck bringing 30,000 pounds of ice to the remote site rolled over, slightly injuring one person, officials said Saturday. Four people were injured Sunday night when their small plane crashed as it attempted to land at the festival's airstrip, about 120 miles north of Reno. (CNN)

5. AUSTRIA, 12 Oct 2004 - Sculpture Kills Artist.
A 28-year-old German sculptor was crushed to death by his own sculpture in the Austrian town of Lofer, police said. The unnamed artist was trying to remove the oak sculpture, measuring 2.5m and weighing 500kg, from its concrete plinth when it fell on him, causing fatal head injuries. (Reuter)

6. USA/JAPAN, 26/31 Oct 1991 - Two Fatal Accidents On Christo Project.
A woman was killed when visiting Christo's umbrella project in Tejon Pass, California. She was killed by the piece after a 40 M.P.H. wind pulled up an umbrella and smashed her against a boulder. The piece was an environmental project consisting of 1,760, 485-pound yellow umbrellas planted throughout the pass.
As part of the same project, Christo had also installed 1,340, 485-pound blue umbrellas in Ibaraki, Japan. On October 31, during the de-installation of the project in Japan, a japanese worker was electrocuted to death when the crane he was operating, which was in the process of removing a sculpture, touched a 65,000 volt high-tension line. (CNN)

7. SOUTH KOREA, 29 May 2001 - Helicopter Crashes Into Sculpture.
An army helicopter installing a sculpture atop a bridge smashed into the structure and plunged into Seoul's Han River on Tuesday, killing all three soldiers on board. The CH-47 Chinook transport helicopter rotors became caught up in a torch-shape decoration being erected to commemorate the 1988 Olympic Games. The helicopter snapped in two. One half fell onto the bridge span and burst into flames, while the other half fell into the river. (TaipeiTimes)

8. USA, 1971 - Killed By Serras "Joplin".
Serra replaced the theater of balancing welded forms that leaned and leapt into the viewer's space with unwelded forms that could, if not properly balanced, kill the viewer. As the work grew in size, one worker was killed by one such piece, "Joplin", and another worker lost a leg during a de-installation. The floors of the Castelli SoHo gallery collapsed under the weight of Serra's work during this period. (ArtNews)

9. ITALY, 22 Sep 2004 - Woman Killed By Crucifix.
A woman was killed Wednesday when a nearly 7-foot-tall metal crucifix fell on her head in a small town in southern Italy, police said. The 72-year-old woman was walking in the main square in the village of Sant'Onofrio, when the crucifix toppled from a monument being restored for a religious celebration, police said. (Reuter)

10. USA, 25 May 1993 - Sculpture Kills Boy.
A four-year-old boy was killed when a small statue of the Virgin Mary fell on him. He was playing on the 60 cm tall statue at the Our Lady Centre in Ellicott on Tuesday when he lost his balance, grabbed at the statue as he fell and pulled it down on him, police said. The child was struck in the head and pronounced dead at a hospital. (AP)

Jan Bünnig & Simon Rühle
Fountain of Youth, 2007
Plastic pool, pump and mud
250 x 60 cm

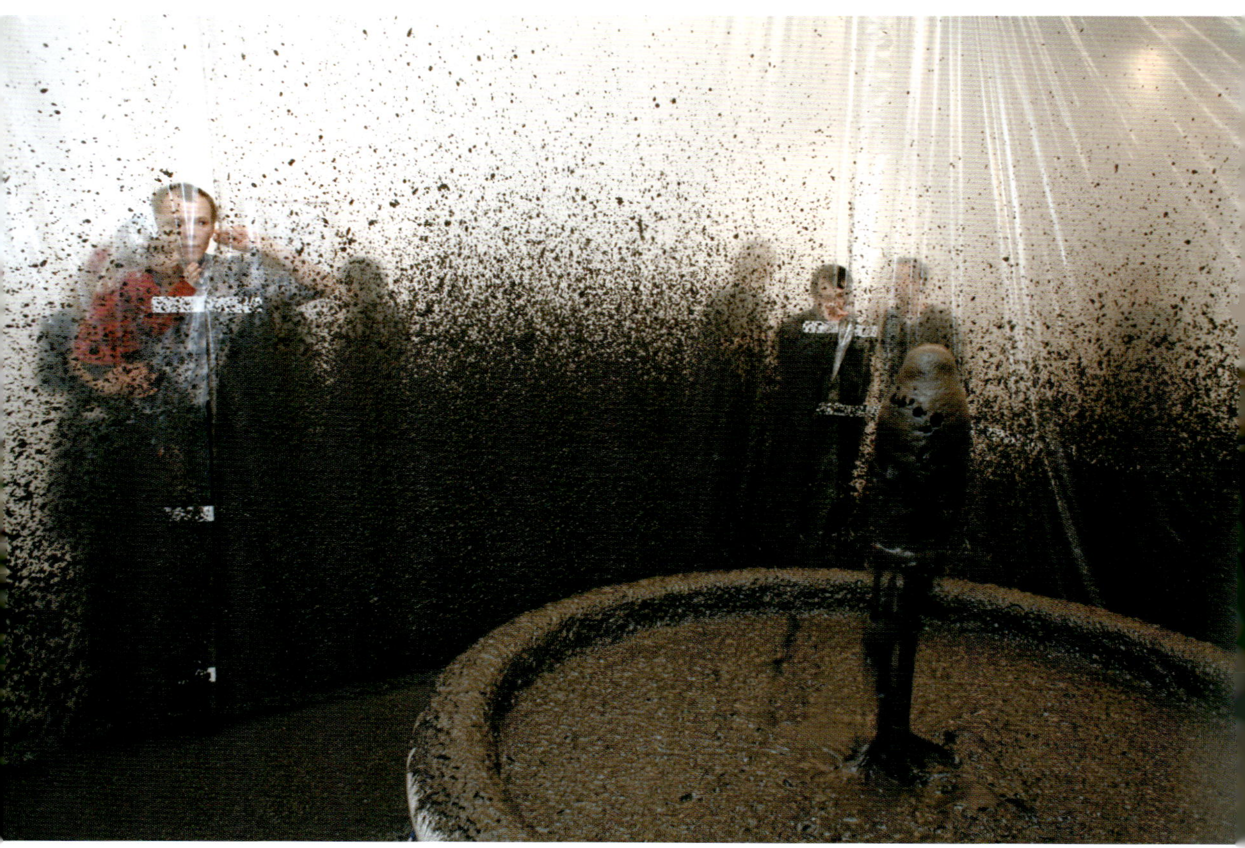

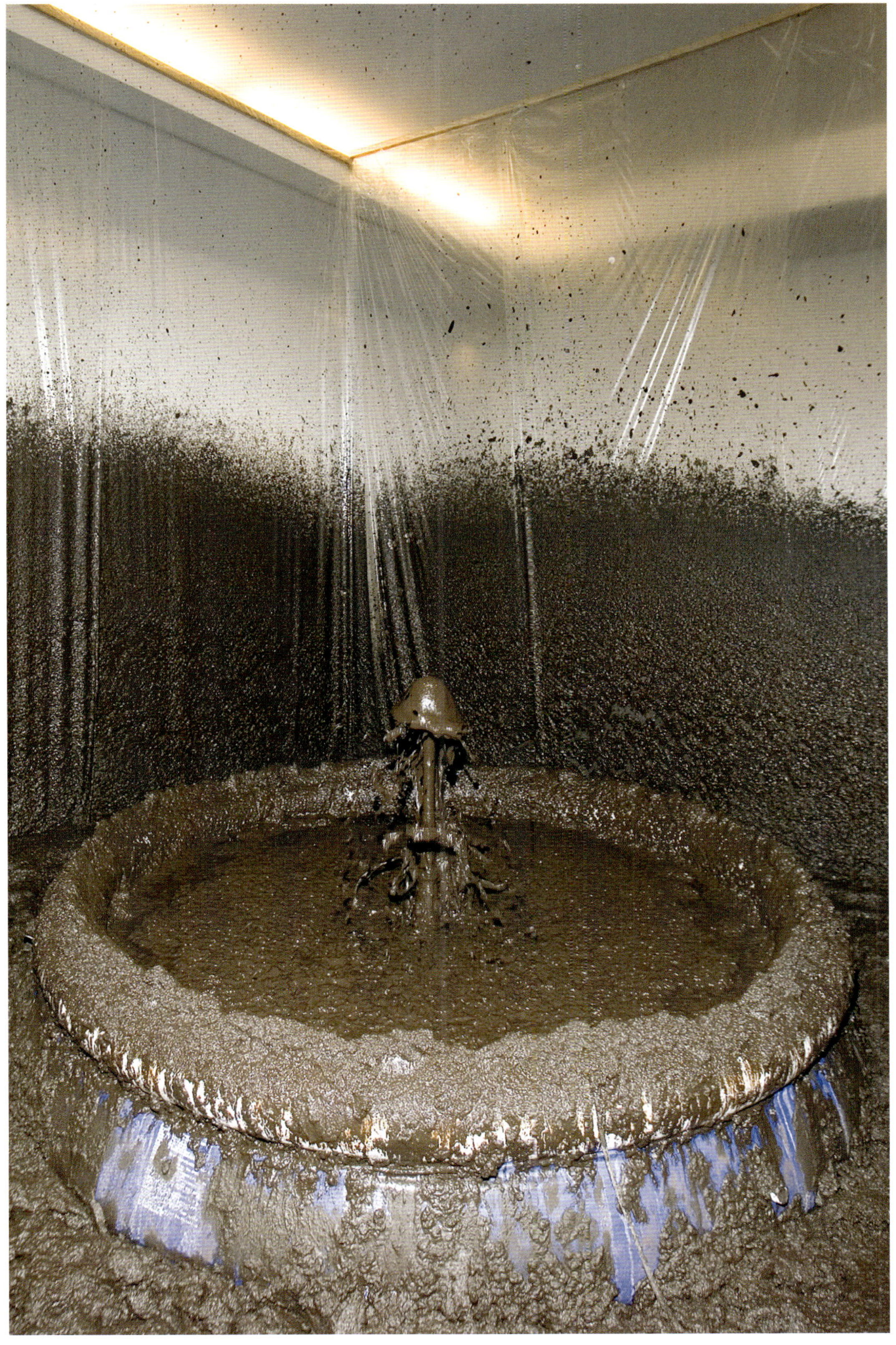

b l u n k

Blunk
31 January – 10 February
What there is and what you see
Curators Lina Berglund, Kristofer
Henriksson, Uta Freia Beer and
Aylin Soyer Tangen

Gallery Blunk is a non-profit gallery run by
young artists and art students in Trondheim.
Started in 2002, its goal is to be an arena for art
students and newly established artists, a place
where they can show their work to the city's
inhabitants. Blunk's membership is usually in a
state of flux, since most of us are also
students and work with our own projects.
Even so, we have built a unique identity as an
experimental gallery – open to exhibiting
finished projects but also those still under
development.
The exhibition room is only fifteen square
metres, and without windows. It is like a small
crooked box; an unpretentious and flexible
format that, due to size,
sometimes demands ad hoc
solutions. Blunk is located
in an old wooden house
squeezed between two
modern buildings, on a
little side-street between

the city centre and Solsiden. It appears as a
somewhat hidden gallery, with only a small
peep-hole in the door, between the street and
the gallery room.

What there is and what you see
Something was about to be thrown away,
the sound underneath others' feet, something
hidden inside, or under, that came to
the surface – without necessarily making
us any wiser.

Gallery Blunk's exhibition *What there is
and what you see* approaches areas on the
outskirts of our everyday consciousness.
The exhibition addresses existential questions
about perception, fiction, reality and change.

Artists Kjersti Foyn, Kristofer Henriksson,
Christina Reenberg Jensen, Lars Skjelbreia,
Lisa Stålspets

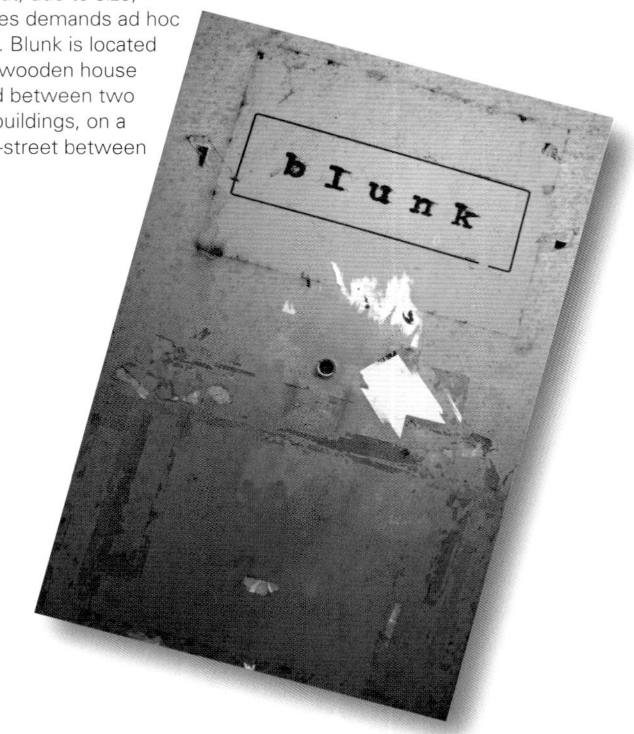

Lisa Stålspets
The giant mermaid, 2007
Video
6:52 min.

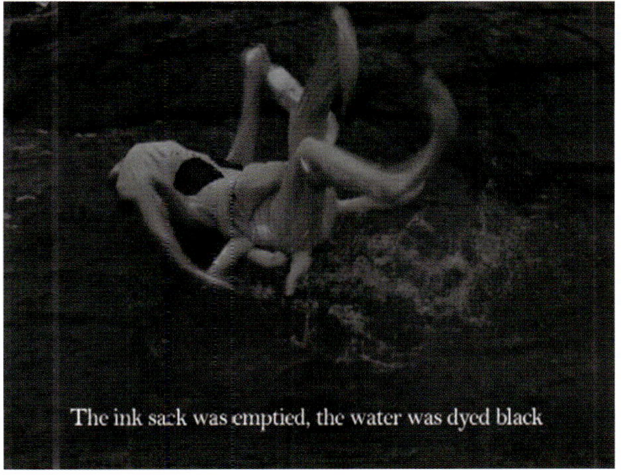

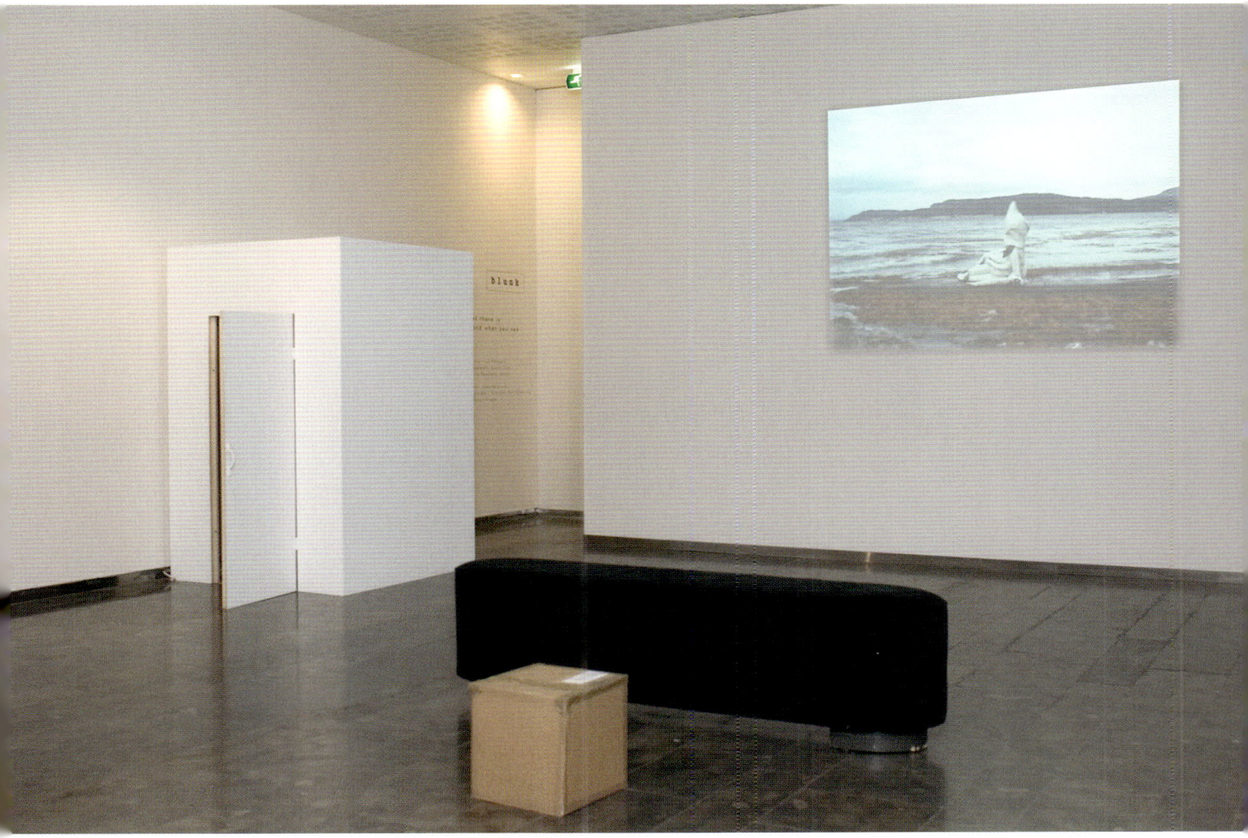

Kjersti Foyn
Change of space, 2007
Acrylic and pencil on chipboard
310 x 316 x 192 cm

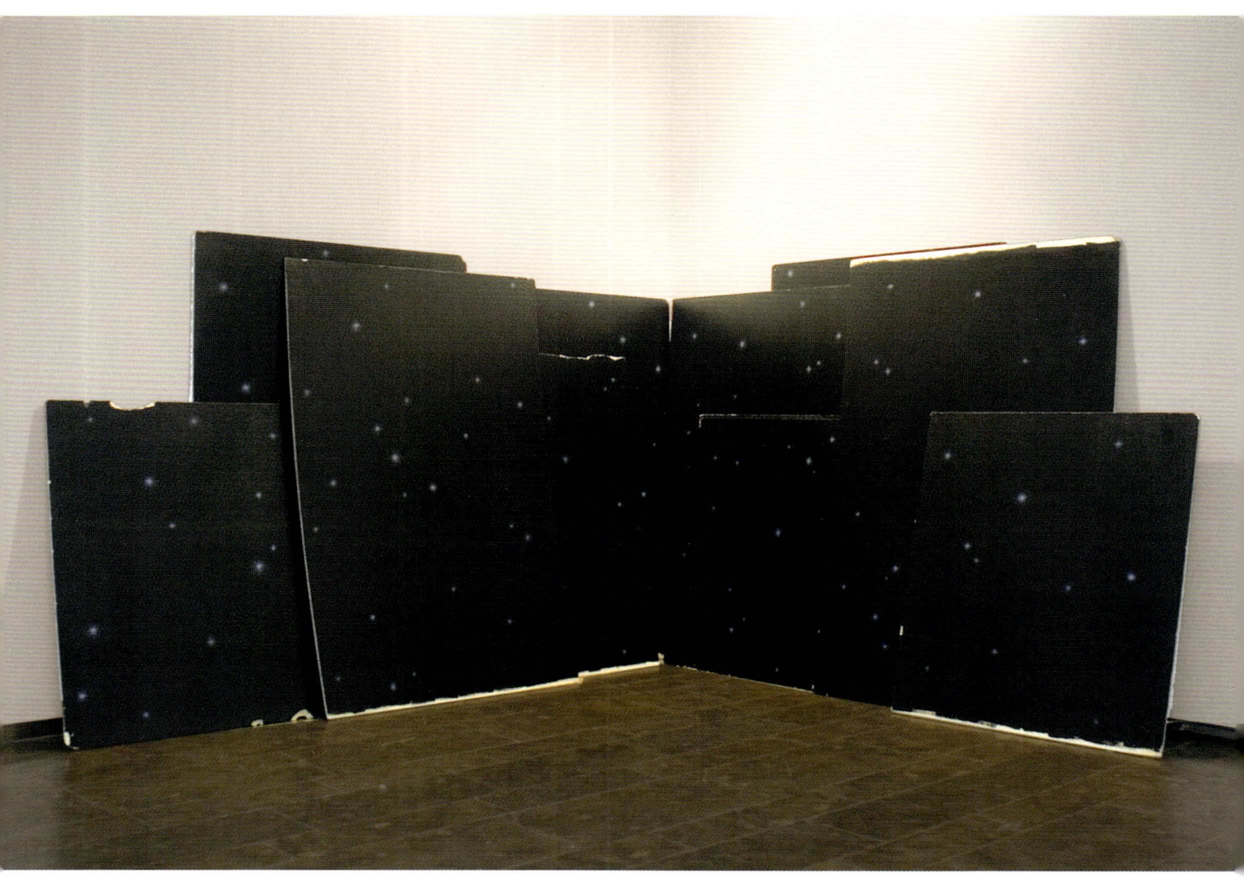

Kristofer Henriksson
A liftetime to live, 2007
Performance 31 January
at 5.30 pm and 10 February
at 2 pm

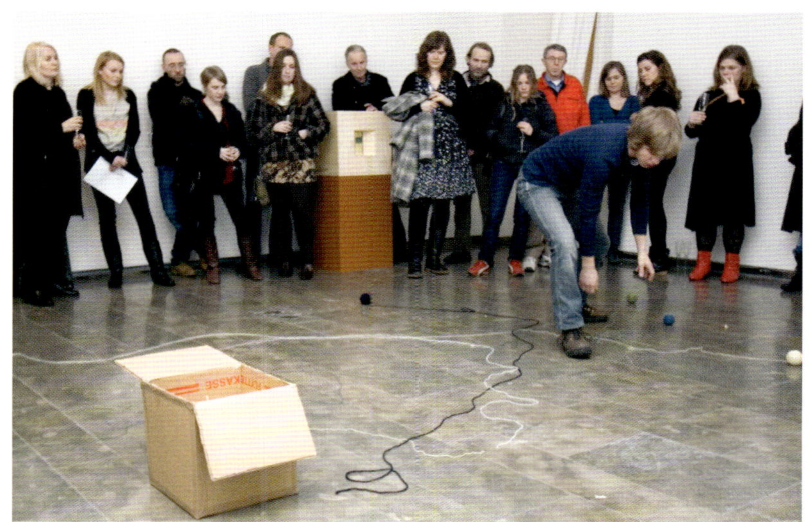

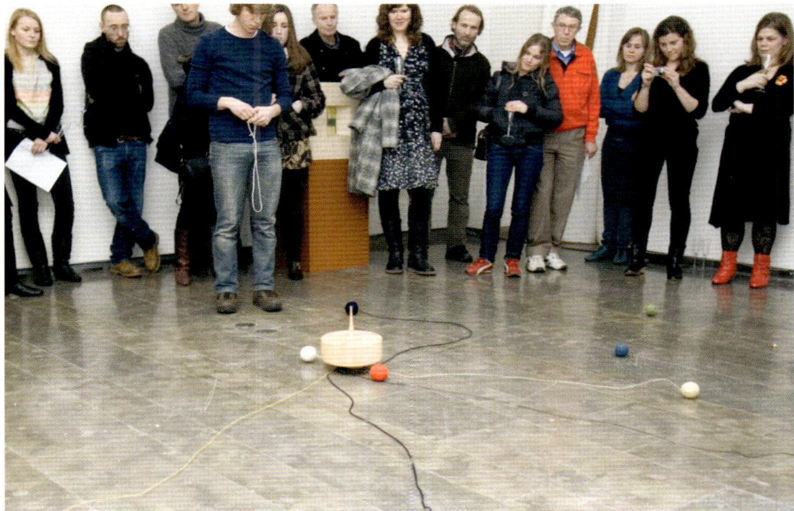

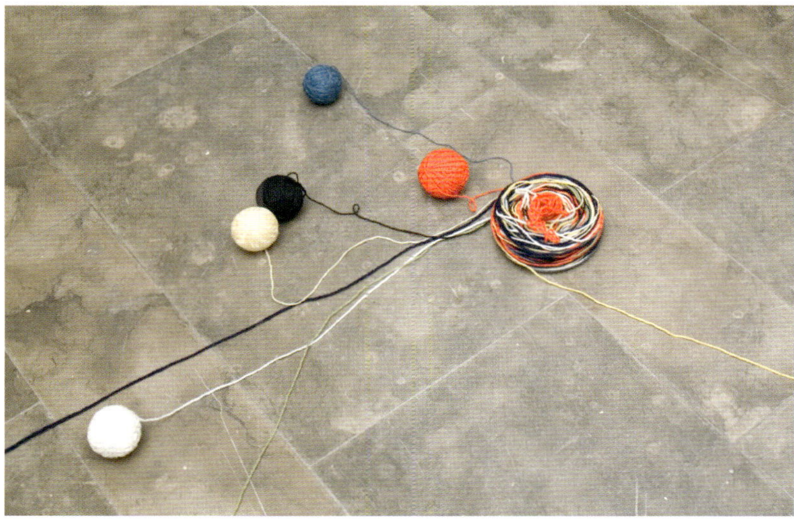

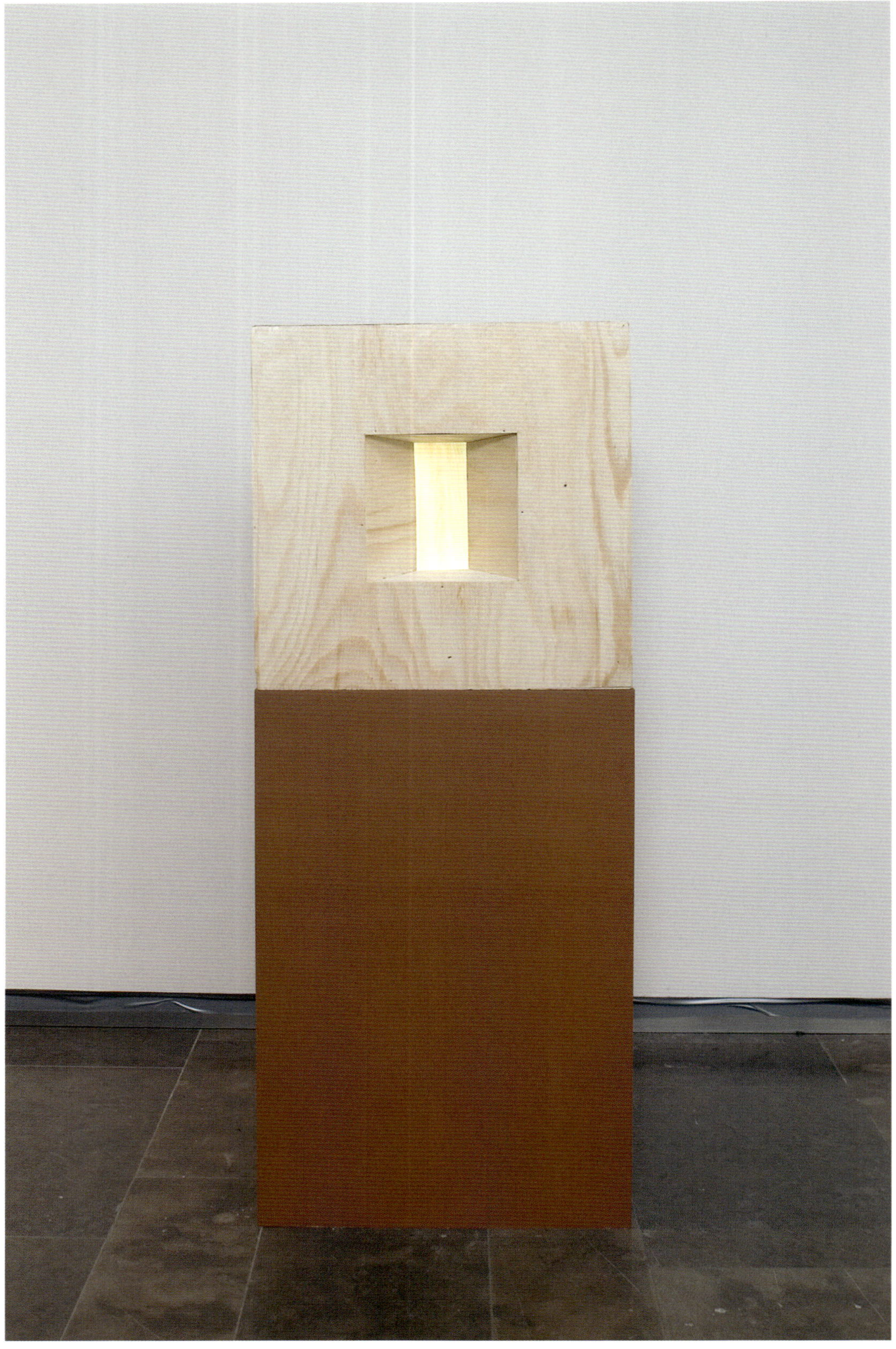

Lars Skjelbreia
Endogen, 2007
Animation/sculpture

Christina Reenberg Jensen
Undertones, 2008
Plug, microphones, loudspeakers,
sound mixer, doormats, MDF
191 x 77 x 77 cm

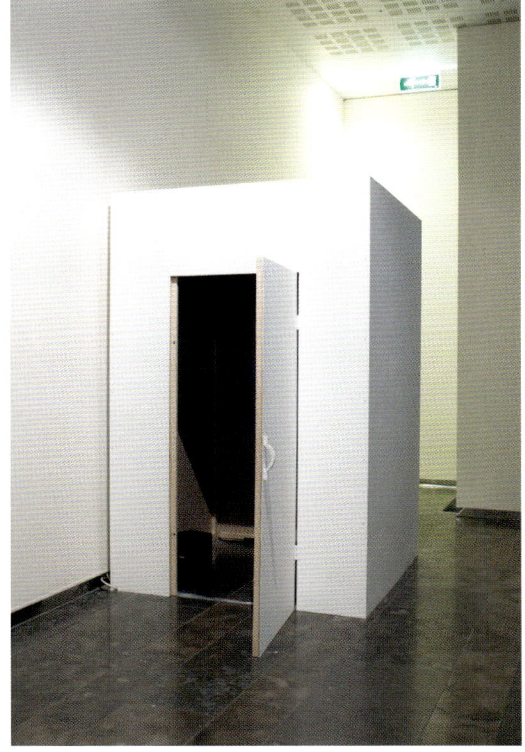

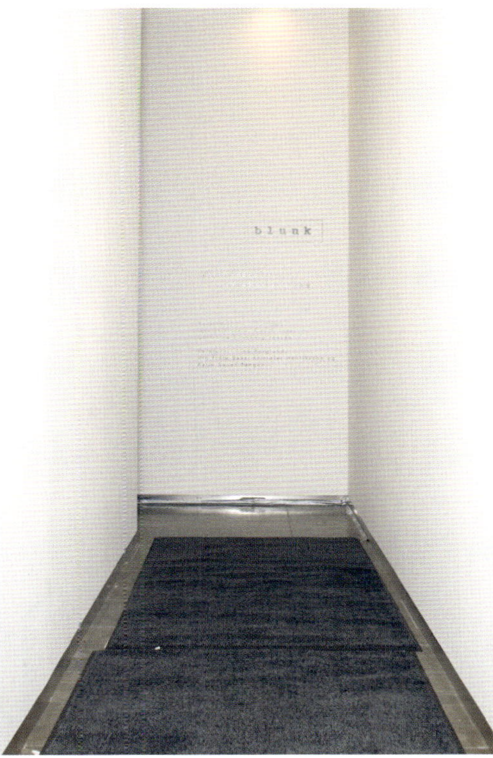

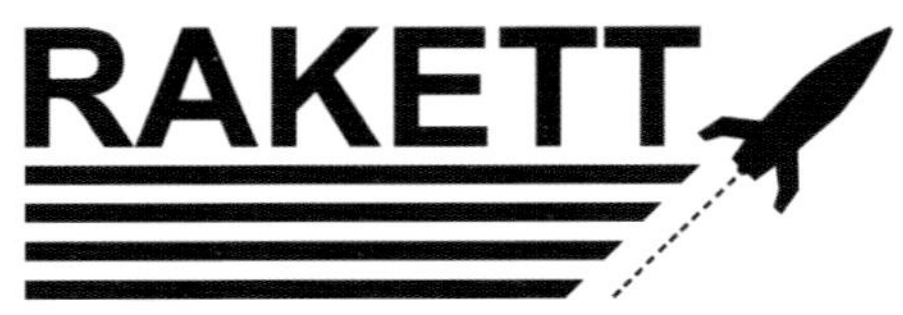

Rakett
14 February – 2 March
**Investigation of a Model of Influence
– including use of subversive strategies
and attempts of aesthetic practice
and experience**
Curators Åse Løvgren and Karolin Tampere
An exhibition project with contributions from
Michael Baers, Centre of the Universe
(Jørgen Skylstad), Arne Skaug Olsen, Espen
Sommer Eide, Søssa Jørgensen, Geir Tore
Holm, Linus Elmes, Magdalena Ziolkowska,
Kristin Tårnesvik, Matt Packer, Ron Sluik,
Maaretta Jaukkuri, Tal Ben Zvi, Tone Hansen,
Camila Marambio, Yvette Brackman, Matei
Bejenaru and Insert Name Here (Jacqueline
Hoang Nguyen and Jenny Yurshansky)

Rakett is not a gallery or an art space, but an
ongoing art project that investigates art as a
potential for activity and collaborative
practice. Here art is seen as a forum or a
public sphere in which negotiations,
investigations and discoveries can be made.
Such a space must not claim consensus
as the ultimate goal, but open up for conflicts
and diverging opinions.
Rakett started in 2003 as a collaboration
between Karolin Tampere and Åse Løvgren.
Within this project we feel free to juggle
between different positions in the field of art;
we act as curators, initiators, context-makers
and artists.
We use different strategies, all in relation to
the kinds of spaces or situations within which
we operate. Rakett projects often function as
lively, temporary platforms for collaborative,
often interdisciplinary, production; we see the
role of the initiator/curator as not only to create
a framework and a stage, but most importantly
to bring together different cultural producers
who have often never met before, to create a
moment of potentiality. Implicitly and explicitly,
Rakett projects touch on a range of questions
around (co)authorship, (im)material production,
the role of artist and curator, and the potential
of mobile and changeable platforms in the
institutional infrastructure of art.
In the exhibition *LIGHTS ON*, we want to
use a discursive approach to 'the Guest
Room' that is devoted to artist-run initiatives.
We have named the project *Investigation of*

*a Model of Influence – including use of
subversive strategies and attempts of
aesthetic practice and experience*. The project
will consist of discursive events and a sound
installation that functions as a platform for
collective investigations and interpretations.
The sound installation is made from a survey
concerning the importance of art and art
institutions. We asked artists, curators and
other cultural producers about what
possibilities there are when working within
the institutional framework. We also wanted
them to consider what kind of negotiations
and strategies are possible and fruitful within
that structure.
We see the whole project as a process-based
investigative work that will present some of
its findings in the Guest Room throughout
the month of February.

• Åse Løvgren is a visual artist living and
working in Bergen, Norway. In her activity as
an artist she uses a great many strategies and
exercises openness in the production of
meaning and experience. Her projects include
the use of photo, video and curatorial
strategies. In 2003, together with Karolin
Tampere, she started her collaboration with
Rakett, and has done a number of projects
which have been shown at Galerie
Neugerriemschneider, Berlin, Sparwasser
HQ, Berlin, Murmansk Art Museum, Russia
and other venues. Løvgren has organized
projects and participated in a number of group
shows. She holds a Diploma of Fine Arts,
a Bachelor in Art History from the University
of Bergen and is currently working on
a MA in creative curatorial practice at the
Bergen National Academy of the Arts.

• Karolin Tampere was born in 1978 in Tallinn,
Estonia. She holds a BA in Visual Arts from
Bergen National Academy of the Arts and did
exchange studies at the Contemporary Art
Centre in Moscow. She followed
interdisciplinary MA studies at Estonian Art
Academy and she took curatorial training at
de Appel arts centre in Amsterdam, 2006–07.
Karolin Tampere has been curating
independently since 2002. In 2006 she
started *ILoveYourWork* at Landmark, the new
media space at Bergen Kunsthall, Norway.

This project is an ongoing investigation of artists working in a hybrid format, in the interdisciplinary field of music and visual art.

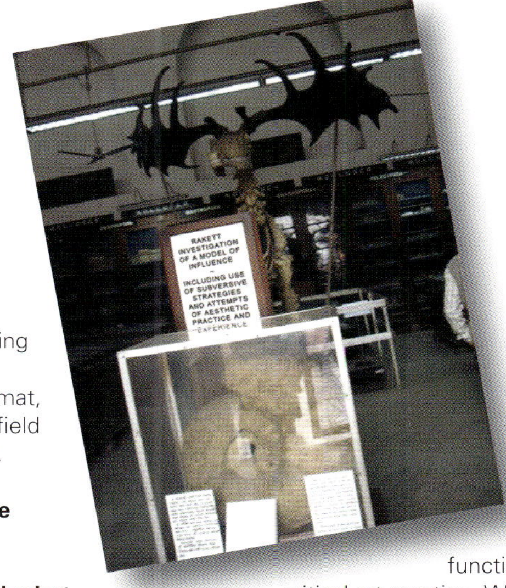

Events included in the project

What are politics, and what is the political function of art?
• Espen Sommer Eide and Arne Skaug Olsen

French philosopher Jacques Rancière has tried to establish a new relation between aesthetics and politics through investigating the two by introducing the concept of 'the distribution of the sensible'. Rancière uses this to reveal a shared aspect of the sphere of politics and the sphere of aesthetics. As an attempt to answer the questions posed above, Espen Sommer Eide and Arne Skaug Olsen invite the public to a collective reading of Rancière's definition of the distribution of the sensible. 'The distribution of the sensible [is] the system of self-evident facts of sense perception that simultaneously discloses the existence of something in common and the delimitations that define the respective parts and positions within it.' Arne Skaug Olsen is a visual artist, director of *Flaggfabrikken* and editor at Ctrl+Z publishing house. Espen Sommer Eide is a musician and philosopher. As part of the musical projects *Alog* and *Phonophani*, he has released several albums on the record label Rune Grammofon.

Who is Gerd Stern and what does he know about Michael Asher?
• Michael Baers

How does institutional critique attempt to resituate the viewer's perception of the institution and the art object? What limits are encountered when attempts are made to redefine the nature of something as concrete and structurally opaque as a museum, or as conceptually entrenched as normative definitions of 'art'? More to the point, what is the lost psychedelic component of institutional critique? Michael Baers seeks to address these and other questions in a talk

show with special guests and entertainment, psychedelic musings and, of course, an incisive interrogation of the nature and function of the museum and critical art practice. While preferring to let the connection between psychedelia and critical practice remain obscure for the moment, as a foretaste of the afternoon's agenda, Baers introduces Timothy Leary's concepts 'set' (as in 'mindset' or attitude) and 'setting' (ambience, décor, and music particularly), the therapist's principal tools in guiding the psychedelic experience. Museums also make use of set and setting in order to ideologically orient visitors in relation to art and its institutions. One might propose institutional critique as instituting a counter-setting, which then hopefully, induces a counter-set. Come re-program your mind and the museum. Michael Baers is an American artist based in Berlin who commonly works with publications and comics. He is currently collaborating with the Dutch publication *Fucking Good Art* on a comic about LSD and Switzerland for their upcoming Swiss issue.

Social Model, open workshop
• Søssa Jørgensen and Geir Tore Holm

This is an open workshop that practically investigates how contemporary art can function in relation to society and on its own terms. Why is art so important? Geir Tore Holm (b.Tromsø, 1966) and Søssa Jørgensen (b. Oslo, 1968) live and work in Oslo, Gildeskål and Tromsø. They studied at the Art Academy in Trondheim (1995) and their individual artistic practices include video, performance and installations. They have also curated, written about art and been art teachers. With Kamin Lertchaiprasert and Rirkrit Tiravanija, they started *Sørfinnset skole/the Nord Land* in 2003. Jørgensen has explored sound art since the mid 1990s through her collaborative project *Ballongmagasinet*. Holm has been project leader for the newly established Art Academy in Tromsø.

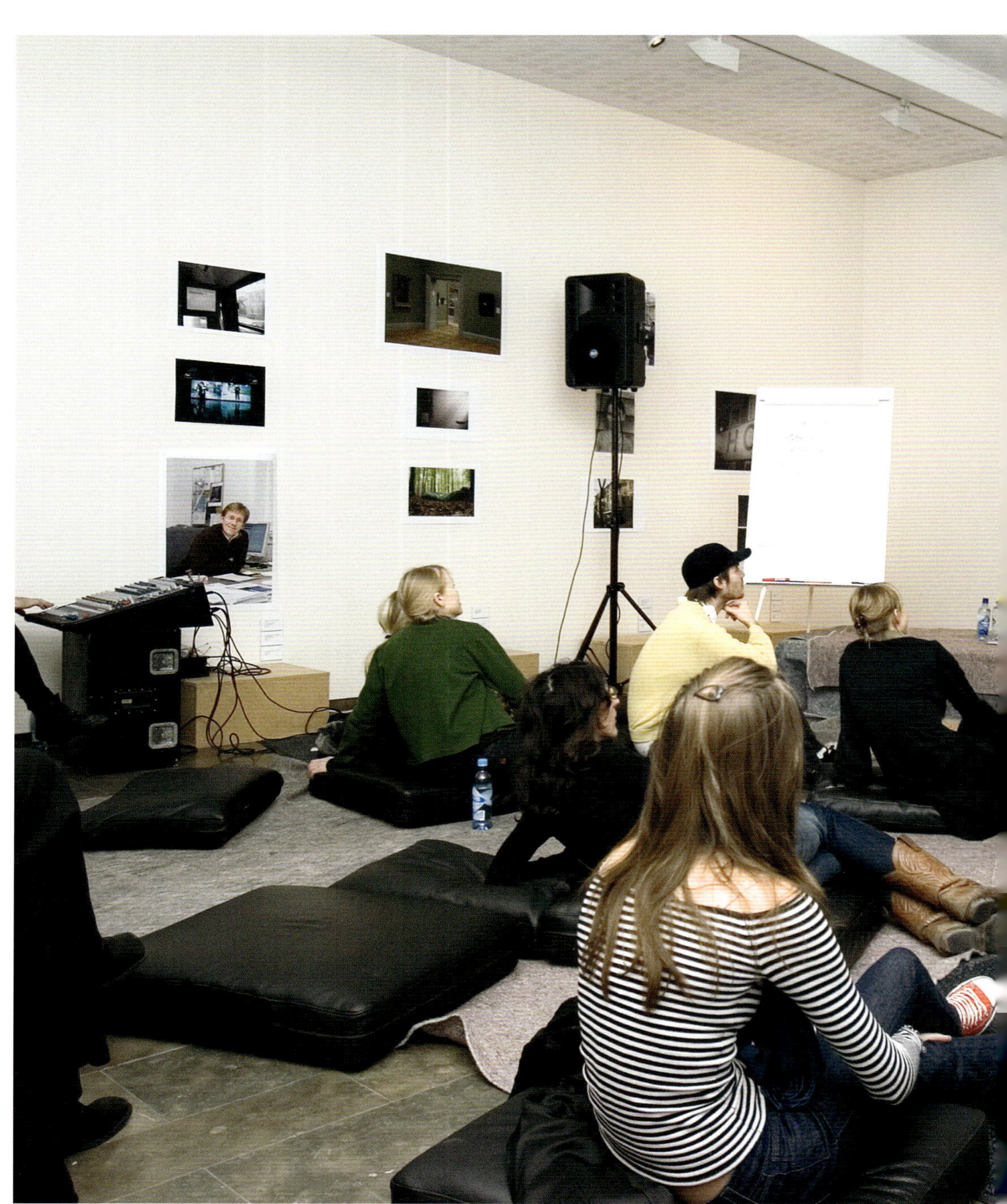

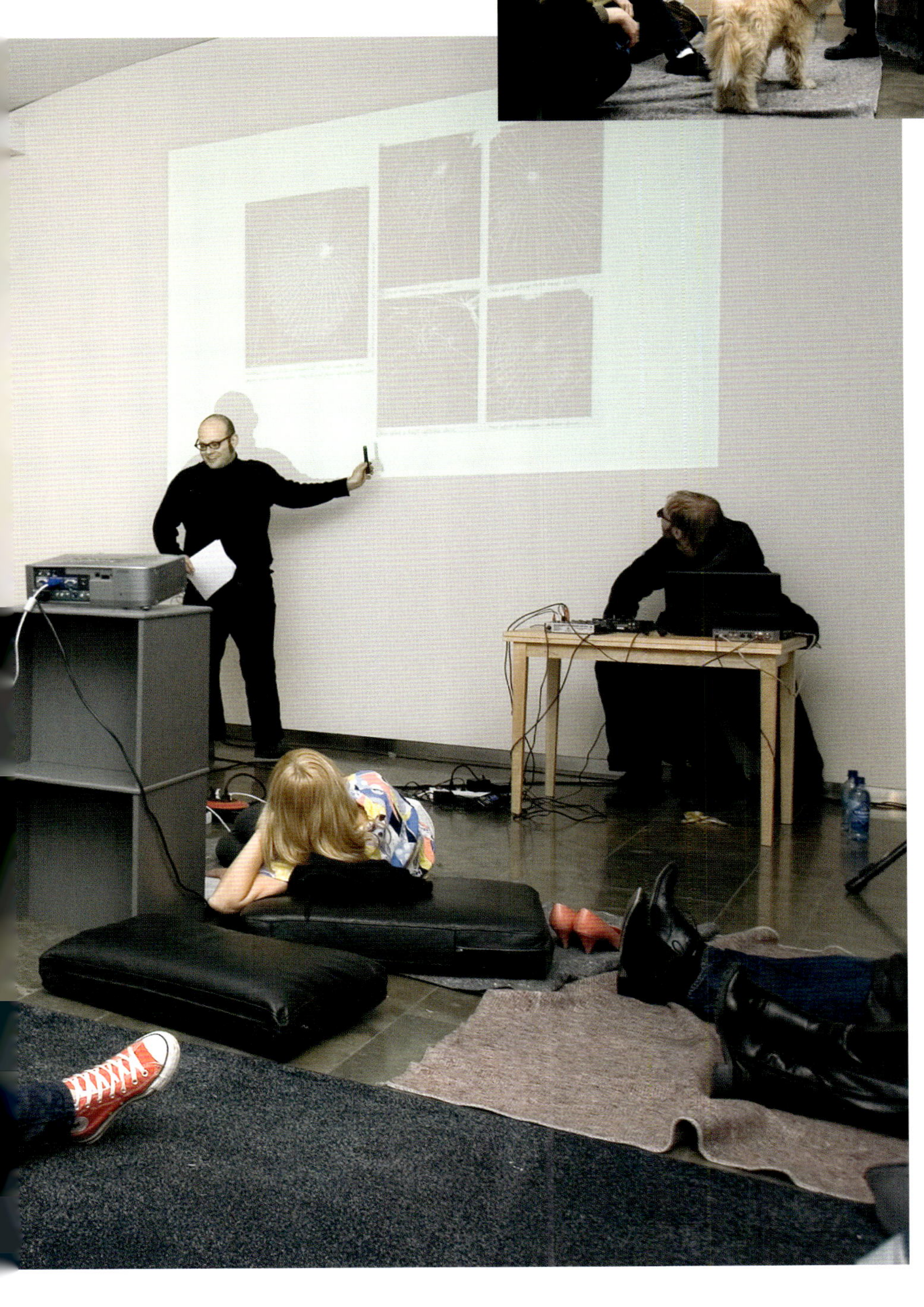

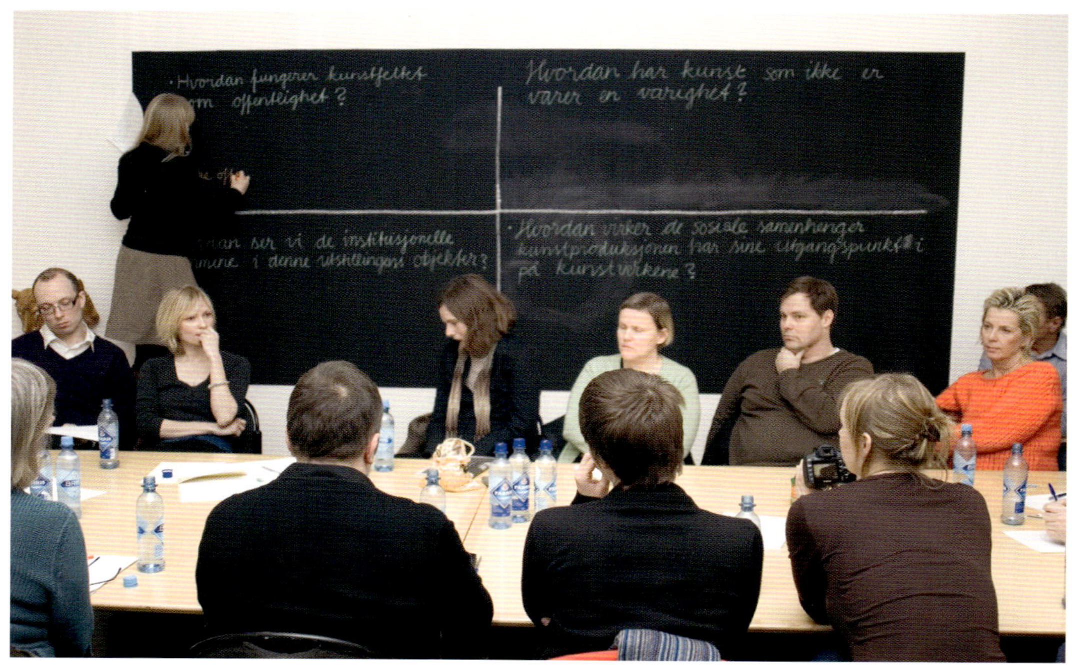

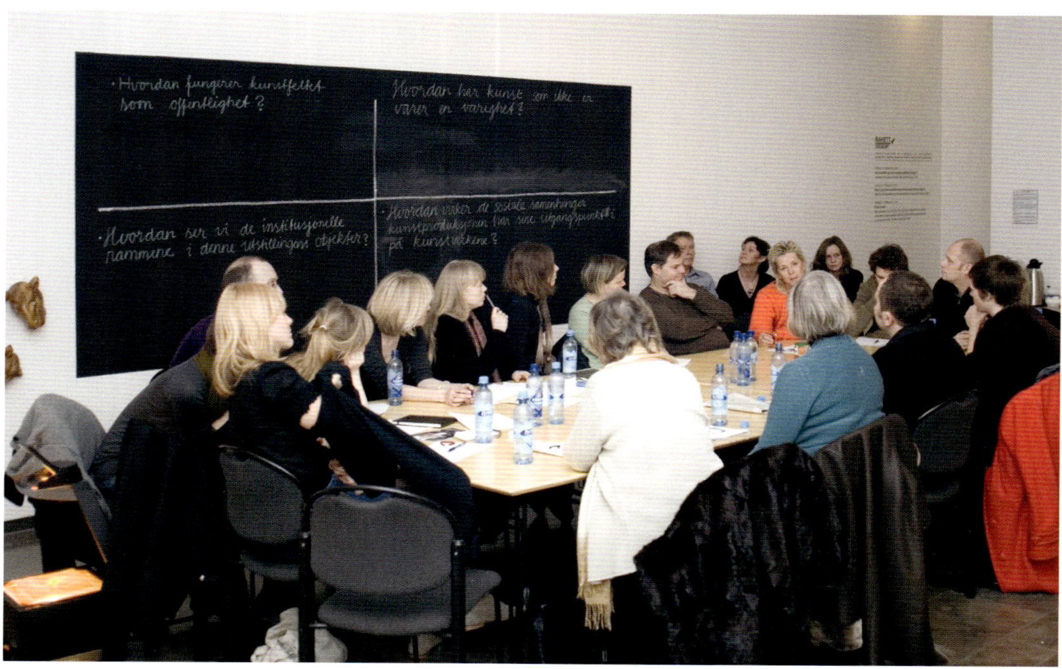

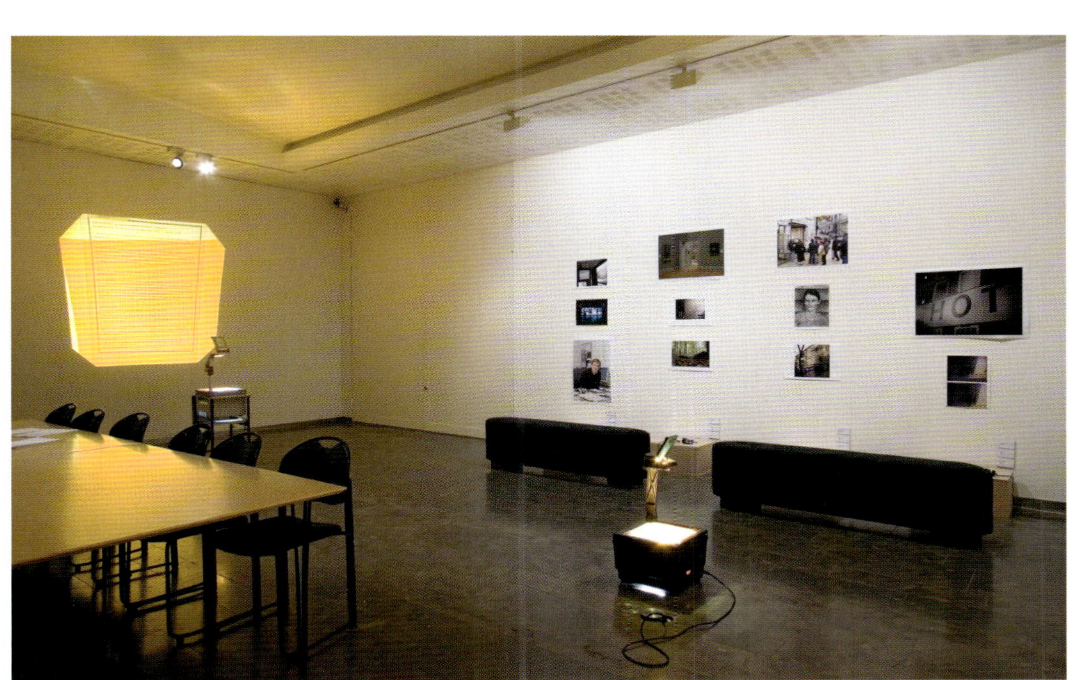

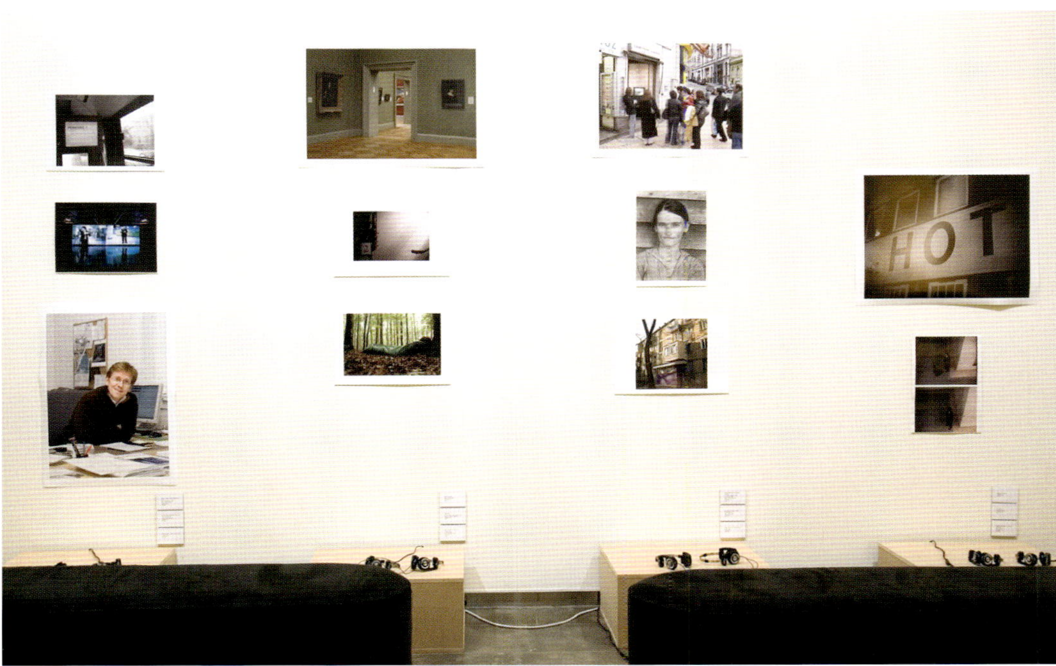

REKORD

Rekord
6–23 March
Pineapple, or knife? Iceberg, or volcano?
Curators Thora Dolven Balke, Ingvild
Langgård and Eirin Støen

*Standby. You're on the air. Buenas noches
Señores y Señoras. Bienvenidos.
La primera pregunta es: Que es mas macho,
pineapple o knife?*

The exhibition title is appropriated from Laurie
Anderson's *Smoke Rings*. We interpret
Anderson's text as discussing the point of
uncertainty between random contrasts, just
as any conceptual pair contains an inherent
degree of irrationality. Several works in the
exhibition pivot on a similar point: the
possibility of implosion. Such a collapse
opens the possibility of breaking away from
formalities and learned conventions.
The exhibited works comment on this by
showing, for instance, how suicide as a
solution is contrasted with insufferable
safety, how crystals glimmer deceivingly,
half hidden in the dark, how the black cloud's
threat of a *major toxic event* is itself as
dissolvable as a watered-out aquarelle, and
how the moral force of definition must be
challenged when half the world condones the
death penalty. Art can redefine and dissect
the concepts we traffic in uncritically, through
a sort of Dada disintegration of language.
Or the opposite: by using text as a manifesto
and assault weapon.
Since Rekord first opened its doors in 2006,
it has presented free and experimental
expressions in divergent media, created by
new and well-established Norwegian and
international artists. Rekord has consistently
focused on situation-dependent expressions,
such as sound, performance and music. The
live performance requires a presence, a space
in which artist and viewer enter into the same
moment. As such this moment represents a
great possibility of failure. It is essentially
unconcealed and direct, and can be theatrical.
It involves potential embarrassment and self-
consciousness to the point of pain, and
functions as a *memento mori*.

All exhibition spaces for art must dare to
include works that shake their own
foundations.
Que es mas macho? Lightbulb, or schoolbus?

Participating artists
Kjersti Andvig
Kristian Øverland Dahl
Trine Falch
Marianne Hurum
Anette Stav Johanssen
Are Mokkelbost
Linn Anita Pedersen
Christina Peel
Kristian Skylstad & Vilde Skylstad
Ulf Styren
Jorunn Myklebust Syversen
Monica Winther & Kjersti Vetterstad
Tori Wrånes

*Thanks to NOTAM and Cato Langnes
for valuable assistance and studio space
for editing and mastering.*

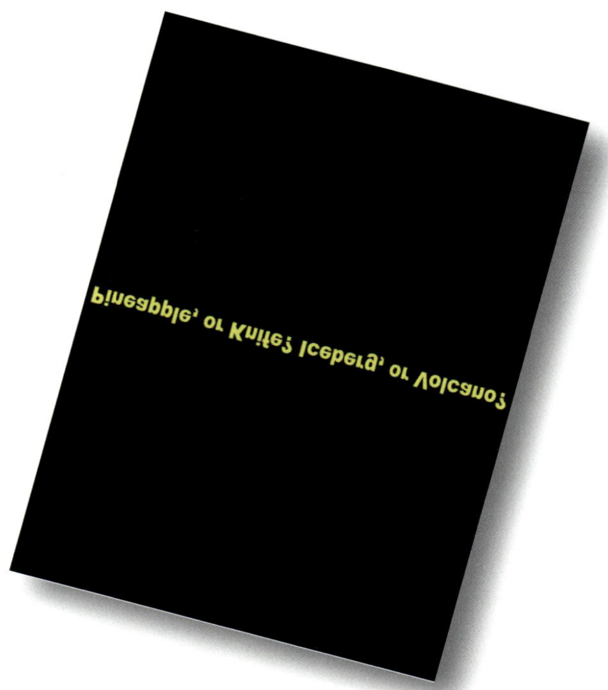

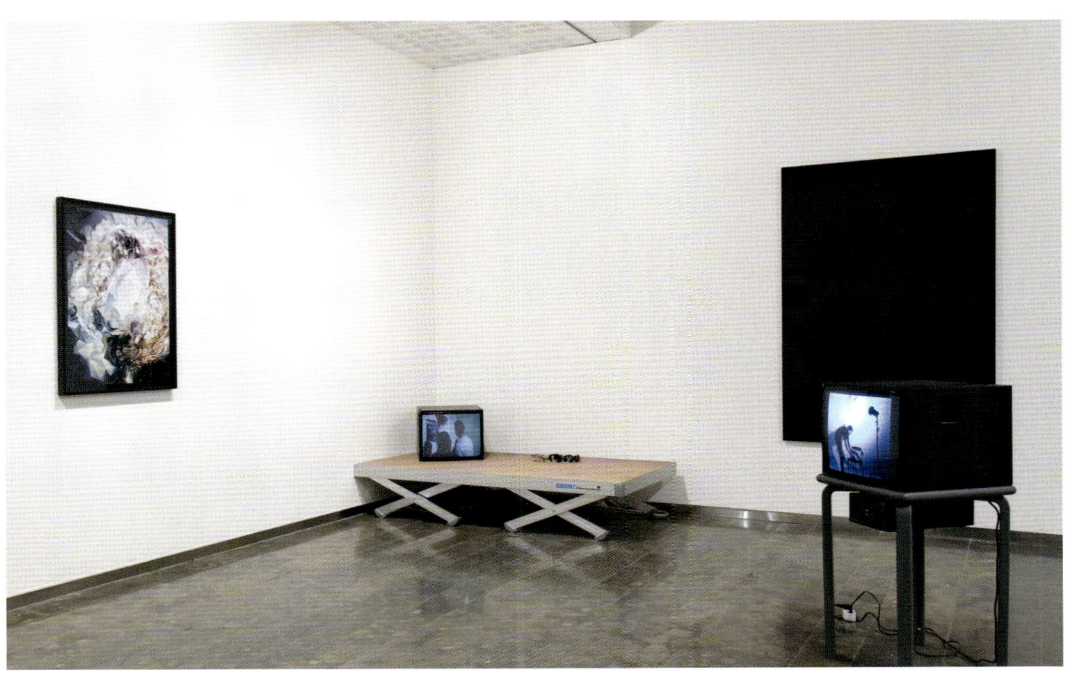

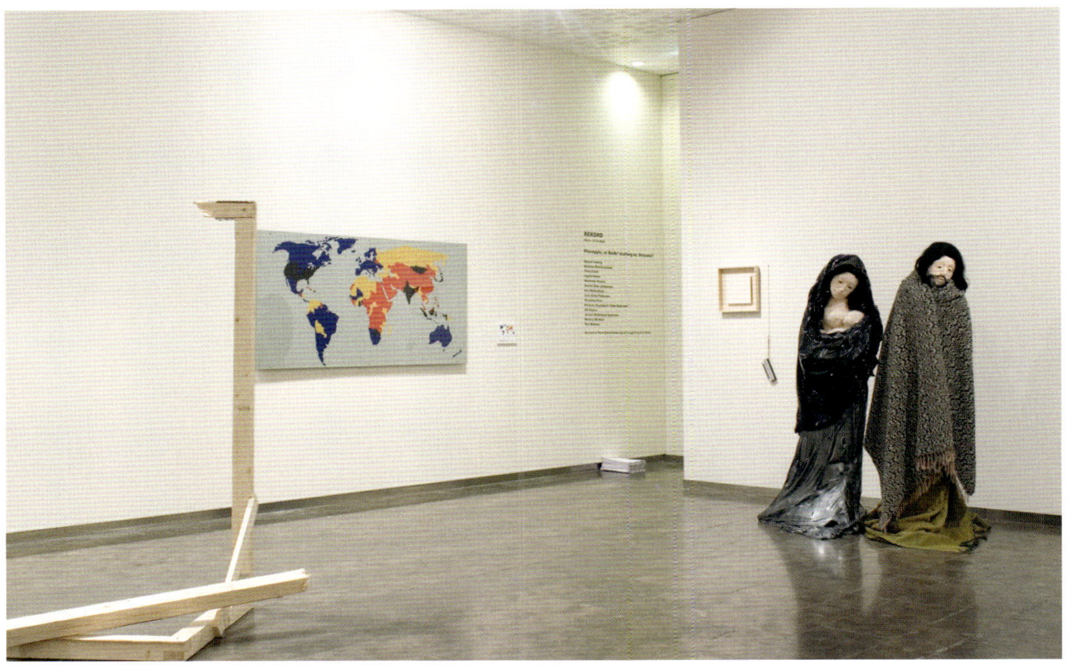

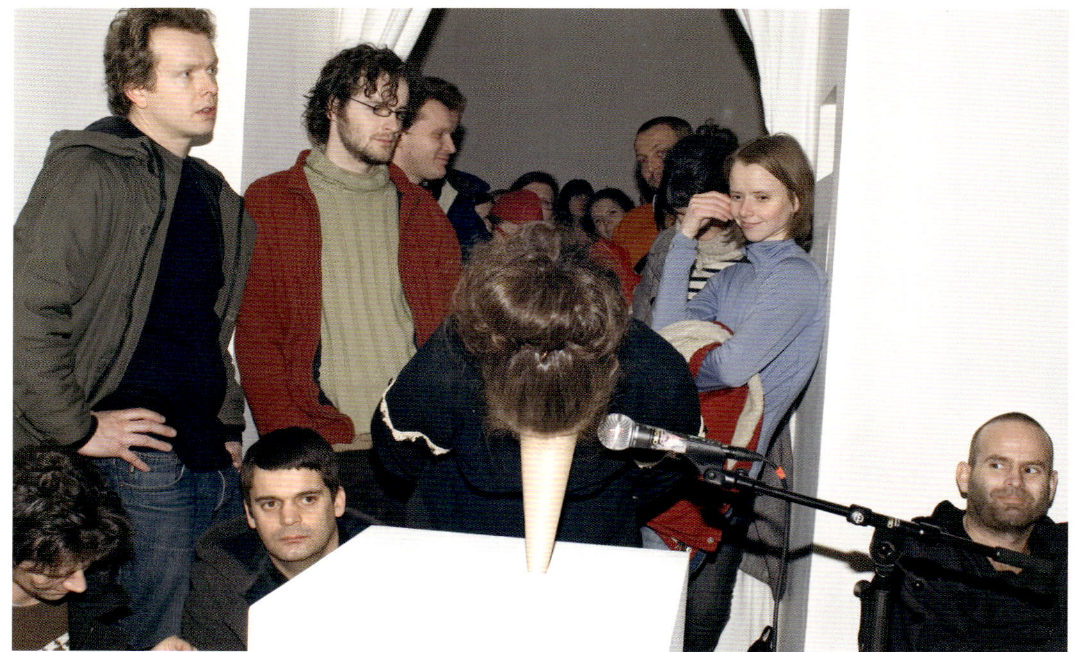

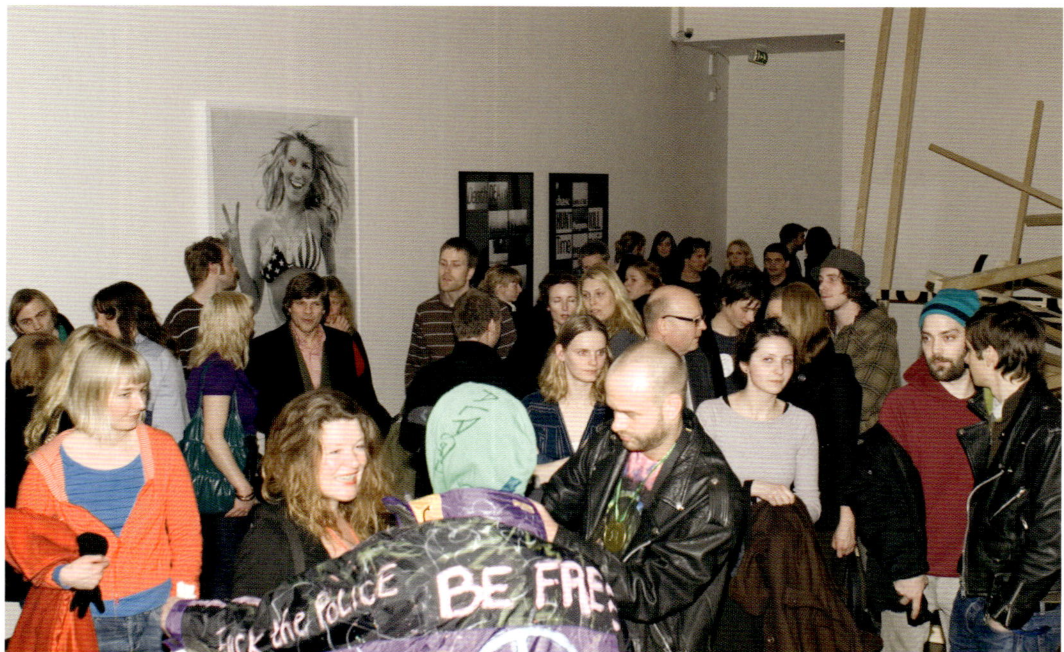

fuck the POLICE
BE FREE

Tori Wrånes
Doubtful Predator
In collaboration with Marte
Gunnufsen (accordeon)
and Jan Erik Mikalsen (saw)

Kristian Skylstad
Changes We Can Believe In, 2008
Performance and wall painting

Annette Stav Johanssen
Hang Safely Die Slowly, 2006
Video performance
Courtesy of the artist

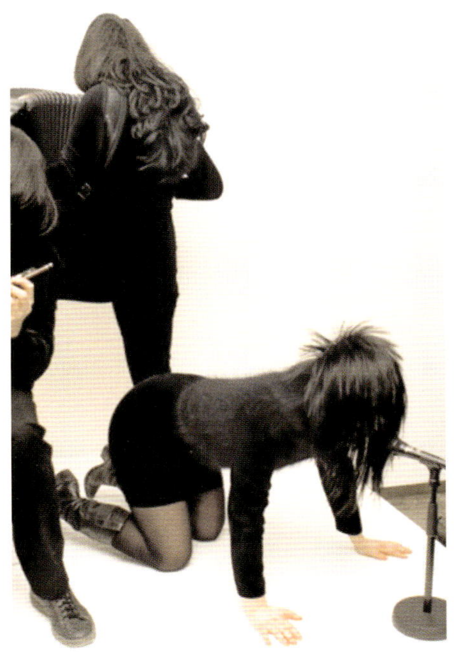

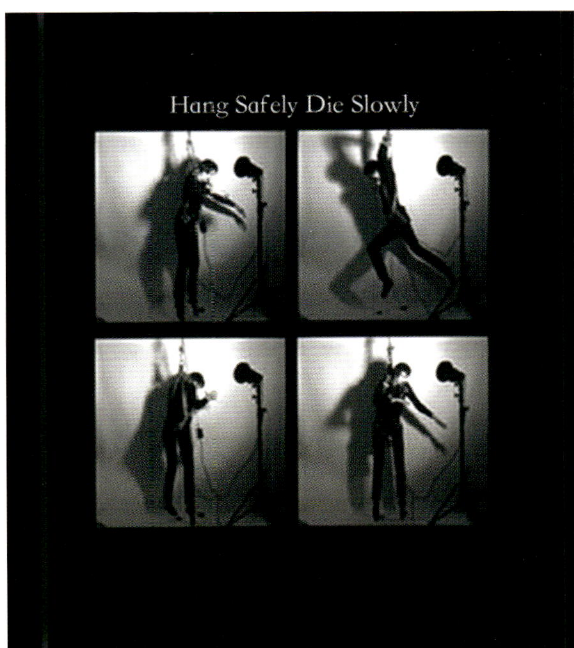

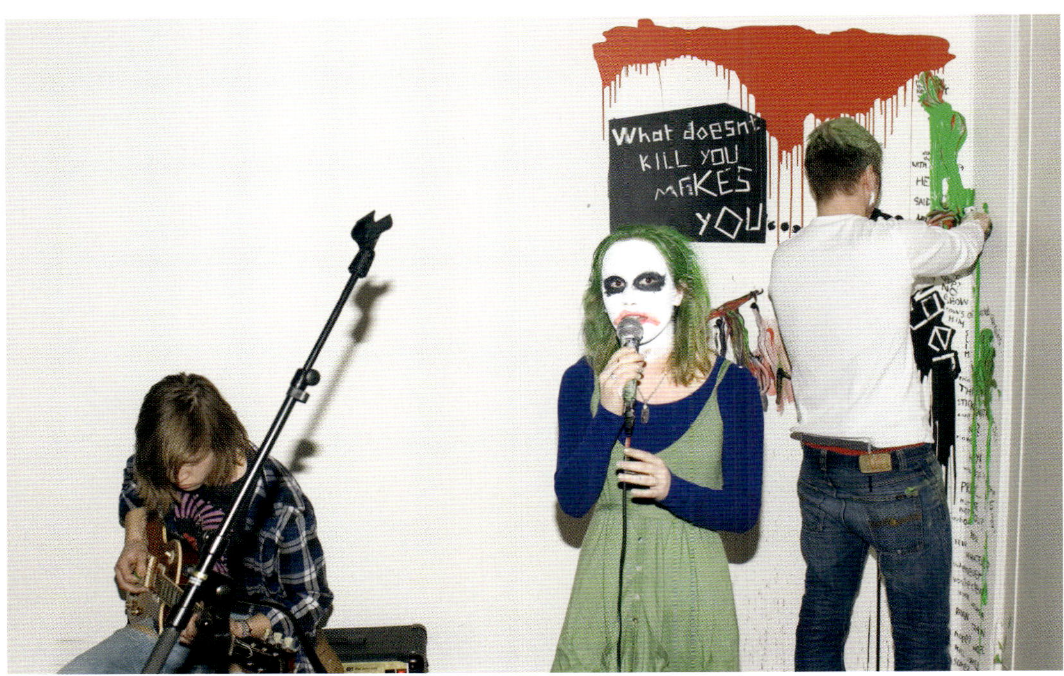

Linn Anita Pedersen
A page, 2008
Photograph, analogue print
50 x 60 cm
Courtesy of the artist

Christina Peel
Shigaraki After Dark, 2007
Silkscreen with fluorescent pigment
on porcelain and black light
30 x 30 cm
Courtesy of the artist

Ulf Styren
*Untitled (Models for a future
disaster)*, 2008
C-print on aluminium
60 x 80 cm
Courtesy of the artist

Are Mokkelbost
ION, 2nd Level, Omni #4, 2008
Paper collage
90 x 60 cm
Courtesy Aaron Turner

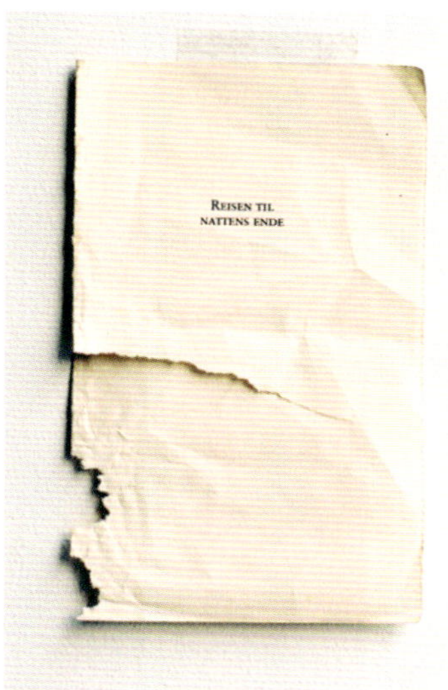

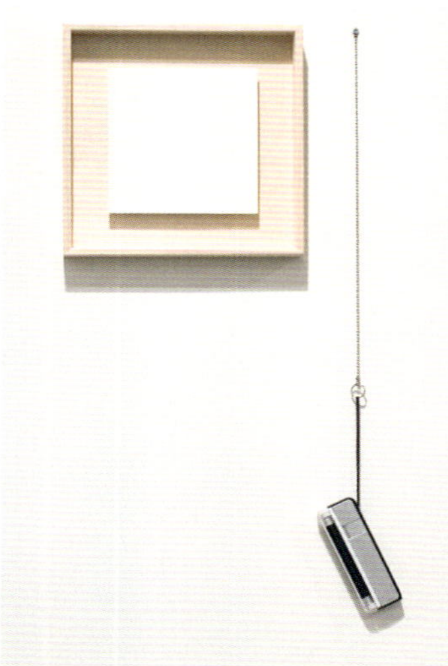

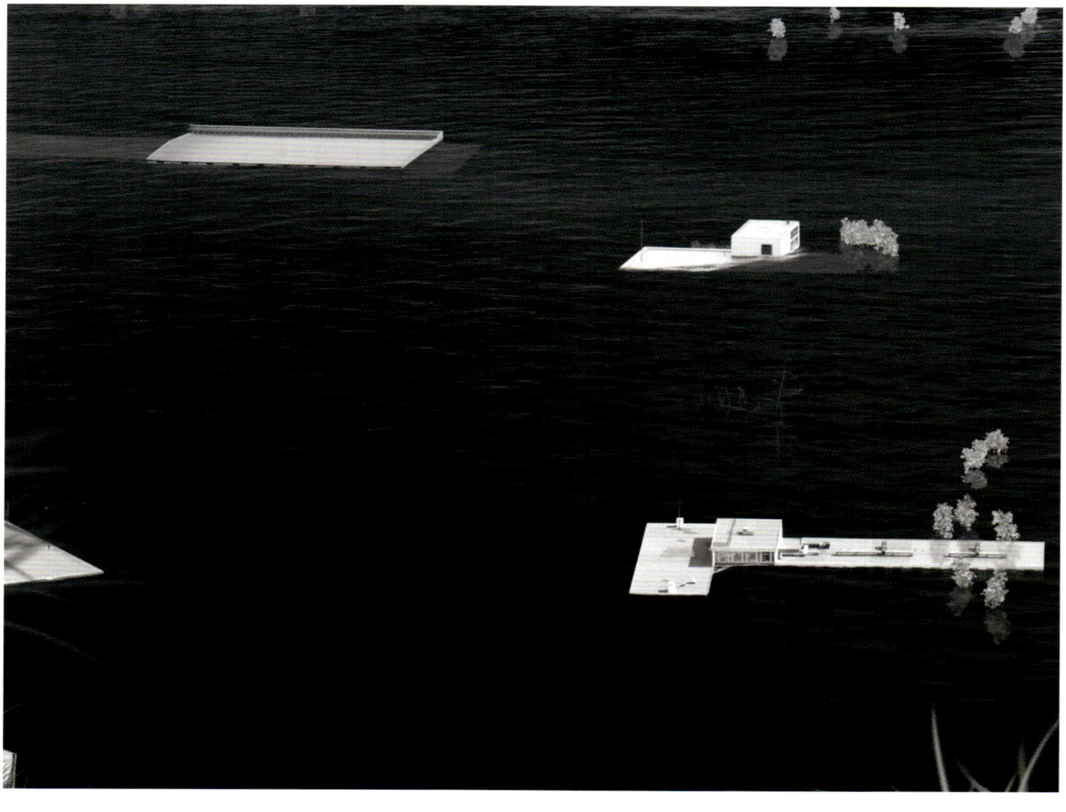

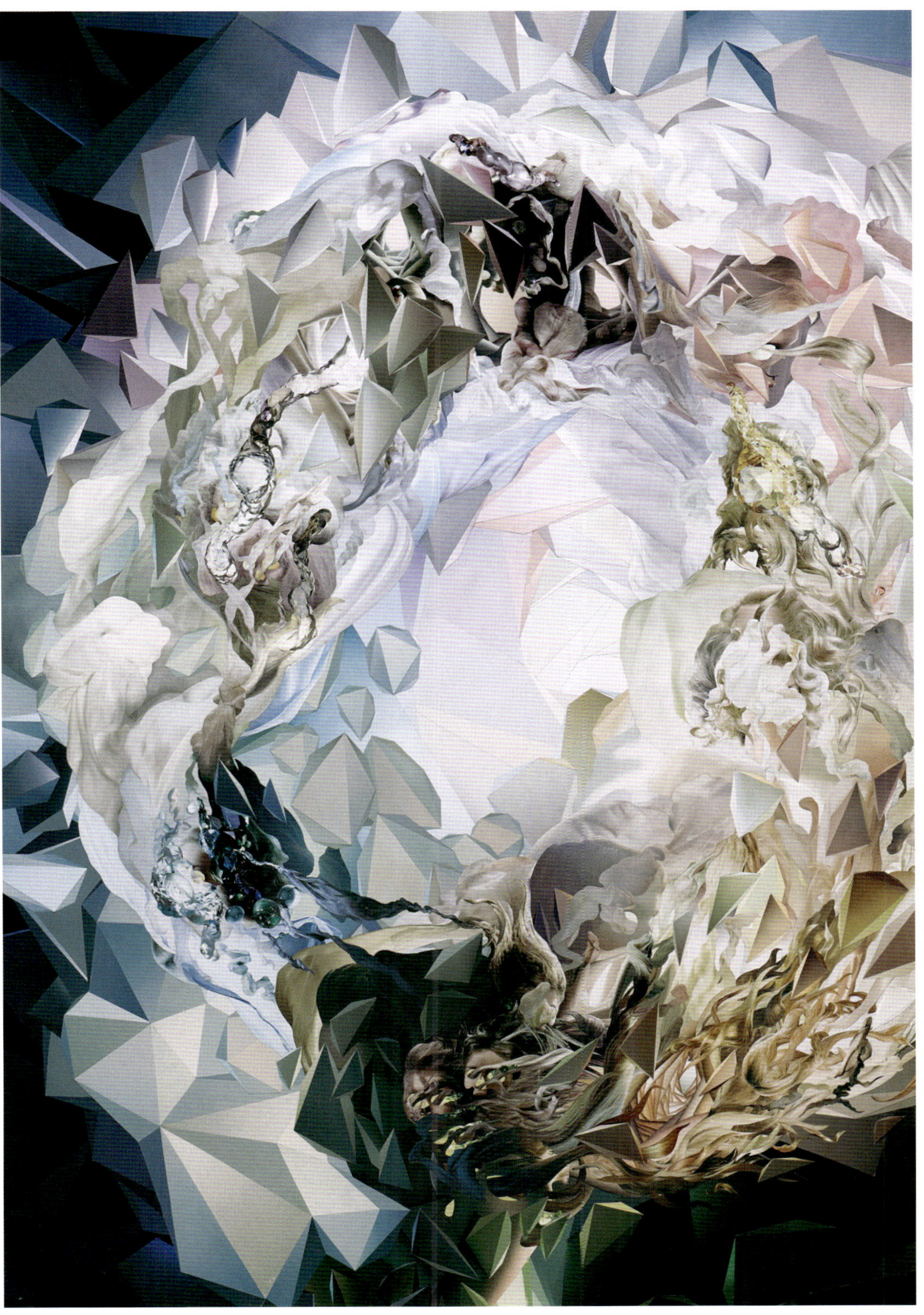

Linn Anita Pedersen
The defying moment, 2008
Sculpture, wood
90 x 173 x 206 cm
Courtesy of the artist

Jorunn Myklebust Syversen
Reach Out and Touch Faith.
Black, 2008
Light jet print, Diasec
186 x 125 cm
Courtesy of the artist

Kristian Øverland Dahl
Family, 2008
Acrylic, plaster, latex, tape,
cardboard, plastic, reinforcement
bars, construction foam,
brick, prosthesis
150 x 70 x 175 cm
Courtesy of the artist

Kjersti Andvig
Untitled, 2006
Knitting
90 x 180 cm
Snare/Christiansen Collection

Marianne Hurum
Creepy, crawly, rusting,
bustling, 2007
Oil on paper
65 x 50 cm
Courtesy of the artist

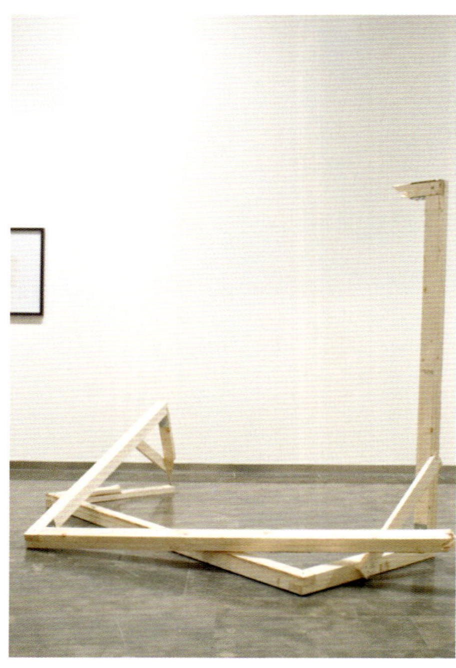

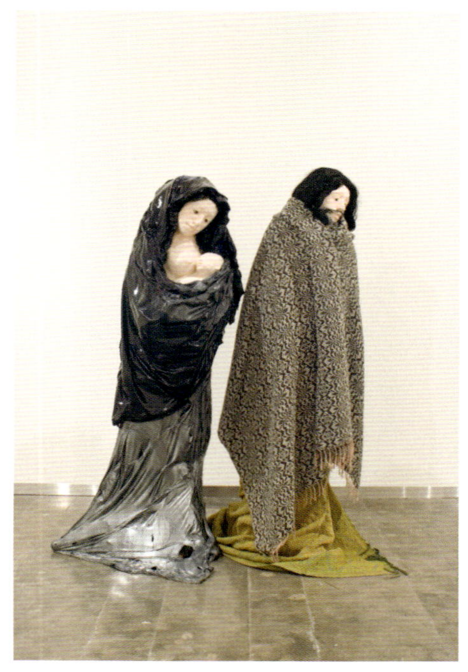

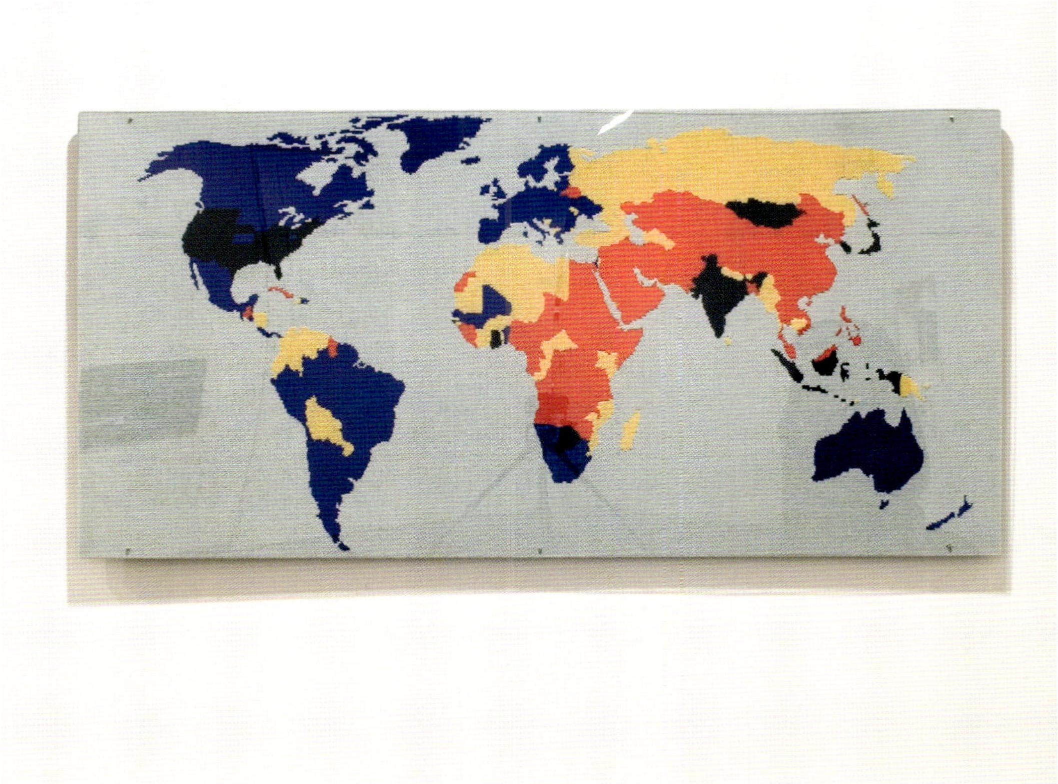

Gallery Overview

Ida Sannes Hansen

This overview presents a selection of commercial galleries profiling young Norwegian contemporary art. These arenas are important for giving exposure to young Norwegian artists, especially since the galleries function as the nexus between artists and private or public art collectors.

One unique aspect of 'Art Norway' is its artist centres: mediational networks run jointly by district organizations for the various artist groups. In all, 15 centres are operated by the district organizations and the following *fylker* (regions) are represented: Agder, Akershus, Buskerud, Hedmark, Hordaland, Møre og Romsdal, Nord-Norge, Oppland, Rogaland, Sogn og Fjordane, Sapmi, Telemark, Trøndelag, Vestfold and Østfold. The artist centres play critical roles in spreading information about young Norwegian art beyond the boundaries of Norway's large cities. Links to the various artist centres are found on the webpage http://www.kunstnersenter.no/

Young artists are also well represented in art societies throughout the country. These societies are gathered under one umbrella organization, Norsk Kunstforeninger (Norwegian Art Societies, NK), which has its main office in Oslo. NK's general goal is to strengthen and stimulate art experiences, to mediate art through the societies' network and to serve members' interests. NK also provides venues for the National Museum of Art, Architecture and Design, other art societies and artists who want to exhibit their works. Links to the art societies can be found on NK's webpage. http://www.kunstnersenter.no/

One of Norway's most important arenas for presenting and selling art by young Norwegian artists is Høstutstillingen, the major national contemporary art show. Begun in 1882 as a protest against the conservative Christiania Art Society, it has had a continuous tradition since its inception. Norske Billedkunstnere (Norwegian Visual Artists' Association) administers the Høstutstilling. http://www.billedkunst.no/hostutstillingen/

In 1988 Høstutstillingen received competition from the exhibition *Norske Bilder* (Norwegian Pictures), presented annually at the Rådhusgalleriet. Norske Bilder is produced in collaboration with Gallery Brandstrup, TV2 and the newspaper *Dagens Næringsliv*. http://norske-bilder.tv2.no/

There are also many important non-commercial actors not included in those mentioned above: for example, Bomuldsfabriken Kunsthall in Arendal, Bergen Kunsthall, Sørlandet's Art Museum, Vestfossen Kunstlaboratorium and Kunsthuset Kabuso in Øystese in Kvam Municipality to name a few. Although the importance of these actors must not be undervalued, they fall outside of the commercial focus of this presentation.

Fotogalleriet, in Møllergata, was established in 1977 through the initiative of Tom Sandberg and Dag Alveng. Its initial *raison d'être* was to set up a separate exhibition venue for photography. The gallery presents work by Norwegian and international contemporary artists working with camera-based art. Its exhibition programme is designed by artistic director Ida Kierulf in collaboration with an exhibition jury. The gallery's professional profile has lately expanded to include video art and photography as integrated aspects of larger expressions. The gallery aims to give young unestablished artists the possibility to produce large-format exhibitions within a professional framework. Fotogalleriet's spring exhibition and the Photographers' Annual Grant Exhibition are instantiations of this, and are produced jointly with *Forbundet Frie Fotografer*. While aiming to present the tradition of photographic art, Fotogalleriet also seeks to explore and expand the boundaries of what photography can be. http://fotogalleriet.no

GAD opened in the autumn of 2005 and is owned by its founder Alexandra Dyvi, who runs the gallery with general manager Knut Blomstrøm. GAD is a mobile gallery consisting of ten steel freight containers (semitrailers). Stacked in three levels, the entirety was designed by architect Magne Magler Wiggen. In autumn 2006 the structure moved from Tjuvholmen to Tøyen and now sits 20 meters from Munch Museum's main entrance. Since opening, GAD has held 18 exhibitions for Norwegian and international artists. It works with younger artists and mediates art through mass media, sales and group and single-artist exhibitions. Most art exhibited at GAD is sold to private collectors. http://www.gadart.no/

Gallery A and **Gallery A Minor** Founded in 2003 at Majorstuen by Andreas Engelstad, Gallery A and A Minor are today run with help from Mie Mortensen. The idea is to cultivate young talented artists who have the ability and desire to breakthrough as important contributors to the Norwegian and international art scene. Efforts are made to draw attention to the 'A team' through so-called UTVALG (selected) exhibitions, in which the gallery's regular artists exhibit their works. Nevertheless, debutants are also invited to participate in exhibitions held in December–January and June–August. Gallery A mostly sells to private customers and businesses, but also to the Norwegian state and to municipalities. http://www.galleri-a.no/

Gallery Brandstrup started in 1984 in Moss, under the management of Kim Brandstrup and his father. It now occupies an old manor house at Madserud allé in Oslo with Kim Brandstrup and Marit Gillespie as owners. Gallery Brandstrup presents national and international contemporary art, including works by Jeff Koons, Robert Morris, Bernd and Hilla Becher, Håkon Bleken and Inger Sitter. The gallery participates in the exhibition *Norske Bilder*, held at the Rådhusgalleriet (see above). This exhibition has been held nineteen times and highlights artists connected with Brandstrup. At the gallery's own premises temporary exhibitions are held monthly (on average), both in the main gallery and in the project room. Gallery Brandstrup also sells a large selection of fine art prints. http://www.brandstrup.no/

Gallery Erik Steen began in 2006 under the auspices of Erik Steen, former director of Gallery Wang. Located at Skøyen, this gallery annually produces six exhibitions of Norwegian and international contemporary art, with emphasis on younger Norwegian artists. Group and solo exhibitions are held in a separate gallery room and are marketed to buyers and actors involved in art institutions. The gallery also presents its artists at international art fairs. Another important aspect is the production and distribution of the gallery's own publications. Gallery Erik Steen contributes to the realization and production of new works which artists would not necessarily manage to carry out through their own economic means. Although buyers are chiefly private, the gallery also sells to key national and international collectors and institutional collections. www.eriksteen.no

Gallery Haaken at Frogner was set up in 1961 by Haaken A. Christensen. It aims to take responsibility for the young artists it represents and distinguishes itself by providing long-range exposure to the artists whose work it exhibits.

Gallery K (Skillebekk) has been a venue for Norwegian contemporary art in Oslo for more than 25 years. Run by gallerists Ben M. Frija and his wife Kristin Kløve Frija, Gallery K has presented important international contemporary art to the Norwegian art scene. Some of its many exhibitors include Candida Höfer, Thomas Struth, Andreas Gursky, Thomas Demand, Matthew Barney, Nan Goldin and Andres Serrano. Gallery K willingly presents young Norwegian contemporary art and focuses mainly on painting and photography. http://www.gallerik.com/

Gallery MGM opened in 2001 under the direction of Marina Gerner-Mathisen, with a view towards promoting young Norwegian artists living abroad. First located at Odinsgate, two years ago it moved into larger premises in the old Frogner fire station. Gallery MGM aims to promote artists internationally via several collaborative partners, its closest being c/o Atle Gerhardsen in Berlin. Recently the gallery brokered several public and private decorative commissions for its young artists. It sells 50/50 to private and public collections. http://www.gallerimgm.com/

Gallery Riis was first instituted in Trondheim in 1972, by Inger and Andreas L. Riis. Their private collection of artworks by the Cobra Group, Ecole de Paris and Norwegian art from the 1960s and 1970s was part of the initial incitement for becoming gallerists. Riis opened a second gallery in Oslo in 1980 and Espen Ryvarden began as director in 1984. Today the gallery is situated at Filipstad and focuses on Nordic contemporary art by promoting a selection of international artists. Its exhibition programme presents work in several media and expressions. http://www.galleririis.com/

KunstVerket opened in 1989 and is today run by Petter U. Morken and nine employees. With 150 square metres of gallery space located at Kampen, its core activities can be divided into three main areas: gallery/exhibitions, fine art print editions and brokering decorative commissions. KunstVerket presents a wide spectrum of techniques and forms of expression. The last three years it has participated in the National Academy of Art's diploma seminar and offered its exhibition room as a space for presenting student projects. KunstVerket's activities mainly focus on private companies, public and private institutions and private buyers and collectors. Its customers are primarily involved in private businesses. www.kunstverket.no

Lautom Contemporary first opened in April 2007 at Collettsgate 6, Oslo, by gallerists Randi Thommessen and Sigrid Haugen. The exhibition profile centres on younger Norwegian and Scandinavian artists and aims to present contemporary art at the frontier between Norwegian and international art scenes. The gallery also employs freelance curators for various projects. Lautom intends to promote its artists internationally, through collaborating with other galleries and via international art expositions. It sells mostly to private buyers. http://www.lautom.no/

STANDARD (OSLO), in the centre of Oslo, came into being in 2005. Its aim is to promote contemporary Norwegian artists internationally and to introduce international artists to a Norwegian audience. Several of STANDARD's artists have been included in internationally notable exhibitions: Venice Biennale (2005); documenta (2007); Sydney Biennial (2004); Istanbul Biennial (2005); Lyon Biennial (2007); Manifesta (2004); and Momentum – Nordic Art Festival (2000, 2004 and 2006). The gallery sells to private and public collections. http://www.standardoslo.no/v1/about.php

BERGEN

Galleri Bouhlou opened in 1994 and is run by Aicha Bouhlou. Located at Allégaten in Bergen's university district, the gallery has profiled key Norwegian artists such as A.K. Dolven, Per Barcley, Bård Breivik and Leonard Rickhard. It aims to distinguish Bergen in relation to Oslo by presenting some of the more prominent Norwegian artists. The gallery offers consulting as well as sales of art. http://www.bouhlou.no/

Gallery Gathe was initiated by Marianne S. Gathe in 2005. It has no deliberate intention of only presenting young artists, but focuses on projects or works that seek to communicate with the public. According to Marianne S. Gathe, the market in Bergen is entirely different from that in Oslo and very little innovative new contemporary art is sold. Insofar as there are sales, it is to private buyers. http://www.gallerigathe.no

Gallery NO. 5 opened in 2000 as Bergen Kunsthall's fifth exhibition room. It presents international and national contemporary art. The gallery seeks to be a flexible venue for newly educated as well as more established artists. Exhibitions cover a wide range: photography, drawing, painting, video and installation art. NO. 5 holds seven temporary exhibitions per year, parallel to Bergen Kunsthall's main exhibitions. It chiefly presents solo exhibitions but sometimes curated group exhibitions. NO. 5 is an important arena for presenting contemporary art, not only for the general art public but also for businesses, insofar as Bergen Kunsthall works actively with national and international collectors. Exhibitors at NO. 5 are continuously evaluated for private and public decorative commissions due to Bergen Kunsthall's brokering activities. The gallery sells 50/50 to private and public customers. http://www.kunsthall.no/no5/index.php

Gallery S·E – International Contemporary Art has been operating for 12 years, now in new premises at the old Hansa Brewery at Kalfaret in Bergen. It has become one of Scandinavia's largest private galleries for international art. The gallery has many customers and good contacts with artists and galleries worldwide. This allows it to present young Norwegian artists and help strengthen their profiles internationally. Gallery S·E has been represented at art expositions such as *LA Art* in New York and *Art Copenhagen*. While most customers are private buyers, the gallery works actively to sell to museums. http://www.galleri-se.no/

ASKER

Gallery Trafo first opened its doors in 2006 in a defunct electricity transformer station in Asker. It consists of three galleries: Trafo 1, 2 and 3. The exhibitions are set up by Bjørn Carlsen and

Halvard Haugerud in partnership with the general manager. The first floor is the main exhibition room of Gallery Trafo 1 and functions more along the lines of a 'kunsthall', i.e., it focuses on more experimental, contemporary artistic expressions. Ingunn Stuvøy manages this gallery. Trafo 2, under the direction of Sigmund Skullerud Bakken, although in many respects similar to Trafo 1, is more focused on commissioned sales. Amongst the many works presented is a wide selection of fine art prints. Trafo 3 is the location of the public Asker Art Collection; this also includes many fine art prints but is a permanent collection. Trafo's ambition is to become one of the most important galleries for contemporary art in Norway. http://www.galleritrafo.no/forside.html

ØSTFOLD

Gallery F 15 began in 1966 and has been a significant promoter of contemporary art in Norway and other Nordic countries since its inception. The name derives from the address 'Fossen 15' in Moss, the gallery's first location. Since 1967 it has borrowed Alby Farm's main building from Moss Municipality, and still operates from that location. Gallery F 15 is a non-commercial gallery run on public funds. It does not own its own collection. The exhibition profile heavily favours Norwegian, Nordic and international contemporary art, but also presents traditional visual art from time to time. In 2006 Gallery F 15 and Momentum Nordic Art Festival consolidated into a new limited company called Punkt Ø, under the direction of Dag Aak Sveinar. http://www.gallerif15.no/

Gallery Henrik Gerner originated in 2003 when Gallery Brandstrup chose to discontinue its activity in Moss. The gallery is run by Dag Modal, former gallerist at Brandstrup. It profiles Norwegian and international contemporary art with main focus on pictorial art. Approximately ten exhibitions are mounted in its main gallery space annually, with as many in its 'intimate' gallery. http://www.ghg.as/

HEDMARK

Kunstbanken Hedmark was founded in 1996 in the old 'Bank of Norway' building in Hamar. Its founders were the County Council and the various artist organizations in Hedmark. Such collaboration between artist organizations and a regional government is unique in the Norwegian context. The art centre's activities span a wide range of initiatives: the gallery, travelling exhibitions, public commissions, seminars, consulting and information services. Kunstbanken presents art from Norway and abroad. Its exhibition profile aims to present a manifold of artistic expressions with emphasis on experimental and innovative art. Recently Kunstbanken has distinguished itself through its autumn performance weekends, collaborative projects with National Academy of Art, Oslo. Kunstbanken sells to both private and public buyers and its exhibition programme varies from year to year. http://www.kunstbanken.no/

BUSKERUD

Gallery Van Bau first opened in 2005 as part of Arena Vestfossen, a defunct factory with 4000 square meters now used for artist studios, production spaces and studios for designers, producers and contemporary artists. Located on the first floor of the building, next to Vestfossen Kunstlaboratorium, Gallery Van Bau has 240 square meters at its disposal. The gallery spotlights young, newly established artists and sells chiefly to private collectors. http://vanbau.no/

STAVANGER

Gallery Opdahl started in 1987 through the initiative of Arve Opdahl. It moved to its present 300 square meter location in 2005. In 2007 it opened a gallery space in Berlin, in the neighbourhood between Mitte and Kreuzberg. Gallery Opdahl has for several years operated vis a vis the international art arena by presenting its artists at international art exhibitions such as *Art Forum Berlin* and *Art Copenhagen*. The interaction between established and young art scenes generates an exciting exhibition activity and gives the public and artists opportunities for new dialogues. Gallery Opdahl caters to private and public customers but its main focus remains on the private sector. www.galleriopdahl.com

Transit Art Space was inaugurated in 2005. Its prime mover, Einar Børresen, started with international group exhibitions of younger artists. The gallery has gradually migrated towards solo exhibitions of young artists. Meanwhile, it also presents solo exhibitions of internationally known artists and more established Norwegian artists. In 2006 Transit Art Space had a stand at *Art Copenhagen* and *VOLTA* in Basel (it was invited as one of eight Nordic galleries in the 'Nordic Focus' section). The gallery has thus far sold to private collectors and businesses. www.transitartspace.com

TRONDHEIM

Gallery Ismene commenced in 1982 with a focus on leading Norwegian and international contemporary artists. Its owner and general director is Per Høiem. As well as holding solo exhibitions, the gallery also focuses on fine art print editions and portfolios. Ismene alternates between presenting established and younger artists, and has shown everything from Håkon Bleken (b. 1929) to the exhibition *Ung kunst I dag II* (Young Art Today II) in November 2007. http://www.ismene.no/

Gallery 7011 was founded in 2006 through the initiative of Sverre Koren Bjertnæs. Today it is run by general manager Svein Roar Grande. 7011's profile is international and its goal is to provide a scene for contemporary art in Trondheim. The exhibition programme mostly shows nationally and internationally known artists, but will also present un-established artists who are deemed to become key actors in future. http://www.7011.biz/

Alternative Art Spaces

Ida Sannes Hansen

Alternative galleries in Norway have experienced a flowering in recent years with the growth of artist-run exhibition spaces and curatorial groups. Line Ulekleiv describes this tendency in *Norsk Kunstårbok* for 2006 (Norwegian Art Yearbook), and points out that artist-run galleries first began in Norway in the 1990s. The most well-known galleries from this first generation are Ole Jørgen Ness's at Herslebsgate 10 in Oslo, Per Gunnar Tverrbak's gallery called Otto Plonk in Bergen, and Frode Saugestad and Bjarne Melgaard's NAF (Norwegian Anarchistic Fraction). Later came Melgaard's Institute for Civil Disobedience at Teatergata in Oslo.

Today's alternative art spaces, Ulekleiv claims, can be a reaction to the consolidation of national museums in 2003, but also a result of the radical increase in artists who have completed their education in the last decade. Nevertheless, it can seem that the motivation for today's alternative galleries is propelled by the freedom artists seek, to produce their own exhibitions and to define for themselves the framework for presenting works. As such, the situation today can be read more as a parallel, yet independent, 'settling of accounts' with established art institutions, rather than a clear opposition.

The alternative galleries have often been described in the Norwegian art news and even addressed in a special edition-supplement in the journal *ArtReview*, in a discussion of the Norwegian art scene. Artist-operated galleries often use mass media and Internet to create debate and interest for their projects. One example is when the young art scene held an art fair 7 May 2007. This was initiated by the Member's Club, a curatorial group from the National Academy of Art in Bergen (KHiB), and PrøveRommet. The exposition appropriated and manipulated strategies used at international art fairs such as the Frieze Art Fair, but focused on non-commercial artist-run galleries and curatorial groups. Invited participants included Bastard Oslo, Drontheim Trondheim, Lautom Contemporary Oslo, Rekord Oslo, Rakett Bergen/Rotterdam, TAFKAG (The Gallery Formerly Known As Galuzin) Oslo, The White Tube Oslo and Torpedo Oslo.

Most alternative art spaces keep regular contact with one another at national and international levels. The Internet page http://www.underskog.no is indispensable for the young art scene, for it provides a closed cultural network through which artists and others in the cultural milieu can keep in touch. Underskog also posts an events calendar of exhibition openings, lectures and happenings.

The following is an overview of the alternative and non-commercial galleries in Norway. Each art space has been contacted via email and the presentation is based on what they themselves offered. In cases where it has been difficult to gather information, the text is based on Internet sources. Our focus is on projects run by graduates from Norwegian art schools and academies. Given the field's constant state of flux, this is far from a complete overview – some art spaces are being discontinued and new projects are in the process of being set up.

OSLO

0047 is an exhibition/project space for non-commercial art and architectural projects. The gallery started in Berlin in 2004 with a view towards promoting Norwegian art and architecture. It quickly gained an international profile through more than thirty exhibitions involving 130 artists, architects and curators. Since 2007, the gallery has been located in an old factory building in Schweigaardsgate 34 at Grønland, and is presently run by Marianne Zamecznik, Espen Røyseland, Øystein Rø and Elisabeth Byre. Public and private sponsors enable 0047 to challenge and expand the exhibition framework. It consists of an exhibition space and an 'event space': both are available for workshops, film presentations and happenings. http://www.projekt0047.com

http://www.artoslo.com/ is a website set up in 2000 as an 'exhibition space' for young Norwegian contemporary artists from Oslo. It is run by artist Andrew Barton. His idea is to bring together clever artists who can create a synergistic network and draw upon one another's network of galleries, curators, collectors and so forth. Although the website is non-commercial, several artists have managed to arrange exhibitions through it.

Atopia was established in 2003 by the artists Farhad Kalantary, Michel Pavlou, Annebeth Grundtvig Hansen, Inger Lise Hansen and Gerg Pope (the latter joined in from 2006). This artist-initiated project space and parallel art project promotes film and video art in Oslo and abroad. As an umbrella organization for diverse projects involving film and video art, Atopia has, since 2003, organized over 100 screenings in its own local as well as other places in Oslo. The chief objective is to create a grassroots movement of experimentation, interaction and discussion between artists on national and international levels. Atopia holds 'Video Forum' once a month; here works in progress, new works and historically important films are presented. The gallery has also experimented with video art in the public sphere. Atopia explores theoretical discourses on film and video art. http://atopia.no

Bastard is an Oslo-based project room located on Uelandsgate, which was opened in 2005 by artists Anders Smebye and Marius Engh. Today the gallery is run by Smebye. Instead of adopting the usual 'alternative' position, part of the impetus for Bastard is the grey area between alternative project rooms, commercial galleries and established institutions. Bastard draws upon an international network of self-organized galleries and collectives, simultaneously as its focus on Oslo's art scene remains intact. Exhibitions are arranged collaboratively and artists mount their own works. Exhibition durations are short and intense – often no more than a fortnight. http://www.bastardene.com

Gallery 21:24, 21:25 and **21:26** are located behind the old Vestbanen (Oslo's former train station for south-west-bound trains). Since 1991 it has functioned as a gallery for the National Academy of Art, Oslo. Originally called Gallery 21.25, during the mid-1990s it developed into two 'white cubes' (21:24 and 21:25). An additional 'flexible gallery' (21:26) can turn up almost anywhere, also on Internet. The galleries are primarily intended for students at Oslo's Art Academy, yet other national and international artists can apply. The three galleries present between forty and fifty exhibitions annually: exhibitions open on Thursday evenings and last through the weekend. http://www.khio.no/Norsk/Aktuelt/Galleri_2124_og_2125/

Galleri 69 opened in the autumn of 2004, in connection with Grünerløkka Airport's tenth anniversary. The gallery was initiated by general director Anja Skjulstad, board member Gidsken Braadlie and artist/curator Cathrine Constanse. Gallery 69 presents monthly exhibitions produced expressly for the space, yet with a non-commercial profile. Exhibitions are based on a wide selection of high-quality artistic expressions. The gallery is under the jurisdiction of the Grünerløkka Lufthavn Foundation, which also operates Café Mir – practice rooms for musicians and work spaces for artists. http://www.lufthavna.no/

Gallery Bang started in 2003 under the motto 'Gallery Bang is contemporary art'. Its founders are Kristian Ø Dahl and Sten Are Sandbeck. Through webpages, exhibitions and participating in art shows, the gallery presents artists for extended periods. The selected artists maintain a high level of artistic practice, but for various reasons are not well-known. The gallery will soon begin presenting art in published form. http://www.galleribank.com

Gallery Barbara Hansen / 33 Basement is an internationally oriented exhibition and project space for contemporary art. It is run by Hjørdis Kurås but is also rented to others who work with exhibiting art, or to artists who need space for temporary projects. Hjørdis Kurås deems the most important curatorial task is to dismantle the commercially-oriented contemporary art scene and to re-evaluate exhibitions as closed circuits. She also aims to dissolve the trend of over-curated exhibitions by offering space to artists who themselves will create the context in which their works are presented. This allows greater room for manoeuvre with regard to trial and error, exploration and research. 33 Basement's purpose is to create an active environment in which to develop and produce free, artistic and non-commercial films, videos and other expressions, and to aid the distribution and presentation of such work. These objectives are realized through exhibitions, seminars and theme nights, and by using the gallery as a national and international forum. http://www.galleribarbarahansen.com/

Gallery Galuzin / TAFKAG (The Art Space Formerly Known As Galuzin) was instituted in 2005 through the initiative of Maria Almås Frantzen, Ivan Galuzin, Kristian Skylstad, Sindre Randen Tufte Johnson. Its purpose is to create dialogue between the international and Norwegian art scenes. Galuzin helped put the alternative art scene on the map, partly because *Osloplus.no* recognized it as Oslo's most important gallery in 2006. The project has since developed into TAFKAG (The Art Space Formerly Known As Galuzin), run by Galuzin and Skylstad until June 2007. In April 2008, Ivan Galuzin will open a project called *The Brown Cube* at Finnskogen, with an opening exhibition and festival called 'The Gathering'. Kristian Skylstad has planned a gallery project with Tommy Olsson on Svalbard called *The Ice Cube*, projected to open in August 2009. http://www.myspace.com/tafkakc

Gallery NB8 is an art presentation space run by National Academy of Art, Oslo. It is used by the Faculty of Visual Arts and the Faculty of Design. Opened in 2007, it presents student work as well as work by external artists. http://www.khio.no/Norsk/Aktuelt/Galleri_Nb8/

Gallery Rekord came into being in September 2006 and is operated by Thora Dolven Balke, Eirin Støen and Ingvild Langgård. It aims to present a wide register of international and Norwegian contemporary art, including performance, music and scenography. Rekord considers alternative gallery spaces as important fora for challenging the definitory power of established art institutions. The gallery actively promotes artists according to artists' own conditions, and presents experimental, situational and temporal projects. www.gallerirekord.no

Gallery Schouberg began in 2006 at a location in Heggedal, through the initiative of Aage Moltke Schou and Marthe Berger Walthinsen. In 2007 the gallery moved to a purpose-built 'white cube' in Asker Kulturhus. As an artist-run, non-profit space for the younger art scene, it is not necessarily restricted to the Asker location and operates according to project periods. Exhibitions are supported by Asker Kulturhus and arranged in collaboration with the *STUP Series* – a cultural series promoting young, innovative expressions within the fields of music, dance and performance. www.gallerischouberger.com

Impromptu Gallery is an artist-run, non-commercial project run by Linn Lervik and Torine Helland. Its purpose is to create a forum for artist presentations and to encourage academic discussions on contemporary art. Impromptu's street address is Maridalsveien 90 in Oslo and it is funded by the *Visual Artists' Compensation Fund*. http://www.impromptu.no/

No. 9 Presentation Room for Contemporary Art / No. 9 in Exile No. 9 was started by Vilde von Krogh in 2001, in Oslo's former Cartoon Series Museum. Christian Arneberg Bould became co-director of the project in 2002. The concept later changed its name to No. 9 in Exile, and although the activity level is limited due to the lack of a permanent location, the project has continued for the last three years in an ambulatory mode. No. 9 in Exile has collaborated with Gallery Galuzin and Gallery Barbara Hansen / 33 Basement. In addition, it continues to arrange the self-initiated Oslo Art Festival, an annual presentation of artist-run alternative spaces in the Oslo area. Open to the public for one long weekend, the festival offers exhibitions, performances and concerts. In the last seven years No. 9 has presented over 170 artists and received two prizes: *Gullpølsa* (Golden Hot Dog) for its extraordinary efforts on behalf of Norway's cartoon series milieu, and *SKA-TV Art Award* for best artist-run gallery of the year 2000.

Nordic Art Info Gallery opened to the public in the spring of 2003 and operates under the aegis of Hanne Storm Ofteland and Jan Valentin Sæther. Nordic Art Info's objective is to inform the public about Nordic contemporary art. Between 2001 and 2003 it published *Barokkminimalist*, an Internet-based magazine for art criticism. Thus far Nordic Art Info has concentrated on working with Norwegian visual artists, but its ambition is to create a platform for young Nordic art. http://www.nordicart.info/

Oslo Project Room is an artist-run arena conjoined with a studio co-operative of c. 75 artists and designers. The gallery's purpose is to present a wide range of exhibitions and projects. A five-artist committee determines the exhibition schedule and evaluates applications from those seeking to use the exhibition space. Exhibitors themselves mount their own works and attend to all practical details of their exhibitions. Oslo Project Room in Lakkegata also holds summer and Christmas exhibitions for its co-operative artists. http://osloprosjek-trom.no/

Podium, at Hausmannsgate 34, has developed along the lines of a monthly club concept since the spring of 2003. Here artists can try out their works at various stages of development in an unpretentious social setting. The idea is to stimulate exploration of one's own and others' expressive forms in ways that cut across disciplinary boundaries and production milieus. Podium arranges live evening art programmes every month – mostly characterized by the actual contributing actors. With its centre of gravity on the live format, Podium evenings can accommodate installation, video, sound and performance art. In addition to live events, PODIUMforum holds workshops, seminars and artist salons. Through PODIUMlab, a wide range of actors are invited to do basic research on their own work methods and expressive forms, which are spawned from a manifold of larger research projects. Podium is run by a network of partners under the present directorship of Snorre Hvamen, Elin Høyland and Miriam Prestøy Lie. It is a collaborative project with Black Box Theatre and Kulturhuset Hausmann BA, and receives funding from Arts Council Norway. http://www.blackbox.no/podium

Sound of Mu, an exhibition and concert location with a bar, first opened its doors in 2005. Since then, its goal has been to create an environment in which so-called alternative cultures can find a foothold. Sound of Mu has a high level of activity, insofar as it held 350 productions in 2007 and opens new temporary exhibitions every fortnight. 15 artists, musicians, and people working with film and computers jointly run the place. Compared to more traditional art spaces, Sound of Mu's hybrid of activities, informal atmosphere and large window onto Markveien at Grunerløkka all work to lower the threshold for encountering contemporary art. The complex profile often creates chance interactions between the public and the various artistic genres. This has inspired the curated exhibition series *Sound of MUtation*, 'genre encounters' between musicians and visual artists. Several artists have also created installations related to the social situation at Sound of Mu. To bring diverse cultural expressions together is a chief goal, and the collaborative partners are many. In addition to visual artists, orchestras, bands, journals and publishing houses, Sound of Mu has collaborated on events with UKS, Atopia, Atelier Nord, Oslo Open, Kortfilmfestivalen I Grimstad, Dans for voksne, Landmark, Cinemateket, Nypoesi, Ny Musikk, Cosmopolite and other entities. http://www.soundofmu.no/

The White Tube (TWT) is an artist-run window showcase gallery in the public passageway at Tøyen subway station. The gallery is operated by G.U.N. Ladies, with support from the public transportation company Oslo Sporveier, Arts Council Norway and Relief Fund for Visual Artists. The artist group G.U.N. Ladies includes Sabina Jacobsson, Camilla Øyhus, Mariken Kramer, Madeleine Park and Hanne Rangul. TWT functions as a hybrid between public art and a gallery space. It uses Tøyen subway station's unique location insofar as it is close to the Munch Museum, Tøyen Swimming Pool and Oslo's Botanical Garden. This gives exhibiting artists great opportunities to reach a wide spectrum of the public – people with disparate backgrounds and tourists from all over the world. The gallery is non-commercial in the sense that its main objective is to present art, but it also sells works if interested parties contact G.U.N. Ladies' webpage. http://www.thegunladies.com/

Torpedo was founded in 2005 and is run by Elin Maria Olaussen, Karen Tandberg, Pia Søndergaard, Anna Carin Hedberg and Eivind Slettemeås. This is Oslo's first independent bookshop specializing in contemporary art publications, theory and visual culture. In addition to the bookshop, Torpedo produces and presents exhibitions, seminars, concerts and book launchings, in collaboration with artists, curators, self-organized networks and institutions. Torpedo established its own publishing house called Torpedo Press in 2006. Visibility and contacts with the public and the artworld happen largely through Torpedo's own catalogues and webpages, but also through alternative forms of distribution and existing archives such as Sjön (Sweden), Kiosk (Denmark), art book expositions and festivals such as NY Art Book Fair (USA) and Small Publishers Fair (UK). http://www.torpedobok.no/

UKS Gallery The Young Artists' Society began in 1921. Since its inception it has sought to ensure the social and artistic rights young artists. During the 1970s UKS was part of the vanguard of artists' battling for economic rights in the welfare society. In recent years the struggle for recognition of new artistic expressions has been a central issue. Meanwhile the embers of the political battle have once again burst into flame. With today's UKS membership at about 1000, it is a pivotal actor in making young contemporary art visible. The journal *UKS Forum* is published biannually. UKS maintains a portfolio archive to be used by the public and curators alike: here young artists who have exhibited in the gallery, or are members of UKS, can post their CVs and archive documentation of works. UKS collaborates with many actors in the cultural arena. Recently it held *Performance Program 2007* in partnership with Black Box Theatre in Oslo. http://www.uks.no/

Willy Wonka Inc. is an artist-run provisional art space and a curatorial group whose members are Lina Viste Grønli, Arild Tveito, Ida Ekblad, Anders Nordby, Lars Laumann and Nils Bech. It has held international exhibitions for, among others, Gallery Karma International, Zurich in August 2007, and Milwaukee International Art Fair in Wisconsin in 2006. http://www.indexof.no/

BERGEN

Flaggfabrikken is a centre for photography and visual art. Founded in 2003 by ten artists/photographers, it is a regional competency centre based in Bergen. The gallery is operated on a volunteer basis by c. ten members. The present group includes Hilde Jørgensen, Anne Szefer Karlsen, Kjetil Kausland, Olaf Knarvik, Åse Løvgren, Kjersti Solberg Monsen, Heidi Nikolaisen, Arne Skaug Olsen, Ulf Styren, Kristin Tårnesvik and Maya Økland. The webpages state that 'Flaggfabrikken's goal is to strengthen competency in camera-based art throughout Bergen and Vestlandet, and to work to make camera-based art in particular, and contemporary art in general, more visible in society'. Flaggfabrikken also holds monthly presentations of work at the art space Landmark at Bergen Kunsthall. http://www.flaggfabrikken.net/

Gallery Fisk is a non-profit student-run gallery. Begun in 2001 in an old fishmonger's shop in Kong Oscarsgate, it is run on a voluntary basis by six students from the National Academy of Art in Bergen (KHiB). Mia Øquist is the present director. Fisk is a space where students from Norwegian and European academies can present their work. It holds approximately nine exhibitions every six months. With support from KHiB and Bergen's committee for cultural affairs, Fisk's goal is to be part of KHiB's external profile and to give Bergensians a glimpse of what is happening at the school in terms of contemporary art and design. http://www. khib.no/khib/visningsrom/galleri_fisk

Lydgalleriet is an experimental arena for Norwegian and international room-based sound art and interdisciplinary artworks with sound as a fundamental element. The gallery is located in a former shop at Østre Skostredet 3 in Bergen centre. The gallery room is 130 sqm and is adjoined to a 50 sqm salesroom. Organized as a foundation, Lydgalleriet was initiated by an interdisciplinary group of artists, art historians and others working in the cultural field. Its purpose is to present sound-based contemporary art to a wide public in an appropriate space. The context and conditions for presentation should be adaptable to each individual artwork. Lydgalleriet wants to inform the public about sound art and audio culture through the production and mediation of sound art, but it also aims to help shape the conditions for the public art discourse. Lydgalleriet seeks to contribute to developing and challenging a field which is presently undergoing expansion, and to initiate new expressions through collaborative partnerships and new models of production. The gallery sells time-based expressions on commission, sound-curiosa, and sells and rents out high-quality sound systems for optimal multi-channel sound art reproductions and related art forms. Lydgalleriet also does technical experimentation in order to develop optimal sound conditions and frameworks for experiencing sound. http://www. lydgalleriet.no

Rakett began in 2003 through the initiative of artists Åse Løvgren and Karolin Tampere. The duo work in a hybrid field between art and curatorial activities, and continuously alternate between the roles of curator, producer, artist, organizer and publicist. Rakett's projects take an interdisciplinary approach and function as platforms for cooperation. The group has produced exhibitions for art institutions, galleries, artist-run project spaces and public spaces, but as a mobile project, their works tend to be site-specific and to focus on creating a meeting point for communication. Curated exhibitions are often short and present non-commercially oriented ephemeral art. http://www.rakett.biz

TRONDHEIM

Babel is the presentation room at Lademoen Kunstnerverksteder (artist workshops) (LKV). It sees itself as something between a gallery and a workshop because every year, between 12 and 18 artists from across the world come to work at LKV for periods of one to three months. It is these artists who use the space. Babel is run and administered by Foundation Lademoen Kunstnerverksteder through the directorship of Kristina Karlsen and funded by Trondheim municipality, Sør Trøndelag Region, Torstein Erbos Gavefond and Arts Council Norway. LKV also offers a studio for one year to a graduate of one of Norway's three art academies. http://babel.teks.no/

Gallery Blunk is a non-profit gallery run by young artists in Trondheim since 2002. Its webpages state that 'the main goal is to be an arena for art students and newly established artists, so they can have the opportunity to present their works to the people of Trondheim'. Gallery Blunk consists of one room without windows, with a wide-angled peep-hole to look through from the street. This simple gallery form can stimulate increased contact between the city's inhabitants and contemporary art insofar as passers-by can peek into the gallery. Blunk is run by Lina Berglund, Kristofer Henriksson, Uta Freia Beer and Aylin Soyer Tangen. http://home. no.net/blunkart/side1.html

Gallery KiT Art Academy of Trondheim's gallery consists of four exhibition rooms with a window onto the street. Gallery KiT is therefore also called a 'window gallery', and principally presents works by the academy's own students. In order to create an exchange of ideas, the gallery aims to present young contemporary art from international academies as well. KiT wants especially to explore the aesthetic differences between the various Nordic schools. http://www.kit.ntnu.no/galleri_kit/index.html

Marienborg studio cooperative started in 2006 through the initiative of a group of newly educated visual artists who wanted to establish practices in Trondheim. The members have backgrounds mainly from Norwegian art academies. Starting as a three-year pilot project intended to promote the young, vital art scene in Trondheim, Marienborg has been supported by, among others, Arts Council Norway, Trondheim Municipality and Sør Trøndelag County. Together with other artist-run spaces, Marienborg was invited to present itself in a larger context: *Supermarket 2007* at the Konstnärhuset in Stockholm. Other than this, Marienborg mostly emphasizes openness and socially related artistic arrangements. The focus is directed towards collaborative partnerships between several artistic disciplines (visual art, music and literature). This has proved to include a wider public. The present board of directors includes Karianne Stensland, Maja Nilsen, Edvine Larssen, Ann Cathrin Hertling, Vigdis Haugtrø and Kjersti Berg. http://www.marienborgkunst.no/

STAVANGER

Galleri 21 m² is an artist-initiated non-profit art space in old kiosk on Stavanger's east side. $21\,m^2$ was started in the summer of 2003 by six artists from the region. From autumn of 2006, two of the original six driving forces remained: Kenneth Varpe and Ingeborg Kvame. Tove Kommedal joined in the spring of 2007. Gallery $21\,m^2$ presents, on average, six to eight projects per year, with local, national and sometimes an international project. The exhibition programme is not planned far in advance, thus there is room for ad-hoc activities, events and presentations of works in progress. With no overriding curatorial agenda, $21\,m^2$ selects and presents projects its backers find interesting.

Mo Money Mo Problems[1]
Subsidy Schemes for Young Norwegian Artists

Ingrid Pettersen

Only a few young Norwegian artists earn a living by selling their art in Norway today. This is due to the limited nature of the market and because there are few private collectors. The chance of receiving a decorative commission from the state is proportionally lower the younger and more unknown an artist is. The most wide-spread form of income a young artist can receive is therefore through grants or some similar form of financial support. In the context of the exhibition *LIGHTS ON – norsk samtidskunst* at Astrup Fearnley Museum of Modern Art, the definition of 'young artist' is linked to age – artists in their twenties through mid-thirties.[2] Giving a complete overview of the various current subsidy schemes has proven to be more complicated than one would have imagined. An exhaustive overview would quickly become too detailed. A general overview would be too vague. Most state funded schemes, such as the various project support schemes, are open to all who apply, young artists included. Some schemes are earmarked for young artists, e.g. *Work Grants for Younger / Newly Established Artists*. Affiliation with place and genre-specific requirements also affect which application possibilities open up to each individual artist. Through the many different support schemes funds are indeed available for the fields of visual art: state grants, the state compensation funds and Arts Council Norway's various grants, regional and municipal funds, and finally private foundations, endowments and sponsors. In the jungle of cultural bureaucracy – including disparate schemes, administrators and specific guidelines for applications – it appears that the various funding bodies carry out their own operations in a parallel mode, but independently of one another.[3]

State subsidy schemes

Every year about 1,700 visual artists apply for state grants. Around 400 are awarded in total. The largest and widest in scope are *State Grants for Artists (Statens Kunstnerstipend)* and *Guaranteed Income for Artists (Garantiinntekter)*, *Relief Fund for Visual Artists (Bildende kunstneres hjelpe-fond)*, *Visual Artists' Compensation Fund (Bildende kunstneres vederlagsfond)* and *Project Grant from Visual Artists' Compensation Fund (Prosjektstøtte fra bildende kunstneres vederlagsfond)*. The lion's share of government grants is awarded through the various artist organizations, e.g., *Norwegian Visual Artists' Association* and *Norwegian Association for Arts and Crafts*. These organizations elect juries or 'grant committees' to award the funds. The committees consist of 12 artists chosen biannually in the autumn. They start their committee work at the new year. The application deadline for such grants is usually 15 October, the exception being the *Compensation Fund*, which has a biyearly deadline, 1 April and 1 October.

State Grants for Artists are apportioned into different types of subsidy schemes. Young artists are eligible for receiving special funds such as the *Work Grants for Younger / Newly Established Artists*. This grant is available to those who are 35 years old and under, and is divided into amounts of kr. 168,500 per year for one to three years. In 2007, 84 such grants were awarded, whereof 25 went to young visual artists. At present, 167 young artists are receiving this type of grant.[4] Other forms of financial support are *Work Grants, Miscellaneous Grants* and *Grant on Completion of Art Studies.* The work grant ranges from one to five years and is set at kr. 168,500 annually. 106 new work grants were awarded in 2007, thus the total number of current receivers is 221. The *Miscellaneous Grant*'s maximum sum is kr. 60,000; starting in 2008, it will replace all previous small grants, e.g., travel or specialized study grants, establishment grants and material grants, etc.

In 2007 the *Relief Fund for Visual Artists* awarded altogether 36 artist grants at kr. 180,000, which range over a period of one to three years. In addition to *Rune Brynestad's Memorial Grant* of kr. 300,000 to a selected artist, the *Visual Artists' Compensation Fund* handed out ten two-year grants for kr. 150,000, and 150 one-year grants of kr. 50,000. *Project Support from the Visual Artists' Compensation Fund* depends entirely on the project for which one seeks the money. In 2007 more than 100 applicants were awarded between kr. 10,000 – 70,000.

Arts Council Norway's grants are principally earmarked for new artistic expressions and forms of mediation '…moneys are awarded through discretionary judgements made by a professional committee, based upon professional and artistic grounds'.[5] Established in 1965, this council administers the *Norwegian Cultural Fund* and carries out duties delegated to it by the *Ministry of Culture and Church Affairs.* Areas for which grants are awarded are *project grants, exhibition grants, exhibition grants for newly established artists, grants for purchasing materials for joint artist studios, art and new technology* and *processes of cultural change. Exhibition grants for newly established artists* involve visual artists making their debut, *kunsthåndverkere* (arts and crafts artists) and photographers. It operates with an open budget. In 2007, 51 artists received between kr. 6,000 and kr. 40,000. Just as with the *Project Grant from the Visual Artists' Compensation Fund*, the *Project Support* from Arts Council Norway depends upon the nature of each individual project. *Arts Council Norway* also administers the *State Exhibition Grant* for visual artists, applied/decorative artists and 'free photographers' (non-commercial photographers); this money does not come from the *Norwegian Cultural Fund.* Kr. 3.8 million was allotted in 2007. Of the 345 artists who applied for the *State Exhibition Grant*, 134 artists received it; the maximum amount awarded being kr. 50,000.

Municipal and regional subsidy schemes

The part of Norway in which an artist lives and works is another criterion in the awarding of grants. Municipal and *fylke* (regional) grants usually require that applicants live and work in the particular region, municipality or city. These grants tend to range between kr. 20,000 and 30,000 and are awarded to persons who live in, or are affiliated with, the area in question, or who are expected to contribute to the cultural life of that region. In principle, grants are awarded only to projects of regional interest, and which coincide with the goals of local, officially adopted cultural resolutions. Regional politicians award the grants.

The largest cities – Oslo, Bergen, Trondheim, Stavanger, Kristiansand and Tromsø – also tend to have their own subsidy schemes for artists. These range between kr. 10,000 and kr. 30,000. *Skien Municipality's Artist Grant* is an example of a municipal scheme that distinguishes itself in a positive sense: Skien offers two kr. 25,000 grants to younger artists who are in the process of establishing their practices, and one artist grant of kr. 150,000.

Private subsidy schemes

The third type of subsidy young artists can seek is from private foundations. The various Norwegian artist societies are here reckoned to be non-governmental actors, even though they often administer state funds.[6] One characteristic common to many of the private application requirements is a focus on specific media; artists seek the grant by virtue of being pictorial artists, photographers, graphic artists, etc. The private foundations offer the same types of grants as the state does, yet there are fewer of them and the amounts are smaller.

The Tegnerforbundet (Drawing Artists' Association) administers the *Norwegian Illustration Fund*: it gives grants to illustrators and pictorial artists so they can accomplish special illustration commissions, and also provides other subsidies with a view towards advancing the art of illustration. Examples of what can be applied for are travel, study and work grants, with sums ranging between kr. 15,000 and kr. 70,000. Grafill (Norwegian Organization for Visual Communication) has a total framework of kr. 610,000 to award. It offers grants for travel, projects, exhibitions, materials and further educational courses for artists working within the field of visual communication.

Every two to three years Norske Grafikere (the Printmakers Association) announces grants for younger print makers. In 2008 they will award two grants at kr. 50,000 to young printmakers, to be used for travel, exhibitions or further artistic development. This grant is a gift from the artist Frans Widerberg. The *Norwegian Photographers Fund* offers grants to artists working with photography and other camera-based forms of expression. These are earmarked for exhibitions, projects, publications or grants for other activities advancing contemporary Norwegian photography. Sums range from kr. 5,000 to kr. 20,000. The *Fond for lyd og bilde* accepts applications from those seeking support for projects within the field of music, CD recordings, scenography, text production and film/video. In addition to project subsidies, separate provisions exist for marketing phonograms and short films/documentaries, as well as scene re-takes. Then there is *Fritt Ord* (*Freedom of Expression Foundation*); its grants are aimed at strengthening and protecting freedom of expression and its conditions in Norway.

Unge Kunstneres Samfund (Young Artists' Society, UKS) has been the principal organization for young Norwegian artists since 1921 and is a subsidiary of the 'behemoth' Norske Billedkunstnere (Norwegian Visual Artists' Association). As of 2008, UKS has ca. 1000 members and administers three types of grants for visual artists. First is the *UKS Work Grant*, allocated to one or two members every third year. It consists of the sum of generated monies from UKS' support fund. The next time it is awarded will be in 2009. Second is the *Painter Ambrosius Egedius and His Wife's Endowment*, divided into two grants for younger 'gifted' artists. The 2007 grants were for kr. 15,000 each. Finally, the *Snorre Andersen's Endowment,* comprised of accrued interest, is awarded to one younger gifted visual artist every third year. The next award will be in 2009.

Travel grants – a distinct genre

By financially supporting artists and curators who are active internationally, the goal of the Office for Contemporary Art Norway (OCA) is to develop collaborative partnerships between Norway and the international contemporary art scene. Grants for staying at OCA's bases in foreign countries are given to artists and freelance curators. At the International Studio and Curatorial Programme (ISCP) in New York, one artist is awarded kr. 150,000 plus a studio for one year, and one curator receives kr. 70,000 and a three-month residency. International Studio Program Künstlerhaus Bethanien in Berlin offers one artist kr. 137,500, plus a studio for one year. Beijing and Istanbul are other residencies for which artists can apply.

Ingrid Lindbäck Langaard's Fund and Foundation for the Advancement of Norwegian Artists is also set up with a view towards Norwegian artists sojourning abroad. It offers three types of travel grants: travel/work grants, grants for post-graduate education in a foreign country, and residency at Cité Internationale des Arts in Paris. Here the foundation has four flats at its disposal. *Forsberg and Aulie's Foundation* also presupposes that its endowments will be for travel and study in foreign countries. In 2007 the foundation offered two grants of kr. 150,000 — one to a painter and one to a drawer, preferably less than 40 years old. In addition to what we have mentioned, there are also bilateral foundations offering cultural funds which cut across national borders. These are geared towards advancing cooperation between the Nordic countries. The *Sleipnir Travel Grant – Nordic Council of Ministers' Travel Grant for Professional Artists under 36 Years Old,* the *Nordic Cultural Fund* and *Culture Contact North* are examples of such subsidy schemes.

Subsidies offered by private financial concerns, businesses and industries

Another type of private subsidy scheme stems from the financial and business/industry sector. These grants are few in number but often consist of kr. 100,000 or more. Juries (usually consisting of artists, art institution leaders and representatives for the specific sponsoring firm) nominate the candidates. This contrasts sharply with application practices for state grants. Some examples: *Royal Caribbean Arts Grant* is designed to support the further international development of young Norwegian visual artists. Artists up to 50 years old are eligible and three grants are awarded, at kr. 150,000 each, plus an exhibition of the produced artworks. Worth mentioning is the *Statoil-Hydro Art Grant,* a work grant of kr. 500,000 paid to one artist over a two year period. Part of this 'prize' is a nomination exhibition at *Kunstnerforbundet Gallery for Contemporary Art.* Statoil-Hydro also purchases the art that is produced. The *Selvaag Group Sculpture Grant* was divided into three grants in 2007, altogether consisting of kr. 250,000. One, for kr. 100,000, was awarded to a younger, unestablished sculptor. The *Sparebanken Øst Group* has established an annual grant distribution divided into four categories, one of which is artist grants. The grants can be as much as kr. 200,000 and are intended for persons or organizations in the geographic region serviced by the bank and its subsidiaries – Buskerud, Vestfold, Oslo and Akershus.

In the Nordic context, the *Carnegie Art Award* is a munificent project: three artists are awarded Swedish kr. 1,000,000; 600,000; 400,000 respectively and there is one grant of Swedish kr. 100,000 awarded to a young artist. Jury-nominated artists send in up to five works each, all of which are then included in an exhibition. The same jury selects the artists who are awarded the prizes.

The Legathåndboken (Endowment Handbook)

The last sub-category of private subsidy schemes consists of a myriad of memorial funds, endowments, grants and subsidies that are listed in an endowment handbook. These funds are usually administered by attorneys and amounts vary. Application criteria reflect the often long deceased benefactor's wishes and interests. *Ingerid, Synnøve and Elias Fegersten's Foundation for Norwegian Visual Artists* distributes two-year work grants of kr. 70,000 annually, as well as some one-year grants ranging between kr. 25,000 and kr. 50,000. These are awarded on even-numbered years. Applicants must be Norwegian citizens and at least 30 years old. The goal of *Sven*

Revold's Memorial Fund is to give memorial grants of ca. kr. 30,000 annually to artists from the various artistic genres. *Ellen and Crix Dahl Foundation* favours giving endowments to pictorial artists, but it varies from year to year as to which groups of artists are invited to apply. There is also the *Harriet Backer Memorial Fund*: it awards grants of kr. 15,000 to one or two visual artists every year. Applicants must have finished a four-year art education and have held a solo exhibition. To give an example of some of the rather original criteria for qualifying for some of these grants, we mention the *Bamsestipendet* from Namsskogan Zoo. Its grant of kr. 25,000 is awarded to one artist – a visual artist, handcraft-artist or photographer – who is interested in studying animals at close range. The grant includes a two-week stay at the Namsskogan Hotel.

'Fighting for the bone'

One could round off this overview of the various subsidy schemes for young artists by underscoring that the endowment handbook's treasure hunt is reserved for creative applicants with time to spare. Private subsidies of a certain sum are too exceptional and exclusive, and thus have little significance for young artists as a group. The conclusion must be that young artists most of all subsist on state grants. The Norwegian state takes responsibility for educating artists and contributes the greatest amount of money in the form of grants. The state is also the largest employer of artists, through decoration commissions for public buildings. On paper the future looks bright. Norway's national assembly has recently increased its allocation to cultural organizations and activities, thus in 2008 the budget will increase kr. 513 million, to a total of kr. 7,687 billion. The Ministry of Culture and Church Affairs' total budget has increased 7.6 percent.[7] According to *Kulturløftet* (the Cultural Endeavour), one percent of the Norwegian state's total budget will go to cultural activities and operations by the year 2014. Meanwhile, although this sounds very positive, the number of graduates from art schools exceeds the state's munificent allocations for artist grants. Every year 50 to 60 students graduate from Norwegian art colleges and academies, in addition to ca. 100 who finish their education in foreign countries. As well as this, a new national academy for art was last year established in Tromsø. *In 2007, 543 younger visual artists applied for work stipends expressly designed for younger artists. 25 of these applicants received a stipend.*[8] Budgetary policy therefore does not keep pace with the growth of art education and artists have, as a result of the stiff competition for grants, developed a tremendous will to organize themselves collectively, *Manifest 2007* being one example.[9]

How, then, do young Norwegian artists survive? One consequence of the Norwegian state's dominant position in subsidy schemes is that artists tend to become rather like cultural bureaucrats. Making a living becomes a matter of the will and ability to produce an ongoing chain of successful applications. Requirements for such applications include giving a project description (the background and goal of the project, what its theme is), sending in pictorial documentation and a CV. The application should also contain information about who is responsible for planning, the budget and financing plan, how much money is required, how the initiative will be carried out, an overview of how the project will progress, the expected starting date of the project and when it will end. Most young artists find it necessary to hold down a part-time job. In applying for grants, however, it is a precondition that one has enough time, energy and the means to produce art in the first place. If one works too much on the side one will have less time to produce art. If one does not produce, one will receive less support. Artists are registered as self-employed businesses owners; they work as freelancers moving from project to project, or they receive short-term contracts. As such, it seems that in general, young artists' social and economic situations are marked by instability and unpredictability.

Thanks to
Marte Johnslien
Sarah Sørheim
Jorunn Myklebust Syvertsen

Links
The Relief Fund for Visual Artists / Bildende kunstneres Hjelpefond:
http://www.kunst.no/kunstavgift
Carnegie Art Award: http://carnegieartaward.com
Forsberg og Aulies legat: http://billedkunst.no/soknadskjema/2008/forsberg_aulie.html
GRAFILL: http://www.grafill.no
Norsk Fotografisk Fonds stipend: http://www.fffotografer.no
Norsk Illustrasjonsfond: http://www.tegnerforbundet.no
Nordic Cultural Fund / Nordisk kulturfond: http://www.nordiskkulturfond.dk/
Arts Council Norway / Norsk Kulturråd: http://www.kulturrad.no/
Norwegian Visual Artists' Association / Norske Billedkunstnere (NBK) og Billedkunst:
http://www.billedkunst.no
The Printmakers Association / Norske Grafikere: http://www.norske-grafikere.no
Nordic Culture Point / Kulturkontakt Nord (KKN): http://www.kknord.org/
Legathåndboken: http://www.legathandboken.no/
Office for Contemporary Art Norway (OCA): http://www.oca.no/
Royal Caribbean Arts Grant: http://www.artsgrant.no/
Selvaaggruppens Skulpturstipend: http://www.selvaag.no
Sleipnir reisestipend: http://www.nifca.org
Statens kunstnerstipend: http://www.kunstnerstipend.no/

1 'Mo Money Mo Problems' is the second single from Notorious B.I.G.'s double album *Life After Death*. Bad Boy/Arista, 1997.

2 Arts Council Norway's definition: 'artists who exhibit work for the first time or who are in the beginning phase of their artistic career". (*Utstillingsstøtte til kunstnere i etableringsfasen*, http://www.kulturrad.no/fagomrader/billedkunst/utstillingsstottetilkunstnerei/ 26 November 2007).

3 For example, no well-functioning joint Internet portal for subsidy schemes exists.

4 *Tildeling av statens kunstnerstipend og garantiinntekter 2007*, Press Release published 29 March 2007. http://www.regjeringen.no/nb/dep/kkd/pressesenter/pressemeldinger/2007/Tildeling-a... 26 November 2007.

5 Arts Council Norway: *Strategi 2006-2009 – Billedkunst og kunsthåndverk* http://www.kulturrad.no/fagomrader/billedkunst/strategi_2006-09/ 21 December 2007.

6 One example is Office for Contemporary Art Norway (OCA), a private foundation set up in the autumn of 2001 by the Ministry of Culture and Church Affairs and the Ministry of Foreign Affairs.

7 Ingvill Henmo: 'Løfter kulturen videre', in *Billedkunst*, no. 6, 3 October 2007. http://www.billedkunstmag.no/Content

8 Ingeborg Stana, director of the *Norwegian Visual Artists' Association* (NBK), quoted by Ingvill Henmo in 'Løfter kulturen videre', *Billedkunst*, 3 October 2007, no. 6. http://www.billedkunstmag.no/Content

9 *Manifest 2007* was a collaborative project initiated by Marianne Heier and a group of art students at the National Academy of Art in Oslo (KHiO). In February 2007, *Manifest* presented a list of demands regarding better conditions for art-related work/occupations. The manifesto was an appeal for a better welfare package for artists, better grants, more subsidized studios and a strengthening of public commissions. The manifesto was exhibited in *The White Tube* at Tøyen Metro Station between 16 February and 18 March 2007. Copies were also delivered to the Norwegian Visual Artists' Association, the Young Artists' Society and Trond Giske, Minister of Church and Cultural Affairs.

JESPER JAMES ALVÆR
Born 1973 Copenhagen
Lives and works in Prague and Oslo

Education
1997–04
Academy of Fine Arts, Prague
2000–01
Cooper Union School of Art,
New York
1994–95
Ecole Brousse, Visual
Communication, Montpellier
1991–93
University of Oslo

Solo exhibitions (selected)
2007
Figure and Ground, Bunkier Sztuki
Contemporary Art Gallery, Krakow
2006
Transkultura: Akt 1, Atrium,
Moravian Gallery, Brno
2005
Next week in your flat, House of Art,
Ceske Budjeovice

Group exhibitions (selected)
2008
LIGHTS ON – norsk samtidskunst,
Astrup Fearnley Museum of Modern
Art, Oslo
2007
Czechpoint, Gallery of Arts, Zilina
Still Here, Artspace Sydney,
Woolloomooloo
Simple Living, Contemporary Art
Gallery of the Brukenthal Museum,
Sibiu

RUNE ANDREASSEN
Born 1976 Tønsberg
Lives and works in Oslo

Education
2000–04
Oslo National Academy of the Arts
1998–2000
Nordland Art and Filmschool, Kabelvåg

Solo exhibitions (selected)
2007
*Bjørkås/Andreassen forfylgjer
synsrandi*, Galleri Rekord,
Oslo
2006
1/32 And Bloody Eclectic II,
Galleri F15, Jeløya

Group exhibitions (selected)
2008
LIGHTS ON – norsk samtidskunst,
Astrup Fearnley Museum of Modern
Art, Oslo
Excentrum, Kabuso, Øystese
2007
Nature is what surrounds us,
KunstVerket, Oslo

THORA DOLVEN BALKE
Born 1982 Oslo
Lives and works in Oslo

Education
2004–06
Oslo National Academy of the Arts

2002–04
Bergen National Academy of the Arts

Solo exhibition
2006
How to swallow a meteorite,
Galleri Fimbul, Oslo

Group exhibitions (selected)
2008
LIGHTS ON – norsk samtidskunst,
Astrup Fearnley Museum of Modern
Art, Oslo
2007
I Wanna be Loved by You,
performance at Hamar Performance
festival, Kunstbanken
Old Bold Neuropa 2, Galerie Area 53,
Vienna
Blackout, Galleri Fimbul, Oslo
2006
Hit that piece of Ivory there,
sound-art group show in Ny
Musikk's space, Oslo
When I leave the world behind, at
Umedalen Sculpture Park 2006 by
Galleri Andersson Sandström, Umeå
2005
Vocal performance at Kjetil Berge's
piece at the Eighth Havana Biennale
Fimbulvinter, Galleri Fimbul, Oslo
Holiday Inn, Galuzin Gallery, Oslo

SIRI BERQVAM
Born 1977 Skedsmo
Lives and works in Oslo

Education
2004–06
Bergen National Academy
of the Arts
2001–04
Bergen National Academy
of the Arts (textile)

Solo exhibition (selected)
2008
liksomheter, Kunstbanken, Hamar
Sámi Art Center, Karasjok

Group exhibitions (selected)
2008
LIGHTS ON – norsk samtidskunst,
Astrup Fearnley Museum of Modern
Art, Oslo
2006
Høstutstillingen, Kunstnernes Hus,
Oslo
The Textile Triennial, Oslo
Kunstforening

KYRRE BJØRKÅS
Born 1979 Sandefjord
Lives and works in Oslo

Education
2000–04
Oslo National Academy of the Arts

Solo exhibitions (selected)
2007
*Bjørkås/Andreassen forfylgjer
synsrandi*, Galleri Rekord, Oslo
2006
1/32 And Bloody Eclectic II,
Galleri F15, Jeløya

Group exhibitions (selected)
2008
LIGHTS ON – norsk samtidskunst,
Astrup Fearnley Museum of Modern
Art, Oslo
Excentrum, Kabuso, Øystese
2007
Nature is what surrounds us,
KunstVerket, Oslo

OLE MARTIN LUND BØ
Born 1973 Stavanger
Lives and works in New York

Education
1998–2002
Bergen National Academy
of the Arts

Solo exhibitions (selected)
2007
(Deceptive outward appearance),
Galerie Opdahl, Berlin
Set-up, Galleri Opdahl, Stavanger
Strategy Breakdown, Fotogalleriet,
Oslo

Group exhibitions (selected)
2008
LIGHTS ON – norsk samtidskunst,
Astrup Fearnley Museum of Modern
Art, Oslo
2007
Space Chase, Galerie Magnus
Müller, Berlin
Partners in Crime, Gallery MC,
New York
2005
*Similarities and differences –
New Norwegian Photography*,
Preus Museum, Horten

BJØRN BÅSEN
Born 1981 Eggedal
Lives and works in Oslo and
Eggedal

Education
2005–07
Oslo National Academy of the Arts
2001–04
The Arts Institute at Bournemouth, UK

Solo exhibition
2006
Looming Laila, Galleri A, Oslo

Group exhibitions (selected)
2008
LIGHTS ON – norsk samtidskunst,
Astrup Fearnley Museum of Modern
Art, Oslo
Galleri Brandstrup, Oslo
2007
Obergeschoss Dritter Finger Rechts,
Ballhaus Ost, Berlin
Norske Bilder, Rådhusgalleriet,
Oslo

JAN CHRISTENSEN
Born 1977 Copenhagen
Lives and works in Berlin

Education
1997–2000
Oslo National Academy of the Arts

Solo exhibitions (selected)
2008
Stenersenmuseet, Oslo
(with Rolf-Yngve Uggen and
Johnny Skalleberg)
2006
Stedelijk Museum voor
Actuele Kunst (SMAK), Ghent
Kunsthaus Baselland,
Basel

Group exhibitions (selected)
2008
LIGHTS ON – norsk samtidskunst,
Astrup Fearnley Museum of Modern
Art, Oslo
2007
Tomorrow, Kumho Museum of Art
and Artsonje Center, Seoul
2006
Super, FRAC des Pays de la Loire,
Carquefou
2005
Post Notes, Midway Contemporary
Art, Minneapolis

GARDAR EIDE EINARSSON
Born 1976 Oslo
Lives and works in New York

Education
2002–03
Independent Study Program,
Cooper Union School
of Architecture, New York
2001–02
Independent Study Program,
Whitney Museum of American Art,
New York
1999–2000
Staatliche Hochschule für
Bildende Künste – Städelschule,
Frankfurt-am-Main
1996–2000
Bergen National Academy
of the Arts

Solo exhibitions (selected)
2007
Südlich des Himmels, Frankfurter
Kunstverein
All my Friends are Dead,
Honor Fraser, Los Angeles
In Practice Projects, Sculpture
Center, Long Island
2006
Population One, STANDARD (OSLO)
Artissima 13, Turin
Tokyo Underworld
Nils Stærk Contemporary Art,
Copenhagen
2005
Leashed or Confined, Team Gallery,
New York
*I Am the Master of My Fate;
I Am the Captain of My
Soul*, Roberts and Tilton,
Los Angeles
Black Iron Prison, Galerie
Loevenbruck, Paris

Group exhibitions (selected)
2008
LIGHTS ON – norsk samtidskunst,
Astrup Fearnley Museum of Modern
Art, Oslo

2007
*In The Poem About Love You Don't
Write The Word Love*, Overgaden,
Institut for Samtidskunst,
Copenhagen; Midway Contemporary
Art, Minneapolis; Artists Space,
New York
Carnegie Art Award, Kiasma,
Helsinki
Time Past – Time Present, Istanbul
Museum of Modern Art
*Paintings, Props and Problems
(Still Unresolved)*, STANDARD (OSLO)
No Context, Taka Ishii Gallery, Tokyo
Bastard Creature, Palais de Tokyo,
Paris
Skate Culture, Bildmuseet, Umeå;
Preus Museum, Horten
2006
Street: behind the cliché, Witte de
With Center for Contemporary Art,
Rotterdam
*KAPITEL VII: Bühne des Lebens –
Rhetorik des Gefühls*, Städtische
Galerie im Lenbachhaus &
Kunstbau, Munich

IDA EKBLAD
Born 1980 Oslo
Lives and works in Oslo

Education
2008
The Mountain School of Arts,
Los Angeles
2002–07
Oslo National Academy of the Arts
2000–01
Central St Martins College of Art,
Department of Fine Art, London

Solo exhibition
2008
Fotogalleriet, Oslo

Group exhibitions (selected)
2008
LIGHTS ON – norsk samtidskunst,
Astrup Fearnley Museum of Modern
Art, Oslo
*Good News for People Who Love
News*, Swiss Institute, New York
Medium Cool, Art in General,
New York
Bakgrunn, Preus Museum,
Horten
2007
The Corny Show, Willy Wonka
Inc for Karma International,
Zurich
2006
Giving People What They Want,
Glassbox, Paris

JAN HAKON ERICHSEN
Born 1978 Oslo
Lives and works in Oslo

Education
2000–04
Oslo National Academy
of the Arts

Solo exhibition
2006
Fury, Kunstbanken, Hamar

Group exhibitions (selected)
2008
LIGHTS ON – norsk samtidskunst,
Astrup Fearnley Museum of Modern
Art, Oslo
Vestlandsutstillingen (travelling)
2007
Demolition!, Site Gallery, Liverpool
Videomedeja, The Museum of
Vojvodina, Novy Sad
2006
Darklight Festival, Dublin
16. Internationales Videofestival,
Bochum

MATIAS FALDBAKKEN
Born 1973 Hobro
Lives and works in Oslo

Education
1994–98
Bergen National Academy of the Arts
1996–97
Staatliche Hochschule für
Bildende Künste – Städelschule,
Frankfurt-am-Main

Solo exhibitions (selected)
2008
Simon Lee Gallery, London
Galerie Giti Nourbakhsch, Berlin
2007
STANDARD (OSLO)
Midway Contemporary Art,
Minneapolis
Statements, Art Basel 38
2006
Galerie Diana Stigter, Amsterdam
Schnittraum, Cologne
2005
STANDARD (OSLO)
The Nordic Pavilion, The Venice
Biennale

Group exhibitions (selected)
2008
LIGHTS ON – norsk samtidskunst,
Astrup Fearnley Museum of Modern
Art, Oslo
The Sydney Biennial 2008
Modern Institute, Glasgow
Johann König, Berlin
2007
STANDARD (OSLO)
Institute of Contemporary Arts
(ICA), London
Cohan and Leslie, New York
2006
PS.1 MoMA, New York
Stadtische Galerie im Lenbachhaus,
Munich
The Wrong Gallery at Whitney
Museum of American Art, Whitney
Biennial, New York
2005
Frankfurter Kunstverein
CAC, Vilnius
Stedelijk Museum, Amsterdam

JAN FREUCHEN
Born 1979 Stavanger
Lives and works in Oslo

Education
2000–04
Bergen National Academy of the Arts

2003
Staatliche Hochschule für
Bildende Künste – Städelschule,
Frankfurt-am-Main
1998–99
Oslo School of Drawing and Painting

Solo exhibitions (selected)
2007
Self Assembly, Galleri Erik Steen,
Oslo
2006
Apocalypse Focus Group, ALP Peter
Bergmann, Stockholm
Internal Combustion, Galleri Fimbul,
Oslo
Pimp My Ride, West Germany, Berlin

Group exhibitions (selected)
2008
LIGHTS ON – norsk samtidskunst,
Astrup Fearnley Museum of Modern
Art, Oslo
2007
Destroy Athens, First Athens
Biennial
Objet Perdu, Pierogi, Leipzig
DUMP, The National Museum of Art,
Architecture and Design, Oslo
Come into the open, 0047, Oslo
Basic Speculations, By the Way,
Bergen
2006
The World State, Galleri Erik Steen,
Oslo
Friction-free, Christansand
Kunstforening

IVAN GALUZIN
Born 1979 Groznyj, USSR
Lives and works in Vadsø

Education
2002–06
Oslo National Academy of the Arts

Solo exhibitions (selected)
2007
Rekord Gallery, Oslo
2006
Gallery No. 9, Oslo
2005
Eka Gallery, Tallinn

Group exhibitions (selected)
2008
LIGHTS ON – norsk samtidskunst,
Astrup Fearnley Museum of Modern
Art, Oslo
The Last Battle, Galleri F15, Moss
2007
Against The Modern World, LNM,
Oslo
2006
Old Bold Neuropa part I, Gallery
Area 53, Vienna
2005
The Idea of North, Gallery F15, Moss

ISABELA GROSSEOVÁ
Born 1976 Prague
Lives and works in Prague

Education
1994–2001
Academy of Fine Arts, Prague

1998
Kungliga Konsthögskolan,
Stockholm
1997
Université Libre de Bruxelles

Solo exhibitions (selected)
2007
Figure and Ground, Bunkier Sztuki
Contemporary Art Gallery, Krakow
2006
Transkultura: Akt 1, Atrium,
Moravian Gallery, Brno
2003
Habitable statues, Art in General,
New York

Group exhibitions (selected)
2008
LIGHTS ON – norsk samtidskunst,
Astrup Fearnley Museum of Modern
Art, Oslo
2007
*Gross Domestic Produc*t, GHMP,
Prague
2005
Systems you have seen, afo –
architekturforum oberösterrreich,
Linz
Past splendour of diversity,
House of Arts, Brno

**ANNA SIGMOND
GUDMUNDSDOTTIR**
Born 1974 Reykjavik
Lives and works in Oslo

Education
1994–97
Bergen National Academy of the Arts

Solo exhibitions (selected)
2007
Living Art Museum. Reykjavik
Galleri 54, Gothenburg
2003
OK Centre For Contemporary Art,
Linz
2002
Sørlandet Art Museum,
Kristiansand

Group exhibitions (selected)
2008
LIGHTS ON – norsk samtidskunst,
Astrup Fearnley Museum of Modern
Art, Oslo
2002
Manifesta 4, Frankfurt-am-Main

ESPEN HENNINGSEN
Born 1981 Holmestrand
Lives and works in Oslo

Education
2003–06
Oslo National Academy
of the Arts

Solo exhibitions (selected)
2007
Sisyfos Minigolfklubb,
Vestfossen Kunstlaboratorium
2006
ROM for arkitektur og kunst
(with Jan Skomakerstuen)

Group exhibitions (selected)
2008
LIGHTS ON – norsk samtidskunst,
Astrup Fearnley Museum of Modern
Art, Oslo
2007
Høstutstillingen #120, Kunstnernes
hus, Oslo (with Lars Kjemphol)
2006
Sommarutstillinga 06, Seljord
kunstforening (with Eivind Blaker)
2005
Adundas, Galleri Van Bau,
Vestfossen

ANE METTE HOL
Born 1979 Bodø
Lives and works in Oslo

Education
2004–06
Konstfack, University College of Arts,
Crafts and Design, Stockholm
2001–04
Oslo National Academy of
the Arts

Solo exhibition
2007
Lautom Contemporary, Oslo
(with Kristin Nordhøy)

Group exhibitions (selected)
2008
LIGHTS ON – norsk samtidskunst,
Astrup Fearnley Museum of Modern
Art, Oslo
The Drawing Biennial, Kunstnernes
Hus, Oslo
2007
Vårsalongen, Liljevalchs Konsthall,
Stockholm
2006
Goods to declare, MFA international,
Tel Aviv, Israel

HÅVARD HOMSTVEDT
Born 1976 Lørenskog
Lives and works in New York

Education
2003
Yale University, School of Art,
New Haven, USA
2000
Rhode Island School of Design
(RISD), Providence, USA
1999
European Honors Program (RISD),
Rome, Italy

Solo exhibitions (selected)
2007
You Will Hardly Know, Galleri Riis,
Oslo
2006
Dud, Kantor/Feuer Gallery, Los
Angeles
End of Work, Medium St Barthelemy,
French West-Indies

Group exhibitions (selected)
2008
LIGHTS ON – norsk samtidskunst,
Astrup Fearnley Museum of Modern
Art, Oslo

2007
Landscapes, Southfirst, Brooklyn,
New York
Black & White, Ibid Projects, London
2006
Farewell to Icon, Anna Helwing
Gallery, Los Angeles
25 Bold Moves, House of Campari,
Los Angeles

LARS KJEMPHOL
Born 1980 Oslo
Lives and works in Oslo

Education
2002–08
Oslo National Academy of the Arts

Group exhibitions (selected)
2008
LIGHTS ON – norsk samtidskunst,
Astrup Fearnley Museum of Modern
Art, Oslo
2007
Sisyfos minihell, Vestfossen
kunstlaboratorium (with Espen
Henningsen, Hans Thorsen)
Killing Vilde von Krogh,
Schweigaards gt 33 Oslo
Høstutstillingen #120, Kunstnernes
Hus, Oslo (with Espen Henningsen)
2006
Sisyfos underground, Catacombs of
Oslo National Academy of the Arts
Diesel New Art, Norsk form, Oslo
Høstutstillingen #113, Kunstnernes
Hus, Oslo (with Hans Thorsen)
National Academy graduation show,
Stenersen-museet, Oslo
2005
Diesel new art, DogA-senteret, Oslo
Sisyfos minigolfklubb, Gallery 21.25,
Oslo

MAREN JUELL KRISTENSEN
Born 1976 Oslo
Lives and works in Oslo

Education
2004
Fine Art, Chelsea College of Art and
Design, University of The Arts,
London
2000
Fine Art, University of Hertfordshire,
Hatfield
1997
Foundation Fine Art, Einar Granum
Kunstfagskole, Oslo

Solo exhibitions (selected)
2007
Dark Matter, Galleri Leif Magne
Tangens, Skien
2006
Nothing to see here, Galleri Fimbul,
Oslo
2005
We Walked Miles For You, Atelier
Nord Projectspace, Oslo

Group exhibitions (selected)
2008
LIGHTS ON – norsk samtidskunst,
Astrup Fearnley Museum of Modern
Art, Oslo

Kunstvisitten, Akershus
Kunstnersenter, Lillestrøm
2007
Climate of change, 235-241 Union
Street, London
Oslo Open, installation at Stortinget
Tube Station, Oslo
Voyeur Collective, 69 Smith Street
Gallery, Fitzroy (AUS)
Prosjekt Galleri Oslo, Galleri
Oslo/Bussterminalen, Oslo
2005
Botschaften+Bring a Friend,
Gemeinschaftshaus der Nordischen
Botschaften, Berlin; Kino Arsenal,
Berlin
2004
Call Me When You Get Here,
Aldwych/The Strand Tube Station,
London

HJØRDIS KURÅS
Born 1974 Oslo
Lives and works in Oslo

Education
2000–03
Oslo National Academy of the Arts

Group exhibitions (selected)
2008
LIGHTS ON – norsk samtidskunst,
Astrup Fearnley Museum of Modern
Art, Oslo
*Mother & Child, Divided #2, Rykk
tilbake til start*, 0047, Oslo
Zeitgeist, Liminal Inception 1&2,
Galleri Barbara Hansen/van Eijk,
Stockholm Supermarket
Bombsquad Mezzoforte,
Tegnebiennalen 2008, Kunstnernes
Hus, Oslo
*BombsquadMezzoforte, Liminal
Inception 1&2*, Galleri Barbara
Hansen/van Eijk, Bridge Art Fair,
New York
Liminal Inception, Festival
de Film et Vidéo de Création,
Beirut

INGVILD LANGGÅRD
Born 1978 Fredrikstad
Lives and works in Oslo

Education
2003–06
Oslo National Academy
of the Arts
1997–2000
The University of Oslo

Solo exhibition
2007
Take Me To The Other Side, Galleri
Leif Magne Tangens, Skien

Group exhibitions (selected)
2008
LIGHTS ON – norsk samtidskunst,
Astrup Fearnley Museum of Modern
Art, Oslo
2007
Vodou, 0047, Oslo
*Hamar Performance festival
(I Wanna be Loved by You)*,
Kunstbanken, Hamar

Blackout, Galleri Fimbul, Oslo
Video Transit, Porsgrunn
Kunstforening
Aftermath, Rom for Kunst, Oslo
2006
Take off, Galleri Brandstrup, Oslo
2005
Holiday Inn, Galuzin Gallery, Oslo

LELLO//ARNELL
Jørgen Craig Lello & Tobias Arnell
Born 1978 Fredrikstad and 1978 Lund
Live and work in Oslo

Education
2002–06
Oslo National Academy of the Arts
(Lello)
2001–05
Oslo National Academy of the Arts
(Arnell)

Solo exhibitions (selected)
2007
Galleri Pictura, Lund
Heimdal kunstforening, Trondheim
2005
Galleri 21:24, Oslo

Group exhibitions (selected)
2008
LIGHTS ON – norsk samtidskunst,
Astrup Fearnley Museum of Modern
Art, Oslo
Snowball Editions, Torpedo, Oslo
2007
0047OSLO, Oslo
2006
Norwegian Sculpture Biennial, Oslo

TRINE LISE NEDREAAS
Born 1972 Bergen
Lives and works in Berlin

Education
1995–99
Slade School of Fine Art, University
College, London
1994–95
UCL, Madness and Society, London
1991–94
Central Saint Martin College of Art
& Design, Fine Art, London
History of Art, University of Bergen

Solo exhibitions (selected)
2007
Galerie Eva Hober, Paris
AR Contemporary, Milan
2006
Luxe Gallery, New York

Group exhibitions (selected)
2008
LIGHTS ON – norsk samtidskunst,
Astrup Fearnley Museum of Modern
Art, Oslo
Ghost in the Machine, Kunstnernes
Hus, Oslo
2007
All About Laughter, Mori Art
Museum, Tokyo
Lambert Collection, Avignon
2006
Into me / Out of me, PS.1 MoMA,
New York

Reality Crossings, Second
International Photo Festival
Mannheim; Ludwigshafen;
Heidelberg

MARTIN SKAUEN
Born 1975 Fredrikstad
Lives and works in Berlin

Education
1998–2002
Oslo National Academy of the Arts

Solo exhibitions (selected)
2008
*There's Plenty of Gold, I've Been
Told*, Galleri MGM, Oslo
Laura Bartlett Gallery, London
Kunstlerhaus Bethanien, Berlin
2006
Dirty work(s), Galleri 21, Malmö

Group exhibitions (selected)
2008
LIGHTS ON – norsk samtidskunst,
Astrup Fearnley Museum of Modern
Art, Oslo
Tang Contemporary, Beijing
Whenever it starts it is the right time,
Frankfurter Kunstverein
The Drawing Biennial, Kunstnernes
Hus, Oslo
Tomorrow Always Belongs to Us,
Göteborgs Konsthall
Hardcore, Sørlandet Art Museum,
Kristiansand
2007
Destroy Athens, First Athens
Biennial

EIRIN STØEN
Born 1974 Oslo
Lives and works in Oslo

Education
1999–2004
The National College of Art and
Design (NCAD/SHKS), Oslo

Group exhibitions (selected)
2008
LIGHTS ON – norsk samtidskunst,
Astrup Fearnley Museum of Modern
Art, Oslo
2006
REFLEKS – Art in public space,
Momentum, Moss
2005
Installation for the music festival
Øya, Oslo, in collaboration with
Ingvild Langgård, Christina Peel and
Benjamin Stenmarck
Holiday Inn, Galuzin Gallery,
Oslo

STIAN ÅDLANDSVIK
Born 1981 Bergen
Lives and works in Oslo

Education
2003–06
Oslo National Academy
of the Arts
2005
Hochschule für bildende Künste,
Hamburg

Solo exhibitions (selected)
2007
Stream Day, The Young Artists
Society, Oslo
2006
Sketches for the meantime,
Fotogalleriet, Oslo (with Lutz-Rainer
Müller)
HAMC jubilee, The National
Museum, Oslo (with Lutz-Rainer
Müller and Frode Markhus)
2005
*It's Not Unlike Being on the
Top of a Snowcovered Mountain*,
Galleri 21:25, Oslo

Group exhibitions (selected)
2008
LIGHTS ON – norsk samtidskunst,
Astrup Fearnley Museum of Modern
Art, Oslo
2007
Be One, Get Three, Cluster Galerie,
Berlin
Play, Gallery Erik Steen, Oslo
2006
Take Off 2006, Galleri Brandstrup,
Oslo

ØYSTEIN AASAN
Born 1977 Kristiansand
Lives and works in Berlin

Education
1999–2003
Oslo National Academy
of the Arts

Solo exhibitions (selected)
2008
Lautom Contemporary, Oslo
PSM, Berlin
Galerie Katharina Bittel, Hamburg
2007
Lautom Contemporary, Oslo

Group exhibitions (selected)
2008
LIGHTS ON – norsk samtidskunst,
Astrup Fearnley Museum of Modern
Art, Oslo
Jones and Truebenbach Galerie,
Cologne
2007
Bare Words, Lautom Contemporary,
Oslo
2006
Liverpool Biennale
Kunstraum NOE, Vienna

List of Works

Jesper Alvær & Isabela Grosseová
• *Trademarks*, 2006
Appropriated objects, video stills
Dimensions vary
Courtesy of the artists

Lello//Arnell (Jørgen Craig Lello
& Tobias Arnell)
• *Vice Admiral Francis Drake's
Expedition to the South Pacific
Aimed at the Disruption of Spanish
Exploration and Conquest I*, 2007
Digital print on aluminium
70 x 100 cm
Astrup Fearnley Collection, Oslo
• *Vice Admiral Francis Drake's
Expedition to the South Pacific
Aimed at the Disruption of Spanish
Exploration and Conquest III*, 2007
Digital print on aluminium
70 x 100 cm
Astrup Fearnley Collection, Oslo
• *Vice Admiral Francis Drake's
Expedition to the South Pacific
Aimed at the Disruption of Spanish
Exploration and Conquest II
(Self Portrait of an Explorer)*, 2007
Digital print on aluminium
70 x 100 cm
Astrup Fearnley Collection, Oslo
• *Inflation, Interest & Investment
(To Infinity) I*, 2007
Digital print on aluminium
70 x 100 cm
Astrup Fearnley Collection, Oslo
• *Inflation, Interest & Investment
(To Infinity) II*, 2007
Digital print on aluminium
70 x 100 cm
Astrup Fearnley Collection, Oslo
• *Inflation, Interest & Investment
(To Infinity) III*, 2007
Digital print on aluminium
70 x 100 cm
Astrup Fearnley Collection, Oslo
• *Knowing about the Universe*, 2008
Powder varnished aluminium
125 x 125 x 5 cm
90 x 60 x 60 cm
Astrup Fearnley Collection, Oslo
Thanks to Water Jet Norge A/S
• *The Seer*, 2008
Plywood
145 x 60 x 60 cm
Astrup Fearnley Collection, Oslo
• *The Oracle*, 2008
Plywood
50 x 25 x 25 cm
Astrup Fearnley Collection, Oslo

Thora Dolven Balke
• *Oh God No*, 2005
5–1 surround sound installation
Dimensions vary
Courtesy of the artist

Siri Berqvam
• *2 hours and 15 minutes*,
2007
Chrocheted, knitted
Life size
Courtesy of the artist
• *Miele Exclusive*, 2005
Sewing, embroidery
Life size
Courtesy of the artist

Bjørkås/Andreassen (Kyrre Bjørkås
& Rune Andreassen)
• *Flat as a birdshit on a buick*, 2006
Acrylic on glass and laminated
parquet, 200 x 125 cm
Courtesy of the artists
• *It's all around you*, 2007
Mixed media
160 x 160 cm
Courtesy of the artists

Ole Martin Lund Bø
• *(deceptive outward appearance)*,
2008
Wooden planks and paint
Dimensions vary
Courtesy of the artist

Bjørn Båsen
• *Termus*, 2007
MDF, wood, gas, chalk, skin glue,
oil paint and gold leaves
80 x 35 x 45 cm
Astrup Fearnley Collection, Oslo

Jan Christensen
• *Nonsense*, 2007
Vinyl
Dimensions vary
c/o Atle Gerhardsen, Berlin and
Galleri MGM, Oslo
• *LIGHTS ON – norsk samtidskunst*,
2008
Illustrated title / logo
Dimensions vary
c/o Atle Gerhardsen, Berlin and
Galleri MGM, Oslo

Gardar Eide Einarsson
• *Untitled (Dining Cluster)*, 2006
ed. 2/3 and 3/3
MDF, aluminium, steel
80 x 172.7 x 172.7 cm
Astrup Fearnley Collection, Oslo
• *Untitled (Barrels)*, 2006
Enamel on aluminium
269.2 x 149.9 cm
Astrup Fearnley Collection, Oslo
• *Untitled (T shirts)*, 2006
500 silk-screened cotton T shirts
and 7 cardboard boxes
Dimensions vary
Astrup Fearnley Collection, Oslo
• *Untitled (Greeting)*, 2008
Acrylic on canvas
183 x 213 cm
Private collection
• *Untitled (No Collaboration)*, 2008
Acrylic on canvas
183 x 213 cm
Astrup Fearnley Collection, Oslo

Ida Ekblad
• *Political Song for Jessica Simpson
to Sing*, 2007
B/w print on paper, chewing gum
175 x 125 cm
Astrup Fearnley Collection, Oslo
• *Poetry Tomb (chase layers of time)*,
2008
C-print
116 x 93 cm
Astrup Fearnley Collection, Oslo
• *Poetry Tomb (Death DEATH)*, 2008
C-print, 116 x 93 cm
Astrup Fearnley Collection, Oslo

Jan Hakon Erichsen
• *Lights Out*, 2006
DVD
2:49 min.
Courtesy of the artist

Matias Faldbakken
• *Untitled (canvas #15)*, 2008
Canvas tape on Belgian linen
and wooden stretcher
152.5 x 152.5 cm
Astrup Fearnley Collection, Oslo
• *Untitled (canvas #16)*, 2008
Canvas tape on Belgian linen
and wooden stretcher
152.5 x 152.5 cm
Astrup Fearnley Collection, Oslo
• *Untitled (canvas #17)*, 2008
Canvas tape on Belgian linen
and wooden stretcher
152.5 x 152.5 cm
Astrup Fearnley Collection, Oslo
• *Untitled (canvas #18)*, 2008
Canvas tape on Belgian linen
and wooden stretcher
152.5 x 152.5 cm
Astrup Fearnley Collection, Oslo
• *Untitled (canvas #19)*, 2008
Canvas tape on Belgian linen
and wooden stretcher
152.5 x 152.5 cm
Astrup Fearnley Collection, Oslo
• *Newspaper Ad #17*, 2007
Inkjet print on Billboard paper
STANDARD (OSLO)
• *Newspaper Ad #16*, 2007
Inkjet print on Billboard paper
321 x 200 cm
STANDARD (OSLO)
• *Newspaper Ad #18*, 2007
Inkjet print on Billboard paper
321 x 200 cm
Astrup Fearnley Collection, Oslo

Jan Freuchen
• *26 Gasoline Stations*, 2007
26 C-prints on aluminium
each 57.5 x 46.5 cm
Courtesy of the artist
Galleri Erik Steen, Oslo

Ivan Galuzin
• *Killed by Death*, 2008
Collage, objects
Dimensions vary
Courtesy of the artist

Anna Sigmond Gudmundsdottir
• *Be extremely careful what you
are thinking and feeling, it affects
everything*, 2008
Installation
Dimensions vary
Courtesy of the artist

Ane Mette Hol
• *Duplication (After Xerox
Untitled)*, 2007
nos. 1–9
Drawings, pencil
each 21 x 29,7 cm
Lautom Contemporary,
Oslo
no. 5 private collection
no. 6 private collection
no. 9 private collection

• *Untitled (Art History Essay)*, 2007
Drawing, pencil and pen
29.7 x 42 cm
Lautom Contemporary, Oslo

Håvard Homstvedt
• *You will hardly know*, 2007
Neon and cables
147 x 412 x 6 cm
Cable installation on floor
Dimensions vary
Courtesy of the artist
Galleri Riis, Oslo

**Lars Kjemphol &
Espen Henningsen**
• *Improvised Wall Piece*, 2008
Mixed media
Dimensions vary
Courtesy of the artists

Maren Juell Kristensen
• *Wish*, 2007
Animation
1:15 min.
Courtesy of the artist

Hjørdis Kurås
• *Liminal Inception #1*, 2004
Digital video
2:15 min
Courtesy of the artist
• *Total Solar Eclipse*, 2007
Digital video installation
4 min. loop
Courtesy of the artist

Ingvild Langgård
• *The Beast*, 2008
5.1 audio and 16 mm film transferred
to DVD, 3:33 min. loop
in black box, mixed media
244 x 308 x 244 cm
Courtesy of the artist
Direction, sound and editing:
Ingvild Langgård
Line producer: Ruben Thorkildsen
Cinematography: Petter Holmern
Halvorsen
Focus puller: Greg Dupre
Electrician: Morten Halfstad
Lighting assistants: Isak Eymundson,
Ruben Steinum
Production assistants: Henrik
Langgård, Elin Conradsson
Grading and editing: Christan
Berg-Nielsen
Thanks to: Norwegian Culture
Council, Nordisk Film Post
Production, Kodak Norge, Norsk
Filmstudio, Sement & Betong, Astrup
Fearnley Museum of Modern Art,
Notam, Rockwool Norge, Kampen
Økologiske Barnebondegård, Oslo
Reptilpark, Naturhistorisk Museum,
Fredric Vogel and Ruben
Thorkildsen

Trine Lise Nedreaas
• *Dead Lift #1*, 2005
16 mm film transferred to DVD,
with sound
Dimensions vary
Courtesy of the artist
Galerie Eva Hober, Paris and Luxe
Gallery, New York

Martin Skauen
• *Felix Culpa, A Handmade
Massacre*, 2007
Video, 5 min.
Galleri MGM, Oslo and Laura
Bartlett Gallery, London

Eirin Støen
• *Black Cloud #1 (dog with bird)*,
2008
Projection
Dimensions vary
Courtesy of the artist
• *Black Cloud #2 (birds on table)*,
2008
Table (Rococo style) and Rapid
prototyping (3D print), nylon
117 x 88 cm
Courtesy of the artist

Stian Ådlandsvik
• *Some Remarks on
Discardedness*, 2008
Plywood, Leitz Pradovit 150 dias
projector, dias
Dimensions vary
Astrup Fearnley Collection, Oslo

Øystein Aasan
• *Display Unit (Also by Tennessee
Williams)*, 2007
MDF, book pages, paper and
mirror foil
186 x 143 x 35 cm
Lautom Contemporary, Oslo, PSM,
Berlin and Galerie Katharina Bittel,
Hamburg
• *Display Unit (Meaning Death)*,
2007
MDF book pages, paper and
mirror foil
186 x 143 x 35 cm
Lautom Contemporary, Oslo, PSM,
Berlin and Galerie Katharina Bittel,
Hamburg
• *Echoplex 1*, 2007
MDF, Celestion loud speaker,
wires, wiretap recording, mirror
foil and plywood
124 x 75 x 60 cm
Lautom Contemporary, Oslo, PSM,
Berlin and Galerie Katharina Bittel,
Hamburg

BOOKSHOP
• Marte Johnslien
One for the Books, 2008
Temporary bookshop with various
dimensions

ARTIST SPACES

Bastard
12–27 January
Monumento Mori
Curator Anders Smebye

• Lars Laumann
La Reine est Morte, 2006
Video
5:18 min. loop
• Lars Laumann
*Morrissey Foretelling the Death
of Diana*, 2006
16 pages, A4-format
Fanzine (edition: 250)

• Marte Johnslien
Untitled (Pink), 2007
Digital print
180 x 110 cm
• Marte Johnslien
Untitled (Blue), 2007
Digital print
180 x 110 cm
• Lina Viste Grønli
The Conclusion, 2006
Paperback, plastic pearl, buttons,
coin, raisin, piece of glass, match
7 x 11 x 18 cm
• Anders Smebye
Hunter´s Funeral, 2007
Felt, vlieseline, thread
180 x 120 cm
• Anders Smebye
Sculpture Kills Top Ten, 2006
Framed A2 poster
60 x 40 cm
• Jan Bünnig & Simon Rühle
Fountain of Youth, 2007
Plastic pool, pump and mud
250 x 60 cm

Blunk
31 January – 10 February
What there is and what you see
Curators Lina Berglund, Kristofer
Henriksson, Uta Freia Beer and
Aylin Soyer Tangen

• Lisa Stålspets
The giant mermaid, 2007
Video, 6:52 min.
• Kjersti Foyn
Change of space, 2007
Acrylic and pencil on chipboard
310 x 316 x 192 cm
• Kristofer Henriksson
A liftetime to live, 2007
Performance 31 January at 5.30 pm
and 10 February at 2 pm
• Lars Skjelbreia
Endogen, 2007
Animation/sculpture
• Christina Reenberg Jensen
Undertones, 2008
Plug, microphones, loudspeakers,
sound mixer, doormats, MDF
191 x 77 x 77 cm

Rakett
14 February – 2 March
Investigation of a Model of
Influence – including use of
subversive strategies and attempts
of aesthetic practice and experience
Curators Åse Løvgren and Karolin
Tampere

An exhibition project with
contributions from Michael Baers,
Centre of the Universe (Jørgen
Skylstad), Arne Skaug Olsen, Espen
Sommer Eide, Søssa Jørgensen,
Geir Tore Holm, Linus Elmes,
Magdalena Ziolkowska, Kristin
Tårnesvik, Matt Packer, Ron Sluik,
Maaretta Jaukkuri, Tal Ben Zvi, Tone
Hansen, Camila Marambio, Yvette
Brackman, Matei Bejenaru and
Insert Name Here (Jacqueline
Hoang Nguyen and Jenny
Yurshansky)

Rekord
6–23 March
Pineapple, or knife?
Iceberg, or volcano?
Curators Thora Dolven Balke
Ingvild Langgård and Eirin Støen

• Trine Falch
100 Years
• Monica Winther & Kjersti Vetterstad
Mum and Jerry
• Tori Wrånes
Doubtful Predator
In collaboration with Marte
Gunnufsen (accordeon)
and Jan Erik Mikalsen (saw)
• Kristian Skylstad
Changes We Can Believe In, 2008
Performance and wall pairting
• Annette Stav Johanssen
Hang Safely Die Slowly, 2006
Video performance
Courtesy of the artist
• Linn Anita Pedersen
A page, 2008
Photograph, analogue print
50 x 60 cm
Courtesy of the artist
• Christina Peel
Shigaraki After Dark, 2007
Silkscreen with fluorescent
pigment on porcelain and
black light
30 x 30 cm
Courtesy of the artist
• Ulf Styren
Untitled (Models for a future
disaster), 2008
C-print on aluminium
60 x 80 cm
Courtesy of the artist
• Are Mokkelbost
ION, 2nd Level, Omni #4, 2008
Paper collage
90 x 60 cm
Courtesy Aaron Turner
• Linn Anita Pedersen
The defying moment, 2008
Sculpture, wood
90 x 173 x 206 cm
Courtesy of the artist
• Jorunn Myklebust Syversen
Reach Out and Touch Faith.
Black, 2008
Light jet print, Diasec
186 x 125 cm
Courtesy of the artist
• Kristian Øverland Dahl
Family, 2008
Acrylic, plaster, latex, tape,
cardboard, plastic, reinforcement
bars, construction foam, brick,
prosthesis
150 x 70 x 175 cm
Courtesy of the artist
• Kjersti Andvig
Untitled, 2006
Knitting
90 x 180 cm
Snare/Christiansen Collect on
• Marianne Hurum
Creepy, crawly, rusting,
bustling, 2007
Oil on paper
65 x 50 cm
Courtesy of the artist